THE FOREIGN POLICIES
OF
MIDDLE EAST STATES

The Middle East in the International System

ANOUSHIRAVAN EHTESHAMI &
RAYMOND HINNEBUSCH,
SERIES EDITORS

THE FOREIGN POLICIES
OF
MIDDLE EAST STATES

EDITED BY
RAYMOND HINNEBUSCH
ANOUSHIRAVAN EHTESHAMI

LYNNE
RIENNER
PUBLISHERS

BOULDER
LONDON

Published in the United States of America in 2002 by
Lynne Rienner Publishers, Inc.
1800 30th Street, Boulder, Colorado 80301
www.rienner.com

and in the United Kingdom by
Lynne Rienner Publishers, Inc.
3 Henrietta Street, Covent Garden, London WC2E 8LU

Library of Congress Cataloging-in-Publication Data
The foreign policies of Middle East states / edited by Raymond Hinnebusch
and Anoushiravan Ehteshami.
(The Middle East in the international system)
Includes bibliographical references and index.
ISBN 1-58826-044-5
ISBN 1-58826-020-8 (pbk.)
1. Middle East—Foreign relations. I. Hinnebusch, Raymond A.
II. Ehteshami, Anoushiravan. III. Series.
JZ1670 .F67 2001
327.0956—dc21   2001041775

British Cataloguing in Publication Data
A Cataloguing in Publication record for this book
is available from the British Library.

Printed and bound in the United States of America

The paper used in this publication meets the requirements
∞ of the American National Standard for Permanence of
Paper for Printed Library Materials Z39.48-1984.

5 4 3 2

Contents

Preface

This volume grew out of a meeting at the University of St. Andrews convened to develop a book badly needed to fill a gap in the study of Middle East foreign policy. The only multicase text in the field, Korany and Dessouki's seminal *Foreign Policies of Arab States,* had gone out of print and had not, in any case, included the major non-Arab actors making up the Middle East system. There was thus a need for a text that would combine an analysis of the Middle East regional system with case studies of how different individual states responded to a similar environment.

The first task of the project was to generate an analytical framework that would incorporate enough of a consensus on the key variables to allow systematic comparison of the country cases while avoiding imposition of an overly rigid and artificial symmetry. This framework, though presented in this book by Raymond Hinnebusch, is the outcome of a collaborative effort involving both the preparation of country studies and interchanges at the St. Andrews meeting that reached a rough, albeit by no means complete, agreement.

This consensus could be described as a modified form of realism. The insecurity of the regional arena was thought to remain the predominant factor shaping Middle East foreign policies, which exhibited with considerable regularity a realist preoccupation with power. While constraints on foreign policy from economic relations with the developed great powers were acknowledged, the group concluded that this asymmetrical interdependence left considerable autonomy to states in the choice of their foreign policies. Moreover, while policymakers could ignore neither transstate identities such as Arabism and Islam nor domestic opposition, several decades of state formation had given decisionmakers

vii

considerable internal autonomy in policymaking. Despite this "majority view," each of the contributors to this book gives a somewhat different weight to the mix of factors, reflective of differences in interpretation and variations in the country cases.

In addition to those of the chapter authors, major contributions to the consensus were made by Jubin Goodarzi, Janet Hancock, Burhan Jaf, Ibrahim Karawan, Joseph Nevo, Francis Outram, Patrick Seale, Hans-Jakob Schindler, and Paul Wilkinson. Special thanks are due to Gerd Nonneman for his trenchant and insightful critique of the framework. Funding was kindly provided by the British Academy, the Foreign and Commonwealth Office, the Honeyman Foundation, and the University of St. Andrews, to each of whom we are grateful.

—The Editors

The Middle East (the Arab League plus Iran, Israel, and Turkey)

1

Introduction: The Analytical Framework

Raymond Hinnebusch

This book takes a modified form of realist theory as a working hypothesis.* It assumes that in the Middle East the state is the main actor in foreign policy and that state elites have an interest in maximizing the autonomy and security of the state. It accepts the realist claim that a built-in feature of a state system, anarchy, has generated profound insecurity and a pervasive struggle for power. Indeed, the Middle East is one of the regional subsystems where this anarchy appears most in evidence: it holds two of the world's most durable and intense conflict centers, the Arab-Israeli and the Gulf arenas; its states are still contesting borders and rank among themselves; and there is not a single one that does not feel threatened by one or more of its neighbors. Finally, the book accepts that states seek to counter these threats through "reason of state," notably power accumulation and balancing, and that the latter is a key to regional order.

Yet realism has several important liabilities in understanding the Middle East. First, neorealism holds that systemic insecurity induces uniform patterns of behavior, notably balancing against threats, but this is merely typical to the extent that a state system of relatively sovereign unified states is consolidated. In the Middle East, however, the state system is still in the *process* of consolidation, hence the dynamics of the "system level," per se, has less effect on state behavior than realism expects, while other levels, addressed by rival theories, have more.

Marxist-inspired "structuralists" argue that the world capitalist system is decisive, that it is a hierarchy, not realism's simple anarchy, and

---

*See the glossary on p. 351 for explanations of international relations terms.

1

that, in this hierarchy, the economic dependency of late-developing states sharply constrains their sovereignty. Constructivists insist that interstate relations are contingent on the way *identity* is constructed; in the Middle East, sub- and suprastate identities compete with state identity, inspire transstate movements, and constrain purely state-centric behavior. For pluralists, Middle East states are not unitary and impermeable, as realism assumes, but fragmented and penetrated and hence less capable of pursuing realist "reason of state."

As such, it is useful to assume that the foreign policies of Middle East states are shaped by the way their leaders negotiate the often conflicting pressures emanating from three conceptually distinct environments: (1) the domestic level; (2) the regional systemic level; and (3) the global (or international) level. Arguably, however, to the extent state formation advances, state decisionmakers acquire greater autonomy of both global and domestic constraints while each state also comes to potentially constitute a greater threat to the other. To the extent this happens, foreign policymaking can increasingly approximate the reason of state whereby rational actors seek regime survival in a dangerous regional environment. Each state actor examined in the book has negotiated a somewhat different course within its three environments.

This chapter looks, first, at the contrary pressures on policymakers emanating from the global capitalist "core" and from conflicting domestic identities, and also examines to what extent state building enables them to master these pressures. Second, it examines the foreign policymaking process; and third, it looks at how the incremental consolidation of the state system increasingly shapes the behavior of its parts along the lines of realist reason of state.

Foreign Policy Determinants

The Global Level: Core-Periphery Relations

The Middle East, once an independent civilization, has been turned into a periphery of the Western-dominated world system. According to L. Carl Brown, the Middle East is a *penetrated system,* one subject to an exceptional level of external intervention and control yet, by virtue of its cultural distinctiveness, stubbornly resistant to subordination.[1] Western penetration has endured in the postcolonial era, motivated by contiguous location and the exceptional concentration of great power interests—oil, transit routes, Israel. To many Arabs and Muslims, imperialism, far from dead, persists in new forms. As Buzan points out, the Islamic world is the only classical civilization that has not managed to reestablish itself as a significant world actor since the retreat of Western empires.[2] This defines the parameters within which Middle East states must operate and is a major issue in the politics of the region.

Structuralism, the international-relations theory most concerned with explaining global core-periphery relations, has been widely used by scholars of the Middle East to understand this reality.[3] According to Galtung's influential "Structural Theory of Imperialism," periphery states, including those of the Middle East, are subordinated within a global hierarchy, dependent on and tied to the core powers while being only very weakly related to each other.[4] Indeed, many scholars argue that the transformation of the Middle East under imperialism produced an outcome that resembles Galtung's model.

First, where once there was a universal trading empire, imperialism fragmented the region into a multitude of relatively weak and, to an extent, artificial states. As Brown shows, these states, at odds with each other and insecure, sought external patrons and resources for the regional power struggle set in motion by this fragmentation. Especially where the new states emerged as Western protectorates against indigenous opposition, they have remained dependent for their security on the Western global powers long after formal independence. Unlike India and China, the postcolonial state system nullifies rather than restores the precolonial universal state.

Second, the parallel incorporation of the regional economy into the world capitalist system shattered regional economic interdependence and restructured the region into a classic dependent economy marked by the production and export of primary products (e.g., cotton and oil) and dependence on imports of manufactures and technology. Oil may be thought to be fundamentally different from other primary products, given the high level of revenues it generates and the dependence of core economies on it, but in fact the recycling of petrodollars has perpetuated overall regional dependency on the import of capital (foreign aid, loans, and investment), and hence high levels of debt, in a way not significantly different from the export of other primary products.[5]

Economic dependency means a major function of foreign policy must be to secure and maximize resource flows from external sources. Because states' revenue bases are exceptionally dependent on external resources—whether foreign aid, taxes on foreign trade, or oil revenues— and not on domestically raised taxes, they may be more responsive to the demands of global powers than to domestic opinion in designing their policies.6 Indeed, some Middle Eastern states explicitly design their foreign policies to serve economic ends, from trading policies favorable to great power patrons in return for aid to merely subordinating nationalism in policymaking to ensuring a favorable investment climate.

Third, according to Galtung, the "bridgehead" that the "core" establishes in "the centre of the periphery nation for the joint benefit of both" is equally important to sustaining the region's subordination to the "core."7 Specifically, imperialism, in implanting "client elites" and fostering "compradors"—traders and exporters—has created shared economic interests between the core and dominant local classes while retarding national bourgeoisies with an interest in autonomous national and regional development. Arguably, the current dominant form of this relation is manifested in the way the overwhelming investment of surplus petrodollars by Arab oil monarchies in the West gives their ruling families a much greater stake in the core economies than in that of the region. According to Bruce Moon, such relations tend to generate a "constrained consensus" that results in significant congruence between the foreign policies of regional states and those of the core. This is a function of the overlap of local elites' economic interests, world views (through Western education), and threat perceptions (fear of radical movements) with those of core elites.8

Fourth, while such manipulation of interests is far more important than crude power in sustaining regional subordination, where there is insufficient overlap of interests, the core powers use economic punishments—withdrawal of aid, economic sanctions, and the like—against economically vulnerable regional states (e.g., U.S. attempts to isolate Iran).9 As a last resort, military force is periodically used by Western powers to prevent, in Brown's words, any regional power trying to "organize the system" against them—as Saddam Hussein found out. Such intervention by the hegemonic powers is consistent with Wallerstein's argument that the maintenance and expansion of the world capitalist system depends on a *hegemon,* a dominant state that defends the system, breaks down barriers to core-periphery economic links (e.g., promoting economic liberalization), and assures reliable access to raw materials, especially the cheap energy concentrated in the Middle East.10 The core-periphery struggle over oil has been a dominant theme in the region's politics from the overthrow of Iran's Mossadeq to the formation of the Organization of Petroleum Exporting Countries (OPEC) to the second Gulf war.

The structuralist view of world capitalist dominance over the region is contested by more realist-centered views and, even in the structuralist view, core-periphery relations are not static. Global penetration does not mean the region lacks all autonomy in the conduct of foreign policy. First, as Oran Young argues, there is always a certain discontinuity between the possession of global power and its exercise in regional arenas: to the extent great powers are unable or uninterested in fully controlling a regional subsystem, the potential for regional autonomy increases.[11]

This has been facilitated when, as during the Cold War, global bipolarity "split the core," so to speak. The superpower rivalry that made local clients valuable actually gave regional states leverage over their patrons, even allowing the "tail to wag the dog" over regional issues where the client's vital interests were more at stake than those of the global patron. It also allowed them to extract enhanced military capabilities that would, ironically, make external intervention more costly. Bipolarity arguably gave local states a crucial three-decade window of opportunity to consolidate their autonomy.[12]

Additionally, as Thompson has observed, the lack of horizontal ties among periphery states in Galtung's model applies in the Middle East chiefly at the economic level and has not prevented the survival in the region of dense transstate cultural and political ties; these provide potential vehicles for the mobilization of region-wide anti-imperialism by nationalist regimes seeking a collective challenge to the dependency system.[13] Thus, in the 1950s superpower competition, in limiting the ability of the Western great powers to use military force in the region, cleared space for Nasser's attempt to use Pan-Arab ideology to organize the Arab states, albeit briefly, against Western intrusion.

Also, at the economic level, local states made efforts to reduce the asymmetry of their relation to the core. For radical states, a statist industrialization strategy, made possible by alternative Soviet markets and technology, aimed to sufficiently dilute or diversify dependency and enhance power capabilities to support nationalist foreign policies challenging Western penetration. Where oil resources, harnessed to such strategies, provided a relatively secure economic base, some regimes— such as Libya, Iraq, and Iran—were better positioned to absorb the economic costs of challenging external power. The limits of such strategies were, however, underlined by the fate of poorer states such as Egypt, where statist failure ended in a post-Nasser dependency on donors who expected and got an end to Egypt's radical nationalism.

Other states, such as the oil monarchies, were less interested in challenging the system than enhancing their autonomy within it. OPEC, in which oil producers banded together "horizontally," altered the "feudal" structure of relations and arguably allowed Saudi Arabia, with its pivotal role in stabilizing oil prices, to transform dependency into asymmetrical interdependence. Even states that began as overt client regimes have sought to defend their autonomy. If dependency holds anywhere, it should do in such extreme cases as Jordan, literally dependent on its annual budget subsidy to sustain the state; but even Jordan briefly defied its patrons in the Gulf war.[14] Israel, with its unique capacity to penetrate the policy process of the U.S. world hegemon, is little constrained by its high dependence on Washington.

However, the post–Cold War transformation in the world system, specifically Soviet collapse and unchecked U.S. hegemony, has once again narrowed the autonomy of many regional states. How far the United States is able to impose its will is debatable, but it is able, as never before, to directly intervene against challenges to its interests, as the ongoing post–Gulf war campaign against Iraq shows. The Libyan case indicates how international sanctions have tempered the radicalism of states that once challenged Western hegemony.[15] In addition, the globalization of capitalism is drawing regional states into ever denser webs of economic dependency—or interdependency. While globalization continues to meet more resistance in the Middle East than elsewhere, notably in the region's evasion of full economic liberalization, increasing numbers of states, such as Tunisia and Egypt, see it as an opportunity for increased investment and markets. They have seemingly made the decision to be players rather than victims, even if this means the sacrifice of some autonomy. But to the extent external penetration of the region tends to generate popular local resistance—recently in the form of political Islam—elites may have to temper such ambitions.[16]

In summation, the impact of the region's position in the world system on the foreign policies of local states is by no means straightforward. (1) Where the interests of local regimes overlap with those of core patrons, reason of state and alliance with a great power coincide and states tend to "bandwagon" with their global patron to contain local threats. (2) On the other hand, penetration generates resistance and where nationalist movements come to power, nationalist regimes have sought to organize a regional coalition to balance against external powers. (3) However, this is only possible under favorable conditions: when the great powers are divided (as in the Cold War)—and hegemonic intervention is thus deterred—and when the region is relatively united (the Nasserite 1950s and 1960s) against the outside, the conditions for regional autonomy may be better than in the reverse case (before 1945; since 1990). Chapters 3 and 4 explore these issues in greater depth.

Between Identity and Sovereignty

The unique features of the Middle East state system, specifically the uneasy relation of identity and state sovereignty, immensely complicate foreign policymaking in the Middle East. The realist model, in which elites represent loyal populations insulated from external influence in the conduct of foreign policy, must be substantially modified in analysis of the region. Many Middle Eastern states lack the full features—impermeability, secure national identity—that realism assumes. The Arab world, in particular, is less well represented by realism's impenetrable "billiard balls" than (in Paul Noble's words) a set of interconnected organisms separated only by porous membranes.[17]

Indeed, the consolidation of a system of nation-states in the region is obstructed by the profound flaws originating in its largely external imposition: the resulting often arbitrary borders and ill fit between states and national identities mean that loyalty to the individual states is contested by substate and suprastate identities. The resultant embedding of the state system in a matrix of fluid multiple identities means that the "national interest" that realism assumes underlies foreign policy is problematic and contested.

Irredentism. One major manifestation of the poor fit of state and nation is the rampant, built-in irredentism—dissatisfaction with the incongruity between territorial borders and "imagined communities." Irredentism is rooted in the way substate (ethnic or religious) communities, in frequently spilling across state borders (becoming transstate), stimulate territorial conflicts. In consequence, states contest each other's borders or "interfere" in each other's "domestic" affairs by supporting dissident transstate communities, a practice that can escalate into actual military confrontation between states.[18] Thus, the Kurdish protonation spreads across Turkey, Iraq, Iran, and Syria, making these states vulnerable to succession movements but also allowing them to manipulate Kurdish dissidents against each other. This transstate conflict was an element in the ongoing Iran-Iraq conflict and the 1998 Turkish-Syrian confrontation. Somewhat similarly, the displacement of the Palestinians by the creation of Israel, and Israel's dissatisfaction with its initial (pre-1967) borders, transmuted a communal struggle over Palestine into an Arab-Israeli interstate conflict. Shi'a Iran's effort to export Islamic revolution found a particular response in Shi'a communities throughout the region and helped touch off the Iran-Iraq war, the world's longest-lasting twentieth-century war. In Lebanon, the power of substate (sectarian) identities and the ties of rival sects with kindred communities in other states produced civil war and state collapse that allowed rival states to make Lebanon a battlefield and unleashed one major war (1982) between Syria and Israel and chronic conflict on Lebanon's southern border with Israel.

Suprastate identity. While irredentism is a feature of much of the Third World, what makes the Middle East region, or more specifically its Arab core, unique is its history of exceptional suprastate identities. Because the state system was imposed on a preexisting cultural and linguistic unity that more or less persists, the mass loyalty to the state typical where it corresponds to a definite nation is, in the Arab world, diluted and limited by strong popular identifications with larger communities— the Arab nation, the Islamic *umma*.[19] The result, according to Kienle, is a system of territorial states, not—so far at least—nation-states.[20] This is most striking in the most artificial states (Syria, Jordan), but even in those such as Egypt, which have their own viable separate identities, suprastate identities sufficiently persist to prevent the consolidation of distinct nation-states. Such variations in identity are examined in greater depth in Chapter 2.

The result, according to Bahgat Korany, is a *duality* where ruling elites are caught between *raison de la nation* (Pan-Arabism) and *raison d'etat* (sovereignty) in foreign policymaking. On the one hand, as Kienle observed, state elites have treated the Arab world as a single arena of political competition and mass publics have believed that shared Arab interests—the Palestine cause, autonomy from the West— should limit the sovereign right to put particular state interests first; on the other hand, leaders have tenaciously defended state sovereignty against suprastate constraints.[21] However, as Michael Barnett's constructivist study argues, identity is "constructed," not given or constant, and the interaction of Arab leaders has determined the evolution of identity over time between Korany's Pan-Arab and sovereignty poles.[22]

Arab leaders' behavior helped to establish Pan-Arabism. They sought all-Arab leadership by competing to win over public opinion through the "outbidding" of rivals in promotion of Arab causes. The conduct of the game involved "symbolic politics," not military force, that is, pressuring or threatening rival state elites by making Pan-Arab ideological appeals to their populations. This would, in a consolidated nation-state system, have been seen as interference in domestic affairs and have had little chance of success; it was natural and successful in the Arab world precisely because of the power of suprastate identity.

Even if states, like Nasser's Egypt, tried to manipulate Pan-Arabism to serve state interests, Pan-Arab movements, autonomous, multiple, and crossing state boundaries, were no mere instruments of regimes; indeed, such movements used Nasser to bolster their local standing as much as he used them and they constantly pressured him into increasing Egypt's commitment to the cause against his own better judgment. The "outbidding" of rival leaders established Pan-Arab norms of behavior: states sought Pan-Arab leadership by raising the standards, states seeking to maintain such leadership had to be seen to live up to Pan-Arabism and states perceived to violate its norms became more vulnerable to subversion. Even Nasser felt constrained to satisfy the expectations of his Pan-Arab constituency, which "entrapped" him and his rivals in a dynamic of nationalist outbidding against Israel and led to the 1967 war, at great cost to state interests.

The interactions of leaders also "deconstructed" Pan-Arabism, so to speak: interstate disagreements over its meaning and the failures of Arab unity projects and of Arab collective institutions disillusioned and demobilized Arab publics, reducing Pan-Arab constraints on state leaders. Ironically, the use of Arabism by ambitious leaders to subvert rivals only heightened the sense of threat from kindred Arab states, reinforced the differentiation between the individual states, and led state elites to promote distinctive state identities and the norm of state sovereignty to legitimize their self-defense. The outcome was, according to Barnett, "normative fragmentation." Identities remain contested, but have become too complex and multiple to sharply or uniformly constrain state elites in their conduct of foreign policy.[23]

This account of the decline of Pan-Arabism must be qualified in two respects. First, constructivism's neglect of power leads it to ignore the extent to which the decline of Pan-Arabism was ultimately rooted in the power struggles unleashed by three major wars—the 1967 Arab-Israeli war and the two Gulf wars. In these wars, it was military power (not public opinion) that counted while the intensified threat to regimes' survival led them to put realist self-help over identity. Anwar Sadat's separate peace with Israel, the classic case where Arab collective interests were sacrificed to reason of state, was legitimized by appeal to the doctrine of sovereignty and precipitated a similar recourse to self-help by the other Arab states that it left more vulnerable to Israeli power.

Second, however, Pan-Arabism continues to have a residual affect on foreign policymaking. Because state identities are still no good substitute for Arab identity in most, if not all, the Arab states, the legitimacy of regimes continues to be contingent on being seen to act for Arab or

Islamic interests, and political Islam, in some respects, has become a surrogate for Pan-Arabism. Foreign policymakers must therefore still disguise, justify, or even modify the pure pursuit of reason of state. As Sela showed, moreover, "dualism" also led to the emergence of the Arab summit system, which institutionalized a version of Arab solidarity more compatible with state sovereignty.[24]

In summary, the Arab world retains some features of an "international society," a community bound by rules and norms; but it is sliding toward merger with the wider Middle East, a mere "system of states" mostly linked by power and interest.[25]

State Formation and Foreign Policymaking

The capacity of Middle Eastern states to cope with the pressures from their multilevel environment depends on a degree of internal cohesion. This is a function of their level of state formation. If they are to conduct foreign policies that rationally cope with external exigencies, state elites must command the legitimacy and institutions to establish a certain autonomy of domestic demands while sustaining some minimum level of public support. While realism tends to take such capacity for granted, in the Middle East state formation remains problematic and a matter of considerable controversy.

According to advocates of what might be called the "domestic vulnerability model" of foreign policymaking, the main threat to unstable Third World regimes is *domestic,* and foreign policy is a key instrument of survival at home, whether used to build domestic legitimacy through nationalism or to secure external support against domestic opposition.[26] This model is relevant insofar as Middle Eastern states, lacking secure national identity and democratic accountability, suffer legitimacy deficits; but it ignores the crucial importance of external threats in foreign policymaking.

The most popular alternative, what might be called the "leadership-dominant model," assumes that leaders, facing few institutional constraints at home, are able to translate their idiosyncratic personal values, styles—and pathologies—into foreign policy.[27] However, this imagines a domestic vacuum that is questionable even in authoritarian regimes, where leaders may face informal domestic constraints, such as the need to protect regime legitimacy. Legitimacy in states where imperialism remains a perceived threat and where little welfare and few political rights are typically delivered tends to be exceptionally dependent on foreign-policy performance.

In the first model, leaders are "too weak," in the second "too strong," but both assume an absence of the institutions (enabling leaders to mediate between domestic demands and external constraints) that are arguably needed for the effective conduct of foreign policy. This, can, however, be misleading if taken too far. As compared to the decade after independence, there is evidence of an increasing durability and stability of Middle Eastern states.[28] Several decades of state formation in the region have arguably resulted in sufficient institution building that foreign policies are less directly shaped by the unconstrained biases of the top leader and less buffeted by internal vulnerabilities than heretofore and are, therefore, more a response to the external challenges assumed by realist thinking.

How far this is so is an empirical question and, in reality, levels of Middle East state formation are very uneven. As such, the domestic politics and leadership-dominant models can be retained as ideal types reflective of more under- and "overdeveloped" regime types at opposite ends of a continuum; while states with more balanced institutional profiles can be located on either side of its midpoint. Individual states are, moreover, likely to *move over time* through several different phases in state formation that are arguably associated with differences in foreign policy. The broad lines of these phases (most relevant for the Arab world) are suggested below.

1. The postindependence period (roughly 1945–1960) in the Arab core and Iran was an era of weak states governed by externally imposed or narrowly based elites chiefly driven by fear of domestic instability from publics inflamed by nationalism. In foreign policy, they opted either to rely on external protection against such threats—embedding themselves deeper into the dependency web—or sought legitimacy by anti-imperialist/anti-Zionist rhetoric. Each strategy had costs: the first risked domestic subversion, the second, foreign defeat or economic loss, in either case resulting in more unstable and vulnerable regimes. By contrast, in Turkey and Israel, where states were more consolidated and institutionalization combined with democratization gave leaders substantial legitimacy and hence autonomy in foreign policymaking, classic reason of state prevailed.

2. By the 1960s (after 1956 in Egypt), state building was under way in the Arab world and Iran, a function of the need to master domestic instability and transstate penetration and/or to dilute international dependency. The different origins and initial social bases of regimes, however, dictated quite different state-building strategies that biased foreign policy in conflicting radical and conservative directions.[29]

In the Arab oil monarchies, state formation took place under Western patronage in small, geopolitically weak and nationally unmobilized societies, although the small middle class was vulnerable to transstate Arab nationalist appeals. Domestic vulnerability was contained by traditional (patriarchal and Islamic) legitimacy and the growing distribution of oil-financed benefits to co-opt the middle class and keep the masses demobilized. Protection from regional threats was provided by the Western great powers. In Iran's larger more mobilized society, the shah had to construct a more elaborate technology of control.

In the opposite strategy, that of the authoritarian-nationalist republics, regimes originating in middle-class overthrow of Western client elites sought to consolidate their power through the mobilization of countervailing popular support and dilution of dependency on the West. Wealth redistribution (e.g., land reform, nationalizations) and public-sector-led development bolstered autonomy of the dominant classes and enabled regimes to access aid, markets, and protection from the Eastern bloc. While these regimes attempted to incorporate the middle and lower classes through party building, because the military remained a vehicle of factional politics and because they lacked a secure social base in a dominant class, they remained unstable. Hence, legitimacy was sought through radical nationalist foreign policies.

3. A third stage was apparent by the mid-1970s, namely the increased consolidation of both kinds of states.[30] The main incentive was now the high threat of war while booming oil revenues and continued superpower patronage provided the means. Successful state building shared certain commonalties across the region.

State bureaucratic structures, modern means of coercion and communications, and the use of political technologies—such as party building or corporatist associations—dramatically expanded and increasingly penetrated society. States tried to indigenize these imported structures by grafting elements of the multiple levels of local identity to them. On the one hand, substate sectarian, tribal, and family *assabiya* (solidarity) was used to construct webs of trusted followers at the state center, commanding the instruments of power, a process of patrimonialization that blurred the distinction between monarchies and republics. On the other hand, political elites tried to legitimize their states in terms of suprastate Arabism and Islam—which, ironically, actually strengthened the capacity of individual states to pursue reason of state: thus, Saudi Islam as well as Syrian and Iraqi Arab nationalism legitimized contrary and often conflicting foreign policies largely expressive of state interests.

More questionable is how far such efforts actually substituted for classic nation-statehood in the Arab world. Political identity is, of course, constructed and need not necessarily be rooted in Arab eth-nonationalism. In the Arab world the *territorial* state, based on habitation of a common territory—especially where boundaries correspond to some historical memory—and equal citizenship rights under a common government could become an alternative basis of identity. To a considerable extent this has happened; but loyalties to individual states will only be consolidated when democratization gives citizens the rights they need to feel the state is "theirs." It is instructive that in Turkey and Israel, the initial much greater coincidence of boundaries and a distinct national identity, plus more substantial democratization, allowed an earlier and smoother consolidation of the state.

Attachment to the state of strategic class interests needed to anchor it against the winds of transstate popular sentiment may substitute for popular identifications. Such classes include bureaucratic strata (whose share in state patronage give them an interest in reason of state) and commercial bourgeoisies (who profit as middlemen between the state and the global economy). Both monarchies and republics gave birth to new state-dependent bourgeoisies, closely linked to officialdom, that had a stake in the status quo.

Stability also requires incorporation of a sufficient segment of the middle and lower strata and, absent democracy, this depends on successful socioeconomic policies. In the authoritarian republics the coincidence in the 1960s and 1970s of economic growth and redistributive policies—land reform, state employment—gave parts of the lower strata some stake in the state. But the failure of the radical states to effectively create a Pan-Arab order eroded their nationalist legitimacy and turned elements of the masses to Islamic-inspired opposition.

In the oil monarchies, command of oil revenues during periods of oil boom enabled the state to incorporate the minority of the population who held citizenship as a privileged constituency with a stake in the status quo—as against the possible demands of migrant labor for similar rights. The oil resources accruing to these states provided them the resources—without resort to taxation and accountability—to establish substantial autonomy from society. They also used the transfer of aid to conservatize the radical states.

In this phase, autonomous elites, balancing social forces and presiding over more stable states less vulnerable to ideology and enjoying greater resources, generally attained greater freedom from domestic pressures and global constraints, increasingly allowing the conduct of foreign policies according to geopolitical reason of state. This tendency drove a considerable convergence in the foreign policies of monarchies and republics.

4. A fourth stage, already apparent in the 1980s, emerged fully in the 1990s with the end to bipolarity. The exposure of grave vulnerabilities in the newly consolidated states—economic crisis and loss of Soviet patronage in the republics and military shock (the Iranian threat, Iraq's invasion of Kuwait) in the monarchies—exposed the limits of regional autonomy and induced movement toward the reintegration of regional states into the global capitalist system.

The "overdevelopment" of the state encouraged by the oil boom and the exploitation of economies for military ends translated into growing economic constraints once the oil boom ended. The most visible policy response, especially in the republics, was *infitah*—economic liberalization. There was a consequent change in the social base of the state, manifested in moves toward power sharing with the bourgeoisie and demobilization or exclusion of popular strata. This was accompanied by a moderation or abandonment of nationalist policies and realignment toward the West. Even as some of these states had previously harnessed their economies to foreign policy, so economic troubles now drove many to harness foreign policy to the economy, that is, to the acquisition of economic aid and investment from the West. In the oil monarchies, the main change was growing Western dependence: a much more overt reliance on Western military protection and a new indebtedness to the West incurred to maintain the distribution state and to make massive weapons purchases in a time of falling oil prices.

To the extent the post–Gulf war intrusion of the U.S. hegemon into the region constrains the regional power struggle, the main threat to elites may again come to be domestic instability. The *infitah* era's replacement of distributive welfarism with trickle-down capitalism has tended to simultaneously give successful capitalists a stake in the state and the economic opening while leaving a more or less large segment of the public excluded from state patronage. While economic troubles make the public more tolerant of whatever policies promise relief, when this coincides with increased subordination to Western patrons, the losers may be mobilized by opposition groups deploying the symbols of sub- or suprastate identity: thus, the marginalized victims of economic liberalization appear to be among the main constituents of Islamic opposition movements. But such movements, so far unable to make Islamic revolution against today's stronger states, may be forced to settle for incremental Islamization of the state.

Foreign Policymaking

A state's particular responses to the three arenas—global, regional, and domestic—that it must negotiate are most immediately a product of leadership and the political process in which policies are drafted and decisions made and implemented.

Policymaking Context

Omni-balancing. Foreign policy in Middle East states, ultimately rooted in state elites' desire to defend their regimes, aims not just at deterrence of external threats, but also at legitimating the regime at home against domestic opposition and mobilizing economic resources abroad. In attempting to balance these needs, elites face potential contradictions: for example, responsiveness to domestic demands mobilized by suprastate ideologies for autonomy from the West clashes with states' dependency on the core powers. Both pressures—from below and from the outside—potentially constrain state sovereignty.

Steven David argues that decisionmakers "omni-balance" between external and internal pressures and the main location of threats (as well as opportunities and resources) shapes the decision context.[31] Thus, when the primary threat is *internal,* a regime may align with an external power to get resources to contain it. But it could also seek to appease domestic opinion and enhance legitimacy by indulging in anti-imperialist rhetoric or irredentist campaigns. Where the primary threat is *external,* a regime may mobilize new domestic actors into politics to expand its internal power base and seek alliances with similarly threatened states. When economic troubles are acute, elites may seek to *contain* domestic nationalism in order to pursue the accommodation with the core powers needed to access economic resources; when the economy is secure, they are more likely to risk *mobilizing* this nationalism to challenge or adjust the impact of external forces on the state. The particular location of threats and opportunities that leaders face obviously varies over time and from state to state and cannot be settled a priori. But few can escape a complex balancing act if they are to survive.

Foreign-policy role. A state's foreign-policy role (or ideology) can be thought of as a durable formula or tradition that incorporates experience by state elites in balancing and reconciling such elements as economic needs, geopolitical imperatives, domestic opinion, and state capabilities. Role implies an identity and defines orientations toward neighbors (friend or enemy), great powers (threat or patron), and the state system (revisionist or status quo).[32]

Geopolitical position seems to have an especially enduring impact on the historical ambitions institutionalized in a foreign-policy role conception. Thus, Egypt's centrality and weight in the system has led its decisionmakers to seek influence in the Arab East, North Africa, and the Nile Valley. On the other hand, the frustration of identity may also produce enduring reactions: artificial or truncated states such as Syria and Iraq have sought protection and fulfillment in a wider Arab role. Israel's conception of itself as a besieged refuge for world Jewry afflicts it with both insecurity and an irredentist need for territorial expansion.

Although manipulated by elites, once a role is constructed and propagated, it sets standards of legitimacy and performance that, to a degree, constrain elites; it also shapes the socialization of the next generation of policymakers. It may therefore impart a certain consistency to foreign policy despite changes in leadership and environment.

Policy Structure and Process

Since roles seldom provide ready-made solutions to particular challenges and because often-incompatible demands require trade-offs, there are many possible rational decisions in any situation. The actual choices of policymaking elites will, therefore, be shaped by their values and interests and, where elites conflict, the power distribution among them that is defined by the state's governing institutions.

The pluralist tradition, which tries to open the black box of decisionmaking, has produced a wealth of literature on how the policy process can produce varied—and often suboptimal—responses to systemic pressures. The "bureaucratic politics" model's stress on conflict between interests over foreign policy and studies of leadership misperception both have their analogues in the literature on Middle East foreign policymaking.[33]

In the personalized authoritarian regimes typical of the Middle East, the choices and style of the leader are decisive, particularly in a crisis or a critical bargaining situation.[34] Whether this is a liability depends in part on the experience and character of the leader. Thus, while Syria and Iraq are ruled by branches of the same party and have similar leader-army-party regimes, big differences between the styles of Asad (the cautious and calculating general) and Saddam (risk-taking ex-street-fighter) seemed to explain key differences in their foreign policies.

Bureaucratic politics plays a greater role in shaping "normal" politics. A limited number of elite actors are involved in this game, such as presidential advisers, senior military and intelligence officers, key cabinet members, and foreign-ministry officials. Each of these may propose different policies, shaped by their special roles and material interests, and they may even constitute veto groups. In the authoritarian republics, the dominance of the president sharply constrains such dynamics, as compared to monarchies such as Saudi Arabia, where the senior princes of the royal family expect to be consulted by the king, and pluralistic states, such as Israel, where the prime minister must keep senior cabinet colleagues satisfied.

The conduct of bureaucratic politics and the range of actors included in it are likely to have bearing on the direction and rationality of decisions and the effectiveness of their implementation. Overconcentration and personalization of power may restrict the information and policy options considered, to the detriment of rational choice; yet where foreign policy becomes a weapon in factional struggles, it may be equally crippled. The salient role of the military and intelligence agencies, even in pluralistic Turkey and Israel, and the relative weakness and limited professionalism of most foreign ministries may bias policy toward coercive options and prioritize "national security" issues over others.

Input into foreign policymaking from outside the governing establishment is typically very limited in the Middle East. Business has only limited access to decisionmakers. Yet economic imperatives require state elites to remain cognizant of business needs: where a "national bourgeoisie" is ascendant, its demands for protection from foreign competition may reinforce a nationalist foreign policy, while satisfying *infitah* bourgeoisies, by contrast, is likely to require a pro-Western policy designed to entice foreign investment.

Broader public opinion is likely to play a greater role in regimes having electoral accountability mechanisms, such as Turkey and Israel. In personalized authoritarian regimes, it may have an indirect impact on foreign policy if leaders must defend legitimacy under attack by rivals or if the mass public is aroused by crisis.[35] In normal times when the public is divided, for example, by class or ethnicity, elites enjoy more autonomy to act as they please.

The effectiveness of policy implementation depends on the instruments of influence available to state elites, notably economic rewards and punishments, propaganda machinery, and military capabilities. Outcomes cannot, however, be adequately explained merely by the balance of such tangible resources among states. The diplomatic skills and bargaining strategies of leaders, including intangibles such as "credibility" and "will," also count. As Telhami observes, even when there is no formal bargaining, much of the relations of states—even war—is tacit bargaining, and the leader's performance can make a decisive difference. Thus, Telhami argues that Sadat's failure to play his hand effectively in the Camp David negotiations produced a suboptimal outcome.[36]

Foreign-Policy Behavior and the
Evolution of the Regional State System

According to neorealism, the state *system*—particularly the distribution of power—is the main determinant of the behavior of its constituent states. Yet, there is never only one possible response to the systemic environment, and the orientations of Middle Eastern states toward it have varied radically. In particular, while some states challenge the status quo, others support it; indeed, the *same* states may change from supporters to challengers of the status quo, as Iran and Iraq did after their respective revolutions. Pluralism and structuralism see domestic and transstate forces as the keys to such variations in state motivation and behavior. In fact, foreign-policy behavior can only be adequately explained as the product of an interaction between the state's domestic needs and the state system in which it operates. The character of this interaction in the Middle East has altered over time.

Revisionism Versus Status Quo:
The Differential Domestic Roots of Foreign Policy

The main initial foreign-policy difference among Middle East states, that between status quo and revisionist orientations, was, in the first instance, a product of subsystemic domestic forces. Revisionism is endemic in Middle East societies, rooted in irredentist conflicts over identity and borders or in reactions against Western penetration and expressed by suprastate ideologies—Arabism, Zionism, Islam, and so on. Such forces have been particularly potent in weak, unconsolidated, or divided states that may be forced to seek legitimacy by championing revisionist causes. Periodically, revisionist movements come to power and harness the capacity of states to their ambitions. Thus, Nasser's Egypt, militant Israel, Ba'thist Iraq and Syria, and Khomeini's Iran have all challenged aspects of the status quo.[37] Such revisionist regimes threaten those wedded to the status quo, typically ruled by landed, tribal, or commercial elites who consolidated their power with Western aid or have a stake in Western markets and who therefore look westward for protection from revisionist neighbors.[38]

Systemic Dynamics and Foreign Policy

Even if domestic forces determine what a state *wishes* to do, it is, according to realism, the system level, starting with a state's position in the distribution of power, that determines what it *can* do. Moreover, state systems have a built-in equilibrium mechanism that tends to preserve them against revisionist challenges. As Rustow argues, "while many Middle Eastern countries individually nurse expansionist or hegemonic ambitions, all of them collectively, by their preference for the weaker side and their readiness to shift alignments regardless of ideology, offer strong support for the status quo . . . ; as such, the system enjoys 'self balancing features.'"[39]

This mechanism depends on state actors adhering to the reason of state deemed rational in the realist tradition: by adopting "realistic" goals (subordinating ideology to the realities of the power balance) and by increasing capabilities or striking alliances against threatening states. Realism also argues that, in fact, the state system itself tends to recast its constituent parts into such "realist" agents of system equilibrium, in part because successful regimes, which play by these rules, are imitated, and in part because those that violate them tend to suffer disaster and are replaced.[40] There is evidence that the logic of the state system has increasingly so impressed itself on the behavior of its parts in the Middle East. The evolution of the regional system is detailed in Chapter 2, but the pattern can be briefly anticipated here.

Balancing. In the early weak oligarchic states, foreign policies were often driven by domestic-rooted revisionism, which largely took the form of rhetoric because states had little power to threaten each other or Western penetration constrained them. However, owing to the unevenness of state formation, some states were consolidated earlier and could, therefore, threaten or constrain other states. In the Arab world, the early consolidation of Nasser's Egypt allowed it to export its Pan-Arab revolution against weaker regimes. Walt, in his classic realist study *The Origin of Alliances,* shows, however, that even at the height of Pan-Arabism, which enjoined inter-Arab cooperation, Arab states widely balanced against each other and specifically against the Egyptian threat.

Not only did the conservative monarchies do so, but even Pan-Arab regimes in Syria and Iraq balanced against their ideologically natural Egyptian leader because the threat from Nasser overrode all ideological considerations.[41] This balancing preserved the state system against the Pan-Arab challenge. What Walt ignores is that just as Nasser's threat was mainly to domestic legitimacy (i.e., was political, not military), so balancing largely took the form of domestic state building to make regimes less permeable to ideological subversion. Pan-Arab transstate movements, having failed to overthrow the state system, gradually declined: states had outlived their main nonstate challengers.

The socialization of revisionist states. The state system was also entrenched by changes in its constituent parts, particularly the decline of revisionism. The pursuit of domestically driven revisionist policies to the neglect of the power balance, notably the Pan-Arab outbidding on the eve of the 1967 Arab-Israeli war or Islamic Iran's attempt to export revolution, typically led to military disasters.[42] These precipitated changes in leadership, the socialization of formerly revisionist states into more "realistic" behavior, and the state building required for survival amidst the anarchy of a state system. This was most dramatic in the case of Syria, where a weak regime's reckless policies toward Israel—partly followed for reasons of domestic legitimation—led to the 1967 military defeat, the rise of new realist leaders, and considerable state building, which gave leaders the internal autonomy of domestic pressures and the military capabilities to effectively balance external threats. This turned Syria from a victim of regional politics into a formidable actor.[43]

The unstable power balance. Throughout the region, heightened external threat fostered the consolidation and militarization of states during the 1970s and 1980s. While, as a result, states were better able to contain internal pressures and subordinate suprastate identity to reason of state, at the same time, this very state strengthening enhanced the potential threat each posed to the other. Regional order was now chiefly dependent on the balance of power, but unfortunately this balance proved widely unstable.

Power imbalances were built into the very fabric of the regional system. The unevenness of state formation allowed states consolidated earlier to threaten late developers—notably, giving the non-Arab periphery the advantage over weaker, less developed Arab states. There was also the arbitrary boundary drawing that created nonviable or ministates (around oil wells—Kuwait; or as buffers—Jordan) alongside large neighbors dissatisfied by these boundaries.

On top of this, power was not static and high insecurity induced states to improve their power position, potentially threatening existing power balances.[44] Indeed, regional power balances were repeatedly upset, in part because of the rapid differential growth in the relative power of certain states owing to their exceptional access to oil revenues and/or foreign aid and hence to arms deliveries from external powers. Thus, Israel and Iraq achieved power superiority over neighbors, providing the occasion—when combined with irredentist leaderships—for, altogether, four wars: Israel's 1967 preemptive war, its 1982 invasion of Lebanon, and Iraq's two Gulf wars. "Buck-passing," that is, the failure of stable alliances to maintain credible collective deterrents against such powerful threatening states, was also part of the problem. To be sure, in the end, power balances were subsequently restored, but only after very costly wars: thus, balancing preserves the system but does not necessarily keep the peace.

Order and power politics. To the degree a state system is consolidated, geopolitics becomes, as realism expects, an increasingly important determinant of foreign policy. A state's capabilities, plus the strategic importance or vulnerability of its location, shapes the main threats it faces and its likely ambitions: hence, small powers (Jordan, Gulf states) are more likely to seek the protection of greater ones and stronger powers are more likely to seek spheres of regional influence (e.g., Syria in the Levant, Saudi Arabia in the Gulf Cooperation Council [GCC] countries). Once ideological revisionism is replaced by geopolitics, the balance of power is more likely to be stable. This tendency is apparent across the Middle East, with the abnormal exception of Iraq, and is, so far, the main source of regional stability.

Realist solutions to the problem of order remain more relevant in the Middle East than elsewhere because, as Yaniv argues, transnational norms restraining interstate conduct are the least-institutionalized there.[45] This, in turn, is arguably because the conditions that pluralists expect to generate the norms that tame the power struggle—democratic cultures and economic interdependence—are absent or weak in the region. Economic dependence on the core states and autarky-seeking neomercantilist reactions against dependence have both stunted the regional economic interdependence that pluralism expects to generate shared interests in the peaceful resolution of conflicts. Moreover, not only do most regimes remain authoritarian but, against pluralist expectations, relative democratization does not necessarily lead to less risky or more status quo foreign policies because populations have remained mobilizable by transstate and irredentist ideology. Thus, democratic Israel has repeatedly attacked its semidemocratic neighbor, Lebanon. In the Gulf crisis, the more democratization permitted public opinion to express itself over foreign policy, the more pro-Saddam opinion forced leaders into distancing themselves from the anti-Iraq coalition. This is consistent with the findings of Mansfield and Snyder that established democratic regimes may be more pacific, but fragile *democratizing* regimes are actually *more* inclined to war than stable authoritarian ones since winning elections encourages resort to the nationalist card.[46]

With the end of the Cold War and the onset of U.S. hegemony and globalization, pluralists such as Etel Solingen argue that zones of peace are spreading. Economic interdependency, she argues, is associated with the rise of internationalist coalitions to power inside states that seek integration into the global economy. This requires moderating nationalist ideology and settling regional conflicts.[47] Certainly, economic liberalization in the Middle East has led to the co-optation of internationalist-minded *infitah* bourgeoisies into power and state attempts to demobilize masses susceptible to revisionist ideology. However, as realism argues, only when threat declines does the pursuit of economic gain displace security atop state agendas. In the Middle East, however, irredentism keeps the Arab-Israel conflict alive while Iraq's defiance of the West manifests the continued resistance to Western penetration. As long as these conflicts continue to generate insecurity, the spread of "zones of peace" will not soon rewrite the dominant realist rules of Middle East international politics.[48]

Plan of the Book

Chapters 2 through 4 look more closely at the international and regional environments in which the foreign policies of Middle East states are conducted. Chapters 5 through 14 examine case studies of key states, and Chapter 15 summarizes their findings. First, the book examines the major Arab powers that have been at the heart of the Arab system, namely Egypt, Syria, and Iraq, as well as Saudi Arabia, the major Arab financial power and the world's major oil producer. In addition, Israel, a major player in the conflicts at the heart of the regional system, is considered here. Additional Arab actors that are distinctive or representative for various reasons are then examined. Libya, an eccentric radical regime seen as a pariah state in the West, is, in some ways, a leftover from the previous age of ideology, while Tunisia, a Maghreb republic that is pioneering economic integration into the global market, may be the wave of the future. Yemen, a rising Arabian Peninsula power that alone has made a unity project successful, is also likely to be a weightier actor in the future. Then, the other major states (besides Israel) of the "non-Arab periphery" are examined, namely Iran and Turkey. The case studies attempt, so far as is practical, to take systematic account of the same variables, as indicated below.

- *Foreign-policy determinants.* The *why* of foreign policy is a function of such durable determinants as (1) the "external" threats, opportunities, constraints, and resources issuing from the international and regional systems; (2) domestic politics, shaped by identity and state formation: specifically the need to preserve regime legitimacy; and (3) economic needs and interdependencies.
- *Foreign policymaking.* The *who* and *how* of foreign policy concerns the effect of (1) elites' goals, perceptions, ideologies, and historic role conceptions; and (2) state institutions and policy processes, notably how the domestic power structure affects (a) the capacity of bureaucratic actors and public opinion to affect policymaking and (b) the leadership autonomy and capabilities that facilitate rational and effective policymaking and implementation.
- *Foreign-policy behavior.* The *what* of foreign policy includes long-term strategies and patterns of persistent behavior as well as watersheds of change in foreign policy—wars and conflict resolution, alignments and realignments—that, together, "construct" the regional system.

Notes

1. L. Carl Brown, *International Politics and the Middle East: Old Rules, Dangerous Game,* Princeton, NJ: Princeton University Press, 1984, pp. 3–5.

2. Barry Buzan, "New Patterns of Global Security in the Twenty-First Century," *International Affairs* 67, no. 3, July 1991, pp. 246–247.

3. Samir Amin, *The Arab Nation: Nationalism and Class Struggles,* London: Zed Press, 1978; Abbas Alnasrawi, *Arab Nationalism, Oil and the Political Economy of Dependency,* New York and London: Greenwood Press, 1991; Simon Bromley, *Rethinking Middle East Politics,* Oxford: Polity Press, 1994; Simon Bromley, *American Hegemony and World Oil: The Industry, the State System and the World Economy,* Oxford: Polity Press, 1990; Jacqueline Ismail, *Kuwait: Dependency & Class in a Rentier State,* Gainesville: University Press

of Florida, 1993; Caglar Keyder, *State and Class in Turkey: A Study in Capitalist Development,* London: Verso, 1987.

4. Johan Galtung, "A Structural Theory of Imperialism," *Journal of Peace Research* 8, no. 2, 1971, pp. 81–98.

5. Roger Owen, *The Middle East in the World Economy, 1800–1945,* London: Methuen, 1981; Alnasrawi, *Arab Nationalism,* pp. 1–23.

6. Bruce Moon, "The State in Foreign and Domestic Policy," in L. Neack, J. Hey, and P. Haney, eds., *Foreign Policy Analysis: Continuity and Change in Its Second Generation,* Englewood Cliffs, NJ: Prentice Hall, 1995, pp. 197–198.

7. Galtung, "A Structural Theory of Imperialism."

8. Bruce Moon, "Consensus or Compliance? Foreign-Policy Change and External Dependence," *International Organization* 39, no. 2, spring 1995.

9. Jeanne A. K. Hey, "Foreign Policy in Dependent States," in L. Neack, J. Hey, and P. Haney, eds., *Foreign Policy Analysis: Continuity and Change in Its Second Generation,* Englewood Cliffs, NJ: Prentice Hall, 1995, pp. 201–213; Adrienne Armstrong, "The Political Consequences of Economic Dependence," *Journal of Conflict Resolution* 25, 1981, pp. 401–428.

10. Immanuel Wallerstein, "The Rise and Future Demise of the World Capitalist System: Concepts for Comparative Analysis," *Comparative Studies in History and Society* 16, no. 4, 1974, pp. 387–415; Wallerstein, *The Modern World System,* New York: Academic Press, 1974.

11. Oran Young, "Political Discontinuities in the International System," *World Politics* 20, no. 3, April 1968.

12. Fawaz Gerges, *The Superpowers and the Middle East: Regional and International Politics,* Boulder, CO: Westview Press, 1994, pp. 1–17, 245–251; L. Carl Brown, *International Politics and the Middle East,* pp. 197–232; Alan Taylor, *The Superpowers and the Middle East,* Syracuse, NY: Syracuse University Press, 1991; Yezid Sayigh and Avi Shlaim, *The Cold War and the Middle East,* Oxford: Clarendon Press, 1997; Yair Evron, *Nations, Superpowers and Wars,* London: Elek Books, 1973; David Lesch, *The Middle East and the United States,* Boulder, CO: Westview Press, 1996.

13. William R. Thompson, "The Arab Sub-System and the Feudal Pattern of Interaction: 1965," *Journal of Peace Research* 7, 1970, pp. 151–167.

14. Laurie Brand, *Jordan's Inter-Arab Relations: The Political Economy of Alliance Making,* New York: Columbia University Press, 1995; Bassel Salloukh, "State Strength, Permeability, and Foreign Policy Behavior: Jordan in Theoretical Perspective," *Arab Studies Quarterly* 18, no. 2, spring 1996.

15. Michael Hudson, "To Play the Hegemon: Fifty Years of U.S. Policy in the Middle East," *Middle East Journal* 50, no. 3, summer 1996.

16. Atif Kubursi and Salim Mansur, "Oil and the Gulf War: An American Century or a 'New World Order'?" *Arab Studies Quarterly* 15, no. 4, fall 1993; Laura Guazzone, *The Middle East in Global Change: The Politics and Economics of Interdependence Versus Fragmentation,* London: Macmillan Press, 1997; Paul Aarts, "The Middle East: A Region Without Regionalism or the End of Exceptionalism?" *Third World Quarterly* 20, no. 5, October 1999, pp. 911–925.

17. Paul Noble, "The Arab System: Pressures, Constraints, and Opportunities," in Bahgat Korany and Ali E. Hillal Dessouki, *The Foreign Policies of*

Arab States: The Challenge of Change, Boulder, CO: Westview Press, 1991, p. 57.

18. F. Gregory Gause III, "Sovereignty, Statecraft and Stability in the Middle East," *Journal of International Affairs* 45, no. 2, winter 1992, pp. 441–467; Mohammed Ayoob, *The Third World Security Predicament: State Making, Regional Conflict and the International System,* Boulder, CO: Lynne Rienner, 1995, pp. 47–70.

19. Michael Hudson, *Arab Politics: The Search for Legitimacy,* New Haven, CT: Yale University Press, 1977, pp. 33–55; Bahgat Korany, "The Dialectics of Inter-Arab Relations, 1967–1987," in Abdullah Battah and Yehuda Lukas, eds., *The Arab-Israeli Conflict: Two Decades of Change,* Boulder, CO: Westview Press, 1988, pp. 164–178.

20. Eberhard Kienle, *Ba'th Versus Ba'th: The Conflict Between Syria and Iraq,* London: I. B. Tauris, 1990, pp. 1–30.

21. Bahgat Korany, "Alien and Besieged Yet Here to Stay: The Contradictions of the Arab Territorial State," in Ghassan Salame, ed., *The Foundations of the Arab State,* London: Croom Helm, 1987, pp. 47–74; Kienle, *Ba'th Versus Ba'th,* pp. 9, 27.

22. Michael Barnett, *Dialogues in Arab Politics: Negotiations in Regional Order.* New York: Columbia University Press, 1999. Constructivism is explicated in Alexander Wendt, *Social Theory of International Politics,* Cambridge: Cambridge University Press, 1999.

23. For other similar explorations of this dynamic, see Noble, "The Arab System," pp. 55–60; Gregory Gause, "Systemic Approaches to Middle East International Relations," *International Studies Review* 1, no. 1, spring 1999, pp. 11–31; Michael N. Barnett, "Sovereignty, Nationalism, and Regional Order in the Arab States System," *International Organization* 49, no. 3, summer 1995; Michael N. Barnett, "Institutions, Roles and Disorder: The Case of the Arab States System," *International Studies Quarterly* 37, no. 3, September 1993; Roger Owen, "Arab Nationalism, Arab Unity and the Practice of Intra-Arab State Relations," in Roger Owen, ed., *State, Power and Politics in the Making of the Modern Middle East,* London: Routledge, 1992, chapter 4, pp. 81–107.

24. Avraham Sela, *The End of the Arab-Israeli Conflict: Middle East Politics and the Quest for Regional Order,* Albany: State University of New York Press, 1998.

25. Hedley Bull, *The Anarchical Society,* London: Macmillan, 1977.

26. Robert Goode, "State Building as a Determinant of Foreign Policy in the New States," in Laurence W. Martin, ed., *Neutralism and Non-Alignment,* New York: Praeger, 1962; Peter Calvert, *The Foreign Policies of New States,* Sussex: Wheatsheaf Books, 1986; Ali E. Hilal Dessouki, "Dilemmas of Security and Development in the Arab World: Aspects of Linkage," in Bahgat Korany, Paul Noble, and Rex Brynen, eds., *The Many Faces of National Security in the Middle East,* New York: Macmillan, 1993, pp. 76–90.

27. For an assessment of this approach, see Bahgat Korany, *How Foreign Policy Decisions Are Made in the Third World,* Boulder, CO: Westview Press, 1986.

28. Adeed Dawisha and I. William Zartman, *Beyond Coercion: The Durability of the Arab State,* London: Croom Helm, 1988; Malik Mufti, *Sovereign*

Creations: Pan-Arabism and Political Order in Syria and Iraq, Ithaca and London: Cornell University Press, 1996, pp. 9–16.

29. Nazih Ayubi, *Overstating the Arab State: Politics and Society in the Middle East,* London: I. B. Tauris, 1995, pp. 196–255; James Bill and Robert Springborg, *Politics in the Middle East,* Glenville, IL: Little, Brown, 1990, pp. 177–299; Michael Hudson, *Arab Politics: The Search for Legitimacy,* New Haven, CT: Yale University Press, 1977.

30. Dawisha and Zartman, *Beyond Coercion;* Mufti, *Sovereign Creations.*

31. Steven David, "Explaining Third World Alignment," *World Politics* 43, no. 2, 1991, pp. 233–256.

32. Kal Holsti, "National Role Conception in the Study of Foreign Policy," *International Studies Quarterly* 14, 1970, pp. 233–309; Ali ad-Din Hillal Dessouki and Bahgat Korany make the case for role as a pivotal variable in "A Literature Survey and Framework of Analysis," in Dessouki and Korany, eds., *The Foreign Policies of Arab States,* Boulder, CO: Westview Press, 1991, pp. 17–18.

33. Graham Allison and Morton Halperin, "Bureaucratic Politics: A Paradigm and Some Policy Implications, *World Politics* 24 (supplement), 1972, pp. 40–79; Gregory Kasza, "Bureaucratic Politics in Radical Military Regimes," *American Political Science Review* 81, 1987, pp. 851–872; Jerel Rosati, "A Cognitive Approach to the Study of Foreign Policy," in L. Neack, J. Hey, and P. Haney, eds., *Foreign Policy Analysis: Continuity and Change in Its Second Generation,* Englewood Cliffs, NJ: Prentice Hall, 1995, pp. 49–70.

34. Tareq Y. Ismael, *International Relations of the Contemporary Middle East: A Study in World Politics,* Syracuse, NY: Syracuse University Press, pp. 35–37; Adeed Dawisha, "Arab Regimes: Legitimacy and Foreign Policy," in Adeed Dawisha and I. William Zartman, eds., *Beyond Coercion: The Durability of the Arab State,* London: Croom Helm, 1988, pp. 264–265.

35. Dawisha, "Arab Regimes," pp. 266, 274.

36. Shibley Telhami, *Power and Leadership in International Bargaining: The Path to the Camp David Accords,* New York: Columbia University Press.

37. Maridi Nahas, "State Systems and Revolutionary Challenge: Nasser, Khomeini and the Middle East," *International Journal of Middle East Studies* 17, 1985; F. Gregory Gause III, "Revolutionary Fevers and Regional Contagion: Domestic Structures and the Export of Revolution in the Middle East," *Journal of South Asian and Middle East Studies* 14, no. 3, spring 1991; F. Gregory Gause III, "Sovereignty and Its Challengers: War in Middle Eastern Inter-State Politics," in Paul Salem, ed., *Conflict Resolution in the Arab World,* Beirut: AUB Press, 1997, pp. 197–215.

38. R. Harknett and J. VanDenBerg, "Alignment Theory and Interrelated Threats: Jordan and the Persian Gulf Crisis," in *Security Studies* 6, no. 3, spring 1997, pp. 112–153.

39. Dankwart Rustow, "Realignments in the Middle East," *Foreign Affairs* 63, no. 3, 1984, p. 598.

40. Kenneth Waltz, *Theory of International Politics,* Boston: Addison-Wesley, 1979, pp. 74–77.

41. Steven Walt, *The Origin of Alliances,* Ithaca, NY: Cornell University Press, 1987. See also Yair Evron and Yaacov Bar-Simantov, "Coalitions in the

Arab World," *Jerusalem Journal of International Relations* 1, no. 2, 1976, pp. 71–72; Alan Taylor, *The Arab Balance of Power,* Syracuse, NY: Syracuse University Press, 1982; Malcolm Kerr, *The Arab Cold War: Gamal Abd al-Nasir and His Rivals, 1958–1970,* London: Oxford University Press, 1971.

42. Janice Stein, "The Security Dilemma in the Middle East: The Prognosis for the Decade Ahead," in Bahgat Korany, Paul Noble, and Rex Brynen, eds., *The Many Faces of National Security in the Middle East,* New York: Macmillan, 1993, pp. 36–75.

43. Yair Evron, *War and Intervention in Lebanon: The Syrian-Israeli Deterrence Dialogue.* Baltimore: Johns Hopkins University Press, 1987. This arguably replicates the European experience where external threats were a major impetus to state formation. See Charles Tilly, *Formation of National States in Western Europe,* Princeton, NJ: Princeton University Press 1969; for Third World experience at defensive modernization, see Ellen Kay Trimberger, *Revolution from Above: Military Bureaucrats and Development in Japan, Turkey, Egypt and Peru,* New Brunswick, NJ: Transaction Books, 1978.

44. This dynamic is examined at the global level in Robert Gilpin, *War and Change in World Politics,* Cambridge: Cambridge University Press, 1981.

45. Avner Yaniv, "Alliance Politics in the Middle East: A Security Dilemma Perspective," in Auriel Braun, ed., *The Middle East in Global Strategy,* Boulder, CO: Westview Press, 1987.

46. Edward Mansfield and Jack Snyder, "The Dangers of Democratization," *International Security* 20, no. 1, summer 1995, pp. 5–38.

47. Etil Solingen, *Regional Orders at Century's Dawn: Global and Domestic Influence on Grand Strategy,* Princeton, NJ: Princeton University Press, 1998.

48. Augustus Richard Norton, "The Security Legacies of the 1980s in the Third World," in Thomas G Weiss and Meryl A. Kessler, eds., *Third World Security in the Post–Cold War Era,* Boulder, CO: Lynne Rienner, 1991, pp. 19–33.

2

The Middle East Regional System

Raymond Hinnebusch

The Middle East regional system is taken here to be comprised of the Arab League members, Turkey, Iran, and Israel. The Arab states, with shared identity, intense interactions, and membership in a regional organization, the Arab League, are judged to make up the core of the system. None of this means that they necessarily act cohesively in foreign policy; but when the Arab world is divided it is much more vulnerable to penetration from the great powers and to threats from its non-Arab neighbors. The non-Arab states Turkey, Iran, and Israel comprise, by virtue of their relative exclusion from the core community, the periphery of the system, but they are, nonetheless, members by virtue of their geographic contiguity and intimate involvement in the region's conflicts. This makes them integral parts of the regional balance of power; in particular, they have tended either to constitute threats to the weaker Arab core or have acted to contain its instability in alliance with external powers.[1] In this chapter, they will mainly be treated in respect to this role in the system, but in the country cases their wider roles will be given more attention.

Between Identity and Sovereignty

The Middle East is marked by high incongruity between the nation (identity) and the territorial state (sovereignty). If, in some respects, the dilemma of the Arab world is "one nation/many states," there and in the non-Arab Middle East, the multinational state ("one state, plural nations") is also the rule rather than the exception. This is bound to complicate foreign policymaking.

The Arab World

The Arab states, mostly successors of the Ottoman Empire, retain a high degree of linguistic and cultural similarity. Similar music and art, food, marriage, and child-rearing practices are recognizable region-wide. Extended family ties frequently cross borders. The common Arabic language—the critical ingredient of nationhood—has, owing to a standard newspaper and media Arabic, become more homogeneous, stunting the evolution of national dialects as the linguistic basis of separate nations. Arab satellite television has reinvigorated a sense of shared experience and identity. This makes the Arab world, in Noble's words, a "vast sound chamber" in which ideas and information circulate widely.[2] Cross-border migration has been constant: in the 1950s, there were major flows of Palestinian refugees; since the 1970s, labor migration to the Gulf oil-producing states has been the norm. Niblock argues that the interests of the separate Arab states are too intertwined—by labor supply, investment funds, security, water, communications routes, and the Palestine issue—for them to develop self-sufficient coherence.[3]

As a result, transstate identities—Arabism and Islam—are, for many people, more emotionally compelling than identification with the state. There is a widespread transstate feeling of belonging to a distinct Arab world (*al-alam al-arabi*). According to 1978 survey data, 78 percent believed the Arabs constituted a nation, 53 percent believed the state boundaries were artificial, and the majority supported doing away with them in favor of a larger, perhaps decentralized state.[4] Uniquely in the Arab world, not this or that border, but state boundaries in general, have been regarded by many Arabs as arbitrarily and externally imposed at the expense of Arabism, depriving them of the legitimacy and sanctity they enjoy elsewhere. It is not that most Arabs reject any state boundaries; indeed, most have not insisted on a single Arab state, but the extreme fragmentation of the region is viewed as a divide-and-rule strategy by imperialism and a cause of Arab weakness. At the level of formal ideology, this sentiment was manifest in the doctrines of Arab nationalism, which viewed all Arabic-speakers as forming a nation, the states of which, at a minimum, ought to act together for common interests, or be constitutionally confederated, or, in its most ambitious form, Ba'thism, be merged into a single state embracing this nation. Arabism is enshrined in state constitutions: Jabbour found thirteen Arab constitutions that defined the nation as the Arab nation, with only Lebanon and Tunisia referring to a Lebanese and Tunisian nationhood.[5]

Historical memories of greatness under unity and experience that the Arabs are successful when they act together (e.g., the 1973 war and use of the "oil weapon"), and are readily dominated when divided, keeps Arabism alive. So does the sense of common victimization: the Crusades are part of every schoolboy or girl's historical world view; the loss of Palestine is seen as a common Arab disaster; the 1967 defeat shamed all Arabs, not just the defeated frontline states. On the other hand, the relative successes in the 1973 war inspired solidarity across the region. In the 1990s, the suffering of Iraqis imposed by the Western economic sanctions was not seen as the affliction of another nation or people that, however regrettable, was not the business of Syrians or Tunisians; to some extent, their pain and humiliation is seen as a common trauma. More recently, all Arabs shared Lebanon's euphoria at Israel's evacuation of southern Lebanon under Hizbollah pressure in June 2000. Foreign policymakers cannot escape the powerful sway of these sentiments to act for common Arab causes, not simple "reason of state."

Nevertheless, there have always been territorial fault lines in the region that could potentially generate identities supportive of territorially based (as opposed to linguistically or ethnically based) separate nations. Harik argues that a viable basis of statehood exists in a multitude of geographical entities with distinct historical experiences: where minority sects established autonomous regimes (Yemen, Oman, Lebanon); where tribal or tribal-religious movements founded states (Saudi Arabia); or where Mamluk elites achieved autonomy as Ottoman power declined (Tunisia). The Western imposition of the contemporary state system on these protonations, defining permanent boundaries that protected them from absorption, and endowing them with ruling elites and state apparatuses, crystallized their statehood.[6]

The result is that multiple levels of identity coexist, albeit in varying ways. In some states, identification with the separate states overshadows without wholly displacing Arabism; in others, state and Arab identities overlap; while in yet others, state identities remain subordinate to or indistinguishable from Arabism. At the first end of the continuum is a rentier city-state such as Kuwait, where Farah's study found state identification came first (24.3 percent), then religious affiliation (14.4 percent), and Arabism last.[7] If Kuwait were acknowledged to be a mere part of the Arab nation, then Kuwaiti oil would be an Arab patrimony to be equitably shared with other parts of the Arab nation, not least the legions of Arab expatriates working in Kuwait. The geographically separate Maghreb (North Africa) has also always identified less with Arab nationalism than local statehood. Some Tunisian writers defend the idea of a distinct Tunisian nation and Morocco has a long history under an independent dynasty.[8] Yet in the 1973 Arab-Israeli war, Morocco's pro-Western ruler thought it to his domestic advantage to send a contingent of troops to the far-off Syrian front; and the strong reaction in the Maghreb to the 1991 Western attack on Iraq showed that Arab-Islamic identities remained powerful, if usually latent.

In Egypt, where a strong sense of territorial identity is based on the Nile Valley and a history of statehood predating the Arabs, theorists such as Louis Awad contrast the reality of an Egyptian nation with the myth of an Arab nation.[9] Yet, Egyptian identity is Arab-Islamic in content, and attempts to construct alternative definitions of Egyptianness— "Pharaonic" or "Mediterranean"—have failed. Thus, even in the late 1970s when Egypt was withdrawing from Pan-Arab commitments, a survey of high-status Egyptians (traditionally relatively unreceptive to Pan-Arabism) indicated that, although 71.3 percent identified with Egypt first, 71.1 percent said Egypt was a part of the Arab nation, indeed the natural leader of the Arabs.[10] This strong sense of kinship with the Arab world meant that decisions taken purely on grounds of state interest— such as the separate peace with Israel and membership in the Gulf war coalition—which would be perfectly natural were Egypt a consolidated nation-state, were extremely controversial and probably damaging to regime legitimacy.

At the other end of the continuum, in many Mashreq (Fertile Crescent) cases, externally imposed borders corresponded to no history of independent statehood, much less nationhood. It is no accident that the main Pan-Arab nationalist movement, Ba'thism, was born in Syria, and was most successful there and in Iraq and Jordan. Thus, if *bilad ash-sham,* historical and geographical Syria, might have supported a viable nationhood, its fragmentation into four ministates (Syria, Jordan, Lebanon, and Palestine) prevented the truncated Damascus-ruled rump from becoming a strong uncontested focus of identity; the attempt to generate a separate non-Arab Syrian national identity by the Syrian Social Nationalist Party came to nothing, and for most Syrians the dominant identity has been Arab. Iraq is the opposite case, a state artificially constructed by imperialism that threw together communally different Ottoman provinces in which, ever since, the political dominance of the Sunnis has been contested by the Shi'a majority and the non-Arab Kurds. A national identity acceptable to all substate groups remained elusive, but Arabism was imposed by the dominant groups.

Identity has of course varied over time. As Pan-Arabism declined after the 1960s, separate state identities became more credible. Yet Pan-Arab decline also seemed to leave an ideological vacuum filled by the rise, in the 1970s and 1980s, of another suprastate identity, political Islam. To be sure, Islamic movements are no mere substitute for Pan-Arabism; rather, they have concentrated more on creating Islamic societies within individual states than seeking a Pan-Islamic order. Individual states have long used Islam to legitimate themselves, and the Organization of the Islamic Conference charter acknowledges state sovereignty.

However, although secular Arabism and political Islam are in some ways ideological rivals, their foreign-policy identities largely reinforce each other. Islam and Arabism both prioritize loyalty to the Arab or Islamic community (*umma*) over citizenship of individual states. Both insist on economic and cultural autonomy of the Western-dominated world system and reject Western penetration. Both reject the legitimacy of Israel; radical Islamic movements such as Hamas and Hizbollah are primarily manifestations of Arab national resistance to Israel rather than promoters of a religious agenda. Particularly in periods of crisis with Israel or the West, when Arab and Islamic identities are simultaneously inflamed, their advocates have combined to put renewed, if temporary, pressures on foreign policymakers. Thus, even in the *maghrebi* (North African) regions long thought to be immune to Arabism, Islamic movements were pivotal in arousing opposition to the Western attack on Arab Iraq that forced local states to distance themselves from Western policy.[11]

The Non-Arab Periphery

In the non-Arab periphery, the incongruity between state and identity is less salient than in the Arab world and, in particular, puts no comparable constraints on state elites' pursuit of reason of state. Turkey and Iran have long histories as separate imperial centers and have constructed modern nations around their dominant ethnolinguistic cores with considerable success despite the unfinished task of integrating a multitude of minorities, above all the Kurds. Israel's very identity as a state is inseparable from its role as a homeland for Jews, despite its Arab minority and diverse ethnic origins.

Vital to understanding the regional roles of the periphery states is that each has, in significant ways, constructed its identity in opposition to that of the Arab core: Israel sees itself besieged by the Arab world and Turkey's modern secularity aims to differentiate it from its Arab-Islamic hinterland. Iran's position is currently more ambivalent. The Persian-Arab cleavage in part shaped Pahlavi Iran's aspirations to act as the regional guardian against Arab instability and radicalism. This was superseded after the revolution by a powerful Islamic identity that made Iran seek a leadership role in the Arab world. But Iran's Shi'ism still differentiated it from the Sunnism predominant in the Arab world, and

Iran's leadership claims, based on Islamic paramountcy, were not recognized by the Arab states, except as a threat. Significantly, each of the non-Arab states is engaged in irredentist-inflamed border conflicts with an Arab neighbor; besides the Arab-Israeli conflict, Turkey has long-standing disputes with Syria while Iran has been in intermittent conflict with Iraq and the United Arab Emirates.

The Evolution of the Regional System

Birth of the States System: Quasi-Independence
Under Oligarchic Multipolarity (1945–1955)

In the years after World War II, the periphery states—Turkey, Iran, and Israel—more advanced in nation building, militarily stronger, and aligned with the West, flanked a weak, fragmented Arab core barely emerging from colonial control. The Arab states were narrowly based oligarchies or dynasties, highly penetrated by the great powers, above all by Great Britain, which retained bases and treaty relations with regimes headed by its clients. The main threat to the system was instability within the individual states: the weak popular loyalty to newly imposed regimes and boundaries, regimes' inability to politically incorporate the rising middle class, gross maldistribution of wealth, still-incomplete decolonization, and the loss of Palestine all soon delegitimized the regimes even as they struggled to consolidate their formal independence. As such, foreign policy was chiefly used to counter domestic threats: either regimes used anti-imperialist rhetoric to shore up their fragile legitimacy or they sought protection from the Western powers against domestic opposition.

The main sources of revisionism included the instability on the Arab-Israeli cease-fire lines and Hashemite ambitions. Iraq dreamed of being an Arab Prussia unifying the Fertile Crescent, while Jordan under King Abdullah promoted a "Greater Syria" scheme and pursued deals with Israel to acquire a chunk of Palestine (the West Bank). Hashemite ambitions precipitated a counteralliance of Egypt, Saudi Arabia, and Syria—which was particularly threatened by Hashemite absorption. This power balancing, plus the restraint put on the Hashemites by their British patron, helped preserve the status quo. So did a shared elitist (dynastic or oligarchic) ideology that facilitated growing acceptance of the rules of a multipolar system, that is, that no state should push its interest so far as to endanger the vital interests of its neighbors.[12]

The Arab League attempted to institutionalize respect for the sovereignty of individual states while acknowledging shared Arab identities and the need for a collective response to the common threat from Zionism. Its legitimacy was, however, tarnished by its failure to coordinate the defense of Palestine, and the most it achieved was a consensus against relations with Israel.

The Rise and Fall of the
Egypt-Centric Pan-Arab System (1956–1970)

Oligarchic multipolarity was transformed by a congruence between the destabilization of oligarchic states amidst the political mobilization of the middle class and the emergence of the radical Nasser regime in Egypt, whose head start in the incorporation of popular support made it the only stable Arab state. Nasser deployed transstate Pan-Arab ideology to challenge the old regimes, upsetting the oligarchic "balance of weakness." He put Egypt at the center of the Arab world, giving it a new cohesion, rolling back Western control, and enforcing Arab solidarity against the non-Arab periphery.

Nasser and the rise of Pan-Arabism. While Nasser may have genuinely identified with the Arab world, his Arab policy served Egypt's aim of replacing Western imperialist influence in the region with Egyptian hegemony. Egypt's Pan-Arab strategy emerged from a contest with conservative Iraq, Egypt's major rival, over the Baghdad Pact. While the pact would have harnessed the Arabs to Turkey and Iran in the containment of communism, Nasser saw the West and Israel as the main threats, saw no role for Iran and Turkey in the Arab world, and proposed, instead, a collective Arab security pact and Arab nonalignment. The independence of the Arab states could only be consolidated by a pooling of resources for their own defense.[13] Nasser's victory in the struggle to win over Syria, Jordan, and Lebanon laid the foundations of Egypt's Arab hegemony.

Egyptian hegemony was not a function of the balance of power as conventionally measured. To be sure, Egypt was the most populous Arab state, having 30 percent of the Arab population, and the only one with a secure identity and a developed state infrastructure. Its large gross national product gave it a modest ability to provide economic aid and enabled it to support the largest Arab army through defense expenditures double those of any other Arab state.[14] But Egypt normally could not use its army to project power, being cut off from the Arab

East by Israel and constrained by international norms. The key to Nasser's hegemony was, therefore, his asymmetrical ability to project transstate influence: while the Egyptian populace was immune to the appeal of Nasser's rivals, he became a Pan-Arab hero who, with the advent of the transistor radio, could reach and mobilize publics across the Arab world against recalcitrant rival leaders at odds with Egypt's Arab nationalist line.[15] Moreover, Egypt was the cultural hegemon of the Arab world and—as the main exporter of books, newspapers, films, and teachers who staffed schools throughout the Middle East—was uniquely positioned to shape the rising generation of opinion leaders.[16]

On the other hand, the superior military power of the non-Arab states, even when allied with great powers, proved impotent or even counterproductive in shaping the regional order. The attempts of Israel, militarily superior but insecure, to compel Arab acceptance and check Nasser's rising prestige resulted in border clashes that inflamed Arab nationalist opinion to Nasser's benefit. These clashes also stimulated Egypt's 1955 Czech arms deal, which enormously boosted Egypt's Arab prestige as the only state with the potential to check Israeli power and, in turn, encouraged Nasser to assume new responsibilities for collective Arab defense. The 1956 Suez war was launched to shatter Nasser's prestige but, despite Egypt's military defeat, actually had the opposite effect, while undermining the pro-Western conservative regimes and destroying remaining British influence. The U.S. attempt to fill the vacuum and contain Syrian radicalism under the Eisenhower Doctrine only pushed Syria into union with Egypt under the United Arab Republic (UAR). Washington's attempt to draw Turkey and, to a lesser degree, Pahlavi Iran, into a conservative pro-Western concert against Arab nationalism only more sharply differentiated the peripheral states from the Arab ones. As Egypt was established as the center of the Arab world, it acquired the capacity to leverage the superpowers; the growing involvement of the USSR in the Middle East checked the ability of the West and its local Turkish and Iranian allies to use their military power, thus forcing them to compete on the ground of ideology and subversion where Nasser enjoyed an unmatched advantage. And, once it seemed clear that Egypt could not be dislodged as Pan-Arab hegemon, Nasser was able to extract aid from both East and West.[17]

Egypt under Nasser came close to, but never achieved, the "organizing" of the region, in Leon Carl Brown's term.[18] The arousal of Arab nationalism precipitated coups and movements against pro-Western regimes across the region and culminated in the UAR, which united Egypt with the most intensely Pan-Arab state, Syria, from 1959 to 1961.

A series of kindred Arab-nationalist regimes arose in Syria, Iraq, Yemen, and later in Sudan and Libya. This revolutionary wave put the conservative Western-leaning monarchies on the defensive and generally enhanced Nasser's ability to pressure all Arab states into observing common Arab-nationalist norms.[19] Indeed, Nasser arguably created an informal "international regime" that, in enforcing already latent Arab-nationalist norms, constrained the unfettered exercise of sovereignty in foreign policymaking by the other Arab states. The power of one such core norm, independence from imperialism, was reflected in the abandonment of Western bases and treaties across the Arab world and the reluctance of conservative states to overtly align with their natural Western protectors as they sought to appease—or "bandwagon" with—Egypt. The result was a more autonomous Arab system, much more impervious to Western influence and intervention than heretofore.[20] A second norm, the rejection of the legitimacy of Israel and support of the Palestine cause (ideally the liberation of Palestine), did not translate into effective common action against Israel, but it did enforce Israel's isolation; thus, Jordan, even when most threatened by its radical neighbors, refrained from alliance with Israel, although the kingdom benefited covertly from an understanding that Israel would intervene if Jordan appeared in danger of absorption.[21] To a degree, elites were socialized into these Pan-Arab norms and subjected to peer pressures to observe them, notably at Arab summits. The main enforcement mechanism, however, was leaders' fear of the domestic legitimacy costs and consequent internal opposition their violation could entail.

Nevertheless, there were disagreements over Pan-Arab norms—the extent of permissible relations with the West, the degree of militancy toward Israel, and so on—and Cairo's attempt to impose its interpretation, especially when this spilled over into a revolutionary challenge to the very legitimacy of rival states, provoked an antihegemonic backlash. When, in 1958, nationalist revolution swept away the pillar of the old order, Hashemite Iraq, and it looked as if the conservative side would be overwhelmed, British paratroopers landed in Jordan and U.S. Marines in Lebanon to check the domino effect and stabilize conservative regimes. After this, Nasser's conservative rivals were less reluctant to defy him and the Arab world became more sharply polarized between radical republics and status quo monarchies resisting Cairo's hegemony. However, Nasser's unwillingness to share power even with ideological allies, manifest in the 1961 breakup of the UAR, stimulated an anti-Cairo reaction among kindred Pan-Arab leaders as well. Thus, the revolutionary camp split when Abd al-Karim Qassim, Iraq's revolutionary leader, rejected Egyptian tutelage and Nasser, in response, joined Jordan and Saudi Arabia in sending troops to protect Kuwait against Qassim's irredentism. While the 1963 Ba'thist coups in Iraq and Syria raised the prospect of a powerful and radical Pan-Arab bloc, the Ba'thists' fear of Nasser's domination caused the failure of the unity talks with Egypt; instead, the weaker Syrian and Iraqi regimes balanced against ideologically kindred Egypt and challenged Nasser's leadership of the radical camp, which again pushed Nasser into détente with the conservative regimes. Thus the ideological bipolarity that had so put pro-Western regimes on the defensive was soon crosscut by phases of "revolutionary polycentrism" in which Nasser tacitly aligned with conservative regimes against Pan-Arab rivals, relieving the pressure on the former.[22] Moreover, in a classic act of realist balancing, the periphery states of Israel, Iran, and Turkey aligned, albeit tacitly and intermittently, in the so-called periphery pact to contain the putative Arab-nationalist threat from the core.

The 1967 war and the decline of Arabism. Nasser's very successes invited his overextension and ended in the 1967 Arab-Israeli war, Arab defeat, and the shattering of the Pan-Arab system. Israel's attack on its neighbors unleashed the war but it was the dynamics of Pan-Arabism that gave Israeli hawks the opportunity to realize their ambitions. In the mid-1960s, Egypt, as Pan-Arab leader, was under growing pressure to act against Israel, which was diverting the Jordan River to absorb more Jewish immigrants. The Palestinians, a permanently dissatisfied diaspora throughout the Arab world, were increasingly impatient for Arab action to resolve their plight; indeed, newly founded groups such as al-Fatah launched a guerrilla struggle against Israel that they hoped would detonate a wider Arab-Israeli war. Nasser argued that the Arab world had to build up its forces, modernize, and unify before it would be ready to take on Israel and, tied down in the Yemen civil war, he could hardly afford a confrontation. But his Arab rivals used the issue to put him on the defensive. Ba'thist Syria, a narrowly based radical regime, was championing the Palestine cause to win domestic legitimacy and outbid Nasser for Pan-Arab leadership. To contain revisionist Syria, Nasser initiated Arab summit meetings to spread responsibility for inaction among the Arab leaders.[23] The summits agreed to counter Israel by diverting the sources of the Jordan River that, since they rose in Syria, would force Damascus to bear the consequences of its own militancy. However, the Syrian Ba'th used Israeli attacks on its river diversion works to embarrass Nasser, criticizing the UN buffer force in the

Sinai (UNEF) that prevented him from deterring the Israelis.[24] When Nasser and Saudi Arabia fell out over Yemen and the conservative regimes joined the criticism of Egypt, Syria took advantage of this to entice Nasser into a radical Cairo-Damascus axis. While Nasser hoped this would remove Syria's incentive for nationalist outbidding, Syria viewed it as the essential backing for its sponsorship of Palestinian guerrilla warfare against Israel.

The war crisis began in May 1967 with Israeli retaliations and threats against Syria and Soviet pressures on Nasser to deter Israel. Despite the unfavorable power balance with Israel, Nasser could not remain passive if he was to protect his Arab leadership, under threat from both left and right.[25] He ordered the withdrawal of UNEF from the Sinai and sent Egyptian troops into the peninsula—with defensive instructions that assumed an Israeli first strike; this precipitated a countermobilization in Israel. Nasser could have de-escalated, but he allowed himself to be pushed into brinkmanship by the expectations raised by his own nationalist rhetoric: he closed the Straits of Tiran to Israeli shipping, thus reversing concessions he had made to Israel at the end of the Suez war. Inflamed public opinion also pushed Jordan's King Hussein, despite knowing it could cost him his territory and army, to join Egypt and Syria in a defense pact. Outbidding on Arab nationalism had entrapped all three Arab frontline states into a war none wanted.[26] Nasser had played into the hands of the Israeli generals who, confident of victory, seized the opportunity to smash the Arabs while Israel still had military superiority, achieve secure borders, force the Arabs to accept Israel and, for some on the Israeli right, to realize "Greater Israel."[27] In the war, Israel took the Sinai Peninsula and Gaza Strip from Egypt, the Golan Heights from Syria, and the "West Bank" from Jordan.

Wars are catalysts for changes in state systems and the 1967 war was no exception. It signaled the decline of Egyptian hegemony and the Egypt-centric Arab regime. Egypt had never enjoyed much capacity to project military power in the Arab world and its one attempt to do so, in Yemen, had ended in stalemate; Egypt's economic superiority was never enough to allow it to provide much economic reward, and by the late 1960s the costs of hegemony—first from Yemen, then from the 1967 defeat—were impoverishing the country, while the growing oil revenues accruing to the oil monarchies decisively shifted the balance of economic power to them. Cairo's hegemony was based largely on the ideological appeal of Arabism, but this was eroded by the failures of unionist schemes and shattered by the 1967 defeat, which some blamed on Arab nationalism.[28]

A second major effect of the 1967 war was that, in giving a mortal blow to Pan-Arab dreams, it started the process of Arab acceptance of the permanence, if not the legitimacy, of Israel. To be sure, Arabism remained sufficiently strong that the survival of the frontline regimes required that they vindicate themselves against Israel, whose occupation of their territory, touching on vital state and regime interests more directly than the Palestinian cause had ever done, locked them into the conflict. However, despite some short-term inflammation of radical sentiment, a longer-term ideological moderation was led by Nasser himself, who ended the ideological cold war with the conservative Arabs in return for economic subsidies and accepted the UN "land-for-peace" Resolution 242, a watershed in the Arab acceptance of Israel. Similarly, Hafiz al-Asad's rise in Syria marked the moderation of radical nationalism there, while the simultaneous 1970 crushing of the Palestine Liberation Organization (PLO) in Jordan marked the defeat of a transnational radical movement by a conservative monarchy. This started the gradual moderation of the PLO leadership itself, among whom the aim of liberating Palestine soon gave way to the much less ambitious drive for a Palestinian state confined to the West Bank and Gaza. Pan-Arab ideological dreams were giving way to the pursuit of limited territorial interests.

If 1967 marked the end of Arab-nationalist revisionism, it had the opposite effect on a triumphant Israel. Israel tripled its territory, achieved defensible borders, and asserted overwhelming military superiority.[29] But instead of this enhanced security promoting a greater willingness to reach a peace settlement, Israel's feeling of invincibility reduced its motivation to reach one while the opportunity to incorporate the remainder of historic Palestine whetted irredentist appetites.[30] The chance to trade the occupied lands for peace was sacrificed to the ambition of Greater Israel—to absorb and settle the occupied territories.

From "Arab Triangle" to Separate Peace (1970s)

The 1973 Arab-Israeli war. With the decline of the Egyptian hegemon, other Arab states acquired greater freedom to pursue their particular interests but those interests were now shaped by the much increased threat from Israel. Before 1967, the expectation that the great powers would restrain Israel, the greater immediate threat Arab rivals posed to each other, and the little practical possibility of liberating Palestine had deterred effective alliance building against Israel.[31] Subsequently, however, a militarily preponderant and expansive Israel had to be contained while the occupied territories were potentially recoverable. This was only possible through inter-Arab cooperation, and the much reduced threat of Cairo made this cooperation less risky for the other Arab states. Military power mobilization—Soviet arms financed by Arab oil revenues—became the preoccupation of the main frontline states, setting the tone for the whole Arab system.

The death of Nasser ended Egypt's hegemonic role as his successor, Sadat, having neither the will or Pan-Arab stature to continue it, subordinated all other concerns to the recovery of the Sinai. Egypt was still the pivotal Arab state that alone could take the leadership in a war for the occupied territories[32] and gradually Egypt and Syria, under new pragmatic leaders, were thrown together by their common interest in this goal; Saudi Arabia took advantage of their need for financial backing to moderate their policies and achieve full partnership in core Arab affairs. If no one state had enough assets to play the hegemon, an axis of the largest (Egypt), the richest (Saudi Arabia), and the most Pan-Arab (Syria) states could pool complementary resources and forge an Arab consensus on war and peace. This "Arab Triangle" or trilateral alliance would, for a period, replace Egyptian hegemony as a new basis of Arab cohesion based on the consensus building made possible by the greater equality, hence trust, between the main leaders, Sadat, Asad, and Faysal.[33]

Sadat sought to enlist U.S. diplomatic patronage of a political settlement with Israel, but war became inevitable when the United States rebuffed his bid. Though Sadat, dissatisfied with Soviet reluctance to provide offensive arms, expelled Soviet advisers as an opening to the United States, Kissinger did not take it up and the Soviets eventually provided the weapons needed for a war.[34] In October 1973, Egypt and Syria launched a coordinated attack on the Israeli-occupied territories while Saudi Arabia deployed the "oil weapon" to force the intervention of U.S. diplomacy. Relative Arab success in the war caused a massive resurgence of Arab nationalism that drove all Arab states to close ranks behind the frontline states: Iraqi and Jordanian forces played crucial roles in containing Israeli counteroffensives against Syria,[35] while Morocco and Saudi Arabia sent token contingents to the front lines and Algeria and the Gulf states provided finance for Soviet arms deliveries. The Arab states failed to liberate the occupied territories, but their ability to challenge and inflict high costs on Israel partly righted the power imbalance against them. This and the oil embargo sufficiently upset the status quo to force U.S. intervention on behalf of a negotiated settlement. At the same time, the relative Arab success in the war endowed the frontline states with a legitimacy windfall that made it possible for them to move toward a peace settlement. The big three agreed on a "comprehensive peace" with Israel on the basis of UN Security Council Resolution 242, legitimized in a round of Arab summits. These summits also designated the PLO as the sole representative of the Palestinians in peace negotiations and marginalized rejectionist states such as Iraq.

There was an expectation that the new Arab oil wealth precipitated by the wartime oil embargo would be shared by the producers, notably with the states that had fought and sacrificed for the common Arab cause. Indeed, significant transfers of oil wealth to the non-oil Arab states and the migration of their excess labor to the labor-scarce oil economies generated a certain economic interdependence over the decade. The ideological cold war and inter-Arab subversion were decisively buried as the conservative states used their aid to moderate the radicalism of the nationalist republics, and interstate diplomacy eclipsed the inter-Arab media wars hitherto typical. The new oil wealth stimulated a popular search for material benefits that spelled the triumph, in Heikel's words, of *tharwa* (resources) over *thawra* (revolution).[36]

Arab summitry: A concert of Araby? A new mechanism of inter-Arab consultation came into its own after 1973, a virtual concert of states, institutionalized in Arab summits held within the framework of the Arab League. Summits were initiated by Nasser in 1964 in an early acknowledgment that Egypt's hegemony could not be imposed and that an Arab order had to be negotiated among equal states. The summit system reaffirmed the qualified sovereignty legitimized by the League, pledging participants to refrain from intervention in each other's internal affairs while attempting to coordinate the Arab states in defense of their common interests.

The summit system was initiated less to promote Pan-Arab action than to contain Syria's demands for it by spreading the responsibility for inaction; as such, it aimed to halt the radicalization of Pan-Arab norms from inter-Arab "outbidding."[37] In the 1970s and 1980s, summits were called to mobilize all-Arab resources, above all financial aid, to counter threats on the non-Arab periphery—from Israel and Iran. They also tried to establish a consensus on the conditions for making peace with them, in particular, trying to resolve conflicts between Egypt and Syria over peacemaking strategy while marginalizing radical states that sought to use outbidding to derail the peace process.

In the 1980s, summits, often boycotted by key feuding states, became less effective, reflective of growing Arab fragmentation after Egypt's separate peace shattered the "Arab Triangle." But Saudi Arabia filled the vacuum for a period, using financial incentives agreed at summits to heal inter-Arab splits; thus the Arab summit of May 1989 readmitted Egypt to the Arab fold and restored relations between it, Syria, and Libya. By 1996, there had been nineteen summits that, with three exceptions (Rabat 1969, Fez 1981, Cairo 1991), had reached their decisions by consensus. While this meant they reflected the lowest common denominator, the system arguably made for a "concert of states," a tradition of practices somewhere between Pan-Arab aspirations of collective action and a purely state-centric system.[38]

The shattering of the Arab Triangle. Just as the conflict with Israel gave birth to the Arab Triangle, so disagreements over the conflict's resolution destroyed the triangle. Egypt's Sadat, believing the United States would deliver Israeli withdrawal from the Sinai and the aid to solve Egypt's economic crisis, sacrificed all other options to appease Washington. Thus, immediately after the 1973 war, Sadat undermined Syria by pushing for a lifting of the oil boycott before there was even a first disengagement on the Syrian front; he also soon abandoned his ties to the Soviet Union and, with them, the military option. Sadat knew Israel was prepared to trade the Sinai for a peace that would get Egypt, the strongest Arab state, out of the Arab-Israeli power balance, and that if he stuck with Syria and the PLO in insisting on a comprehensive settlement and a Palestinian state, he might get nothing. He therefore entered into piecemeal deals with Israel and finally accepted a separate peace settlement that restored Egypt's lost land but reduced the likelihood a comprehensive peace could be attained. At the second Baghdad summit, Iraq and Syria jointly forced Saudi Arabia and other wavering states to ostracize Egypt for its 1979 peace treaty with Israel. This forced Cairo into greater dependence on the United States, allowing the virtual neutralization of the core Arab state by a superpower deeply biased toward Israel.[39]

Sadat's separate peace had profound consequences for the Arab system. Just as Egypt's hegemonic role had established Pan-Arab constraints on sovereignty, so its promotion of sovereignty over Arabism released many remaining such constraints. It also generated deepened insecurity throughout the Arab system that intensified the retreat to state-centric self-help by the individual states, notably Syria; similarly, it intensified Palestinian irredentism. The first and most destructive symptom of these tendencies was the Lebanese civil war, unleashed in 1975 by conflicts over the Palestinians in Lebanon, precipitated by the so-called Sinai II agreement in which Egypt seemed to abandon Syria and the PLO. This sparked a showdown between a coalition of Palestinians and radical Lebanese Muslims who wanted to challenge Israel in southern Lebanon and Maronite Christians determined to eradicate this disruptive threat to Lebanese security and sovereignty. At the same time, Syria, left extremely vulnerable to Israeli power by the collapse of its Egyptian alliance and seeking to redress the imbalance, tried to use the Lebanese civil war to impose its leadership in the Levant, especially on Lebanon and the PLO. This precipitated a PLO-Syrian conflict that would never be wholly healed. Thus, if, in the 1973 war, cooperation between the Arab states benefited them all, thereafter—caught in a classic prisoner's dilemma—none could trust the other not to seek individual gains unilaterally. When such vital interests as recovery of territory, perhaps even political survival, were at stake, each actor fell back on the self-help typical of a state system.[40]

A Centerless Arab World
and Conflict on the Peripheries (1980s)

State consolidation and sovereignty. If the 1973 war and associated oil boom fueled Arab interdependence, at the same time, relative wartime success restored some of the legitimacy of the individual states and oil revenues financed individual state building. The distribution of oil revenues across the system allowed states to build large armies and bureaucracies, foster new bourgeoisies with a stake in regimes, and co-opt the middle class, which—once the constituency of Pan-Arabism—now became or aspired to be part of the new state establishments. States became far less vulnerable to Pan-Arab ideological subversion than hitherto as the Pan-Arab movements, so readily manipulated by Nasser against his rivals, virtually disappeared or were "statized": thus Ba'thism became the official ideology and the Ba'th Party an instrument of state co-optation in Syria and Iraq. The Sadat regime fostered an Egypt-centric reaction against Arabism, exploiting resentment of the failure of the "rich" Arabs or "ungrateful" Palestinians to fund and appreciate Egypt's long sacrifice of its economic well-being to defense of the Arab cause.[41] By the middle 1980s, major Arab leaders were insisting that Arabism had to take a back seat to sovereignty in foreign policymaking. Thus, Mubarak told the Arabs that the only way to limit inter-Arab conflict was tolerance of a diversity of foreign policies since each state knew its own interests best. Saddam Hussein conceded that there were "many tents in the Arab house."[42] The very durability of the states as the customary framework of political life fostered their growing acceptance, if not strong affective support for them.

But, while mass Arabism seemingly declined in the 1980s, identifications did not necessarily fully attach to the states since the negative side effects of state building—the resort to personalism and sectarianism, the enhanced corruption and inequality accompanying the oil bonanza, and the repression rather than incorporation of political activism into institutionalized participation—left states with legitimacy deficits and no convincing substitute for Arabism or Islam as legitimating ideologies. Indeed, the vacuum left by the decline of Arabism was filled by heightened identification with either smaller substate communities (e.g., sects) or the larger Islamic *umma;* thus, in the Lebanese civil war, nationalist movements fragmented along sectarian lines or were displaced by transnational Islamic movements such as Hizbollah.

Political Islam, an alternative suprastate ideology that challenged the legitimacy of the existing states, was greatly accelerated by the example of the Iranian Islamic revolution and Ayatollah Khomeini's effort to export revolutionary Islam. As Meridi Nahas argues, the decline of Pan-Arabism made regimes especially vulnerable to revolutionary Islam because the same ills and identities that fueled the rise of Pan-Arabism persisted, but the disaffected now turned to Islam because many states had appropriated Arab nationalism as their legitimating ideology while blatantly violating its norms.[43]

While stronger states facing less mobilized, more fragmented publics were now better positioned to pursue reason of state to the neglect of Arab-Islamic norms, they nevertheless still paid a legitimacy cost when they did so. The rise of Islamic opposition in Egypt and Sadat's assassination were in part a function of the regime's loss of its Arab nationalist legitimacy after its peace with Israel, while the 1980s Islamic rebellion in Asad's Syria was partly a function of the delegitimation issuing from Syria's attacks on the PLO in Lebanon.[44] Iraq was especially threatened by Iran's transstate penetration of its large Shi'a population. Even Saudi Arabia and the Gulf states, which sought legitimation through Islam, were vulnerable to Islamic Iran's denunciation of their "American Islam."

Fragmented multipolarity. By the 1980s, a multipolar struggle for power raged among several contending states pursing state-centric policies yet still ambitious to exercise regional leadership. This was a consequence of both Egypt's relative decline and the rise of other Arab powers. In 1965, Egypt's gross national product (GNP) was still almost three times Saudi Arabia's, but by 1977 its percentage of Arab GNP had declined from 23.4 percent to 7.9 percent, making it economically dependent on the oil states. Economic decline was paralleled by the displacement of Cairo as the Arab world's political hub and the eclipse of Egyptian domination of inter-Arab institutions, which were now funded and under the increased influence of the oil monarchies. Military capabilities were much more equally distributed as well: in 1970 Egypt's military expenditures were still much higher than other Arab states, but by 1979 Syria and Iraq each matched it and Saudi Arabia had surged ahead. Other states also caught up with Egypt in their levels of state formation: the conservative states were now stabilized through the use of oil wealth to incorporate middle strata, while Ba'thist Syria and Iraq grew organizational muscle to control their fractious societies.[45]

But no new hegemon emerged. Iraq, in a peripheral location and long contained by hostile Turkey and Iran, was finally internally consolidated and, strengthened by oil and Soviet arms, made a bid for Arab leadership. Initially it remained marginalized under the banner of rejectionism, but when Sadat forfeited Egypt's Arab leadership and the Pahlavi gendarme of the Gulf collapsed, Saddam Hussein perceived power vacuums Iraq could fill; however, he soon dissipated Iraq's potential in his war with Iran. Asad's Syria, internally stabilized and enjoying diversified (Gulf and Soviet) resources, took advantage of Egypt's isolation and Iraq's embroilment in its war with Iran to assert Pan-Arab leadership against Israel; but Syria was handicapped by the decline of Pan-Arab sentiment and the preoccupation of Arab regimes with the Gulf conflict. Saudi Arabia quietly accumulated inter-Arab influence from the leverage it could potentially wield in the West on behalf of Arab interests, as the swing producer in OPEC and by using its wealth to moderate inter-Arab conflicts; indicative of this, in the 1970s it became the focus of most inter-Arab official visits. However, its military weakness made it vulnerable and therefore extremely cautious; the decline of its oil revenues after the mid-1980s oil bust and its growing dependency on the United States for protection from Iran checked its rising influence.[46]

Revisionism and power imbalances. As such, each Arab state was strong enough to prevent hegemony by another, but, equally, too driven by particular interests to forge an axis of states able to engineer all-Arab cohesion. This fragmentation made the Arab world exceptionally vulnerable to the powerful revisionist impulses being unleashed on its peripheries, which radically upset the regional power balance.

The Iranian revolution, turning this regional great power from defender of the status quo to exporter of revolution threatening its Arab neighbors, but also snapping the Tehran—Tel Aviv axis against Arab nationalism, threatened to shift the power balance against Israel. Instead, however, the Iraqi invasion of Iran, unleashing the eight-year Iran-Iraq war, immediately reshuffled the deck to Israel's advantage. The effective removal of both Iraq and Egypt from the Arab-Israeli power balance freed Israel, where the revisionist Likud government took power, to project its power in the Arab world with little restraint. Lebanon became the main arena of struggle between Israel, the PLO, and Syria, and the Begin government seized the opportunity to break the stalemate there and establish regional hegemony. With U.S. complicity, Israel's 1982 invasion of Lebanon sought to drive the PLO and Syria from Lebanon, install a client government, impose another separate peace, and encircle Syria.[47] At the same time, the Soviet invasion of Afghanistan, plus Soviet activity in the Horn of Africa and in its client state of Democratic Yemen, when combined with the Iranian threat, produced a heightened feeling of vulnerability among the Gulf monarchies.

These threats, rather than uniting the Arab world, polarized it into two rival coalitions, not on the basis of ideology or identity but the location of the greater threat. A "moderate" pro-Western coalition that came to include Iraq, Egypt, Saudi Arabia, and the Gulf Cooperation Council (GCC) states, as well as northern Yemen and Jordan, combined against the Iranian and Soviet threats. Owing to the Gulf states' intense fear of Iran, massive resources were diverted from the Israeli front to support Iraq's war with Tehran. The need for Egyptian arms and manpower in this conflict drove Cairo's inter-Arab rehabilitation, despite its adherence to its separate peace with Israel. The United States was allowed to expand its presence and influence in the Gulf despite the Reagan administration's complicity in the Israeli invasion of Lebanon, its designation of Israel as a U.S. strategic asset, and its 1986 bombing of Libya. Against the "moderate" bloc, a so-called Steadfastness Front of radical states—Libya, Democratic Yemen, Algeria, and Syria—was drawn together in opposition to Israeli revisionism. More important, the sense of threat from Israel, Iraq, and the United States shared by Syria and Iran drove them into a defensive counteralliance; Iran mobilized Lebanese Shi'a on behalf of Syria's resistance to Israel in Lebanon, and Syria obstructed the isolation of Iran in the Arab world. Iran was thus brought directly into the heart of inter-Arab politics, eroding the boundaries between the Arab core and the periphery.

The decline of Pan-Arab norms and institutions, far from making for a more stable Middle East, merely meant the supersession of ideological conflicts waged by subversion and propaganda by much more violent and sustained military conflicts on the Arab–non-Arab fault lines. The massive intensification of threats and ambitions translated into a search for security through arms races and militarization, which only exacerbated the security dilemma. The two wars on the peripheries resulted from a coincidence between revisionist leaderships (Likud, Khomeini, Saddam), overarmed states, and power imbalances—in one case a result of Egypt's withdrawal from the Arab-Israeli power balance, and in the other by the seeming (albeit temporary) collapse of Iranian power in the revolution.

The balance of power became the main, albeit precarious, source of order: in the end, the ambitions of revisionist states (Israel, Iran, Iraq) were in each case blunted and the status quo preserved by countervailing power. In the east, the two dominant Gulf powers wore each other down; Iran's military threat was contained and no state succumbed to Islamic revolution. On the western front, Syria, sheltered by a Soviet deterrent, used the mobilization of Lebanese Muslims to frustrate Israeli plans in Lebanon; Syria thereafter reached sufficient military parity with Israel to establish a "deterrence relationship," making a new war more costly and probably unwinnable for both. The Syrian-Iranian alliance, in continuing to defend the Arab-Islamic core issues at stake in the conflict with Israel, substituted in some degree for the collapsed Arab center.[48]

The Gulf War and the Shattering of the Arab System (1990s)

The second Gulf war further enervated the remnants of Arab solidarity. Saddam Hussein used Arabism to justify his invasion of another Arab state while anti-Iraqi Arab regimes manipulated the Arab League to engineer Western intervention against another member of the League and abort an "Arab solution" to the crisis.

The formation of the anti-Iraq coalition showed that decisionmaking in the Arab states was, by this time, driven almost exclusively by such factors as individual geopolitical interest and/or Western dependency. Saudi Arabia initially hoped for a diplomatic solution but could not resist U.S. demands to host the Western juggernaut if it was to retain protection against the much increased Iraqi threat. Having thereby made an enemy of Saddam Hussein, the Saudis acquired an interest in his overthrow but feared the destruction of Iraq would benefit Israel or Iran. Egypt's Mubarak, who was pivotal in engineering the Arab League resolution inviting Western intervention, was partly driven by Egypt's deepening economic dependency on the West. Egypt's ability to win Western aid by acting as a "moderating" state in the region had been threatened by Saddam Hussein's bid for Arab leadership—manifest at the 1990 Baghdad summit—through confrontation with the United States and Israel; however, the invasion presented an opportunity to "bandwagon" with the United States, demonstrate Egypt's continued importance to regional stability, and thereby win debt relief. The coalition's most reluctant member, Syria, saw an opportunity to weaken Saddam Hussein, a rival for Pan-Arab leadership; to win gratitude and aid from its Saudi patron; and, as Soviet protection receded in the post–Cold War era, to gain U.S. recognition as a responsible power whose interests should be accommodated in any settlement of the Arab-Israeli conflict.[49]

Saddam Hussein's effective use of Pan-Arab themes—Western interference, Palestine, the distribution of "Arab" oil wealth—to win support from the Arab "street" cast doubt on the "death of Arabism." Indeed, those Arab states that were experimenting with democratization—Tunisia, Jordan, Yemen, and Algeria—proved most vulnerable to public sentiment and distanced themselves from the anti-Iraq coalition.[50] On the other hand, authoritarian regimes proved much less vulnerable to Saddam's transstate manipulation of domestic opinion than states had been at the height of Pan-Arabism. Moreover, the Pan-Arab arousal receded in the wake of Iraq's defeat and ceased to be a constraint on states in the postwar Arab-Israeli negotiations started at the Madrid conference. Militant Islam remained more consequential but was contained by increasing state repression and Iran's inability, enervated in war with Iraq, to sustain the export of revolution.

The inter-Arab institutions designed to reconcile identity and sovereignty were much weakened by the Gulf crisis. The Arab League secretary-general, presumably the keeper of the common interest, announced that henceforth no Arab state could interfere in another's definition of its own interest and security. The Arab League was paralyzed, with no agreement possible on holding an Arab summit between 1990 and 1996 even though momentous decisions were being taken affecting the common Arab interest, notably in the Arab-Israel peace process. Brief hopes for the creation of a new Arab security framework embracing Egypt, Syria, and the GCC under the Damascus Declaration failed when the latter chose to rely on Western treaties, further enervating the Arab norm against overt foreign treaties and bases.[51]

The collapse of Pan-Arab solidarity and institutions left little restraint on the realpolitik of individual actors, which, however, only
made it easier for hostile periphery states to exploit Arab divisions.
Thus, Israel was able to exploit the enduring distrust rooted in Camp
David—that other Arab parties would not refrain from Sadat-like sepa-
rate deals—to split the PLO from Syria. The Oslo Accords, in which the
PLO assumed full responsibility for the fate of the Palestinians, released
remaining constraints on the Arab states to pay even lip service to the
Palestinian cause. It prompted both Jordan's peace treaty with Israel and
Syria's bid for a settlement on the Golan regardless of the doubtful like-
lihood that Oslo would lead to the realization of Palestinian rights.
Moreover, the virtual collapse of Arab collective security was sharply
exposed by the failure of the Arab states to back Syria against a Turkish-
Israeli pincer and overt Turkish war threats against Damascus over its
support for the Kurdistan Workers Party in the late 1990s.

In the wake of the second Gulf war, there was much talk about the
dissolution of the Arab core in a wider Middle East system embracing the
non-Arab periphery as full members. No such formal or institutionalized
new system emerged, but the enhanced postwar fragmentation of the Arab
core meant that reference to an "Arab world" sharing interests and identity appeared obsolete for much of the 1990s. No Arab concert existed to
provide leadership and the Arab League rarely met, and never effectively.
U.S. penetration of the region reached levels comparable to the Western
presence of the pre-Nasser age. While U.S. stewardship of the Arab-Israeli peace negotiation was sharply biased in Israel's favor, and although
U.S. force was regularly directed at Arab targets, above all Iraq, Washington's influence was not seriously jeopardized in Arab capitals. At the
same time, Israel and Turkey, though continuing to employ military superiority against Arab states and interests, were nevertheless increasingly
accepted as players—even partners—in regional politics. Only at the turn
of the millennium were there some tentative signs that Arab institutions
were reviving. But, as no new Arab or "Middle Eastern" security system
emerged, states continued to rely on realist self-help manifest in unrestrained arms races and/or on U.S. protection. Chapter 4 provides an
analysis of these developments throughout the 1990s.

Notes

1. Louis J. Cantori and Steven L. Spiegel, *The International Politics of Regions: A Comparative Approach,* Englewood Cliffs, NJ: Prentice Hall, 1970,

pp. 192–207; Tareq Y. Ismael, *International Relations of the Contemporary Middle East: A Study in World Politics*, Syracuse, NY: Syracuse University Press, pp. 5–13.

2. Paul Noble, "The Arab System: Pressures, Constraints, and Opportunities," in Bahgat Korany and Ali E. Hillal Dessouki, eds., *The Foreign Policies of Arab States: The Challenge of Change*, Boulder, CO: Westview Press, 1991, p. 56.

3. Tim Niblock, "The Need for a New Arab Order," *Middle East International*, 12 October 1990, pp. 17–18.

4. Bahgat Korany, "Alien and Besieged Yet Here to Stay: The Contradictions of the Arab Territorial State," in Ghassan Salame, ed., *The Foundations of the Arab State*, London: Croom Helm, 1987, pp. 54–55.

5. Cited in Nazih Ayubi, *Overstating the Arab State: Politics and Society in the Middle East*, London: I. B. Tauris, 1995, p. 146.

6. Iliya Harik, "The Origins of the Arab State System," in Ghassan Salame, ed., *The Foundations of the Arab State*, London: Croom Helm, 1987, pp. 19–46.

7. Tawfiq Farah and Feisal Salam, "Group Affiliations of Children in the Arab Middle East (Kuwait)," *Journal of Social Psychology* 111, 1980, pp. 141–142.

8. Ayubi, *Overstating the Arab State*, p. 144.

9. Ibid.

10. Raymond Hinnebusch, "Children of the Elite: Political Attitudes of the Westernized Bourgeoisie in Contemporary Egypt," *Middle East Journal* 36, no. 4, 1982, pp. 535–561.

11. P. J. Vatikiotis, *Islam and the State*, London: Routledge, 1987; David George, "Pax-Islamica: An Alternative New World Order," in Abdel Salam Sidahmed and Anoushiravan Ehteshami, eds., *Islamic Fundamentalism*, Boulder, CO: Westview Press, 1996, pp. 71–90.

12. Bruce Maddy-Weitzman, *The Crystallization of the Arab State System, 1945–1954*, Syracuse, NY: Syracuse University Press, 1993, pp. 175–176; Malik Mufti, *Sovereign Creations: Pan-Arabism and Political Order in Syria and Iraq*, Ithaca and London: Cornell University Press, 1996, pp. 21–59; Patrick Seale, *The Struggle for Syria*, London: Oxford University Press, 1965, pp. 5–99.

13. Michael N. Barnett, *Dialogues in Arab Politics: Negotiations in Regional Order*, New York: Columbia University Press, 1998, pp. 100–103; Fawaz Gerges, *The Superpowers and the Middle East: Regional and International Politics, 1955–1967*, Boulder, CO: Westview Press, 1994, pp. 21–40; Michael Ionides, *Divide and Lose: The Arab Revolt of 1955–58*, London: Geoffrey Bles, 1960.

14. Steven Walt, *The Origin of Alliances*, Ithaca, NY: Cornell University Press, 1987, p. 53; Noble, "The Arab System," pp. 61–65, 74–75.

15. Charles Cremeans, *The Arabs and the World: Nasser's Arab Nationalist Policy*, New York: Praeger, 1963; Ayubi, *Overstating the Arab State*, pp. 142–143; Barnett, *Dialogues in Arab Politics*, p. 128.

16. Adeed Dawisha, *Egypt in the Arab World: The Elements of Foreign Policy*, New York: Wiley, 1976, pp. 174–175.

17. Seale, *The Struggle for Syria*, pp. 100–326; Walt, *The Origin of Alliances*, pp. 57–66.

18. L. Carl Brown, *International Politics and the Middle East: Old Rules, Dangerous Game*, Princeton, NJ: Princeton University Press, pp. 88, 162–172.

19. Malcolm Kerr, *The Arab Cold War: Jamal Abd al-Nasir and His Rivals, 1958–1970*, London: Oxford University Press, 1971.

20. Gerges, *The Superpowers and the Middle East*, pp. 245–251.

21. Walt, *The Origin of Alliances*, pp. 206–212.

22. Ibid., pp. 79, 204; Kerr, *The Arab Cold War.*

23. Avraham Sela, *The End of the Arab-Israeli Conflict: Middle East Politics and the Quest for Regional Order*, Albany: State University of New York Press, 1998, p. 80; Janice Stein, "The Security Dilemma in the Middle East: The Prognosis for the Decade Ahead," in Bahgat Korany, Paul Noble, and Rex Brynen, eds., *The Many Faces of National Security in the Middle East*, London: Macmillan, 1993, pp. 62–67; Kerr, *The Arab Cold War*, pp. 96–128; Walt, *The Origin of Alliances*, pp. 86–87.

24. Sela, *The End of the Arab-Israeli Conflict*, p. 75.

25. Gergis, *The Superpowers and the Middle East*, p. 213.

26. Barnett, *Dialogues in Arab Politics*, pp. 146–159.

27. Charles Smith, *Palestine and the Arab-Israeli Conflict*, New York: St. Martin's Press, 1992, pp. 195–200; Yoram Peri, *Between Battles and Ballots: Israel's Military in Politics*, Cambridge: Cambridge University Press, pp. 244–251.

28. Barnett, *Dialogues in Arab Politics*, pp. 165–176; Bassam Tibi, "Structural and Ideological Change in the Arab Subsystem Since the Six Day War," in Yehuda Lukas and Abdalla Battah, eds., *The Arab-Israeli Conflict: Two Decades of Change*, Boulder, CO: Westview Press, 1988, pp. 147–163.

29. Michael Brecher, *The Foreign Policy System of Israel*, London: Oxford Press, 1972, p. 64.

30. Ilan Peleg, "The Impact of the Six-Day War on the Israeli Right: A Second Republic in the Making?" in Yehuda Lukas and Abdalla Battah, eds., *The Arab-Israeli Conflict: Two Decades of Change*, Boulder, CO: Westview Press, pp. 54–66.

31. Walt, *The Origin of Alliances*, pp. 265–266.

32. Sela, *The End of the Arab-Israeli Conflict*, p. 148.

33. Alan Taylor, *The Arab Balance of Power*, Syracuse, NY: Syracuse University Press, 1982, pp. 49–56; Fouad Ajami, "Stress in the Arab Triangle," *Foreign Policy* 29, 1977–1978, pp. 90–108.

34. Walt, *The Origin of Alliances*, pp. 117–121.

35. Sela, *The End of the Arab-Israeli Conflict*, p. 145.

36. Mohamed Heikel, *The Sphinx and the Commissar*, New York: Harper & Row, 1975, pp. 261–262; Ali E. Hillal Dessouki, "The New Arab Political Order: Implications for the Eighties," in Malcolm Kerr and El Sayed Yassin, eds., *Rich and Poor States in the Middle East*, Boulder, CO: Westview Press, 1982, pp. 319–347; Barnett, *Dialogues in Arab Politics*, pp. 152–153.

37. Kerr, *The Arab Cold War;* Sela, *The End of the Arab-Israeli Conflict*, pp. 75–94; Barnett, *Dialogues in Arab Politics*, p. 122.

38. Sela, *The End of the Arab-Israeli Conflict*, especially pp. 2–23, 341–346.

39. Taylor, *The Arab Balance of Power*, pp. 54–81; Sela, *The End of the Arab-Israeli Conflict*, pp. 153–173; Edward R. F. Sheehan, "How Kissinger Did It: Step by Step in the Middle East," *Foreign Policy*, no. 22, 1976.

40. Sela, *The End of the Arab-Israeli Conflict*, pp. 189–213; Patrick Seale, *Asad: The Struggle for the Middle East*, Berkeley: University of California Press, 1988, pp. 185–315.

41. Noble, "The Arab System," pp. 65–70.

42. Barnett, *Dialogues in Arab Politics*, pp. 6–7.

43. Maridi Nahas, "State Systems and Revolutionary Challenge: Nasser, Khomeini and the Middle East," *International Journal of Middle East Studies* 17, 1985.

44. Noble, "The Arab System," pp. 53–54.

45. Shibley Telhami, *Power and Leadership in International Bargaining*, New York: Columbia University Press, 1990, pp. 96–97; Malik Mufti, *Sovereign Creations: Pan-Arabism and Political Order in Syria and Iraq*, Ithaca and London: Cornell University Press, 1996.

46. Walt, *The Origin of Alliances*, p. 137; Mufti, *Sovereign Creations*, p. 80; Noble, "The Arab System," pp. 65, 71–72.

47. Zeev Schiff and Ehud Ya'ari, *Israel's Lebanon War*, New York: Simon & Schuster, 1984.

48. Anoushiravan Ehteshami and Raymond Hinnebusch, *Syria and Iran: Middle Powers in a Penetrated Regional System*, London: Routledge, 1997, pp. 101–105.

49. Ahmad Abdalla, "Mubarak's Gamble," *Middle East Report*, January–February 1991, pp. 18–21; Raymond Hinnebusch, "Syria's Role in the Gulf War Coalition," in Andrew Bennett, Joseph Lepgold, and Danny Unger, eds., *Friends in Need: Burden Sharing in the Gulf War*, New York: St. Martin's Press, 1997, pp. 219–240.

50. Walid Khalidi, "Why Some Arabs Support Saddam," in Micah Sifry and Christopher Cerf, eds., *The Gulf War Reader*, New York: Times Books, 1991, pp. 161–171; Tareq Y. Ismael and Jacqueline S. Ismael, "Arab Politics and the Gulf War: Political Opinion and Political Culture," *Arab Studies Quarterly* 15, no. 1, winter 1993, pp. 1–11; Maxime Rodinson, "The Mythology of a Conqueror," *Middle East Report* 21, no. 1, January–February 1991, p. 12.

51. Barnett, *Dialogues in Arab Politics*, pp. 227–228.

3

The Impact of the International System on the Middle East

B. A. Roberson

The International-Regional Dynamic

The modern Middle East, in the path of European expansion, felt the brunt of European imperialism and the influence of its emerging capitalist industrialization. The area was engulfed in the strategies and the political and economic rivalries of the great powers and became a fertile ground for exploitation. Yet, as L. Carl Brown argued, even as the Middle East became a factor in the calculations of the European balance of power, regional players also utilized relationships with the great powers to achieve their own objectives.[1] With the emergence of independence followed by the rise of nationalist movements and regimes, Middle East states, seeking to establish their credibility and viability, continued trying to implicate the great powers of the day in their efforts to establish a favorable balance of power. The great powers, in their turn, "thoroughly penetrated" the Arab region in an attempt to influence, manage, and control events in the area.

These aspects of the relationship between the great powers, and later the superpowers, and the states in the region have now been sufficiently documented to show that though the external powers continued to involve themselves in the region, there remained considerable scope for independent action available to the Middle East states.[2]

Nevertheless, despite the superpowers' many policy failures, at the end of the day, the states in the region have very little to show for their attempts to exploit superpower rivalry during the Cold War. In the absence of the Cold War, it is clear that neither the region's cultural commonalties nor ideological commitments to unity were enough to overcome the catastrophic political and military decisionmaking of key states—Egypt in 1967 and Iraq in 1990—which have placed the future security of the region yet again in the hands of an outside power.

Impact of the International System

Western Penetration

External influences and interventions emanating from the international system have been an enduring recognizable feature of the Middle East.[3] The ongoing impact of the industrialization and modernization of the nineteenth and twentieth centuries brought to the Middle East the globalizing effects of technological developments in production, transportation, and communications. The organizational and economic changes that had been developing in Europe over the previous several hundred years—the institutions and processes of capitalism and the modern sovereign state model—began to penetrate the Middle East. These developments brought changes to traditional Middle Eastern societies and economies and stimulated indigenous political and ideological responses. The political responses were reflected in organizational reforms and the acquisition of new military technologies, beginning with the efforts of the Ottoman reformers and Egypt's Muhammed Ali, as they sought to enhance their security against external threats. The ideological responses to these developments, including Arab nationalism and Islamism, reflected a sense of interrupted unity and of threatened autonomy.

The Formation of the Middle East State System

With the end of World War I and the breakup of the Ottoman Empire, what had been previously a largely unified region was fragmented, in the style of the 1878 Congress of Berlin, into bounded territories that had little regard for the idea of nation. This was the enduring European legacy to the region.[4] A partitioned Middle East became a ward of European power.[5] The attitude of the great powers was that the peoples outside the European region were not really in a position to govern themselves.[6] In the case of the Middle East, the mandatory arrangements of the great powers were designed to cloak the wartime agreements that Britain and France had made regarding the Arab provinces of the Ottoman Empire and where the principle of self-determination of peoples would not immediately apply.[7] The great powers restructured the region using an Arab elite that was divided and unprepared for rule.[8] This set in motion the development of a nationalism, both defensive and negative, that aimed in its various strands at ridding each part of the region of foreign occupation.[9] It also contributed to the destruction of the population's trust in the Western-oriented elite that had cooperated with Europe, destabilizing the region's nascent polities.[10] This formative period contributed significantly to the authoritarian character of the emerging regimes as well as the rules and trading structures that circumscribed the relations among the states of the region.

The Cold War and Superpower Involvement

World War II led to the recognition that the oil of the Middle East was of strategic importance.[11] From this time onward, and as the colonial powers exited from the region during the 1950s, the Middle East would figure prominently as part of a U.S. global Cold War strategy. The United States attempted to assume the responsibility of the old imperial powers for protecting Western (and Japanese) interests in the region and erecting a sphere of influence against Soviet penetration.[12]

While U.S. policymakers, at least publicly, declared their overriding concern to be Soviet expansion in the region, they in fact had to worry about internal threats in the Middle East arising from a variety of sources that had little to do with communism or Soviet expansion, but from which the Soviet Union could benefit. For one, British policy in the Palestine Mandate fostered a Jewish homeland without protecting the interests of the Arab population. The emergence of the state of Israel inflamed anti-Western, anti-Zionist nationalism. U.S. involvement in the active support of Israel thereafter complicated its ambitions for the region.[13] Another factor was Washington's misperceptions of the rise of radical ideologies that, whether Arab nationalism, local communism, or political Islam, in large part expressed a reaction against outside intervention and a desire for autonomy from Western domination. However, the United States equated aspirations for a "third way" free from foreign alliances, especially when professed by governments that purchased Soviet arms, with a sympathy for Soviet aims that threatened U.S. strategic objectives in the Middle East.[14]

The United States used several strategies to contain threats to Western interests. First, it tried to contain the Arab-Israeli conflict by establishing a regional balance of power, notably through the Tripartite Agreement with Britain and France, which limited arms sales to states involved in the conflict. Second, through the Baghdad Pact or Central Treaty Organisation (CENTO), it attempted to forge an alliance system against Soviet and radical influence without directly involving its own forces. Third, it tried to pressure nationalist governments into eschewing relations with the Soviet Union through the denial of economic and military assistance and occasionally through outright subversion.[15] The United States could not, however, prevent the spread of radical ideology across the region, maintain a status quo where the interests of regional powers remained unsatisfied, or prevent Soviet penetration of the region. Its preoccupation with the global-level power struggle had, by the 1960s, pushed the Middle East into a lowered priority in Washington's strategic thinking.[16]

The 1967 War:
Watershed in Superpower-Regional Relations

Although the origins of the 1967 war were lodged in regional and not international conflicts,[17] the war entrenched the superpowers in their competitive relations on opposing sides of the Arab-Israeli conflict. It drew the United States back into the region and posed a dilemma for it. On the one hand, the sudden crisis of the war and its aftermath introduced the possibility of confrontation between the two superpowers that both viewed as dangerous.[18] On the other hand, Israel emerged from the war much strengthened and in possession of significant Arab territories, an outcome seen by U.S. policymakers as having the potential to open up greater opportunities for achieving its objectives in the Middle East.[19]

The years of stalemate between the Arab states and Israel immediately after 1967 were acceptable to the United States as long as discussions among the parties remained at a negotiating level. However, the stalemate brought the Soviet Union into a greater commitment to the confrontation states of Egypt, Syria, and Iraq. Moreover, the 1969–1970 Egyptian-Israeli War of Attrition and the October war of 1973 brought the United States into an awareness that it had to become more actively involved diplomatically if it was to protect its regional interests without direct military involvement.[20] U.S. policy had failed to prevent the Arab states from establishing close relations with the Soviet Union, but the events of 1967 allowed Washington to impress upon the Arab states that its good offices with Israel offered a more effective solution to the Israeli occupation of Arab lands than did Soviet arms.[21] The United States was also in a good position to offer aid to Arab governments having economic difficulties.[22]

In fact, an opening to the United States emerged from the chronic economic difficulties and the insecurity of the regime in Egypt. For Anwar al-Sadat, the successor of Nasser, a solution to the problems facing Egypt lay in the abandonment both of the war with Israel and the alliance with the Soviet Union, and the formation of a new alliance relationship with the United States.[23] This gave the United States the opportunity to assume the role of broker between Egypt and Israel, which began with Henry Kissinger and culminated with Jimmy Carter.[24]

While the United States could feel that it had achieved a degree of stability in the Middle East with the signing of the 1979 Egypt-Israel Peace Treaty, its other policy in the 1970s of constructing an Iranian hegemony in the Persian Gulf in the wake of British withdrawal from "east of Suez" unexpectedly collapsed with the Iranian revolution in 1979. Under the Nixon Doctrine, the United States had armed regional allies—Israel and Iran—in order that it could avoid a direct military presence in the region and remain "over the horizon." The breakdown of the balance of power in the Gulf, meticulously constructed by the United States, radically altered the dynamics of strategic relations in the region. This, together with the introduction of Soviet troops into Afghanistan and the outbreak of war between Iraq and revolutionary Iran, brought into sharp focus, if not the failure of U.S. policy, at least the need for greater substantive involvement in the region. This took the form of increasing its "over the horizon" military capabilities.[25] The United States also pursued piecemeal tactics to try to limit as much as possible Soviet gains in the region and, in the latter part of the Iraq-Iran war, the United States had reestablished an indirect alignment with Iraq, a Soviet ally, on the basis of their mutual hostility toward Iran. Thus, while the Iraq-Iran war had concluded with a UN-negotiated cease-fire in which both countries could claim victory, the United States could view these results with some equanimity and could feel that its policy of containment of the Soviet Union was finally paying off.

The Post–Cold War World

The end of the Cold War meant the end of the superpower competition that had so affected the structure of the international system and the Middle East. While a "new world order" was still clarifying in Europe, Iraq's 1990 invasion of Kuwait made clear the implications for the Middle East of the post–Cold War era. Iraq miscalculated the U.S. response to a direct threat to the security of the oil resources of its Persian Gulf allies at a time when, crucially, the Soviet Union no longer acted to deter U.S. intervention in the region. The United States, with support from countries in the Middle East and Europe and the acquiescence of the Soviet Union, for the first time, intervened massively and decisively with its troops in the Middle East. In the process, it demonstrated a preponderance of U.S. military power, which left an enduring impression on the region.

Thus, by the beginning of the 1990s, with the threat of Iran and Iraq eliminated, together with the collapse of the Eastern bloc, which had weakened the strategic position of radical nationalist states, no state, by itself or in concert with others in the region, was in a position to establish a Middle Eastern order independent of U.S. influence. Moreover, by 1991, the Arab-Israeli conflict had reached an impasse: with the demise of the Soviet Union and the defeat of Iraq, a military solution was not possible while a diplomatic solution would have to recognize U.S. interests in the region, in which a crucial element was the security of Israel. These events provided the United States with an unprecedented opportunity to project influence into the region.[26]

Dual Containment and U.S. Interests in the Persian Gulf

The balance of power in the region had collapsed with the Iranian revolution. It was with the Iraqi attack upon Kuwait that the stark reality of the innate instability of the region and threat to the national interest of the United States was displayed. It fell to the Clinton administration to attempt to readjust U.S. strategy to cope with these realities. The United States sought to advance a vision of a global order that included a particular balance of power operating in favor of its allies in the region.[27]

By the end of the twentieth century, the main lines of U.S. strategy in the Middle East had emerged: they rested on its previous Cold War goal of containment, but were now aimed at perceived *regional* threats.[28] The main regional threats were seen to be Iraq and Iran. Iran was a threat by virtue of its hostility to the U.S. presence, attempts at acquiring weapons of mass destruction, support for terrorism in the region, and opposition to the peace process.[29] Iraq, in addition to all this, also posed a direct military threat to its neighbors.

The U.S. response was twofold. First, it now accepted that it would have to maintain a permanent military presence in the Gulf. Iraq's attack on Kuwait had disabused Washington of its earlier assumption that Israel's "military superiority in the Middle East, . . . [would] deter attack and prevent a call for direct American intervention."[30] The acceptance of a U.S. presence became tolerable in the region when the Gulf monarchies recognized that they were powerless in the face of regional hegemons willing to use force to reorder the region. The security of their regimes and the maintenance of a Middle East order that suited them could only be guaranteed by the United States. It would be a symbiotic relationship that expressed a coincidence of interest and profoundly held needs.

The second leg of U.S. policy, "dual containment,"[31] emerged when it became clear that the long-standing policy of maintaining a militarily dominant role for Israel in the region was under threat. The objectives of the policy were to alter the balance of power by weakening the military and economic capabilities of both Iraq and Iran through a single policy that would impose restricted sovereignty on Iraq with military force and a sanctions policy regarding trade and investment in Iran. The policy was, however, constrained by Washington's inability to win sufficient sustained support from key Western powers in its efforts to isolate Iraq and Iran.[32]

Europe's Interests in the Middle East

The European powers have had a lesser regional role since World War II exhausted their economies and their ability to play a major role in international affairs. European interest in the Middle East centers on commerce, energy, and the stability needed to contain terrorism and mass migration. Europe's interest in regional stability overlaps with that of the United States, and where differences exist, they are matters of priorities and tactics. The United States tends to deal with the region as a global power with global interests, while Europe, with its limited power capability, has a less expansive view of its interests and needs. While the United States divided the region into enemies and allies, Europe seeks relations with all states in the region. While the United States had, in the 1990s, moved away from an "evenhanded" approach to the peace process, Europe believes a stable peace requires the formation of a Palestinian state with East Jerusalem as its capital. It also believes that if the interests of all frontline states were not to be incorporated into any agreements that emerge from the peace process, they would not endure and that Europe would bear the brunt of a breakdown. While Europe supported the U.S.-driven UN sanctions imposed on Iraq, as the decade wore on, it increasingly became disillusioned with their effectiveness and chafed against them. There also has been a significant divergence of view as regards Iran. Europe has preferred a "critical dialogue" with Iran [33] and resisted the U.S. dual containment policy with its attempted extraterritorial enforcement of U.S. domestic legislation through the Iran-Libya Sanctions Act of 1996.[34]

Europe's policy toward the Middle East is, however, weakened by its considerable difficulty in arriving at a common policy. Under the Maastricht Treaty of the European Union (EU), the heads of state and government set the general guidelines for foreign-policy decisions. The council of the EU, that is, the foreign ministers of the member states, can then decide to take joint action but a unanimous decision is necessary. Under the Amsterdam Treaty of 1997, the EU can take a common strategy by qualified majority vote rather than unanimity, with those in disagreement opting out under the new principle of "constructive abstention."[35] However, the problem of the different world perspectives and interests of member states remains and there are still significant divergences among them regarding the Middle East.[36] This, compounded by the lack of an integrated European military power, has limited the role of the EU. Ultimately, because Europe lacks the capability on its own to influence developments in the Middle East, its concerns are not allowed to undermine the common fundamental interests it has with the United States in this region, even though they may have divergent views on tactics, strategy, and costs.

Globalization and the Middle East

The Middle East has inevitably been affected by the contemporary globalization of economic activity—the universalization of a liberalized capitalist economy as the accepted model of domestic and international economic relations—and the accompanying ideological pressures for the liberalization of politics and the quickening pace in the development and use of communications technology.[37]

The character of economic development in the region has not, however, led to much increased engagement with globalization processes. A major impetus for economic development has come from the production of energy resources and the investment of its profits abroad. The non–oil and gas producer states have depended disproportionately on labor migration and remittances, and on foreign aid from the oil producers and/or Cold War superpowers. In these circumstances, Middle East governments were able successfully to structure rentier economies with heavy investment in state enterprises. However, the manufacturing sectors continued to be small and the service sectors large,[38] while diversification was limited to traditional sectors that did not allow for the responses to global changes that other regions of the world were able to make. In effect, massive oil revenues provided a cushion that permitted resistance to liberalization during the 1980s and 1990s by elites and vested interests in the Middle East. This allowed the Middle East, in contrast to other regions, to avoid the effects of the ending of the economic underpinnings of the Cold War.

There were, however, high costs. The annual average gross domestic product growth of Middle East countries declined from 6.1 percent to 2.9 percent during the period 1965–1980. With the collapse of oil prices in 1985, real per capita incomes declined 2 percent per year.[39] Regional gross national product declined by a further 4 percent in the wake of the second Gulf war.[40] The Middle East has fallen strikingly behind global growth rates: for the years 1990 to 1995, average annual economic growth rates were 1.3 percent for Egypt, 1.2 percent for Morocco, 1.7 percent for Saudi Arabia, and 0.1 percent for Algeria.[41] As high population growth exceeded sluggish economic growth, per capita income declined measurably.[42] Despite these onerous statistics, Middle East governments were able to absorb the considerable costs of the two Gulf wars without the strength of vested interests opposed to liberalization being seriously jeopardized.[43]

The problems of the Middle East reside not only in the structure of their economies. In large part, the instability of the Middle East also is due to unsustainable concentration of power in regimes that appear incapable of a style of governance that would provide the economic and subjective needs of their peoples. They appear equally incapable, to date, of reforming themselves or adapting adequately to changing economic conditions induced by the effects of globalization.[44]

Diverging Economic Interests

Effective solutions to the dilemmas facing the Middle East have been elusive. Middle East governments have made some efforts at regional economic cooperation but, to succeed, these would require rebuilding infrastructural networks of trade, harmonizing government policies, and providing a safety net for those that would be adversely affected by these developments, and this has not happened.[45] Although Middle Eastern governments may have preferred traditional preferential trading arrangements with the EU and United States as a less disruptive form of economic arrangement,[46] both the EU and United States are pursuing different political and economic objectives.

The EU, since 1995, has pursued its Euro-Mediterranean Partnership Initiative, which has called for a free-trade area among Middle East countries and the EU by 2010.[47] The concern of the EU has been political stability on its periphery. It would like to see the Middle East region economically integrated into the norms of the international system, which it believes would result in a less conflict-prone environment. There is, however, little indication that this scheme will be sufficient to solve the Middle East's economic problems, in part because the protectionist policies of the EU have closed off agricultural and textile products as "sensitive" and because of the inability of Middle Eastern enterprises to compete with European producers. Preferential trade agreements do give some beneficial market access to certain Middle East exports. The hope is that the agreements might help to "lock in" beneficial liberal economic reforms that could create pockets of prosperity within Middle East economies. While this might have some spillover or trickle-down effects, if the experiences of other parts of the world are an indication, the result could be more economically divided and, hence, politically unstable societies.[48]

The United States, for its part, promoted the Casablanca economic program, which would open up Middle East economies to the world market without particular regional linkages and would ensure, through the establishment of a Middle East and North Africa development bank, a deepened involvement of Israel in the regional economy. This initiative foundered on the failure of the Middle East peace process to progress, together with the suspicion that it might lead to Israeli dominance of the regional economy. More recently, the United States has been pursuing what is labeled the Eizenstat Initiative, which is designed to cut across the Arab Maghreb Union (AMU) by promoting economic relationships between the United States and Morocco, Algeria, and Tunisia, to the exclusion of Libya and Mauritania, who are also members of the AMU. In effect, Washington gave notice to the EU that the United States "has no intention of relinquishing the commercial opportunities in North Africa to Europeans or others."[49] Despite the competition between the United States and EU over the future ordering of Mediterranean relations, the aim of both is to create a regional bloc within an international liberal economic order.[50] The Middle East order, if it is to emerge from such plans, will inevitably reflect the disparities between these economic giants and the Middle East.

Conclusion

Once the Middle East escaped the constraints of colonialism, the countries of the region had a greater control over their internal affairs within the structures and expectations inherited from the colonial era. However, their inability to develop a regional security system, or resolve their antagonisms through force, imparted a tumultuous and anarchic character to regional politics that endures today.

The process of change from the colonial to the postcolonial era contributed to early ideological divisions in the region between those willing to continue a cooperative postcolonial relationship with the West and those who were not willing to do so. This led into alignments either with the United States or the Soviet Union. Superpower rivalry provided Middle East governments the opportunity to resist Western encroachments on their independence as well as the material means and diplomatic support that allowed regional states to pursue their own military objectives and enhance their regional roles.

The rival superpowers continued to exert influence in the region primarily as a result of the disparities in power as well as the political and economic fragmentation of the region. The superpowers could not "control" what policies states pursued, but they could impose constraints and costs, construct obstacles, push or draw them into preferred alignments, and channel their activities through the international institutions by which they tried to manage the international system.

When the Cold War ended, the international political environment changed radically. The elimination of the Soviet Union as a credible counterforce in the region left the United States as sole arbiter in the region's politics and in pursuit of interests that often failed to correspond to those of regional governments or publics. This post–Cold War transformation imposed constraints on the policies of Middle East governments, but it has not been sufficient to alter the basic fragmented, anarchic pattern of relations in the region, which continues to keep states deeply insecure. Unable to strike upon a convergence of interests that would allow them to arrive at an effective collective-security arrangement; and faced with deteriorating economic conditions that threatened political consequences, Middle East governments increasingly pursued policies accommodating to U.S. objectives.

The United States, for its part, having acquired a dominant position in the Middle East, has been unable to exploit this position fully to settle the disputes that destabilize the region. Unable to create a lasting order, the United States has reconciled itself to the management of conflict in the area until such time as the expected growth in economic interdependence from incorporation into the emerging liberalized world market generates the political stability and conflict-resolution that it anticipates will naturally follow. This leaves the Middle East largely emasculated of any ability to determine a path to its own future.

Notes

1. L. Carl Brown, *International Politics and the Middle East: Old Rules, Dangerous Game,* London: I. B. Tauris, 1984.

2. Fawaz A Gerges, *The Superpowers and the Middle East,* Boulder, CO: Westview Press, 1994; Malik Mufti, *Sovereign Creations: Pan-Arabism and Political Order in Syria and Iraq,* London: Cornell University Press, 1996; Alan Taylor, *The Superpowers and the Middle East,* Syracuse, NY: Syracuse University Press, 1991.

3. In analyzing these relationships between the region and external powers, as well as other international and global processes, conceptualization of the external influences on a region have depended on the perspective taken. International relations academics often make reference to an international system from which influence and intervention upon a region emanates. The concept of the international system that has emerged from the realist/neorealist perspectives has seeped into more general usage. Hedley Bull, Kenneth Waltz, and Barry Buzan et al. have viewed the idea of an international system as the collective relationship of sovereign states in their interactions that have a binding effect to the extent that the behavior of the members is constrained by agreements, informal undertakings, threats, and deterrences. The structure of the system is defined in three main ways—by its membership (sovereign states), the pattern of relationships, and hierarchy of power among these states. The overall characteristic of the international system as understood by them is its anarchical nature, with neorealists recognizing that the international system as a consequence is not wholly conflictual but also produces cooperative relations among states. See Hedley Bull, *The Anarchical Society: A Study of Order in World Politics,* London: Macmillan, 1977; Barry Buzan, Richard Little, and Charles Jones, *The Logic of Anarchy: From Neo-Realism to Structural Realism,* New York: Columbia University Press, 1993; Kenneth N. Waltz, *Theory of International Politics,* Reading, MA: Addison-Wesley, 1979.

4. B. A. Roberson, ed., *The Middle East and Europe: The Power Deficit.* London: Routledge, 1998, pp. 4–5.

5. Roger Adelson, *London and the Invention of the Middle East: Money, Power, and War, 1902–1922,* London: Yale University Press, 1995.

6. B. A. Roberson, "The Superpowers and the Middle East," in *Global Politics.* Milton Keynes: Open University, 1988, pp. 11.

7. James Gelvin, "The Ironic Legacy of the King-Crane Commission," in David W. Lesch, ed., *The Middle East and the United States: A Historical and Political Reassessment,* Boulder, CO: Westview Press, 1996, pp. 11–16.

8. Rashid Khalidi et al,, eds., *The Origins of Arab Nationalism,* New York: Columbia University Press, 1991; Zeine N. Zeine, *The Emergence of Arab Nationalism, with a Background Study of Arab-Turkish Relations in the Near East,* 3d ed., Delmar, NY: Caravan Books, 1976.

9. Bassam Tibi, *Arab Nationalism, A Critical Enquiry,* edited and translated by Marion Farouk-Sluglett and Peter Sluglett, London: Macmillan, 1990, pp. 116–122.

10. Abbas Alnasrawi, *Arab Nationalism, Oil, and the Political Economy of Dependency,* London: Greenwood, 1991.

11. Daniel Yergin, *The Prize: The Epic Quest for Oil, Money and Power,* London: Simon & Schuster, Pocket Books, 1993.

12. Roberson, "The Superpowers and the Middle East," p. 23.

13. See Paul W. T. Kingston, "The 'Ambassador for the Arabs': The Locke Mission and the Unmaking of U.S. Development Diplomacy in the Near East, 1952–53"; Richard Parker, "The United States and King Hussein," p. 103; Malik Mufti, "The United States and Nasserist Pan-Arabism," pp. 167–170, all in David W. Lesch, ed., *The Middle East and the United States: A Historical and Political Reassessment,* Boulder, CO: Westview Press, 1996; see also, Peter Mansfield, *A History of the Middle East,* London: Penguin Books, 1992, pp. 162–165.

14. T. G. Fraser, *The USA and the Middle East Since World War II,* London: Macmillan, 1989, pp. 71–73.

15. For Egypt as one of a number of examples, see Mufti, "The United States and Nasserist Pan-Arabism," pp. 167–169; Parker, "The United States and King Hussein," pp. 103–104; and Peter Hahn, "National Security Concerns in U.S. Policy Toward Egypt, 1949–56," pp. 96–97, all in David W. Lesch, ed., *The Middle East and the United States: A Historical and Political Reassessment,* Boulder, CO: Westview Press, 1996.

16. Warren I. Cohen and Nancy Bernkopf Tucker, eds., *Lyndon Johnson Confronts the World: American Foreign Policy, 1963–68,* Cambridge: Cambridge University Press, 1994, pp. 279–281; George Lenczowski, *American Presidents and the Middle East,* London: Duke University Press, 1990, p. 91.

17. Gerges, *The Superpowers and the Middle East,* pp. 175–197.

18. Richard Cottam, *Iran and United States: A Cold War Case Study,* Pittsburgh: University of Pittsburgh Press, 1988, pp. 51–55.

19. William B. Quandt, *Peace Process: American Diplomacy and the Arab-Israeli Conflict Since 1967,* Washington, DC, Berkeley, and Los Angeles: The Brookings Institution and University of California Press, 1993, pp. 58–62.

20. Naseer Aruri, "US Policy Toward the Arab-Israeli Conflict," in Hooshang Amirahmadi, ed., *The United States and the Middle East: A Search for New Perspectives,* Albany: State University of New York Press, 1993, pp. 100–101.

21. Quandt, *Peace Process,* p. 73.

22. Fraser, *The USA and the Middle East,* p. 93.

23. Aruri, "US Policy," pp. 104–108.

24. Quandt, *Peace Process,* pp. 183–331.

25. Anthony Cordesman, *Western Strategic Interests in Saudi Arabia,* London: Croom Helm, 1987; David Long, *The United States and Saudi Arabia: Ambivalent Allies,* Boulder, CO: Westview, 1985.

26. Gary G. Sick, "The United States in the Persian Gulf: From Twin Pillars to Dual Containment," in David W. Lesch, ed., *The Middle East and the United States: A Historical and Political Reassessment,* Boulder, CO: Westview Press, 1996, pp. 280–291.

27. Amr Sabet, "Dual Containment and Beyond: Reflections on American Strategic Thinking," *Mediterranean Politics* 4, no. 3, 1999.

28. Eric Davis, "The Persian Gulf War: Myths and Realities," in Hooshang Amirahmadi, ed., *The United States and the Middle East: A Search for New Perspectives,* Albany: State University of New York Press, 1993, p. 254.

29. Adam Garfinkle, "NSC-68 Redux," *SAIS Review* (special issue, "NSC-68 and U.S. Foreign Policy Today") 19, no. 1, winter/spring 1999, pp. 41–54, 44–45; Sabet, "Dual Containment," p. 31.

30. Aruri, "US Policy," pp. 99–100.

31. Sabet, "Dual Containment," p. 1.

32. Graham E. Fuller, "Repairing US-Iranian Relations," *Middle East Policy* 6, no. 2, October 1998, pp. 140–144.

33. Fred Halliday, "An Elusive Normalisation: Western Europe and the Iranian Revolution," in B. A. Roberson, ed., *The Middle East and Europe: The Power Deficit*, London: Routledge, 1998.

34. Phebe Marr, "The United States, Europe, and the Middle East: Cooperation, Co-optation or Confrontation?" in B. A. Roberson, ed., *The Middle East and Europe: The Power Deficit*, London: Routledge, 1998, p. 83.

35. Alan Dashwood, "External Relations Provisions of the Amsterdam Treaty," in David O'Keefe and Patrick Twomey, eds., *Legal Issues of the Amsterdam Treaty*, Oxford-Portland, OR: Hart Publishing, 1999, pp. 211–224; Laurence W. Gormley, "Reflections on the Architecture of the European Union after the Treaty of Amsterdam," in David O'Keefe and Patrick Twomey, eds., *Legal Issues of the Amsterdam Treaty*, pp. 58–62.

36. Dashwood, "External Relations," pp. 212–213, 223–243; Wim Van Eekelen, "EU, WEU and NATO: Towards a European Security and Defence Identity," Sub-Committee on Defence and Security Cooperation Between Europe and North America, Defence and Security Committee, *NATO Parliamentary Assembly*, International Secretariat, AS 257, DSC/DC(99)7, November 1999, pp. 8–9.

37. Diana Tussie, "Multilateralism Revisited in a Globalizing World Economy," *Mershon International Studies Review* 42, 1998, p. 192; Peter Nunnenkamp, "Winners and Losers in the Global Economy: Recent Trends in the International Division of Labor, Major Implications and Critical Policy Challenges," *German Yearbook of International Labor* 39, 1996, p. 42; Benjamin Coriet, "Globalization, Variety and Mass Production: The Metamorphosis of Mass Production in the New Competitive Age," in J. R. Hollingworth and Robert Boyer, eds., *Contemporary Capitalism: The Embeddedness of Institutions*, Cambridge: Cambridge University Press, 1997, pp. 242–243.

38. S. Fischer, "The Middle East," in Jarrie de Melo and Arvind Panagariya, eds., *New Dimensions in Regional Integration*, Cambridge: Cambridge University Press, 1993, pp. 423–448.

39. World Bank, *Claiming the Future: Choosing Prosperity in the Middle East and North Africa*, Washington, DC: World Bank, 1995, p. 3.

40. Gary G. Sick, "Defining Security: The Case of the Gulf," paper presented at the University of Virginia, 1994.

41. World Bank, *Claiming the Future*, pp. 90–112.

42. Harry Brown, "Population Issues in the Middle East and North Africa," *RUSI Journal*, February 1995, pp. 32–43.

43. Roberson, ed., *The Middle East and Europe*, pp. 1–19.

44. Paul Aarts, "The Middle East: A Region Without Regionalism or the End of Exceptionalism?" *Third World Quarterly* 20, no. 5, October 1999, pp. 911–925.

45. Richard Gibb and Wieslaw Michalak, eds., *Continental Trade Blocs: The Growth of Regionalism in the World Economy,* New York: Wiley, 1994, pp. 251–253; Riccardo Faini and Enzo Grilli, eds., *Multilateralism and Regionalism After the Uruguay Round,* Basingstoke, England: Macmillan, 1997, pp. 194–200.

46. Charles Oman, "Globalization and Regionalization in the 1980s and 1990s," in Marjan Svetlicic and H. W. Singer, eds., *The World Economy, Challenges of Globalization and Regionalization.* Basingstoke, England: Macmillan, 1996, pp. 137–152.

47. European Commission, *Strengthening the Mediterranean Policy of the European Union: Establishing a Euro-Mediterranean Partnership,* Supplement 2/95 to the Bulletin of the European Union. Luxembourg: Office for Official Publications of the European Communities, 1995.

48. George Joffé, ed., *Perspectives on Development: The Euro-Mediterranean Partnership,* London: Frank Cass, 1999.

49. Statement by U.S. Undersecretary of State for Commerce Stuart Eizenstat in Mary-Jane Deeb, "Paying Attention to Tunisia," *Journal of Commerce* 22, January 1999, p. 4A.

50. Marr, "The United States," pp. 74–103.

4

The Challenge of Security in the Post–Gulf War Middle East System

Nadia El-Shazly and Raymond Hinnebusch

Regional Order or Disorder?

The end of the second Gulf war stimulated much speculation about the construction of a new Middle East order, under the aegis of a Pax Americana, to replace the collapsed Arab-centered system. The Middle East's rampant insecurity made it an anomaly in a dawning post–Cold War era when "zones of peace" seemed to be spreading; the end of the Cold War and the subsequent Gulf war, however, seemed to present a unique opportunity to construct a new security architecture in the region. The defeat and discrediting of Iraq's militaristic Arab nationalism and the replacement of superpower rivalry with great-power cooperation in the region seemed to reduce the likelihood of aggression. The beginnings of the Arab-Israeli peace negotiations, with their associated confidence-building measures, promised to resolve or reduce the region's most enduring conflict. The final displacement of Pan-Arabism by the doctrine of state sovereignty would allow "normal" state-to-state relations based on shared interests and accord non-Arab states such as Turkey and Israel legitimate membership in a "Middle East system."

In this new environment, the more cooperative security arrangements needed to end the unrestrained struggle for power could be established. The consequent dilution of insecurity and the exhaustion of economies from arms races would allow economic development to push military ambitions off of state foreign-policy agendas. Interdependence fostered around economic ties and cooperation in resolving common problems such as water scarcity would create interest in peace and generate confidence. Public opinion, exhausted by war and acquiring enhanced weight from democratization experiments, would restrain state

71

leaders. In consequence, the regional system would move, in Korany's words, "from warfare to welfare." Pax Americana would provide the essential external support for movement toward this new order. In terms of international-relations theory, the expectation was that realist power politics would be tamed by pluralism's complex interdependence and democratic peace.[1]

In fact, few of these benign expectations for regional order were realized in the first decade after the Gulf war. The region continued to be marked by protracted conflicts throughout the decade. Civil war continued in Sudan and high-stakes confrontation in Iraq. Chronic warfare raged throughout the 1990s in those places where interstate security threats overlapped with persisting irredentism: in Israel's so-called security zone in southern Lebanon and along Turkey's frontiers with Iraq and Syria where Ankara fought a war against Kurdistan Workers Party (PKK) guerrillas. Meanwhile, peace processes between Israel and the Palestinians and Israel and Syria had, at the beginning of the new millennium, foundered.

In this scenario of continuing insecurity, the old power politics not only persisted, but, with the collapse of solidarity among the Arab states after the invasion of Kuwait, it was accompanied by the increasing dominance of the non-Arab periphery over the Arab core, notably in the form of a new Israeli-Turkish alliance. And ironically, the new magnitude of U.S. postwar penetration actually exacerbated the region's underlying instability even as Washington sought, through such contested policies as the "dual containment" of Iraq and Iran, to contain its consequences.

Pax Americana?

In the 1990s, the Middle East regional system was subject to a new magnitude of penetration by the U.S. world hegemon. Although justified in the name of a "new world order" or Pax Americana, its effects were far more ambiguous.

The U.S. Navy in Troubled Waters

The major new pillar of the U.S.-sponsored order in the region was its enhanced overt military presence in and tightened security links with the Gulf states. In essence, the United States had used the two Gulf conflicts to establish itself as the major naval power in the Gulf. The U.S. presence significantly increased during the Iran-Iraq "Tanker War" and the accompanying reflagging of Kuwaiti tankers in the late 1980s. Following the second Gulf war, the United States accomplished its long-hoped-for strategic objectives in the Gulf. The early 1990 memoranda of understanding signed with several Gulf Cooperation Council (GCC) states allowed access to naval and air bases, the pre-positioning of war matériel, combined exercises, and vast arms sales. U.S. policy aimed to secure unconstrained access to Gulf oil at "acceptable" prices.[2] The new penetration also increased the short-term security of key Gulf allies, especially Saudi Arabia, that were pivotal to the protection of U.S. interests.

Dual Containment

The second pillar of the U.S.-imposed new regional order was the "dual containment" of the region's two most powerful nationalist states with a record of contesting U.S. hegemony, Iran and Iraq.

The U.S.-led coalition smashed Iraq's power in the second Gulf war and a continued U.S. military presence was seen by many regional states as indispensable to containing the militarism manifest in Saddam Hussein's two aggressive wars and his pursuit of weapons of mass destruction. But Washington's postwar policy exacerbated rather than solved the Iraqi problem. Long after Iraq had been defeated and its strategic weapons substantially destroyed, Washington continued to wage a campaign against Baghdad, including continued bombing, economic blockade, and an intrusive international sanctions regime that openly aimed to permanently destroy Iraq as a regional power and impose enough suffering on Iraqis to cause Saddam Hussein's overthrow. The resulting conflicts between Iraq and the Anglo-U.S. *combinazione* over "no-fly zones," Kurdish autonomy, and the UN Special Commission (UNSCOM) inspections of Iraqi disarmament kept the regional pot boiling while failing to either remove or reach agreement with the Iraqi regime.

Even in the short term, U.S. policy was often ineffective or actually counterproductive. Thus, CIA support for the opposition in Iraqi Kurdistan collapsed in 1996 when Iraqi tanks were invited to enter the region by the Iraqi Kurdish Democratic Party, a member of this opposition. Later, U.S. missile attacks on Iraq ended UNSCOM's mission and the so-called degrading of Saddam's weapons capabilities by aerial attacks was no substitute for on-the-spot monitoring. These attacks may also have increased Iraq's incentive to attain a weapons of mass destruction (WMD) deterrent.

Moreover, U.S. policy actually deterred Iraq from the postwar reconstruction that could have turned it inward to its own problems. The sanctions regime allowed limited imports of food and medicine under the "Oil for Food" program, but its overall effect, in preventing the reconstruction of the county's infrastructure, ensured that Iraq remained debilitated. The irony was that Saddam Hussein was arguably strengthened by the sanctions regime. The dependence of the Iraqi population on rationed food supplies gave the regime a new instrument of control and he profited from Iraqi resentment of the West and Arab empathy with his people's plight. It was hard to avoid the conclusion that Washington was less interested in a solution to the Iraqi crisis than in containing Saddam Hussein at whatever cost to Iraq and to the region.[3]

However, the unprecedented violations of Iraq's sovereignty and the massive use of coercive measures against it—including the arbitrary imposition of a border with Kuwait and the near genocidal victimization of a whole Iraqi generation by economic sanctions, blamed by Iraqis and many Arabs on the United States and Britain—generated enduring resentments that were bound to have negative long-run political consequences. The high costs of Saddam's policies for Iraqis may well deter a future Iraqi leadership from acting on these feelings. However, Iraq, by virtue of its geostrategic location, human resources, and oil reserves on a par with Saudi Arabia's, retains the potential to reemerge as a regional great power, and Washington's policy only postponed the unavoidable problem of rehabilitating and readmitting it to the regional system. Worse, it increased the likelihood that when Iraq does recover its power it will be a threat to the region. The Versailles-like dictat to which it was subjected sowed ample seeds of revanchism that future Iraqi politicians may have little trouble in harvesting, potentially making Iraq a chronic source of future revisionism.

Anglo-U.S. unilateralism toward Iraq provoked unease across the region. What the U.S. secretary of state defined as "containment plus regime change" met with widespread criticism in Middle Eastern capitals. The refusal by Egypt and the United Arab Emirates (UAE) of U.S. requests to host meetings of the Iraqi opposition-in-exile and the unwillingness of Saudi Arabia, Bahrain, the UAE, and Turkey to allow use of their air bases to attack Iraq for its alleged violation of UN resolutions showed how far the United States was operating outside any regional or international consensus. The governments of the United States' own regional allies, sensitive to public opinion, insisted that they could only support such measures if Israel also complied with the UN resolutions it had so long ignored. Indeed, there was, by the late 1990s, a sea change in regional opinion, which increasingly sought to reintegrate Iraq into the region. Signs of this included the expansion of commercial and air links with Iraq, increased popular and official calls for the lifting of sanctions as penalizing the Iraqi people, not the regime, and near-unanimity in denouncing the punitive air campaigns against Iraq, with their repeated "collateral damage." In the words of former U.S. national security advisor Zbigniew Brzezinski: "Our policy is either strike them or starve them, and neither accomplishes our objectives."[4] But the policy of provoking Saddam did keep the lower Gulf states utterly dependent on U.S. protection from him.

At the same time, Washington aimed, under dual containment, to isolate Iran, the other power that contested its hegemony. The supposed Iranian threat Washington sought to contain was more political and ideological than military. Tehran's aspiration for acceptance as a regional power meant opposition to the U.S. role in the region, including its brokering of an Arab-Israeli peace process that Iran believed threatened Palestinian rights. Rejecting U.S. claims to be defending a new world order, Iran held that the United States used its global hegemony to promote double standards and to manipulate international institutions for its own ends. The tools of dual containment included U.S. military power in the Gulf, and efforts to economically isolate and demonize Iran for its rejection of the Madrid peace process.[5] The containment of Iran was, however, ineffective since Iran used its commercial and military links to Russia and diplomatic bridge building with Western Europe and the Arab Gulf states to obstruct Washington's attempts to make it an international and regional pariah. It was also counterproductive in that it stimulated a defensive military buildup in Iran, including a possibly increased readiness to pursue the nuclear option.

Flawed Peace Process

The third pillar of the Washington-orchestrated new security order was the effort, initiated at the 1991 Madrid peace conference, to resolve the Arab-Israeli conflict that had so long inflamed the region against the United States for its support of Israel. To be sure, Madrid and, thereafter Oslo, were watersheds in Arab acceptance of Israel. As the Arab-Israeli relation was reduced from an ideological war to a competition over the terms of a settlement, Arab leaders were increasingly confident they could legitimize accommodationist policies toward Israel even if these violated Arab nationalist norms.[6]

Yet the peace process proved so flawed that many doubted it could deliver a durable settlement. This was rooted in the power imbalance in Israel's favor, whose military superiority was enhanced by the defeat of

Iraq and the decline and collapse of the Arabs' Soviet patron, and massively reinforced rather than offset by Washington's continued pro-Israeli bias. Two of the Arab parties, the Palestine Liberation Organization (PLO) and Jordan, needed a settlement more than Israel did in order to escape the marginalization imposed on them for their tilt toward Iraq in the Gulf war. Arab weakness was compounded by the structure of the negotiating process that the United States imposed to Israel's advantage. The separate individual negotiations of the Arab parties with Israel made it impossible for Syria, the PLO, and Jordan to hold to a common strategy, enabling Israel to play them off and weaken each individual party. Their leverage was also weakened by U.S. pressure for the premature start of normalization of relations with Israel, begun by certain Gulf states made vulnerable by their total dependence on Washington for protection from Iraq. All this meant that unequal power, not justice or even UN resolutions, would dictate the outcome, making an equitable—hence legitimate and durable—settlement highly doubtful.

To be sure, Jordan and Israel, whose territorial differences were minor, readily reached an acceptable arrangement. Agreement reached in principle on a land-for-peace settlement between Israel and Syria, where more of a power balance existed, may well be realized in practice. However, the Israeli-PLO Oslo Accord, reached between such grossly unequal parties, was so profoundly structured against the Palestinians that it risked conferring international legitimacy on a settlement that totally frustrated their national rights.

The Oslo Accord did embody the breakthrough of Israeli-PLO mutual recognition and it did permit the establishment of a Palestinian Authority (PA) on several patches of the occupied West Bank and in Gaza. But, ironically, as handfuls of its officials were co-opted by new privileges, the PA seemed reduced to the role of enforcing Israeli security demands against its own people, thus relieving Israel of the costs of occupation. Most crucially, Oslo failed even to halt Israeli colonization of Palestinian land, which actually accelerated, plus the construction of a web of so-called security roads linking them to Israel. In 2000, seven years after the Oslo Accord, Israel kept full control of 60 percent of the West Bank and 20 percent of Gaza, controlled water rights, and continued to limit Palestinian freedom of movement within the occupied territories. The course of negotiations over the final status agreement suggested that Israel would offer the Palestinians limited self-rule over perhaps three-quarters of the West Bank and Gaza, scattered in "Bantustans" lacking territorial contiguity and surrounded by security roads and settlements. The Palestinian entity would be demilitarized, lack free access to its Arab hinterland or the outside world, and remain profoundly dependent economically on Israel and international donors and always vulnerable to reoccupation. Moreover, Israel refused to surrender sovereignty over Arab East Jerusalem and expected the PLO to renounce the rights of return or compensation of the Palestinian diaspora that are enshrined in UN resolutions. The Al-Aqsa *intifada* starting in the autumn of 2000 suggested that such a false peace would not be easily imposed and, even if accepted by the PLO, was unlikely to have the legitimacy needed to endure.[7]

The peace process, in the U.S. design, was to be accompanied by increasing economic cooperation between the Arabs and Israel that would supposedly build confidence and create transstate interests with a stake in peace. However, the proposed "Middle East market"—in which Israel would contribute technology, the Arab oil states capital and markets, and the non-oil states labor—was obstructed by the lack of a political settlement, which in turn sustained Arab perceptions that economic integration was an Israeli bid to conquer economically what it could not take militarily.[8]

Magnet for Terrorism

Washington's intrusiveness and continuing use of force against Arab targets was bound to stimulate widespread popular resentment. Its actions were all the more inflammatory because of the transparent double standards it applied: visible to all, for example, was the gross disparity between Washington's tacit support for Israeli violations of UN resolutions in Lebanon and the occupied territories and its punitive measures against Iraq for similar violations. Given the powerlessness of the region in the face of U.S. hegemony, opponents inevitably resorted to the weapon of the weak—terrorism. There were attacks on the World Trade Center in New York, the Khobar military complex in Dhahran, and U.S. embassies in Tanzania and Kenya. In the latter case, the United States responded with counterviolence, launching cruise missiles against a Sudanese pharmaceutical factory Washington claimed was producing poison gas and was linked to master terrorist Osama bin Laden. Middle East public opinion rejected Washington's action as disproportionate, lacking in legal justification, and motivated by President Clinton's domestic troubles. A year later, the CIA admitted Washington lacked evidence of nerve gas production or of links with terrorists and in May 1999, the United States released the frozen funds of the factory's owner.[9]

The Turkish-Israeli Pact
and the Regional Power Balance

Since the Gulf war, Turkey has emerged as a Middle East great power much more actively involved in regional alignments and conflicts than heretofore. On the one hand, Turkey seized the opportunity to recover its strategic value to the West, lost with the end of the Cold War, by allowing its bases to be used for strikes against Iraq in the Gulf war and by enforcing economic sanctions against Iraq. At the same time, however, Turkey suffered from sharp internal cleavages in which the military-dominated secular establishment confronted Islamic movements and a Kurdish insurrection. The core army commanders, the ultimate arbiters in Turkish politics, viewing the Kurdish question purely as a "terrorist problem" to be dealt with by military means, mobilized 250,000 troops in a relentless campaign against the PKK guerrillas and forcibly vacated thousands of Kurdish villages.

This war inevitably spilled over in conflicts with Iraq, Iran, and Syria, who had sizable Kurdish populations and were believed to harbor PKK guerrillas used to pressure Turkey. Damascus and Ankara conducted a complex geopolitical game, using the issues of water sharing and security as bargaining counters against each other. Syria manipulated Abdullah Ocalan's PKK against its neighbor and Turkey exploited its dominion over the headwaters of the Euphrates and Dejla Rivers, essential to Iraq and Syria. From 1984, Syria had given shelter to the PKK, allowing it to set up training camps in Lebanon's Beqa' Valley, in the face of Turkey's constant rejection of regional or bilateral discussions of water sharing. The vast Ataturk dam network in the southeast, which diverted the flow of water, caused critical shortages in Syria, which Turkey exploited for political ends.

A major watershed in the region was the emergence of a Turkish-Israeli pact aimed at Syria and, to a lesser degree, Iran. Turkey was the first Muslim state to recognize Israel in 1948; in 1959, one year after Egypt and Syria formed the United Arab Republic, the Ben Gurion–Menderes Peripheral Treaty allowed intelligence sharing between Turkey and Israel. This relation declined beginning in the 1960s in deference to rising pro-Palestinian domestic opinion and Turkish need for Arab markets and oil. However, the February 1996 military cooperation agreement between the two states revived and strengthened this old partnership of the non-Arab periphery against the Arab core of the regional system. Rooted in a convergence of Israeli and Turkish interest in deterring Syrian use of Lebanon-based guerrillas (Hizbollah, PKK) against these states, it can be seen as a case of classic checkerboard balancing to counter the long-standing Syrian-Iranian alliance.

The Turkish-Israeli alliance was a clear strategic threat to Syria, Iraq, and Iran. It expanded Israeli airspace in the eastern Mediterranean by allowing Israeli reconnaissance flights along the borders of these states with Turkey. Israeli intelligence officers also trained the Turks to work along these states' frontiers, ostensibly to track down PKK guerrillas, and assisted Turkish troops when they overran Iraqi Kurdistan.[10]

When Turkey, Israel, and the United States carried out their first combined maneuvers, with a Jordanian observer, it became a focal point of alarm in the Arab world. Although the trilateral Operation Reliant Mermaid was described as an innocent search-and-rescue mission, Israel's defense minister, Yitzhak Mordechai, acknowledged its "security aspect."[11] Paris, Moscow, and Tehran shared the view that, with U.S. consent and Jordan's tacit backing, Syria had been encircled, sharply weakening its leverage in the peace negotiations with Israel. The Turkish-Israeli pact was viewed as the centerpiece of the new U.S.-dominated regional order under which Turkey was enlisted to help maintain Israeli superiority, preserve the dual containment of Iraq and Iran, and combat terrorism.

The pact was accompanied by an extraordinary new assertiveness on the part of Turkey. Turkey imitated Israel's south Lebanon policy by imposing a *cordon sanitaire* in northern Iraq and launching periodic forays against PKK bases there and, occasionally, in Iran. In October 1998, Turkey's threats of war against Syria unless it evicted all PKK guerrillas and their leader were underlined by troop and air force movements along the border.[12] Syria's compliance with this application of coercive threat was a measure of how far the power balance had shifted against it. The widely suspected complicity of Israeli, U.S., and Turkish intelligence officers in abducting PKK leader Abdullah Ocalan from Kenya in February 1999 underlined the close cooperation between the United States and its two closest non-Arab allies in the Middle East.

It is the conventional wisdom that common dangers create mutual interests. However, Turkish and Israeli perceptions of threat do not entirely coincide. Israel considers Iraq, Iran, and Syria as major enemies, while Turkey has both differences and interlocking strategic and economic interests with them. Ankara signed security agreements with Baghdad (April 1983), Damascus (October 1998), and Tehran (August 1999), and all have consistently opposed Kurdish autonomy in northern Iraq. In the 1980s, Turkey was Iran's and Iraq's second-largest customer and supplier. A decade later, Turkey signed a $23 billion agreement for

Iranian natural gas. UN Security Council Resolution 986 permits Iraq to sell an amount worth $10.6 billion annually of crude oil, most of which is transshipped through the Kirkuk-Ceyhan pipeline from which Turkey profits. As such, the Israeli connection, imposed by the Turkish military on purely strategic grounds and in defiance of a section of the political elite and significant sectors of public opinion, could hardly be said to reflect a consensus on Turkey's national interest.

The Turkish-Israeli alliance did not precipitate an effective counterbalance in the region. The Damascus Declaration, aligning Syria, Egypt, and the GCC member states, was seen at its founding during the Gulf war as the basis of an explicitly Arab regional security order. But it remained moribund throughout the 1990s. Significantly, Egypt did not fully back its Syrian partner in this nominal alliance when it needed help against Turkey, and instead sought to mediate between the two.[13]

Iran, the largest, most populous, and potentially most powerful state in the region, sought to counter the U.S.-dominated regional order through its alliance with Syria and its geopolitical centrality in the Gulf. The Syrian-Iranian alliance had proved its value against Israel and Iraq in the 1980s, but its failure to protect Syria in its showdown with Turkey underlined its limits. Iran under Presidents Rafsanjani and Khatami sought to break out of U.S. containment by cultivating pragmatic relations with the Arab Gulf states and advocating a Gulf collective security arrangement that would reduce the U.S. presence in the area. But this initiative was obstructed by remaining tensions, such as the dispute over Iran's continued hold on three Gulf islands claimed by the UAE. Iran insisted it had to keep them to prevent their being turned into U.S. bases controlling the Strait of Hormuz, the jugular of its oil lifeline.

Lastly, although the three states most at odds with Washington—Iran, Iraq, and Syria—could make up a very powerful counteraxis, the conflicts of interest between them effectively neutralized this potential throughout the 1990s. As such, at the beginning of 2000, no regional state or axis was positioned to build a regional order that could dampen the insecurity that kept the struggle for power alive. Worse, the regional power constellations on which order therefore inevitably rested seemed distinctly unbalanced, as an assessment of the regional arms race will make clearer.

Arms Proliferation in the Middle East

In this environment, the security dilemma, wherein each state, in seeking security through arms acquisitions, only heightens general insecurity, was given full rein. The region headed the world arms-procurement list for most of the last two decades of the twentieth century. While the outcome of the Gulf war—the smashing of Iraqi power and the start of the Madrid peace talks—was seen as an opportunity to construct cooperative security arrangements and advance arms control, the arms race actually accelerated. Thus, 1997 defense budgets rose, with Saudi Arabia in the lead ($18.4 billion), followed by the non-Arab states Turkey ($8.2 billion), Israel ($7 billion, *excluding* U.S. military aid, in addition to $2 billion from arms sales), and Iran ($5.8 billion). They were followed by Kuwait ($4 billion), the UAE ($3.7 billion), Egypt ($2.8 billion), Oman ($1.8 billion), Syria ($1.7 billion), Iraq and Libya ($1.3 billion each), Qatar ($1.2 billion), Lebanon ($592 million), Jordan ($548 million), Yemen ($414 million), and Bahrain ($402 million).[14]

In addition to pervasive insecurity and continuing unresolved conflicts, arms acquisition was accelerated to cement alliance relations between regional and external powers, above all between the United States and recipient states. Competing arms dealers, backed by their governments, were also eager to absorb the foreign exchange surpluses of oil-rich states.[15] Washington, the supposed author of a new order in the region, actually led the way in the transfer of arms to its allies Saudi Arabia, Turkey, and Israel. At the same time, the United States threatened sanctions against Russian companies that sold Syria and Iran arms or weapons-related technology. As such, U.S. policy not only increased the level of regional militarization but also threatened to create a regional imbalance, and hence greater insecurity for disadvantaged states.[16]

Military spending by states such as Saudi Arabia served Western interests, notably in recycling petrodollars, but were of less obvious benefit for the kingdom. Saudi Arabia underwrote the costs of two Gulf wars: it partially funded Iraq's war effort to frustrate revolutionary Iran, then paid the United States $62 billion to bankroll the war against Iraq. In its aftermath, the Saudis bought $14.8 billion worth of U.S. arms and continued to negotiate large new acquisitions long after Iraq's defeat.[17] Partly to finance such purchases, the Saudis and other Gulf states overproduced oil, plunging prices to $10 a barrel in the late 1990s, a twenty-five-year low in real terms. In 1998, the Saudi government, with a $12 billion budget deficit, had to reschedule payments and cut domestic spending. Sophisticated arms acquisitions also required the Gulf Arab governments, which lacked the capacity to maintain such equipment, to import skilled foreign personnel and some U.S. arms contracts stipulated that U.S. crews permanently supervise some features of the weapons systems' operations. This has been true, for example, in transfers of F-16s to the UAE, and of Airborne Warning and Control Systems (AWACS) to the Saudi kingdom.[18] Such dependence on expatriate experts gave foreign powers direct influence over Gulf defense establishments, including access to the strategic planning by which threats were designated.

Turkey also expanded its military. With the third-largest military budget in the region, it was also a main recipient of heavy weapons, free of charge under the 1992 Cascade program that allowed NATO states to transfer surplus weapons to other members. This enabled Turkey, which had almost four thousand tanks, to obtain over a thousand more during the first year alone, while refusing to mothball its older-vintage models. By 1993 Turkey had the second-largest army in NATO and had enlarged its naval and air forces as well, threatening to upset the power balance in the Middle East and the Balkans.[19]

Israel, the second-largest military spender, also had the most sophisticated military-industrial complex, with a high-technology electronic warfare capability underpinned by thousands of highly qualified Russian immigrant scientists and by U.S. and German subsidies. Israel also benefited from Washington's commitment to keep it militarily superior to any combination of regional enemies. In 1983, President Ronald Reagan announced a strategic cooperation agreement, the dimensions of which were continuously amplified in the following fifteen years, during which Israel acquired offensive forces that could intimidate any of its perceived enemies, be it Iran, Syria, or Iraq. Ironically, progress in the Arab-Israeli peace negotiations seemed to merely whet Israel's appetite for more arms and, in a November 1998 memorandum of agreement, Washington went considerably beyond earlier guarantees to ensure "Israel's qualitative military edge."[20] In particular, Israel's Arrow-2 antiballistic missile, unique in the region, was largely funded by the United States at a cost of $1.6 billion.[21] In addition, Israel acquired three German-made Dolphin-class submarines fitted with nuclear-capable missiles. They made up the third leg of an emerging land-, air-, and sea-based nuclear triad comparable to those of the major nuclear powers, of which Israel is now estimated to be the sixth in the world. These developments widened the Arab-Israeli technological gap and made Israel's overwhelming military supremacy incontestable.

Not only weapons but intentions define the threat a state poses to its neighbors, and Israel adheres to an offensive-minded military doctrine stressing the overwhelming use of force and preemptive strikes to minimize casualties and neutralize its geographic vulnerability. Hence, an emerging power imbalance, in which Israel may be attaining the capacity to attack any of its enemies from behind the safety of U.S.-funded antimissile systems, threatens regional stability. In particular, it could undermine such deterrence relationships as that with Syria, which has maintained the peace on the Syrian-Israel front since 1982.

Inevitably, the imbalance in favor of Washington's clients stimulated a counter-buildup, albeit a much more modest one, among states who felt their deterrent capabilities threatened. Syria, surrounded by Turkey and Israel, sought new arms purchases in Paris and Moscow.[22] But it is doubtful that its aging Soviet-equipped military can keep up with the advances of its enemies. On the contrary, Syria's challenge is to prevent further deterioration of its forces after Soviet/Russian demand for payment in hard currency denied it enough ammunition and spare parts and forced the storage of more than one-quarter of its 4,600 main battle tanks and most of its artillery.[23]

The Gulf war and the subsequent regional arms buildup also stimulated Iran's attempt to restore the military capability so degraded in the Iran-Iraq war. Iran's military acquisitions were by no means unreasonable. It had lost half its military capability in the war and much of the rest was obsolete. Its scramble to buy arms was also a reaction to a "decade of near total [arms] embargo [during that war] and a sense that it might be reimposed at any time."[24] The second Gulf war, in which U.S. air power, high-tech electronics, and intelligence—exactly Iran's weaknesses—effortlessly won out, underlined the threat from the United States.[25] Since the war, Iran's military buildup has therefore also been driven by the U.S. maintenance of a enhanced presence in the Gulf and by its militarization of the Gulf monarchies while seeking to cut off Iran's access to arms.[26]

Iran's experience with the arms embargo and continued U.S. attempts to isolate it made military self-reliance and diversification indispensable.[27] Thus, Iran diverted scarce resources into the further expansion of its indigenous military industry and into joint arms development with Syria, Pakistan, and North Korea; with assistance from Russia and China, it acquired the capability to produce tanks, missiles, and artillery.

Iranian equipment levels—aircraft and tanks—are, however, still only about half of prerevolutionary levels. Moreover, Iran's buildup was tailored to defense, not offense. Its navy, built around mine-laying capability and submarines, aims at denying a foreign force control of the Persian Gulf. Although the acquisition of three ex-Soviet Kilo-class submarines and ten Chinese Hudong-class missile boats, aroused furor among U.S. officials, strategists agreed that they did not alter the balance in the Gulf.[28] Similarly, Iran acquired relatively cheap missiles as a deterrent because its air force and air defense had low capabilities.[29]

Egypt, once the main Arab power, was, in key ways, hobbled as a potential component in an Arab security alliance. In the aftermath of the peace agreement with Israel, it made significant reductions in the size of its armed forces and increasingly depended on U.S.-made weapons. Cairo is now at the mercy of Washington, where weapon sales to "moderate" Arab countries are repeatedly vetoed by the powerful Jewish congressional lobby and by Israel. Egypt has, in spite of this, managed to acquire significant advanced arms from its patron.[30] Yet it would be extremely difficult, given Washington's control over its supplies, for Egypt to make these arms part of any strategy of political compulsion against the country its planners still consider its main security threat, namely Israel.

The Proliferation of Weapons of Mass Destruction

The Middle East is threatened by the proliferation of weapons of mass destruction. Israel is the sole regional nuclear power but Iraq acquired, and used, chemical weapons and was pursuing a uranium enrichment program before its efforts were hobbled by the Gulf war and UNSCOM. Both Iraq and Israel justified their need for such capabilities by the asymmetries with their neighbors' manpower and strategic depth, but it is these states alone that have militarily attacked their neighbors in recent decades.

A decade ago, Anthony Cordesman, a leading writer on Middle Eastern strategic affairs, predicted Israel's nuclear capability and its development of intermediate-range ballistic missiles would set off a chain reaction in the Middle East, in which other states would seek to match that capability or acquire more easily produced and concealed biological weapons, as an essential deterrent.[31] Israeli and Iraqi acquisitions did in fact force their rivals, Iran and Syria, to right this imbalance through acquisition of chemical and biological agents; Iran is suspected of efforts to acquire a nuclear capability as well.

While a few experts argue that WMD deterrents kept the peace in the Cold War, this rested on a rough bipolar balance of power quite unlike the imbalance in the Middle East where Israel, alone possessing nuclear weapons, faces several rivals possessing biological or chemical weapons. Moreover, because WMD-tipped missiles may give first-strike advantages in the absence of stable mutual deterrence, they could, in a time of crisis, plunge the area into a holocaust.

Deterrence is also jeopardized by the fact that Israeli strategic doctrine does not even limit WMDs to a purely deterrent role. In 1962, Shimon Peres, the architect of Israel's nuclear program, referred to the idea of "nonconventional compellence," that is, the use of nuclear weapons to force the other side to accept Israeli political demands.[32] Almost a quarter of a century later, defense minister General Yitzhak Mordechai suggested that Israel "had tactical nuclear weapons and would be prepared to use them."[33] Israel's alteration of its military doctrine, shifting from hinting at its nuclear power to publicizing it and pledging no first use, then threatening to wield it—as well as its creation of a triad of nuclear forces—heightens insecurity across the region.

As peace with the Arabs seemed increasingly possible, Israel started to claim that Iran posed an "existential threat," although it was one of the main suppliers of sophisticated arms and aircraft spare parts to Iran during its war with Iraq. This new enmity was a rationale for Israel to forcefully oppose transfers of missiles and dual-use technology to Iran while also legitimizing the retention and expansion of Israel's strategic and conventional arsenals.

Iran does, indeed, appear to be the next Middle Eastern state with the greatest potential to acquire nuclear weapons. However, unlike Israel, it has acceded to the chemical-weapons convention of 1993 and the Nuclear Non-Proliferation Treaty (NPT). For the past decade, at least, Israeli intelligence reports have been warning that Iran was two years away from having a nuclear bomb, while U.S. and British estimates suggested five to ten years.[34] It would be rational for Iran to acquire some such capability as a deterrent against Iraq and Israel. Such weapons would also enhance Iran's regional leadership claims.[35] Chubin is probably right, however, that Iran's nuclear program is embryonic, designed as a hedge, an option to be nursed rather than a determined effort to produce a weapon.[36]

Efforts to limit and reduce WMDs in the region have faltered on the rock of Israeli obduracy. The Arab states and Iran have acceded to the NPT and their nuclear-power facilities are open to inspections by the International Atomic Energy Agency. By contrast, Israel, the only Middle Eastern country to refuse to adhere to the NPT and to block entry to its own nuclear plants, is one of a handful of states that operate "unsafeguarded nuclear facilities."[37]

Israel's unwillingness to discuss its WMDs was the single reason for the breakdown of the regional multilateral arms control negotiations in December 1995. In the words of General Ahmad Fakhr, a member of the Egyptian delegation to the 1991 Madrid Conference and of the Working Group on Arms Control and Regional Security:

> The Arabs had argued that these were talks to shape a new Middle East, one that was moving towards a lasting peace. They insisted that

all types of weapons, whether conventional or non-conventional, such as nuclear, biological and chemical be discussed, in order to build confidence and ease tensions. They also pressed for mutual transparency on their inventories, as well as inspections of sites by specialised agencies. Israel's representative exclaimed: "This is a non-starter." Negotiations ended then.[38]

The issue was again on the agenda at the Nuclear Non-Proliferation Conference where Egypt sponsored agenda item 74, "The Risk of Nuclear Proliferation in the Middle East," on behalf of Arab League members of the UN, none of which has a nuclear military capability. It calls for a nuclear-free Middle East, notes that "Israel remains the only state in the Middle East that has not yet become party to" the NPT, and urges "universal adherence to the Treaty." Israel and the United States voted against it, while 158 members voted for, with 11 abstentions.[39] Before the renewal of the NPT, Egypt campaigned among members of the Non-Aligned Movement to refrain from signing the treaty unless Israel acceded. Although Cairo eventually succumbed to U.S. pressure to remain a party to the NPT, Egypt and other states stayed out of the Chemical Weapons Convention—enforced in April 1997 and signed by more than 160 countries. Israel's refusal to accede to the NPT sparked an ongoing debate in the Arab academia and press, especially in Egypt, about matching Israel's nuclear capability.

Washington, the supposed guarantor of a new world order limiting WMDs, bears major responsibility for their introduction and proliferation in the Middle East. On the one hand, it long had tacit knowledge of Israel's thermonuclear bomb program yet regularly subsidized Israel's budget, notwithstanding the Glenn-Symington amendment that proscribes aid to countries that acquire nuclear weapons.[40] On the other hand, the United States, though a signatory and determined promoter of the NPT, supported Israel's refusal to sign the NPT, while—characteristically—rebuking those Middle East states that refused, as a result, to sign the Chemical Weapons Convention.

Conclusion

The failure of regional institutions, multilateral or bilateral alliances, and of the regional power balance to give local states security, brutally exposed by the Iraqi invasion of Kuwait, opened the door to acceptance of a heightened role for the non-Arab periphery states and for the U.S. hegemon in the region. In the post–Gulf war era, inter-Arab disputes continued to paralyze the Arab League/summits system as an arena for collectively addressing security threats.

The result is a security situation that serves Western interests and narrows Arab autonomy in a way the architects of the Baghdad Pact could only dream of. The quasi-permanent U.S. military presence in the Gulf, partly funded by Arab oil and aimed at Iran and Iraq; the devastation and siege by which Iraq's power was destroyed and its revival prevented; the neutralization, through economic and security dependency, of Egypt and Saudi Arabia; and the Israeli-Turkish encirclement of Syria, all keep any regional state or coalition that might seek to reorganize the regional system for collective indigenous purposes effectively hobbled. The notion of an autonomous Arab system has been virtually nullified.

Was this the price of increased regional security? Pax Americana, far from uniformly enhancing the security of the Middle East, had a contradictory effect. On the one hand, the United States exacerbated power imbalances, sowed the seeds of future Iraqi revanchism and Palestinian frustration, and encouraged the spread of strategic weapons, arguably the single most serious challenge to Middle Eastern security. Instability was contained largely by the deterrent power of the hegemon and its ties to the pivotal Arab states of Egypt and Saudi Arabia, plus the counterbalancing of the Turkish-Israeli and Syro-Iranian axes. As such, rather than a stable new Middle Eastern system replacing the old Arab-centered system, security rests on fluid ad hoc arrangements.

This "system" has several potentially fatal flaws. As Barnett argues, a stable order depends on congruence between the normative expectations of society and those of state elites.[41] While the international hegemon and key state elites may believe there is no viable alternative to the status quo, significant parts of indigenous society retain visions of an Arab-Islamic order free of Western intrusion and Israeli dominance; this taints the legitimacy of those states seen to support a status quo order devoid of these expectations. As Barnett observes, the separation between elites and society was sharply underlined in the 1994 Sharm al-Shaikh meeting of a concert of state leaders, both Arab and Israeli, who identified the main security threat as internal—from radical Islam.[42]

To a very considerable extent, therefore, the status quo, lacking indigenous popular legitimacy, is erected on hegemonic external force and on economic and security relations that benefit a relative few. The continued application of U.S. force in the region is thus essential to maintain the status quo, but paradoxically further undermines its legitimacy. As such, should that force falter, it seems likely that the regional order would again face destabilizing challenges from below and within.

Moreover, the Middle East's instability and insecurity cannot be confined to the region. The September 11, 2001, attacks on the World Trade Center and the Pentagon only reaffirm what the Guf war a decade prior made clear: at least once per decade unresolved regional crisis spills over into a world crisis. In the latest case, the particular character of the crisis is shaped by the dominant features of the current global configuration, namely U.S. hegemony and globalization. On the one hand, the grievances expressed by Osama bin Laden and his following of "Arab Afghans" are a reaction against the unprecedented scale of post–Cold War U.S. penetration of and impact on the Middle East. This includes the U.S. presence in Saudi Arabia, site of Islam's holy places, its ongoing campaign against Iraq, and its perceived support of Israel's denial of Palestinian statehood. On the other hand, the resulting Middle East ferment seems increasingly likely to take the form, not just of state-to-state conflict, but to spill out of the region via transnational terrorist networks such as al-Qa'ida. One unforeseen consequence of the acceleration of transnational communications and transportation in an age of globalization is that, more than ever before, Middle East insecurity spells global insecurity.

Notes

1. Bahgat Korany, "The Old/New Middle East," in Laura Guazzone, ed., *The Middle East in Global Change: The Politics and Economics of Interdependence Versus Fragmentation,* London: Macmillan, 1997, pp. 135–149; Michael N. Barnett, "Regional Security After the Gulf War," *Political Science Quarterly* 111, no. 4, 1996–1997, pp. 597–617; Bassam Tibi, *Conflict and War in the Middle East: From Interstate War to New Security,* London: Macmillan, 1998; Anoushiravan Ehteshami, "Security Structures in the Middle East: An Overview," in Haifaa Jawad, ed., *The Middle East in the New World Order,* London: Macmillan, 1997, pp. 101–102.

2. *Independent,* 20 September 1991; and *San Diego Union,* 26 January 1992; M. A. Armacost, Undersecretary of State for Political Affairs, "U.S. Policy in the Persian Gulf," Department of State, Special Report No. 166, Senate Foreign Relations Committee, July 1987, in *International Legal Materials* XXVI, nos. 4–6, 1987, pp. 1429–1431.

3. Sarah Graham-Brown, *Sanctioning Saddam: The Politics of Intervention in Iraq,* London: I. B. Taurus, 1999; Tim Niblock, *"Pariah States" and Sanctions in the Middle East,* Boulder, CO: Lynne Rienner, 2001, pp. 97–198; Geoffrey Simons, *The Scourging of Iraq: Sanctions, Law and Natural Justice,* London: Macmillan, 1996.

4. *New York Times,* 21 December 1998.

5. Shahram Chubin, *Iran's National Security Policy, Capabilities, Intentions, Impact,* Washington, DC: Carnegie Endowment for International Peace, 1994, pp. 20–55.

6. Barnett, "Regional Security," pp. 603–605.

7. Ghada Karmi, "A Binational State in Palestine," *Middle East International,* 7 May 1999; Amira Hass, "Beaten and Betrayed," *The Guardian,* 3 October 2000, p. 21; Atif Kubursi, "Prospects for Arab Economic Integration After Oslo," in Michael Hudson, ed., *Middle East Dilemmas: The Politics and Economics of Arab Integration,* London and New York: I. B. Tauris, 1999, pp. 308–309.

8. Emma Murphy, "The Arab-Israeli Conflict in the New World Order," in Haifa Jawad, ed., *The Middle East in the New World Order,* Basingstoke: Macmillian, 1997, pp. 110–139; Bahgat Korany, "The Old/New Middle East."

9. *International Herald Tribune,* 31 July–1 August and 23 August 1999; and *Independent,* 10 August 1999.

10. The accord includes, inter alia, intelligence sharing and jointly combating terrorism, and military-industrial cooperation, including the equipping of fifty-four Turkish F-4 Phantom jet fighters—and forty-eight F-5s at a later stage—with modern avionics and radar systems by Israel; the development of the Popeye surface-to-air missile at a cost of $80 million; combined training in strafing and hitting of targets; the use of Turkish ports by Israeli vessels; and regular consultations between the high echelons of the military. General Ahmad Fakhr, interview, 8 October 1998; see also Nadia El-Shazly, "Arab Anger at Axis," *World Today* 55, no. 1, January 1999, pp. 25–27; *al-Ahram,* 10 July 1999; *International Herald Tribune,* 20–21 December 1997; and *al-Hayat,* 15 July 1999.

11. *Independent,* 8 January 1998.

12. For instance, General Husseyn Kivriloglu, the chief of staff, said that "there is a state of undeclared war between us and Syria," in *International Herald Tribune,* 3 and 5 October 1998; and *Independent,* 5 October 1998. Also, a Turkish general warned that the army would "drive through one end of Syria and out through the other," in *International Herald Tribune,* 23 February 1999.

13. Arab diplomat, interview, 7 October 1998; *Independent,* 22 June 1996.

14. *Al-Ahram Strategic Report 1998,* table 3, Cairo: Al-Ahram Publishing, p. 256. See also Nadia E. El-Shazly, *The Gulf Tanker War,* Basingstoke, England: Macmillan, 1998, p. 154; *SIPRI 1993,* pp. 444–445, tables 10.10 and 10.11, *SIPRI Yearbook,* Stockholm International Peace Research Institute, Oxford University Press; and *Military Balance 1998,* London: International Institute of Strategic Studies, pp. 116–118, 124–134, 137–145, table 16, pp. 119–122.

15. Abdel Moneim Said Aly, "The Middle East and the Persian Gulf: An Arab Perspective," in Andrew J. Pierre, ed., *Cascade of Arms: Managing Conventional Weapons Proliferation,* Washington, DC: Brookings Institution Press, 1997, pp. 253–284.

16. *International Herald Tribune,* 30 July 1998, 22 July, 5 and 28–29 August 1999; *Middle East International,* no. 605, 30 July 1999, pp. 8, 9; *Hayat,* 20 July 1999; *Independent,* 21 July 1999; and *Independent on Sunday,* 4 April 1999.

17. *Financial Times*, 27 November 1989; *Independent*, 7 January, 27 February, and 2 September 1992, and 8 January 1994; *Hayat*, 13 January 1999; *Military Balance 1996*, p. 121; and *Al-Ahram Strategic Report 1998*, p. 261.

18. *International Herald Tribune*, 7 August 1999.

19. *Independent*, 21 July 1993.

20. *International Herald Tribune*, 3 November 1998.

21. *International Herald Tribune*, 3 November 1998, 16 September 1998, and 2 November 1999.

22. *International Herald Tribune*, 6 and 8 July 1999; *al-Ahram Strategic Report 1998*, p. 262.

23. *Military Balance 1998*, p. 142.

24. Chubin, *Iran's National Security Policy*, p. 75.

25. Ibid., p. 20.

26. John Calabrese, *Revolutionary Horizons: Regional Foreign Policy in Post-Khomeini Iran*, New York and London: St. Martin's/Macmillan, 1994, pp. 3–22.

27. Chubin, *Iran's National Security Policy*, pp. 18–19.

28. Above data on Iran's arms acquisitions are from *al-Hayat*, 25 August 1999; *International Herald Tribune*, 5 April and 16 September 1999; and *Military Balance 1998*, p. 119.

29. Calabrese, *Revolutionary Horizons*, pp. 34–44.

30. *Military Balance 1998*, pp. 117–118, 119; *al-Ahram Strategic Report 1998*, pp. 262, 269.

31. Anthony H. Cordesman and Abraham R. Wagner, *The Lessons of Modern War*, vol. 1. London: Mansell, 1990, p. 356.

32. Yair Evron, "Israel and the Atom: The Uses and Misuses of Ambiguity, 1957–67," in Stephen Green, *Taking Sides*, London: Faber & Faber, 1984, pp. 151–152.

33. *Independent on Sunday*, 8 February 1998; see also *Independent*, 22 May 1995; and *International Herald Tribune*, 19 December 1997.

34. *Independent*, 15 February and 30 November 1992, and 11 January 1995; *Military Balance 1998*, p. 117.

35. Chubin, *Iran's National Security Policy*, pp. 20–55.

36. Ibid., p. 75.

37. NPT/CONF. 1995/6 Clause 3 (a) subparagraph, p. 1; also ibid., Decision 2, Clause 1, p. 9, and Clause 3, p. 10 in 1995 *Review and Extension Conference of the Parties to the Treaty on the Non-Proliferation of Nuclear Weapons*, Final Document, Part I, Organization and Work of the Conference, New York, 1995, NPT/CONF. 1995/32 (Part 1).

38. Interview, 8 October 1998.

39. Senior Arab diplomat at the UN, telephone interview, 3 August 1999.

40. On Israel's nuclear program, see Green, *Taking Sides*, pp. 151, 153, 164–167, passim.

41. Barnett, "Regional Security After the Gulf War," pp. 614–616.

42. Ibid., p. 617.

5

The Foreign Policy of Egypt

Raymond Hinnebusch

The modern Egyptian republic is the product of a long history. Egypt has been a proto-nation from the time of the pharaohs who centralized rule in the Nile Valley. The Arab invasion of the seventh century led to the Arabization and Islamization of the population. Egypt's centuries of subordination to foreign rule and the long independence struggle against Britain generated a powerful nationalism that made defense of independence crucial to the legitimacy of ruling elites. Gamal Abdul Nasser harnessed this sentiment to consolidate his regime, challenge Western dominance, and make Egypt a regional great power. However, his successors, Anwar Sadat and Husni Mubarak, faced tightening constraints forcing them to put economic survival over nationalist ambitions in Egypt's foreign policy.

Foreign-Policy Determinants

Geopolitics

Egypt's geopolitical position is a constant that has shaped the foreign policies of successive rulers. Egypt occupies a strategic position as a land bridge between two continents and a link between two principal waterways, the Mediterranean and the Indian Ocean. As the preeminent civilization center of the region, and the most cohesive and weighty Arab state positioned astride the eastern and western wings of the Arab-Islamic world, Egypt naturally seeks regional leadership.

On the other hand, Egypt's position on the route of potential conquerors has made it a target of external powers throughout history,

91

generating a sense of vulnerability and a belief that Egypt had to either dominate its regional environment or become the victim of these forces. Also, Egypt's survival depends on the waters of the Nile, and it therefore also considers satisfactory relations with the states on the river's headwaters a matter of national security.

As such, Egyptian rulers traditionally tried to project their power into the Sudan and into Syria and Arabia—often in contest with other powers in Anatolia or the Euphrates Valley. For some six hundred years, Cairo was the center of Arab-Islamic dynasties—the Fatimids, Ayyubids, and Mamluks—that carved out empires to the west and east and defended the Islamic world from Crusader and Mongol threats.[1] Under the Ottoman Empire, Egypt became a province, but, as Istanbul's power waned, local dynasties reappeared; Muhammed Ali, a modernizing ruler, challenged the Ottomans for regional dominance and projected Egyptian power into the Arabian Peninsula and Syria, precipitating a European great-power coalition against him.

As, in the twentieth century, Egypt gradually achieved independence, state elites needed a foreign-policy orientation and, given Egypt's strategic weight in the emerging Arab states system, they naturally were drawn into the competition for Arab leadership. Egypt was pivotal to an Egyptian-Syrian-Saudi concert that sought to check the ambitions of the pro-British Hashemites in the *mashreq*. In the 1940s and early 1950s, Egypt sought to use the Arab League to mobilize regional pressure on the British to abandon their bases in Egypt.[2]

Under the post-1952 republic, Egypt's strategic position similarly shaped its ambitions. Egypt, Nasser believed, was at the center of three "circles," the African, the Arab, and the Islamic. Egypt came to view itself as the Arab "nucleus state" and the Arab world as its natural sphere of influence.[3] It therefore worked to roll back the penetration of the region by the Western powers. At the same time, the perception of threat from Israel, backed by a superpower, situated on Egypt's border, and blocking its access to the Arab East, became one of the single most determining factors in Egypt's security policy.

Egypt in the 1950s and 1960s was the only Arab state with the political and military capability to pursue hegemony in the Arab world and to assume its defense against Israel. Under Nasser, Egypt's defense expenditure was geared to match Israel's and frequently exceeded the combined expenditures of Iraq, Syria, and Jordan, the next-ranking military powers.[4] Nasser discovered that Egypt's Arab leadership bolstered his stature at home and deepened the country's strategic weight in world affairs, allowing him to play off and extract resources from both superpowers.

Egypt's hegemony in the Arab world invited, as under Muhammed Ali, a reaction against it—Western backing for Nasser's Arab rivals and the 1967 Israeli occupation of Egyptian lands. This defeat forced a major contraction in Egyptian ambitions and, after Egypt's separate 1979 peace with Israel, its temporary isolation in the Arab world. Under Mubarak, Egypt was able to break out of this unnatural isolation, but other Arab powers had by then consolidated themselves, and Egypt was only one of several actors in a multipolar Arab arena, its role constrained by its treaty with Israel. But both Sadat and Mubarak, no less than Nasser, saw a leading inter-Arab role as the key to extraction from the international system of the resources needed for survival at home.

Identity and Domestic Politics

A second constant that shaped Egypt's foreign policy was its Arab-Islamic identity. To be sure, Egyptian's national identity was never merged in an undifferentiated Arabism; Egypt's long pre-Islamic heritage and its partially isolated Nile Valley–centered civilization combined with its ethnic homogeneity have given it a distinct and assured identity. In periods such as the British occupation, it developed separately from the Arab world and a portion of the most Westernized upper class came to see Egypt as "Mediterranean" or "Pharaonic." Even the great nationalist leader Saad Zaghlul professed a distinctly Egyptian nationalism. But for the vast majority of Egyptians, the content of Egyptian identity was Arab-Islamic. Egyptians speak Arabic and 90 percent are Muslim. Egypt is the largest Arabic-speaking country and the intellectual and political center to which the whole Arab world has looked in modern times. It is also a center of Islamic civilization, its al-Azhar University one of Islam's major religious institutions, and its popular culture profoundly Islamic.

As mass politicization advanced after the 1930s, the content of Egyptian identity became ever more Arab-Islamic. This politicization was fueled by the resonance in an Egypt struggling for independence of the similar anti-imperialist struggles in other Arab states. Most decisive was the threat perceived from Zionist colonization of Palestine, which Islamic movements such as the Muslim Brotherhood adopted as their cause in the 1930s.[5] As Arab-Islamic sentiment was aroused, rival political leaders, notably King Faruq and the Wafdist leader Mustafa al-Nahhas, adopted it to bolster their popular support.

But it was Nasser who consolidated the Arab content of Egyptian identity. He was himself politicized as an army officer in the Palestine war, where he viewed the fighting as self-defense, not a conflict over foreign territory. Since all the Arab states faced the same imperialist and Zionist enemies, Arab solidarity against the outside was, he came to believe, the key to independence.[6] As Nasser's Pan-Arab message evoked Arab enthusiasm, his regime made systematic attempts to propagate an Arab identity in Egypt through schools, the media, and the single party. The 1962 National Charter blamed the failure of the 1919 Zaghlul-led revolution on its inward-oriented leaders, who were incapable of deducing from Egypt's history that there was no conflict between Egyptian patriotism and Arab nationalism.[7]

Yet, Egypt's Arabism remained relatively shallow: kinship was acknowledged and, indeed, Egypt saw itself as the leader of the Arab world entitled to preeminence in proportion to the heavy burdens it bore in defense of the Arab cause. But few Egyptians had an emotional commitment to Arabism or to unity with other Arab states. Even Nasser remained jealous of Egyptian sovereignty and preferred foreign-policy solidarity behind Egyptian leadership to the unity schemes that preoccupied the eastern Arabs.[8] The responsibilities that accompanied Arab leadership were accepted as long as the benefits exceeded the costs, but when the balance was reversed, Egypt tended to lapse into greater isolationism. Under Anwar Sadat, the regime began to disengage from Pan-Arab commitments and to promote a more Egypt-centric identity. Once his march toward a separate peace with Israel brought him into growing conflict with other Arab leaders and the Palestinians, Sadat successfully exploited Egyptians' feeling that they had made enough sacrifices for the Arab cause and their growing resentment of the "rich and ungrateful" Arabs for whom Egypt had shed blood and treasure but who were niggardly in sharing their unearned new oil wealth with Egypt. However, as Mubarak's regime attempted to consolidate itself against Islamic opposition in the 1980s, it quickly jettisoned a stance so at odds with Egypt's cultural roots and sought to don the mantle of Nasserism—albeit in symbol, not substance.

Between Anti-Imperialism and Dependency

Finally, Egypt's foreign policy was pulled in contrary directions by the ideals of anti-imperialist nonalignment and the webs of economic dependency in which the country was increasingly enmeshed. On the one hand, the long history of subordination to foreign rulers, especially European imperialism, produced an intense anti-imperialism, a quest for dignity, and, particularly under Nasser, a powerful nationalism among

Egyptians. Egypt's national ideal was to be independent of both East and West.

Yet, as a poverty-stricken developing country suffering a permanent structural imbalance between an excess population and limited resources, especially land, and a nearly permanent balance-of-payments deficit, Egypt could not do without large amounts of aid from the advanced economies. Egypt lost the capacity to feed itself and has depended on U.S. food aid since the 1960s. Moreover, Egypt had a classic primary-product-producing dependent economy, with cotton and cotton products accounting for 60 percent of total exports in the 1960s and oil somewhat diversifying this after the mid-1970s. The main geo-economic constant for Egypt, its high level of dependency on external markets and resources, has meant both potential constraints on its foreign policies and a recurrent effort to use foreign policy to access the resources that would allow the country to continue to live above the level that could be sustained by purely domestic resources.

Nasser, convinced that excessive dependence was incompatible with foreign-policy independence, tried to limit and diversify Egypt's dependence. Economic diversification through import-substitute industrialization was to provide the base of national power. However, Nasser's ambitious effort to combine industrialization, a modest welfare state, and military power exacerbated the resource imbalance and created new dependencies on imported machinery and technology. This could not be sustained without drawing on major external resources; between 1952 and 1975, foreign aid financed over a third of imports and development investment. But Nasser minimized the potential constraints from such dependency through a policy of balancing between East and West that won aid from both sides. At Nasser's death, Egypt's debt was modest.

Nevertheless, Egypt paid a mounting economic cost for Nasser's foreign policies. The United States punished his anti-imperialist stance by withdrawing food aid in the mid-1960s. U.S. support for Israel after the June 1967 war made Egypt ever more dependent on the Soviet Union for military aid and protection. But this was, in part, balanced by growing financial aid from the conservative Arab oil states; moreover, according to Nasser himself, the Soviets were generous and put no strings on their aid: the Soviet interest in Egypt's anti-imperialist nonalignment and its post-1967 ability to resist capitulation to the U.S.-Israeli *combinazione,* coincided with Egypt's own interests.

Under the pro-Western Sadat, however, the Soviets began to insist on payment for arms in hard currency. Military expenditures, originating in the drive to overcome the 1967 defeat, escalated and Egypt purport-edly spent $25 billion from 1967 to 1975.[9] The defeat had also cost Egypt $350 million annually from Suez Canal income, oil, and tourism while the Arab oil states' subsidies made up only $250 million.[10] From 1967 onward, Egypt labored under an intractable economic crisis and part of Sadat's motivation, when he realigned Egypt westward, was to win economic relief.

But the result of Sadat's policies was a totally new order of eco-nomic dependency, at first on Arab oil aid and the remittances of Egyp-tians working abroad and then, after Egypt's separate peace with Israel, on $2 billion in yearly U.S. aid. Ironically, much of the latter was spent unproductively on arms: the peace with Israel did not substantially re-duce military burdens since the break with the Soviets required the re-equipping of the army with very expensive U.S. arms. Moreover, Sadat's economic liberalization, notably its associated import booms and inflow of foreign resources, radically deepened Egypt's debt and dependency. This made Egypt ever less self-sufficient and more vulner-able to the demands of Western donors and the International Monetary Fund (IMF), which constrained, if it did not entirely preclude, foreign-policy decisions displeasing to Israel and Washington. This sharply lim-ited Egypt's ability to pursue a vigorous independent and Arab-oriented foreign policy. By the late 1980s Mubarak, facing the prospect of de-fault on Egypt's debt, took the opportunity of the second Gulf crisis to trade alignment with the West against Iraq for debt relief.

Omni-Balancing and the Search for a Role

The challenge of Egyptian foreign policy is to preserve the country's autonomy and security while also mobilizing economic resources for de-velopment. Egypt's geopolitical centrality and weight in the Arab world defines a natural strategy in which Egypt invests in the power resources to make itself the hub of the Arab states system and thereby presents it-self as the bridge between the regional and international systems. Bal-ancing between external powers and the region gives it the potential to extract geopolitical "rent" while protecting its autonomy and security.

Nasser initially used foreign policy to combine nationalist achieve-ment and economic benefits and this set a standard of legitimacy that his successors have been unable to live up to. His Arab nationalist legitimacy allowed him to win economic aid from both superpowers. Yet security needs and foreign ambitions also absorbed scarce economic resources and, after the 1967 war, the economy had to be sacrificed to the demands of defense. Thereafter, Sadat opted, instead, to sacrifice Nasser's nationalist foreign policy in return for massive U.S. economic subsidies and diplomatic assistance in the recovery of Egypt's lost territory. Since then, Egypt has had to choose between autonomy and economic benefits. Complicating the trade-off is the fact that the intimate connection between internal legitimacy and a nationalist profile means trading foreign policy for economic resources may appease more privileged elements of domestic society that stand to most benefit while inflaming those who do not. This dictates a constant "omni-balancing" between external constraints and threats and domestic needs and demands.

Foreign Policymaking

State Formation

The 1952 coup against the traditional monarchy, led by Gamal Abdul Nasser's group of nationalist-reformist "Free Officers," gave birth to the contemporary republic. Nasser, the first true Egyptian to rule Egypt for centuries, forged the new state. He suppressed the rudiments of pluralism and created a presidential-dominated, military-led, authoritarian-bureaucratic regime with a single party and a subordinated parliament, press, and judiciary. Nasser's charismatic leadership and the populist achievements of the 1952 revolution—particularly land reform, welfare programs, and state employment—built a base of mass support for the regime. But it was Nasser's foreign-policy successes—the "victories" over "imperialism," notably the Czech arms deal and Suez; the wide acknowledgment of Nasser's leadership across the Arab world; and his deft manipulation of Egypt's Arab leadership to extract resources from both superpowers—that made Nasser's personal rule unassailable. Nasser gave the state a broader base of support than it had hitherto enjoyed, embracing a populist coalition of the army, bureaucracy, the middle class, and the masses. This strong state enjoyed the autonomy of domestic constraints that allowed Nasser to conduct a foreign policy successfully exploiting Egypt's geopolitical advantages, but also to take the risks that led to the 1967 war. This defeat threw the regime into crisis.

Although Anwar al-Sadat assumed power as Nasser's vice-president and was a veteran of the 1952 revolution, the legitimacy windfall he won as "Hero of the Crossing" positioned him to launch his "de-Nasserization" and to pursue new solutions to the regime's main vulnerabilities, namely its alienation from the Egyptian bourgeoisie and from the United States, the superpower whose support was needed to resolve the conflict with Israel. A major economic and diplomatic opening (*infitah*) to the West shifted the base of support of the state from Nasser's populist coalition to the bourgeoisie. The political system remained essentially authoritarian but, in a tacit deal with the political class, Sadat assumed a free hand in foreign policy, but conceded greater political pluralism in which parliament, opposition parties, interest groups, and the press all acquired greater though still limited freedom to influence domestic policy. Resistance to Sadat's foreign policy eventually led to mass arrests of regime opponents, precipitating Sadat's assassination to "warn those who come after," in the words of the perpetrators. But the survival of most of his policies after his death suggests that, more successfully than Nasser, Sadat had partially institutionalized them—in an alliance with the dominant social forces and in a web of economic and diplomatic dependency that constrained significant change.

Husni Mubarak, Sadat's vice-president and successor, maintained the major lines of Sadat's policies, while trying to overcome some of their excesses. Nasserist policies—from Arab nationalism to food subsidies and the public sector—had created durable interests and standards of legitimacy that Sadat had threatened and with which Mubarak initially attempted to identify. But, locked into the U.S. alliance and the separate peace with Israel, he faced rising Islamic opposition. The regime sought to defuse domestic threats through a mix of limited liberalization, limited repression, and limited accommodation with the conservative wing of the Islamic movement. However, rising Islamic violence together with the regime's gradual abandonment of the residues of populism under IMF pressures, forced an ever greater resort to repression.

In spite of enormous pressures on it, however, the post-1952 state showed a remarkable capacity to survive and adapt. The ruling elite remained autonomous enough to shape foreign-policy decisions in response to perceived geopolitical or geo-economic opportunities and threats, without fear of uncontainable reaction at home.

The Foreign-Policy Process

The great risks and opportunities inherent in Egypt's foreign relations made it inevitable that foreign policy would dominate the leader's political agenda. Foreign-policy performance can make or break the leadership. Nasser's charisma was rooted above all in his nationalist victories over "imperialism," and the decline of Nasserism was a direct function of the 1967 defeat by Israel;[11] similarly, Sadat's achievements in the October 1973 war gave him legitimacy, while his separate peace with Israel enervated it.

Presidents therefore seek to make foreign policy their exclusive prerogative, and the constitution of the authoritarian state accords them appropriate powers: the president is supreme commander, declares war, concludes treaties, proposes and vetoes legislation, and may rule through decree under emergency powers that were regularly delegated by parliament. The extent of the president's consultation with the top elite and with foreign-policy professionals in the policy process is, therefore, very much a matter of his personal choice, while the relative influence of such elites depends more on their personal relations with the president than their official position.[12]

Nasser, although initially consulting with his fellow Free Officer revolutionaries, alone took the crucial decision to nationalize the Suez Canal; the success of this venture so raised him above his colleagues that he soon ceased to seek consensus and became overbearing in cabinet discussions of policy.[13] Sadat asserted a similar presidential prerogative; a major issue in his power struggle with left-wing Free Officers after Nasser's death was Sadat's insistence on his unilateral right to make foreign-policy decisions, such as his offer to open the Suez Canal in return for a partial Israeli withdrawal from its east bank. While Sadat's purge of these rivals gave him a freer hand, the planning and decision to go to war in 1973 was made in close consultation with the military and political elite.[14]

Once Sadat consolidated his power and legitimacy in that war, however, he continued and exaggerated the tradition of presidential unilateralism in the postwar peace diplomacy brokered by the United States. He tolerated no domestic dissent and Mohammed Hassanein Heikel, Egypt's premier press baron and most prestigious presidential adviser, was purged for daring to question Sadat's postwar strategy. Sadat took crucial decisions in defiance of elite opinion and in disregard of professional military and diplomatic advice; in negotiations over the disengagement agreements with Israel after the 1973 war—Sinai I and Sinai II—he excluded his top advisers from key sessions with U.S. secretary of state Henry Kissinger and overrode their objections to many details of these agreements. He made his momentous decision to go to Jerusalem without even bothering to create an elite consensus behind him. He allowed his top generals little say at Camp David. Three successive foreign ministers resigned in protest over his tactics in the negotiations with Israel, indicative of his unwillingness to create or depend on a national consensus for his decisions. His unilateral concessions so often undermined the hand of his diplomats in the negotiations over the peace treaty with Israel that they sought to keep the Israelis away from him.

Sadat was no more prepared to accept constraints from public opinion. He brushed aside numerous attempts by a near-parliamentary consensus, remarkable in a body dominated by the government party, to restrain his march toward a separate peace. These included parliamentary resolutions to break off the negotiations with Israel, to give the Arab Defense Pact priority over the peace treaty with Israel, to make normalization of relations with Israel contingent on a comprehensive settlement, and to link it to the West Bank autonomy provided for in the Camp David Accords. Eventually, a fed-up Sadat dissolved this parliament and made sure elections to its successor eliminated all leading critics.[15]

Despite presidential dominance, the Egyptian foreign-policy bureaucracy was the most sophisticated and influential in the Arab world. Under the minister of foreign affairs were a minister of state for foreign affairs and a series of undersecretaries in charge of geographical areas and functional departments (economic affairs, cultural affairs, and the like). Al-Ahram's Centre for Political and Strategic Studies acted as a think tank in support of decisionmakers. Career diplomats were recruited chiefly through competitive examinations and trained at the Egyptian Diplomatic Institute. In 1982, Egypt had diplomatic relations with ninety-five foreign countries and more than a thousand foreign service officers. This apparatus should have permitted Egypt's presidents to make more informed and effective policies if they were willing to consult with it. In fact, although Husni Mubarak inherited the tradition of presidential dominance in foreign policy, he seemed to make his decisions in consultation with close advisers such as Usama al-Baz and Boutrus Ghali, and his foreign ministers, Ismat Abd al-Majid and Amr Musa.

Foreign-Policy Behavior

Despite certain constants, Egyptian foreign policy underwent substantial evolution shaped by the differing values and perceptions of the country's presidents and the changing constraints and opportunities of its environment.

Foreign Policy Under Nasser

The core of Nasser's ideology and the very basis of his legitimacy was his insistence on real independence for Egypt. Nasser sought to end

Egypt's long political subordination to Western imperialism, to restore its Arab-Islamic identity diluted by a century of Westernization, and to launch independent national economic development. He also aimed to replace Western domination of the Arab states system. Hence his first major foreign-policy initiative was to oppose the Baghdad Pact under which the West sought to harness the Middle East to an anti-Soviet Western alliance. Rejection of the pact led Nasser to neutralism and to advocacy of Arab collective security as a substitute for Western security dependence. It became a matter of conviction with Nasser that the main instrument by which the West and Israel sought to dominate the post-colonial Middle East was by dividing the Arabs states and that their best defense was unity under Egyptian leadership. When the Arabs were divided they were readily dominated, but when they were united they could face up to outside threats.[16]

Yet Nasser's foreign policy emerged less from a preconceived ideology or strategy than through the experience of interaction with the great powers, regional opponents, and the mass public. The new stress on Arabism reflected a popular-level alteration in identity as Egypt, long separated from the Arab world by British occupation and a Westernized Turko-Circassian ruling class, was, even before Nasser's revolution, reclaiming its Arab-Islamic identity amidst the rise of popular Islam and the Palestine struggle. Part of Nasser's calculations was the need to consolidate his position at home, where powerful opponents such as the Muslim Brotherhood could be neutralized by playing the nationalist card.

In other key respects, Nasser's policy unfolded largely as a reaction to external threat: Nasser himself said, "I don't act, I react." Thus, arguably, it was the Israeli threat that precipitated a chain of events that consolidated Nasser's Pan-Arab policy. Israel's 1955 attacks on Egyptian positions in Gaza exposed the Egyptian army's inability to confront Israeli military superiority. This precipitated the Czech arms deal, breaking the West's embargo on arms supplies imposed in the absence of peace with Israel. This began an Egyptian realignment toward the Eastern bloc, and was the first step in the generation of Nasser's heroic stature in the Arab world. In alienating the United States, it also led to the withdrawal of its financial support for the Aswan High Dam, which in turn precipitated Nasser's nationalization of the Suez Canal to acquire the needed resources to build the dam. This unleashed the Suez invasion, which cemented Nasser's Pan-Arab stature. It reinforced the perception of threat from Israel and the West that had to be countered by the mobilization of alliances in the Arab East, drawing Egypt further into its drive for Arab leadership. Moreover, the remarkable surge of Pan-Arab support unleashed by Egypt's challenge to imperialism further sensitized Nasser to the possibilities of asserting region-wide leadership.[17]

Nasser's Pan-Arab strategy also varied in response to the challenges and opportunities he encountered in the Arab world. Nasser first promoted a "unity of ranks," seeking to force the Arab states into alignment with Egypt's rejection of Western security pacts. His Pan-Arabism did not envision a Ba'thist-style challenge to independent statehood, and he only accepted union with Syria in the United Arab Republic (UAR) as the price of maintaining his mass Pan-Arab constituency. Thereafter, however, Egyptian ambitions appear to have been whetted to extend the UAR to other states and Egypt supported Pan-Arab movements that threatened the sovereignty of Jordan and Lebanon. When the Iraqi monarchy was overthrown in 1958, an unexpected opportunity to realize, at the very least, a more ambitious Arab concert under Cairo's leadership appeared to present itself.

The first major check to the Pan-Arab wave was the failure of revolutionary Iraq to defer to Egypt or join the UAR. This enervated the momentum than Pan-Arabism had built up and threatened Nasser's leadership; but ironically, his attempt to isolate Iraq's revolutionary leader, Abd al-Karim Qassem, required détente with the conservative Arab states and hence respect for their sovereignty. Egypt reverted to its previous, more pragmatic goal of Arab solidarity, calling merely for cooperation among Arab states; this stance, less threatening to other Arab leaders, was an opportunity grasped with alacrity by the conservative states.[18]

The breakup of the UAR, however, reversed this new pragmatism. It was a mistake, Nasser declared, to coexist with reactionaries who were inevitably the enemies of Arab nationalism; Arab unity was only possible once social revolution had removed the backward Arab client regimes, and Egypt would therefore seek to export its revolution. For awhile, this isolated Egypt, whose rivals—not just the monarchies, but the Iraqi and Syrian republics as well—combined against Nasser's hegemonic ambitions. But Nasser grasped at the opportunity presented by the 1962 Yemeni revolution to expand the "progressive camp" at the expense of his rivals.[19] Then, the 1963 Ba'thist coups in Iraq and Syria, which brought ostensibly Pan-Arab movements to power, ushered in the tripartite unity negotiations for a new three-state Arab federation that could have transformed the region. However, Nasser's profound distrust for the Ba'thists, whom he accused of complicity in the breakup of the UAR, and their determination not to be swept into a new form of Egyptian domination, aborted the negotiations. This failure cast doubt on

Nasser's claim that exporting revolution would prepare sounder ground for Arab unity. This episode exposed the vulnerability of Nasser's style: an inability to collaborate with other Arab leaders on an equal basis.[20]

The next alteration in policy, a swing back to mere Arab solidarity, was precipitated by the failure of revolutionary unionism, the mounting economic burdens of the Yemen intervention, and the challenge from Israel's 1964 diversion of the headwaters of the Jordan River. The return to "unity of ranks" was manifest in Nasser's sponsorship of several Arab summit meetings meant to share responsibility for Arab action— or more accurately inaction—for Nasser's aim was to deflect demands by his radical rivals, notably the Syrian Ba'thists, that he shoulder responsibility for confronting Israel. Nasser also sought to use summitry to reach an agreement with Saudi Arabia, whose backing of the Yemeni royalists had prevented the consolidation of the republican regime and entangled Egypt in an ever more costly civil war. Yemen had been a testing ground, as Kerr put it, between the forces of revolution and conservatism, and the contest had stalemated. However, the failure to reach an agreement precipitated Egypt's return to the ideological cold war with the conservative regimes.[21]

If Nasser's Pan-Arabism was initially an instrument of Egypt's foreign policy that enhanced its power and autonomy, it soon turned into a constraint. Once Nasser had mobilized a Pan-Arab constituency, he was henceforth bound to live up the role of Arab hero, and this led him into a deepening struggle with the West and Israel. As the Palestinian movement and nationalist opinion in general were radicalized in the 1960s, the credibility of his leadership rested on championing the Palestine cause and challenging Israel. Although Nasser sought to evade these pressures, they eventually led him into the brinkmanship that unleashed the disastrous June 1967 war with Israel (see Chapter 2). The rapid collapse of the Egyptian army in the war showed how far Nasser's foreign-policy ambitions had exceeded his capabilities. Israel occupied Egypt's Sinai Peninsula and henceforth Pan-Arab ideology would have to be subordinated to the realist policies that could permit the recovery of Egyptian territory.[22]

Nasser's new realism was first evident in his Arab policy, which reverted to a stress on all-Arab solidarity against Israel, burying permanently the Arab cold war in return for financial aid from the conservative states needed to rebuild Egypt's military capability. Second, his 1970 acceptance of Washington's Rogers Plan signaled Egypt's readiness for a peaceful settlement of the Arab-Israeli conflict; this meant the acceptance of Israel and acknowledged the United States' role as a dominant power broker in the Middle East. But, convinced that diplomacy alone would never recover the Sinai and skeptical of U.S. intentions, he launched a major overhaul and expansion of his armed forces. Then, in the War of Attrition (1969–1970), he contested Israel's hold on the peninsula and although he was forced to accept a cease-fire in 1970—the year he died—Nasser left Egypt in a far better military position to challenge Israel.

Nasser's foreign policy seemed, until 1967, a qualified success. Adeptly exploiting changes in the international balance of power, namely the local weakening of Western imperialism, the Soviet challenge to Western dominance, and the national awakening of the Arab peoples, he achieved the long-sought British withdrawal from Egypt, defeated the Western security pacts, nationalized the Suez Canal, and put Egypt at the head of an aroused Arab nationalist movement that forced a substantial retreat of Western control from the Middle East. Nasser's Egypt failed to become the Prussia of the Arab world, but it played the decisive role in the emergence of an Arab state system independent of overt foreign control.

Nasser's success was, of course, only relative to the failure of previous leaders and his policies had mounting costs. The other Arab states resisted Egyptian hegemony and, although largely on the defensive, worked to thwart Nasser's effort to impose a foreign-policy consensus on the Arab world. The effort to project Egyptian influence drained the country's resources. And the same nationalist foreign policy by which Nasser had ended the Western domination of Egypt led him into a trap that in 1967 entrenched a new foreign presence on Egyptian soil. This shattered Egyptian self-confidence. Moreover, the fear that the Soviet Union would not supply the offensive weapons for a military recovery of the Sinai and that the United States would keep Israel strong enough to repulse such a recovery, convinced a growing portion of the Egyptian political elite that the United States held the cards to a solution. Egypt would have to come to terms with Washington, Israel, and the West, and this would require abandoning Nasser's Arab nationalist policy.[23]

Foreign Policy Under Sadat

Sadat came to power ready for a compromise, even partial, solution to the crisis of Israeli occupation and seeking a U.S.-sponsored peace. His expulsion of the Soviet advisers in 1972 was in part an effort to court U.S. favor. He also struck a close alliance with the conservative Arab oil states headed by Saudi Arabia, whose influence in Washington, money, and potential to use the "oil weapon" were crucial elements in building Egyptian leverage over Israel; the Saudis, for their part, sought to use oil aid to pry Egypt out of its dependency on the Soviet Union. Only once it was clear that Egypt's interests would be ignored until Egyptians showed they could fight and upset a status quo comfortable to Israel and the United States, did Sadat turn seriously to the war option. He astutely prepared for war by building solid bridges to the Arab world, in particular Saudi Arabia and Syria, whose army was crucial to the two-front war needed to budge Israel. Sadat's Arab policy, seeking partnership rather than domination, was less threatening than Nasser's and, in the end, more productive.

Sadat opted for a strictly limited war to establish a bridgehead on the East Bank of the Suez Canal as a way of breaking the Israeli grip on the Sinai; such a limited war, he reasoned, would rally the Arab world around Egypt, bring the oil weapon into play, challenge Israel's reliance on security through territorial expansion, and, above all, pave the way for a U.S. diplomatic intervention that would force Israel to accept a peaceful settlement.[24] The October 1973 war did upset the status quo and ended with Egyptian forces in the Sinai. But since Israeli forces had penetrated to the West Bank of the Suez Canal, Sadat badly needed and accepted a U.S.-sponsored disengagement of forces. "Sinai I," as this agreement was called, removed the Israelis from the West Bank but, in defusing the war crisis, also reduced Arab leverage in bargaining for an overall Israeli withdrawal. In subsequently allowing his relations with the Soviet Union and Syria to deteriorate—and hence the viability of the war option—Sadat became so dependent on U.S. diplomacy that he had little choice but to accept a second partial and separate agreement, "Sinai II." Egypt recovered further territory, which included economically important oil wells, but was allowed a mere token military force in Sinai. This so undermined Arab leverage that negotiations for a comprehensive peace stalled.

At the same time, Sadat was under escalating international and domestic economic pressures; on the one hand, Western donors and economic institutions were using Egypt's dependency to pressure it into economic reforms, including the removal of the food subsidies on which the mass public depended; when Egypt removed the subsidies, the 1977 food riots shook the regime. Sadat seemed to see further movement in the peace process as the solution to his problems at home. But Israel was refusing further withdrawals on the Syrian and Palestinian fronts and Sadat had no way of restarting the negotiations expect to offer further concessions that would entice Israel to reciprocate. He decided on "shock diplomacy": he hoped his dramatic trip to Jerusalem would win world and especially U.S. support and undermine Israeli hardliners. He must also have calculated that, even if Israel refused concessions to Syria or the Palestinians, it might thereby be brought to relinquish the rest of the Sinai in return for a separate peace that took Egypt out of the Arab-Israeli power balance. Egypt would also become eligible for a "new Marshall Plan" to rescue its economy, which, not getting enough Arab aid and investment to overcome its troubles, remained in chronic crisis.

Simultaneously, Sadat gradually abandoned Nasser's policies of balancing between the superpowers. Wanting U.S. diplomatic help and economic largesse, he started portraying Egypt as a bulwark against Soviet penetration of the area. When the Soviets refused to reschedule Egypt's debt, Sadat suspended repayments in 1978. As the Soviet share of Egyptian exports fell from 50 percent to 10 percent, Egypt's once dense economic ties to the East were finally snapped. Under these conditions, Soviet relations naturally turned hostile and diplomatic relations were broken in 1980.[25] Particularly after the fall of the shah in Iran, Sadat openly sought to assume the role of guardian of U.S. interests in the area. Joint military maneuvers were held, facilities granted U.S. forces, and Egyptian troops deployed to prop up conservative pro-Western regimes, such as the government of Zaire. The Egypt that had led the fight to expel Western influence from the Arab world now welcomed it back.

Sadat seemingly reasoned that Washington's support for Israel derived from its role in protecting U.S. interests in the area, and if he could arrogate that role to himself, Egypt would be eligible for the same aid and support and the importance of Israel to Washington would decline.[26] However, he discovered that serving U.S. strategic interests did not necessarily change U.S. Middle East policy, which was affected at least as much by the Zionist lobby in Washington. And once Egypt could no longer credibly threaten to tilt toward the USSR, U.S. leaders were unlikely to antagonize Israel for its sake: hence Sadat could only get the political settlement Israel wanted, not one acceptable to the wider Arab world.

At Camp David and in the subsequent negotiations over a peace treaty, Sadat found out just how much his new diplomatic currency would purchase: a return of Sinai and, at most, a relaxation of Israeli control over the West Bank ("autonomy"), but no Palestinian state. By 1979, Egypt was finally at peace and U.S. aid was flowing in. But since the separate peace removed any remaining incentive for Israel to settle on the other fronts, Egypt was ostracized from the Arab world, forfeiting its leadership and the Arab aid to which this had entitled the country.[27]

Foreign Policy Under Mubarak

Husni Mubarak's main foreign-policy challenge was to resolve the contradiction between the standards of nationalist legitimacy established under Nasser and the combination of close U.S. and Israeli connections and isolation from the Arab world brought on by Sadat's policies. It took him nearly a decade to make significant progress, but, although Sadat's legacy proved quite durable, Mubarak succeeded in reintegrating Egypt into the Arab world.

Mubarak's Arab policy. Mubarak's astute diplomacy and the mistakes of his rivals allowed him to achieve a gradual reintegration of Egypt into the Arab world without prejudice to Cairo's Israeli links. The first break in Egypt's isolation came when Arafat's 1983 quarrel with Syria enabled Egypt to extend him protection and assume patronage of the Palestinian resistance. Then, the Arab oil states, fearful of Iran and of the spread of fundamentalism, looked to Egypt for a counterbalance. Egypt's claim to be indispensable to the Arabs and the natural hub of the Arab world was thus at least partially acknowledged, and Egypt's 1989 readmission to the Arab League crowned Mubarak's efforts. Another breakthrough was Egypt's 1989 formation, with Iraq, Yemen, and Jordan, of the Arab Cooperation Council, a new moderate bloc of non-oil states that seemed poised to become the center of gravity in inter-Arab politics—until Saddam's invasion of Kuwait destroyed it.[28]

In contrast to Nasser's Egypt, which claimed leadership in championing Arab revolution and independence from the West, Mubarak's Egypt promoted itself as moderator and stabilizer of the Arab world. Mubarak worked, in this capacity, to establish good relations with all Arab regimes. Relations were quickly restored with the conservative Arab oil states, above all Saudi Arabia, which had been the key Egyptian alliance before Camp David. But Egypt also repaired its links with nationalist Libya and Syria, promoting itself as a shield against U.S. wrath over their alleged use of terrorism. Egypt also took the lead in trying to mediate conflicts between Arab states, notably between Iraq and Kuwait in the summer of 1990. Egypt promoted its large well-armed army as a deterrent force, part of the Arab balance of power, against potential threats from Israel and Iran. Finally, Mubarak sought to establish Egypt as the pivotal Arab country, positioned to deliver an equitable settlement of the Arab-Israeli conflict, which was widely desired by nearly all Arab states. It presented its U.S. alliance as a conduit for securing U.S. pressure on Israel and promoted itself as an indispensable facilitator of peace negotiations by virtue of its status as the only Arab country having good relations with Israel.

The main obstacle to Egypt's strategy throughout the 1980s was Israel under the Likud, which had little interest in furthering the peace process. Moreover, Israel's heightened military activism exposed the hollowness of Egypt's pretension to defend Arab security. Egypt remained passive in the face of Israel's bombing of Iraq's nuclear reactor and of the Palestine Liberation Organization's Tunis headquarters. Israel's 1982 invasion of Lebanon was only possible because of the neutralization of Israel's southern front under Egypt's separate peace.

The Egyptian-U.S. alliance. Since Sadat, Egypt's strategic alliance with the United States has been its main bridge to the international system and its main route of access to external resources. In return for U.S. economic subsidization, military aid, and security coordination, Egypt gave Washington a key door into the Arab world. Egypt now acted as a force for stability against anti-Western radicalism and played a pivotal role in getting the Arabs to accept Israel.

Mubarak sustained this policy. Yet, the U.S. relationship had costs for his regime throughout the 1980s, owing to Washington's strong support for Israel at a time when Tel Aviv was widely seen in Egypt as having "betrayed" the peace settlement by its attempt to keep the Sinai enclave of Taba and its resistance to Palestinian national rights. The making into a folk hero of Sulayman Khater, a policeman who killed Israeli tourists (1985), indicated the deep-seated public resentment of Israeli policy. Economic dependency on the United States was also resented, and the United States' forcing down of an Egyptian airliner after the 1985 *Achille Lauro* incident was taken as a national insult and set off the first nationalist street disturbances in years. This sentiment did not become a mass movement able to force a policy change despite demands by opposition leaders and isolated attacks on Israeli and U.S. officials by disgruntled "Nasserist" officers. But there is little doubt that Egypt's foreign policy was a legitimacy liability at home.[29]

Sensitive to the asymmetrical character of the U.S. alignment, Mubarak worked to diversify Egypt's international connections.[30] Egypt sought the intervention of Western European governments with its international creditors and to put pressure on Israel, but the Europeans were, in the latter respect, no substitute for Washington. Under Mubarak, amicable, but still low-key relations were reestablished with Moscow, which, however, was in no position to offer economic aid or diplomatic leverage over Israel and hence to present a credible threat to U.S. influence. Thus Egypt had little choice but to carry on with Sadat's attempt to make itself indispensable to U.S. Middle East interests. Sadat had served Washington by defusing the threat of another Arab-Israeli war in the absence of a peace settlement and by helping to roll back Soviet and radical influence in the Arab world. After the demise of the Soviet Union, Mubarak repositioned Egypt as a bulwark against the United States' new enemy, Islamic terrorism.

Precisely because Egypt was such a valued client, it enjoyed some counterleverage over Washington, which could not afford to alienate it or abandon it to an Islamic take-over that would threaten the peace with Israel and U.S. influence across the region. As such, Mubarak could count on continued economic largesse even while recovering some foreign-policy independence; thus, he rejected Reagan administration pressures for joint antiterrorist action against Libya (1985) and for a permanent military base at Ras Banas. He contested the exemption of Israel from the Nuclear Non-Proliferation Treaty, although ultimately succumbing to U.S. pressure to sign up without a similar Israeli commitment. He rejected Washington's entreaties to attend the Multilateral Economic Conference in Doha in protest against the Netanyahu government's obstruction of the Oslo Peace Accords. He also distanced Egypt from Washington's hard line over sanctions against Iraq in the late 1990s.

There remained fundamental contradictions in Egypt's policy toward Washington. Egypt's utility to the United States depended in good part on its centrality in the Arab world. Yet the strategic alliance with the United States was a very ambiguous asset for a state seeking such Pan-Arab stature, for it sharply circumscribed the extent to which Egypt could champion Arab interests as Nasser had once done. For example, Cairo's acquisition of U.S. arms was meant to bolster its position as an Arab power and to this end Egypt also maintained 300,000 well-equipped and trained troops and a substantial indigenous arms industry.[31] Yet, while defense planners continued to see Israel as the main military threat to Egypt and the Arabs, Egypt's military dependence on Washington sharply circumscribed the potential role of its forces in protecting Arab security against Israel.

Egyptian foreign policy in the second Gulf war. Cairo's Gulf war policy was rooted in Egypt's tradition of bartering its political-strategic position in the Arab world for economic benefits. In this respect, Mubarak's strategy of positioning Cairo as a broker in the Arab-Israeli peace process was threatened by Saddam Hussein's bid, at the 1990 Baghdad summit, to force a new era of confrontation with the United States over its support for Israel and the seeming exhaustion of the peace process in the face of the obdurate Likud government. In essence, Baghdad was bidding to displace Cairo as the hub of a new, more muscular Arab diplomacy resting on threats rather than the U.S.-sponsored peace process. The Iraqi invasion of Kuwait also showed Egypt to be ineffective as an Arab moderator since Mubarak had invested his prestige in mediating the Iraq-Kuwait conflict and had obtained a pledge from Saddam Hussein not to resort to force. Economics was also determinant in a very immediate sense, for Egypt was on the brink of economic collapse, forced to stop payments on its debt, and in danger of becoming a financial pariah. Iraq threatened the geopolitical rent Cairo's stabilizing role purchased, while the invasion was a perfect opportunity to demonstrate Egypt's indispensability to the West and the Gulf oil monarchies.

Mubarak short-circuited Arab diplomacy in favor of U.S. intervention, sent Egyptian troops to give the United States "legitimizing cover," and backed the U.S. goal of a military over a negotiated solution to the crisis. This not only pleased his U.S. patron but also permitted the full restoration of the Egyptian-Saudi alliance, which had not until then fully recovered from Camp David. In fact, Egypt won massive, globally unprecedented debt relief and a promise of aid as a result of its role in the conflict.[32]

The Mubarak regime, in placing Egypt so overtly in the service of a foreign power attacking an Arab state, risked its domestic legitimacy. It initially exploited Egyptians' mistrust of Saddam's challenge to Egypt's Arab preeminence, their resentment of Iraq's maltreatment of Egyptian workers, and their disapproval of aggression against Kuwait. But public opinion turned ambivalent as Mubarak appeared to be an accomplice to the U.S. destruction of Iraq. The Muslim Brotherhood and the secular Egyptian left united in declaring that to back Western armies against Iraq was a worse offense than the original invasion of Kuwait. The war unleashed simmering antiregime and anti-Western feeling in Egypt, manifest in four straight days of clashes between thousands of students and police. For *whose* new world order, Egyptians asked, was the war waged? That such sympathy should be felt for a rival state, and that the nationalist opposition could condemn an attack on Iraq in which Egyptian troops took part, is a symptom of how far Egypt remained from a true nation-state with an identity separate from Arabism.[33]

Egypt's postwar policy. During the war, Egypt expressed an ambition to organize a new Arab security system and, in the Damascus Declaration, Egypt and Syria agreed to provide peacekeeping troops in the Gulf area in return for major economic assistance from the oil emirates. This plan was stillborn, however, when the Gulf states, led by Kuwait, concluded direct security agreements with the United States and invited Egyptian and Syrian troops to leave. The ease with which both Washington and the Gulf states bypassed Egypt undercut Cairo's attempt to sustain the role of regional moderator. Rebuffed in the Gulf, Egypt aimed, all the more, to assert and capitalize on its supposed indispensability as the only Arab state at peace with Israel, in the Madrid-initiated peace process. Cairo's high-profile mediator role in PLO-Israeli negotiations over implementation of various phases of the Oslo agreement won credit both in Washington and with the PLO. Oslo and the Jordan-Israel peace accord helped neutralize the legitimacy deficit from what had formerly been Egypt's separate peace with Israel. Egypt was able to claim that Sadat had, after all, been correct that his peace with Israel was only the first and crucial step in a resolution of the conflict.[34] While there was the risk that, as the peace process advanced, Egypt would lose some of its former unique value as an Arab-Israeli interlocutor, in fact the negotiations frequently encountered roadblocks and Cairo found continued opportunity to play a mediating role valued by both Washington and the Arabs.

Conclusion

In his groundbreaking article "Pre-Theories and Theories of Foreign Policy," James Rosenau suggested that pressures from the international system and the personal leadership factor would dominate foreign policy in Third World countries.[35] This is seemingly borne out in the Egyptian case, although only because Egyptian leaders successfully extracted resources from the international system to consolidate stable personal rule at home.

The need to cope with the external world facilitated and legitimated the concentration of presidential power and a leader-dominated foreign-policy process, giving considerable insulation from domestic pressures. Leaders did, of course, manipulate foreign policy to serve domestic economic and legitimacy needs, but presidents enjoyed the autonomy at home to play the game of realpolitik abroad.

Presidents shaped the broad lines of Egyptian foreign policy within parameters set by geopolitics and geo-economics. Egypt, a potential

Arab hegemon, secure in its identity but with a massive population confined to the cramped Nile Valley, naturally sought Pan-Arab leadership enabling it to both contain and manipulate the impact of external powers on the region while extracting economic resources in the process. This strategy was pursued most successfully under Nasser, whose foreign-policy achievements legitimized and stabilized the state and consolidated Egypt's independence. However, the costs of regional leadership, especially the Israeli occupation of the Sinai, dictated a radical scaling down of such ambitions under Sadat, whose Egypt-first policy traded foreign-policy decisions, and autonomy, for geo-economic rent. Egypt fell into an economic dependency that radically narrowed its subsequent foreign-policy options under Mubarak.

If external constraints and opportunities carried the heaviest weight in determining Egypt's policy, presidential autonomy, nevertheless, enhanced the impact of the idiosyncratic factor on the way Egypt played its cards in the great game. It explained crucial differences in Egypt's behavior: thus, Nasser's vision was the key to the emergence of an autonomous Arab state system while his brinkmanship brought on the 1967 disaster. Sadat's diplomatic style opened the door to renewed Western penetration and a suboptimal Arab-Israeli settlement that undid much of his predecessor's work; but his preference for the West over the East undoubtedly better positioned Egypt for the post–Cold War era of U.S. hegemony and globalization.

Notes

1. Adeed Dawisha, *Egypt in the Arab World: The Elements of Foreign Policy,* New York: Wiley, 1976, p. 2.

2. Patrick Seale, *The Struggle for Syria,* London: Oxford University Press, 1965, pp. 17–23.

3. Dawisha, *Egypt in the Arab World,* p. 78; R. Hrair Dekmejian, *Egypt Under Nasir: A Study in Political Dynamics,* Albany: State University of New York Press, 1971, pp. 105–108.

4. Dawisha, *Egypt in the Arab World,* p. 87.

5. Israel Gershoni and James Jankowski, *Redefining the Egyptian Nation, 1930–1945,* Cambridge: Cambridge University Press, 1995; Dekmejian, *Egypt Under Nasir,* pp. 91–96.

6. Seale, *The Struggle for Syria,* p. 192.

7. Dawisha, *Egypt in the Arab World,* p. 35; Malcolm Kerr, *The Arab Cold War,* London: Oxford University Press, 1971, p. 32; Dekmejian, *Egypt Under Nasir,* pp. 39–40, 76–80, 101–108.

8. Seale, *The Struggle for Syria,* p. 226.

9. Ali ad-Din Hillal Dessouki, "The Primacy of Economics: The Foreign Policy of Egypt," in Ali ad-Din Hillal Dessouki and Bahgat Korany, eds.,

The Foreign Policies of Arab States, Boulder, CO: Westview Press, 1991, pp. 163, 178.

10. Michael Brecher, *The Foreign Policy System of Israel,* London: Oxford University Press, 1972, p. 115.

11. Dekmejian, *Egypt Under Nasir,* pp. 37–47.

12. Dessouki, "The Primacy of Economics," pp. 168–171; Raymond Hinnebusch, *Egyptian Politics Under Sadat,* Cambridge: Cambridge University Press, 1985, pp. 78–79.

13. Dawisha, *Egypt in the Arab World,* pp. 104–105, 115; Charles Cremeans, *The Arabs and the World: Nasser's Arab Nationalist Policy,* New York: Praeger, 1963, p. 33.

14. Bahgat Korany, *How Foreign Policy Is Made in the Third World,* Boulder, CO: Westview Press, 1986, pp. 96–99.

15. Dessouki, "The Primacy of Economics," pp. 168–171; Ehud Yaari, "Sadat's Pyramid of Power," *The Jerusalem Quarterly,* no. 14, 1980, pp. 111–112; Anwar Sadat, *In Search of Identity: An Autobiography,* New York: Harper & Row, 1978, pp. 306–308, 331; Muhammed Hassanein Heikel, *The Autumn of Fury: The Assassination of Sadat,* London: Corgi Books, 1983, pp. 75–79, 113–116.

16. Robert Stephens, *Nasser: A Political Biography,* New York: Simon & Schuster, 1974, pp. 140–343; Cremeans, *The Arabs and the World;* Anouar Abdul Malek, *Egypt: Military Society,* New York: Vintage Books, 1968, pp. 223–287.

17. L. Carl Brown, *International Politics and the Middle East,* Princeton, NJ: Princeton University Press, 1984, pp. 162–167; Dawisha, *Egypt in the Arab World,* p. 125; Fawaz Gerges, *The Superpowers and the Middle East: Regional and International Politics, 1955–1967,* Boulder, CO: Westview Press, 1994, pp. 13–17; Kenneth Love, *Suez: The Twice-Fought War,* New York: McGraw-Hill, 1969.

18. Dawisha, *Egypt in the Arab World,* pp. 30–32.

19. Kerr, *The Arab Cold War,* pp. 26–43; Dawisha, *Egypt in the Arab World,* pp. 33–36, 77.

20. Kerr, *The Arab Cold War,* pp. 44–76; Dawisha, *Egypt in the Arab World,* pp. 41–42.

21. Kerr, *The Arab Cold War,* p. 111; Dawisha, *Egypt in the Arab World,* pp. 43–49, 148–149.

22. Kerr, *The Arab Cold War,* pp. 106–156; Stephens, *Nasser,* pp. 435–492.

23. Brown, *International Politics and the Middle East,* pp. 169–175; Dawisha, *Egypt in the Arab World,* pp. 50–59; Muhammed Hassanein Heikel, *The Road to Ramadan,* New York: Reader's Digest Press, 1975, p. 50; Stephens, *Nasser,* pp. 511–520, 545; John Waterbury, *Egypt: Burdens of the Past, Options for the Future,* Hanover, NH: The American Universities Field Staff, 1976, pp. 317, 340–341.

24. Mahmoud Riad, *The Struggle for Peace in the Middle East,* London and New York: Quartet Books, 1982, pp. 39–50, 75, 90–91, 141–146, 184–211, 215–217, 230–231; Heikel, *Road to Ramadan,* pp. 53–57, 114–120, 146–179, 184–206; Heikel, *The Autumn of Fury,* pp. 52–60; Sadat, *In Search of Identity,* pp. 210–244, 276–289.

25. Dessouki, "The Primacy of Economics," pp. 166, 171–175.

26. Shibley Telhami, *Power and Leadership in International Bargaining: The Path to the Camp David Accords,* New York: Columbia University Press, 1990, pp. 12–14.

27. Raymond Baker, *Egypt's Uncertain Revolution Under Nasser and Sadat,* Cambridge, MA: Harvard University Press, 1978, pp. 136–148; Sadat, *In Search of Identity,* pp. 302–304; Heikel, *Road to Ramadan,* pp. 214–216; Heikel, *Autumn of Fury,* pp. 72–81, 101–108; Ismail Fahmi, *Negotiating for Peace in the Middle East,* Baltimore: Johns Hopkins University Press, 1983, pp. 45–51, 69–81, 164–165, 170–175, 186–187, 283, 292–308.

28. *Middle East International,* 9 January 1987, pp. 9–10; 21 November 1987, pp. 6–7; 23 January 1988, pp. 12–13; *The Middle East,* September 1988, p. 21; Dessouki, "The Primacy of Economics," pp. 181–184.

29. *The Middle East,* September 1985, pp. 49–53; January 1986, pp. 10–12; March 1986, pp. 9–11; *MERIP Reports,* January 1985, pp. 3–9.

30. Dessouki, "The Primacy of Economics," p. 167.

31. Ibid., p. 164.

32. Ahmad Abdalla, "Mubarak's Gamble," *Middle East Report,* January–February 1991, pp. 18–21; Dina Haseeb and Malik S. Rouchdy, "Egypt's Speculations in the Gulf Crisis: The Government's Policies and the Opposition Movements," in Haim Bresheeth and Nira Yuval-Davis, eds., *The Gulf War and the New World Order,* London: Zed Books, 1991, pp. 70–76; Daniel Brumberg, "From Strategic Surprise to Strategic Gain: Egypt's Role in the Gulf Coalition," in Andrew Bennett, Joseph Lepgold, and Danny Unger, eds., *Friends in Need: Burden Sharing in the Gulf War,* New York: St. Martin's Press, 1997, pp. 91–112; Sherif Hetata, "What Choice Did Egypt Have?" in Phillis Bennis and Michel Moushabeck, eds., *Beyond the Storm: A Gulf Crisis Reader,* New York: Olive Branch Press, 1991, pp. 241–247.

33. Haseeb and Rouchdy, "Egypt's Speculations in the Gulf Crisis," pp. 77–78.

34. *The Middle East,* December 1991, p. 12.

35. James Rosenau, "Pre-Theories and Theories of Foreign Policy," in R. B. Farrell, ed., *Approaches to International and Comparative Politics.* Evanston, IL: Northwestern University Press, 1966, pp. 27–93.

6

The Foreign Policy of Israel

Clive Jones

It has become almost an axiom to view Israel's foreign policy through a realist prism. The perception of Israel as a regional superpower that views its relationship with the wider Arab world in terms of a "zero-sum" game appears to negate, a priori, any substantive multilateral cooperation with its neighbors on a whole range of security issues facing the Middle East. Indeed, despite the seismic shifts in the contours of the international system since 1989, the old mantra that "Israel has no foreign policy, only a defense policy" remains the dominant prism through which the Jewish state views its immediate external environment. It would be churlish to ignore the formal peace treaties that Israel has signed with Jordan and Egypt, or, more immediately, the recognition of Palestinian national rights, however circumscribed, under the Oslo Accords.

But equally, Israel's burgeoning strategic relationship with Ankara, its concerns expressed forcefully over the acquisition—real or otherwise—of weapons of mass destruction (WMDs) by Baghdad and Tehran, as well as the continued importance placed upon the special relationship with the United States, delineate a continuity of thinking seemingly immune from changes in the broad arena of global politics. As Robert Bowker has observed with regard to the Arab-Israeli conflict, "'Peace through Strength' strategies have a strong emotional, political and cultural appeal. Even with the conclusion of peace agreements, skepticism is bound to remain regarding the idea of seeking security *with* other countries rather than *from* them."[1]

Yet, while Israeli foreign policy has become synonymous with national security, this fails to capture the process of foreign-policy decisionmaking peculiar to the Jewish state, particularly since the 1980s when the consensus among Israelis over what constitutes national security began to fragment under the impact of Israel's invasion of Lebanon in 1982 and the outbreak of the Palestinian *intifada* in 1987.[2]

Initially, societal consensus over the strategic threat faced by Israel in a hostile Arab world held in abeyance ideological debates within Zionism over territory to be claimed as part of a Jewish sovereign state. It is ironic that Israel's military victory in the June 1967 war, while reducing substantially the existential threat to the Jewish state, witnessed a recrudescence of these divisive debates. Since 1967, Israel's domination of the physical and political space in the West Bank and Gaza Strip has not only appeared incongruent with Israel's democratic tradition, but exposed deep rifts in a society that even seasoned observers of Israel's political scene have come to believe contain the future seeds of internecine conflict.[3]

In this respect, Israel's foreign policy is as much about defining the political boundaries of Zionism as it is about determining the future physical borders of the Jewish state. While still wrapped and presented in the language of national security, pressure groups and public opinion, as well more traditional intergovernmental actors, have informed the formulation and implementation of foreign policies in Israel to an extent hitherto unknown. The fact that Benyamin Netanyahu, a staunch opponent of the Oslo Accords on both strategic and ideological grounds, grudgingly sustained a peace process is a reflection of popular support among Israelis for some form of rapprochement with the Arab world in general and the Palestinians in particular. But equally, Netanyahu's failure to invigorate the peace process with sufficient momentum—seen in the failure to implement further Israeli troop withdrawals from the West Bank under the Wye River Memorandum, as well as Ehud Barak's attempts to secure "quick" peace agreements with Syria and the Palestine National Authority (PNA) on his terms—highlights the influence that ideology, the influence of pressure groups, as well as the world view of an individual leader can have upon the conduct of foreign policy.

Foreign-Policy Determinants

Systemic Level

The tendency to view foreign policy through the prism of realism still dominates Israeli perspectives of the international system. While acknowledging the unipolar character of the post–Cold War world and the subsequent Arab loss—at least among the so-called radical Arab states—

of a superpower patron, Israelis regard the Middle East as a region still wracked by turmoil in which, despite the strides made toward regional accommodation, recidivist tendencies still determine interstate relations. One is tempted, to paraphrase Alexander Wendt, to say that the international system is what states, including Israel, actually make of it, a position that suggests an emphasis upon multilateralism would do much to assuage the security dilemma facing nation-states.[4] But as Efraim Inbar has argued:

> Attempts to establish a new Middle East order have failed and it is still a region where the use of force is widely considered a policy option and one which receives popular support. The negative effects of the systemic changes on the international arena and on the Middle East have been similarly overlooked. Israel's [security] predicament has hardly changed. It is still a small state facing various challenges from powerful regional foes.[5]

A consensus has existed among all Israeli governments upon the need to ensure that foreign policy is shaped to national security, ensuring in the process that a premium is placed upon continuing and maintaining the "special relationship" with the United States. In structural realist terms, the relationship between Washington and Tel Aviv can be explained in terms of "bandwagoning," the idea that states seek to optimize their position within the international system through a matrix of alliances with other, usually stronger states.

Certainly Israel has been a huge beneficiary of Washington's munificence, being the single largest recipient of U.S. economic and military aid, estimated to have totaled some $65 billion for the period 1948 to 1996.[6] This would suggest a dependency relationship, and one that limits severely the sovereign autonomy of the Jewish state. The fact, however, that the relationship is deemed special negates either a purely realist or indeed structuralist account of a symbiotic relationship constructed around both "soft" and "hard" variables. Soft variables include the identification of Israel with democratic, Western values and, more tangibly, the influence that U.S. Jewry, and in particular the powerful pro-Israel lobby groups on Capitol Hill, can and do wield in both houses of Congress. Hard variables center on the perceived confluence of strategic interest between the two states, a position, however, that has yet to be enshrined in a formal strategic or defense treaty between Washington and Tel Aviv. Indeed, the extent of financial assistance given to Israel has not always produced a linear subservience to Washington's foreign-policy aims or aspirations. Israel's attack on the Iraqi nuclear reactor at Osirak in June 1981 remains a case in point, while the construction and expansion of Jewish settlements in the occupied territories remains incongruent with wider U.S. policy objectives in the region.[7]

As such, it is perhaps inaccurate to describe Israel's relationship with Washington as falling within a traditional patron-client paradigm. Despite the huge inflows of U.S. capital into an economic system that has yet to shrug off the last vestiges of central planning, the structure of the relationship between Israel and the United States has immunized the Jewish state to a large extent from great-power leverage usually associated with core-periphery relations in the international system. Moreover, structuralist accounts of economic dependency—the means by which the core states in the international system both dominate and penetrate the Middle East—need to be tempered with regard to Israel. The Jewish state is now a permanent fixture in the core, rather than the periphery, of the global economy. In 1996, its gross domestic product (GDP) was worth $99.3 billion, a sevenfold increase in twenty years and some 50 percent more than the combined GDPs of Syria, Jordan, and Egypt, while per capita income stood at $16,980, a rate that withstands comparison with the developed economies of the European Union.[8] Concentrated in its very own "silicon valley," Israel now has the largest concentration of software firms outside of the United States, and a high-tech industrial base thought to be equal to, if not more advanced than, that of the United Kingdom.[9] Accordingly, the proportion of gross national product committed to defense spending dropped from an all-time high of 33 percent in 1975, to 9 percent in 1995, although Washington still offsets the costs of weapons development programs such as the Chetz antiballistic missile system.[10]

Regional System

Defining precisely the current matrix of relationships in the Middle East remains problematic. State nationalism, Middle Easternism, and Euro-Mediterranianism have been some of the descriptions applied to characterize the regional state system. Shimon Peres, perhaps more in hope than expectation, made much of a new order emerging in the region following the signing of the 1993 Oslo Accords, a new order based on regional mutilateralism "in which people, goods and services can move freely from place to place."[11] Such hubris aside, for many Israelis, the Arab Middle East remains one of the few places on earth where men rule for life despite the massive changes brought about by the process of globalization and rapid demographic change, both deemed sufficient elsewhere to undermine the vertical means of state control. The argument put forward here is that the state still remains the most important regional actor and, as such, any resolution to the Arab-Israeli conflict will be based on vertical (state-to-state) security regimes rather than on the emergence of a new horizontal economic order.

This points to the efficacy of the security dilemma in continuing to explain the contours of interstate relations in the Middle East. Indeed, Shlomo Gazit, former head of Israeli military intelligence, defined the Arab-Israeli conflict from an Israeli perspective as consisting of three concentric circles—Israel/Palestine; Israel/Egypt, Syria, and Jordan; and Israel/Iran, Iraq, Saudi Arabia, Libya, and Sudan—each with its own level of hostility and threat capability.[12] The great importance of the bilateral peace treaties with Cairo and Amman should not be overlooked, but equally, as Israeli strategists remain quick to point out, this does not discount recourse to the use of force by individual states, or an alliance of all or some of the above to break a perceived political deadlock in the region.

Given that Israel perceives regional security relations as vertical—that is, exclusive, state-to-state, and biased toward maintaining a strong military posture—rather than horizontal, inclusive, or multilateral, effective deterrence remains the bedrock of Israel's strategic thinking. This includes not just the possession of a nuclear-weapons capability, but the maintenance of what has been termed an "offensive-minded defense posture" with regard to the use of conventional forces. This posture originates from a perceived lack of strategic depth, requiring that the Israeli Defense Force (IDF) prosecute any conflict on the soil of its enemies, rather than inside Israel proper. The result has been a tendency toward preemption, most visibly demonstrated in the June war of 1967 but, more recently, with the attack on the Iraqi nuclear reactor at Osirak in June 1981. This offensive mindset has also been a feature of Israeli government policy where threats to the security of the state outside any immediate existential danger have arisen. Falling under the rubric of "regime targeting," the bloody removal of individuals or groups has included the bombing of the Palestine Liberation Organization (PLO) headquarters in Tunisia in 1985, the killing of Khalil Wazir (Abu Jihad) in April 1988, the assassination of Hizbollah leader Shaykh Hussein Abbas Musawi in February 1992, as well as the attempted politicide of the PLO as an effective symbol of Palestinian resistance between June and September 1982.[13] More recently, the assassination of individuals in Palestinian-controlled areas of the West Bank and Gaza Strip associated with Arafat's Fatah movement and the so-called Tanzim militia remained key components in Israel's strategy to counter the so-called al-Aqsa *intifada*.[14]

Whether such actions can be considered "rational" remains a moot point, but Israel's military alliance with Ankara, and allegations of developing technological and strategic links with New Delhi, fall within a classic realist paradigm of an order based on power politics and regional alliances.[15] The close military relationship with Turkey that has developed since 1995 is, according to Neill Lochery, "as important a development in the Middle East region as any of the peace treaties that [Israel] has signed with the Arabs."[16] Tel Aviv has stated its desire to see this axis develop into the dominant security structure for the region, though Ankara has made such development contingent on political progress with the Palestine National Authority.[17] Still, given Turkey's history of tense relations with Syria, the alliance with Ankara acts as a natural force multiplier as Israel seeks to maintain both its conventional and nonconventional military advantage over Damascus.

It is in the area of nuclear weapons that Israel remains the regional power par excellence. All Israeli governments since the 1960s have embraced "nuclear ambiguity" by stating that the Jewish state will not be the first to introduce such weapons to the region. Such opacity aside, Israel is believed to possess some two hundred nuclear weapons and appears set on developing a survivable deterrent capability. Apart from advanced delivery platforms based upon the indigenous Jericho 3 ballistic missile system and U.S.-supplied F-15I strike aircraft, Israel has taken delivery of three Dolphin-class diesel attack submarines from Germany. The importance of these boats is that the IDF is thought to be developing a sea-launched nuclear cruise missile system that, if fitted to the Dolphins, would give Tel Aviv a survivable nuclear triad and thus enhance its deterrent capability vis-à-vis the second and third circles of Arab and Muslim states.[18]

In the logic of a multipolar regional subsystem, the strength derived from its alliance with Washington and its own economic, technological, and military capabilities have helped sustain Israel's position at the apex of the regional order. Indeed, the shift among Arab elites toward tacit acceptance, if not formal recognition of the Jewish state would have been impossible without the development and maintenance of such capabilities. Yet the strategic success of the Jewish state in ensuring its survival amid the animus of its surrounding neighbors obscures ongoing internal debates in Israel that undermine a purely realist context in which the formulation and implementation of foreign policy are played out. Indeed, it is these very debates, centered upon both the physical and spiritual boundaries of the Jewish state, that have exercised the most profound influence on the scope and direction of Israel's foreign policy.

State Formation and Identity

The immediate strategic threat Israel faced between 1948 and 1967 held in abeyance debates inherent within the very concept of Zionism over the exact territory to be claimed as part of a Jewish sovereign state. The need to maintain a strong military, absorb new immigrants, and settle the more inhospitable areas of the newly established state required considerable self-sacrifice on the part of Israelis, including heavy taxation and long periods of service in the armed forces. In return, Israelis could expect the state to offer an extensive package of welfare benefits. This was the indigenous expression of statism, or *mamlachtiyut*.

The demands of *mamlachtiyut*—not least the need to build a coherent polity from a largely immigrant society—as well as the continuous demands of ensuring external security offset potentially divisive debates over the normative character of Zionism. While successive Israeli governments remained convinced that the cease-fire lines established following the 1948–1949 Arab-Israeli war remained indefensible, Zionism per se had never reached a consensus over defining the territorial dimensions of the Jewish state. While a cross-party consensus justified retention of territories captured in the June 1967 war both on strategic grounds and in the absence of peace overtures from surrounding Arab states, a confluence of interest emerged between revisionist Zionists who believed a priori in the unity of Eretz Yisrael on historical grounds, and religious-nationalist Zionists who regarded the capture and settlement of the occupied territories in eschatological terms.[19]

The approbation placed upon the maintenance and expansion of Jewish sovereignty over the occupied territories by settler organizations such as Gush Emunim exposed a clear bifurcation in Israel's claims to be both a Jewish and democratic state. Whatever physical security control of the West Bank, Gaza Strip, and Golan Heights bought, the price paid in terms of Israel's democratic credentials has proven to be high. Sudden absorption of Palestinians from these areas who, by 1995, numbered 1,816,000 would clearly dilute the Jewish Zionist character of the state if (1) Israel annexed the formerly occupied territories and/or (2) conferred Israeli citizenship upon its inhabitants.[20] The struggle to square this particular circle has dominated Israel's approach to dealing with its intrastate conflict with the Palestinians and in turn has shaped policy toward the wider Arab world.

Since 1967 a correlation can be traced in the reduction of external security threats to the Jewish state against a corresponding rise in the internal challenges, both political and religious, to the democratic structures of

Israel. Thus, while the growth and development of Israel's economic base has been truly impressive, the paradox remains that its democratic structures have come to be increasingly circumscribed by what Ilan Peleg has referred to openly as Israel's *kulturkampf*. [21] The main cleavages that are seen by many to now define the political landscape in Israel—communal divisions between Ashkenazim Jews and those of an Oriental background, religious dissonance between the *haredim* (Ultra-Orthodox Jews) and the main body of secular Israelis, and the continued marginalization of Israel's Arab minority—stem in no small part from the ongoing debates within Israel's polity over the very nature of Zionism itself and how, therefore, an Israeli identity is to be defined. The assassination of Premier Yitzhak Rabin in November 1995 at the hands of a young religious-nationalist remains the most infamous manifestation to date of such deep-rooted divisions over identity.

Yet despite, or perhaps more accurately, because of the pressing need to assuage communal differences, external security issues have always dominated a vertical axis along which Israel's internal political agenda is organized. The election in May 1992 of Yitzhak Rabin was in large part due to his reputation as a military man who would not unduly jeopardize Israel's security. Similarly, the defeat of Shimon Peres by Benyamin Netanyahu in the 1996 elections can in part be traced to his failure to counter the spate of Hamas terrorist bombings in February and March 1996, followed in April by the disastrous attempt to crush Hizbollah guerrilla activity in south Lebanon. Netanyahu's election slogan "Peace with Security" therefore conflated neatly with the primordial instincts of a large swath of the Israeli populace, as well as members of the political elite who have yet to embrace a broader conception of Israel's security needs. [22]

Foreign-Policy Role

Central to Israel's foreign-policy role is its conception of itself as an embattled Zionist outpost besieged by a hostile Arab world. Thus, foreign policy in Israel has remained subordinate to the demands of ensuring national security. For many Israelis, the "war of independence is not over yet," a statement that reflects a profound belief that the external animus faced by Israel continues to remain a constant feature of Middle East politics. Having been involved in six major conventional conflicts in its half-century of existence (in addition to innumerable border clashes of varying intensity), the culture of national security remains the compass around which foreign policy is orientated. Maintenance of an exceptionally powerful military, as well as ensuring strong ties with Washington, have become the enduring themes of Israel's search for security. Located in the heart of what Benyamin Netanyahu referred to as a "tough neighborhood," the logic of realism has an appeal to a society conditioned by war. In this respect, Israel's recourse to the use of force is best explained by the logic of a security dilemma particular to a state that lacks substantial human resources, strategic depth, and until recently, any tangible regional alliance. As such, a broad consensus among Israelis greeted recourse to the use of force by the state until 1982. Rabin's description in the 1960s of periods of peace as constituting "dormant war" struck a chord among Israelis whose experience of the region—and for many in a largely immigrant society, of life in Europe—had been nasty and brutish, if not short.[23]

Some would equate this position with a prevailing militarism—defined as a tendency to view organized violence, or the threat of organized violence, as a legitimate tool in solving political problems—that has so marked the development of Israel, both as a state and a society.[24] Viewing the Arab world through a "gun sight" may be simplistic, but it remains the legacy of an ethos derived from a "nation in arms" where identity could easily be defined against the three concentric circles that were the "Other."

Some Israelis have argued that militarism, while benefiting Israeli democracy because the energies of the military have been directed toward countering the Other, has simultaneously constrained alternative avenues of foreign policy less confrontational in their approach toward the region.[25] For example, Israeli academics have questioned the extent to which Israel's portrayal of Tehran as a modern day Golem—a mythical figure of fear and loathing in Israeli children's books—has helped to create and perpetuate a self-fulfilling security dilemma. While Iran's attempt to acquire WMDs is interpreted as a clear threat to Israel and all too congruent with the vitriol of its anti-Zionist propaganda, Ehud Sprinzak has argued that such threat perceptions have been much exaggerated. Aside from their own concerns over Israel's nuclear capability, Sprinzak places Tehran's program within the context of its own circle of regional threats and challenges, not least the continued concerns over Afghanistan, U.S. forces in the Gulf, Iraq with its record of using chemical weapons, Saudi Arabia, and Turkey. Such an interpretation has led Sprinzak to conclude that successive Israeli governments have applied what he terms a "political-strategic concept," some two decades after the Iranian revolution, that fails to distinguish between "inflammatory Islamic rhetoric" and the reality of Iran's need to match military means to its immediate geopolitical environment.[26] This is congruent with Wendt's notion that the insecurity of a state system, far from being inevitable, is "constructed" by the hostile interactions of state actors.

Another pivotal aspect of Israel's role is its conception of itself as the homeland of global Jewry. Israel remains one of the few states worldwide to encourage immigration on ideological grounds alone, irrespective of constraints imposed by resources or geographical space. Because of the emotive appeal of fulfilling the highest ideal of Zionism, the state continues to actively promote the value of *aliyah* (migration to Israel) throughout the Jewish diaspora and among governments able to facilitate Jewish immigration to Israel. Accordingly, such activity has become a foreign-policy value rather than just another foreign-policy objective, given the decimation of European Jewry during World War II. In his seminal study *The Foreign Policy System of Israel*, Michael Brecher describes the dominant Jewish character of the state as the prism through which all foreign-policy decisions are made. He declared, "For Israel's high policy elite, as for the entire society, there is a primordial and pre-eminent aspect of the political culture—its *Jewishness:* this pervades thought, feeling, belief and behaviour in the political realm."[27]

Brecher noted that David Ben Gurion regarded the population of the state of Israel and those Jews living in what was termed *galut* (exile or the diaspora) as indivisible. In perhaps the most explicit declaration of the Jewish state's raison d'être, Israel's first premier declared that "the two groups are interdependent. The future of Israel—its security, its welfare, and its capacity to fufill its historic mission—depends on world Jewry. And the future of world Jewry depends on the survival of Israel."[28] It is this claim to be the protector of heterogeneous Jewish communities worldwide, irrespective of their national allegiance, that is perhaps unique to Israel in the construction of its national identity. The "ingathering of the exiles" has, since Israel's foundation, remained an ideological totem around which the broad spectrum of Zionist opinion concurs. As such, the Law of Return passed by the Israeli Knesset in 1950 remains central to the *external* identity of Israel as a Jewish state, conferring as it does the right of Israeli citizenship upon all Jews who make *aliyah* to the Jewish state. It should be noted, however, that defining the *internal* character of the Jewish state and, in particular, the exact balance to be struck between religious and secular identities, remains, as the assassination of Rabin demonstrated, a contemporary issue of bitter debate.

Israel has, nonetheless, gone to extraordinary lengths to rescue diaspora communities deemed to be under threat. The airlift of 35,000 Jews from Yemen between May 1948 and November 1949 provided a template for similar operations involving Ethiopian Jewry in 1984 and 1991. More recently, some 1,000 Jews were smuggled out of Sarajevo in 1994 by representatives of the Jewish Agency and the Israeli intelligence agency Mossad during the Bosnian war.[29]

But support among all parties and groups that fall under the Zionist rubric for a strong, secure, and sovereign state remains *the* point of departure, both in the relationship between large sections of the Israeli electorate and the state elite, and between Israel and its regional neighbors.[30] While national solidarity against a clear existential threat marked Israeli society during the wars of June 1967 and October 1973, as well as the 1990–1991 Gulf crisis, the invasion of Lebanon in 1982 and the Palestinian *intifada* in December 1987 exposed deep rifts within Israeli society over exactly how to address Palestinian nationalism, rifts based increasingly on a complex web of ideological, religious, ethnic, and social-economic demands. For example, the mass protest of 400,000 Israelis in Tel Aviv in September 1982 against the war in Lebanon undermined the political aims of the invasion as envisaged by then defense minister Ariel Sharon: the destruction of the PLO as a symbol of the national aspirations of the Palestinian people and the redrawing of the Lebanese political map under a Christian Maronite ascendency.[31]

It remains clear, nonetheless, that Israel does not see its foreign policy in revisionist terms but rather seeks to maintain a status quo based on a strong defense posture. The debate in Israel is not about the goals themselves—ensuring the security of the state—but about the actual process of preference formation to achieve such goals among those charged with the implementation of Israel's foreign policy. In turn, preferences are by their very nature multidimensional and subject to a host of variables that include the cognitive disposition of key individuals, formal and informal political alliances, as well as the efficacy or otherwise of existing channels charged with both the formulation and implementation of foreign policy. In the case of Israel, however, such variables not only inform foreign policy, but have also shaped the internal political milieu of a state still struggling to define a consensual national identity.

Foreign Policymaking

The Policymaking Elite

Determining what constitutes *the* national interest remains a vexed question. In his treatment of preference formation in U.S. foreign policy,

Stephen Krasner argued forcefully that the national interest was all too often a product of inductive reasoning among key decisionmakers, rather than simply being determined by the relative position of a state within the international system.[32] In the case of Israel, core values—the need to secure the Jewish state against external threat while preserving a Jewish majority internally—provide a framework in which the process of inductive reasoning determines the national interest. As such, ideological, pragmatic, and geostrategic dispositions of key decisionmakers—attitudinal prisms—remain key variables in determining policy preferences. This is not to suggest that such prisms vary markedly between decisionmakers over a period of time. From 1967 through to 1987, Israeli foreign policy was marked more by continuity than change in its approach toward both the Arab world and Washington.

On the one hand, the structure of foreign policymaking in Israel allows considerable latitude for the expression of personal preference by a prime minister, irrespective of political or ideological agendas. This level of individual executive authority is perhaps peculiar to Israel, not because such patterns are never replicated in other democracies in times of crisis—one only has to look at the position of Margaret Thatcher during the Falklands war—but because it represents the very essence of Israel's foreign-policy decisionmaking process during the longer periods of "dormant war."

On the other hand, an impressive continuity of approach stems in no small part from the dominant backgrounds of those charged with maintenance of Israel's national security, with key decisionmakers having been, to quote Efraim Inbar, "socialised in the defense establishment."[33] Such socialization is best personified by the figure of Yitzhak Rabin, who held the portfolios of prime minister twice and minister of defense twice, having already served as IDF chief of staff and Israel's ambassador to Washington. More recently, Rabin's personification of the military-political symbiosis allowed him to provide strong leadership in presenting the Oslo Accords to the Israeli public, while also enjoying the confidence of his generals and security chiefs charged with overseeing the implementation of the accords.

It came as little surprise to Israelis when, upon his retirement as Israel's chief of staff in 1994, Ehud Barak was persuaded by Rabin to join the Labor Party. The fact that he became the leader of that self-same party is testament to the perceived efficacy of his military record among Israelis, rather than any innate political acumen he may or may not have possessed.[34] Other key individual decisionmakers steeped in the ethos of Israel's military culture have included Yigal Yadin, Ezer Weizmann,

Moshe Dayan, Yigal Allon, Ariel Sharon, and Yitzhak Mordechai, all former generals who at one time or another have held the portfolios of prime minister, foreign minister, or defense minister. Given this process of socialization, it is not surprising that foreign policy in Israel has been viewed as complementing, rather than determining, the value placed upon ensuring the maintenance of Israel's military superiority.

The bias in the decisionmaking structure toward those individuals and bureaucracies with direct experience of and influence over security issues can also inhibit, if not negate, the executive authority of a premier lacking perceived grounding in or experience of security issues. Thus, during his short tenure as prime minister between December 1953 and February 1955, Moshe Sharrett lost control over the defense ministry, thereby undermining his own secret diplomacy with Nasser. It became known that his own defense minister, Pinchas Lavon, had sanctioned covert sabotage operations in Egypt against British and U.S. targets designed to alienate Cairo still further from Washington and London.[35] Levi Eshkol, Israel's premier on the eve of the June 1967 war, faced strong pressure from his chief of staff, Yitzhak Rabin, to turn the defense ministry—a portfolio held by Eshkol himself—over to former chief of staff Moshe Dayan, thereby creating a critical mass within the cabinet for the option of launching a preemptive strike against Egypt.

As such, foreign-policy decisionmaking remains restricted by security concerns, and one in which strong personalities can emasculate the role of the institutions charged with formulating and implementing foreign policy. David Ben Gurion, Golda Meir, and Yitzhak Rabin based their leadership in government upon highly stratified lines with relatively few people party to broad policy formulation beyond their respective "kitchen" cabinets. Nowhere is this demonstrated most visibly than in the role played by the ministry of foreign affairs. In the competition for influence within the Israeli cabinet, the views of the foreign ministry have carried less weight than either the views expressed by the prime minister's office or the defense ministry. Indeed, even though Uri Savir, director general of the foreign ministry, was responsible for brokering the negotiations that led to the signing of the Oslo Accords, senior representatives of the defense ministry and the IDF dominated negotiations over implementation of the accords once they were signed. As one former ministry official opined:

> This phenomenon can only be understood in the Israeli context. All of Israel's interests are determined according to security considerations, and that's why the security establishment became dominant in defining

the state's vital interests . . . political considerations were pushed aside. It was so in the talks with the Palestinians, as well as the contacts that preceded the signing of the peace treaty with Jordan.[36]

Accordingly, the foreign ministry has all too often been left to deal with issues of presentation rather than substance.[37] Conversely, in this hierarchy of influence, the intelligence services have become entrenched as the prime arbiters in defining Israel's key foreign-policy interests, a position that has led to a process of cognitive dissonance that some, including former premier Benyamin Netanyahu, have argued has undermined rather than reinforced Israel's national security. Three main intelligence agencies exist in Israel: military intelligence (Agaf Modi'in or AMAN), the Mossad (HaMossad LeModi'in U'Letafkidim Meyuhadim—Institute for Intelligence and Special Duties), and Shin Beth (Sheruth Bitachon—General Security Service or GSS). Of these, AMAN carries the most weight, with the director of military intelligence and the head of AMAN's assessment division serving as intelligence advisers to the Israeli cabinet. They remain subordinate to the minister of defense and chief of staff of the IDF, who attends all cabinet meetings. Mossad and the GSS operate under the auspices of the prime minister's office and coordinate intelligence gathering and assessment with AMAN through the Varash (Va'ad Rashei Sherutim—The Committee of the Chiefs of the Services). Yet assessing the objectivity of attitudinal prisms through which an intelligence assessment or "product" is presented to the consumer, in this case the prime minister or Israeli cabinet, has, particularly under the premiership of Netanyahu, proven increasingly problematic. Known for his antipathy toward the whole Oslo process, Netanyahu demonstrated visible unease on assuming office at the role played by the intelligence agencies in implementing the agreements with the Palestine National Authority. Netanyahu believed that as appointees of the previous Rabin/Peres government, the heads of the intelligence services had become politicized into an uncritical acceptance of the Oslo process.[38]

Suspicions of political bias in formulating policy preferences are not new to a state where ideological disposition has influenced decisionmaking. Accordingly, much debate surrounded the establishment by Netanyahu of a National Security Council (NSC) based on the U.S. model. The creation of an NSC was first recommended by the Yadin-Sharaf committee in 1963, set up following the intelligence scandal surrounding the Lavon Affair in the mid-1950s. Intermittent calls for the establishment of an NSC have punctuated political debate in the Jewish state ever since, usually following major lapses in intelligence gathering and assessment as occurred in the October 1973 war. Such a move was resisted by Rabin during his tenure as premier, not least because of entrenched bureaucratic resistance from the heads of the existing intelligence bureaucracies and government ministries. Yet the argument to proceed with the creation of an NSC was to be the main recommendation of the Ciechanover Commission, convened in the aftermath of the failed Mossad attempt on the life of Hamas activist Khalid Meshal in Amman in September 1997. Its recommendation that the NSC become a forum for balanced assessment of foreign-policy aims and objectives was indeed laudable. Certainly, foreign ministry officials let it be known that they were not approached to assess the implications of the attack on Israel's relations with the Hashemite kingdom. While its existence has been justified by the commission's report, the areas of responsibility assumed by the NSC remain circumscribed. Established in March 1999, the emphasis of the NSC has been placed upon combating regional proliferation of WMDs, rather than acting, as was the original intention, as a coordinating body overseeing objective assessment on a broad range of foreign-policy issues, including continued negotiations with the Palestinians.[39]

The Extra-Elite Policy Process

The security bias in the decisionmaking structure is also manifested in the role of parliament in foreign policymaking. The Israeli Knesset committee system, based on the Westminster model, convenes a cross-party forum but it is one that combines foreign affairs and defense rather than treating them as distinct areas. Moreover, the influence that such committees have on preference formation in foreign policy remains limited. Indeed, once the horse trading involved in the formation of a coalition government has been completed, the Knesset remains circumscribed from any real input into the decisionmaking process dominated by the national security bureaucracies.

If bureaucracies dealing with national security dominate the foreign-policy decisionmaking process, the agenda in which that process operates has been influenced heavily by pressure groups or grassroots activists representing a distinct ideological, ethnic, or religious outlook associated with policy toward the occupied territories. The extraparliamentary group Gush Emunim (Bloc of the Faithful), formed in the aftermath of the October 1973 war, became the most high-profile of such groups. Between 1977 and 1992, and often acting with government

approval, Gush Emunim spearheaded the establishment of Jewish settlements across the West Bank. Settlements associated with the movement were accorded the same status as *kibbutzim,* a move that allowed
public money to be used in the process of ideological construction while
suggesting that Gush Emunim were now seen officially as the true in-
heritors of the pioneering ideals behind Zionism.

The discourse surrounding the issue of the territories continues to
be cloaked in the language of national security. Certainly, for organizations representative of the ideological and religious right in Israel, policy toward the territories remains internal to the Jewish state: recognition of the future status of the occupied territories as constituting a
foreign-policy issue negates claims over sovereignty inherent within the
very concept of Eretz Yisrael.

In this regard, the emphasis placed upon national security disguised
the core debates surrounding the West Bank by justifying settlement
policy in terms of protection against the "Other," rather than dealing
with the recrudescence of a debate concerning the very identity of the
Jewish state. It is such concerns over the debilitating impact of the occupation on Israel's political culture and social cohesion that first led
to the emergence of peace groups in Israel. Prominent among these remains Shalom Achshav (Peace Now), formed in 1978 by a group of
reserve officers in the IDF concerned at Prime Minister Begin's reluctance to invest the critical dialogue initiated by President Anwar Sadat
with sufficient urgency. It reached its apogee in 1982, organizing a mass
demonstration of some 400,000 Israelis—10 percent of the population—against the war in Lebanon following the massacres of Palestinian refugees in the Sabra and Chatilla camps in West Beirut. This
demonstration, more than anything else, undermined the claims of
Prime Minister Begin that the invasion was a "just war," leading ultimately to the removal of Ariel Sharon as defense minister and the resignation the following year of Begin himself as Israel's premier. More
recently, the activities of the "Four Mothers Movement" did much to
persuade a critical mass of Israelis to support a unilateral withdrawal of
the IDF from south Lebanon. Such was the resonance of the movement
across all sections of Israeli society that Ehud Barak, previously identified as a hawk with regard to the bloody if limited war fought against
Hizbollah, made such an Israeli withdrawal a central feature of his electoral campaign in the May 1999 Israeli general election and, on winning
the election, carried out a unilateral Israeli withdrawal.[40]

Such events have proven to be symptomatic of a broader evolution
away from the traditional demands of self-sacrifice incumbent within

the original concept of *mamlachtiyut*. Questioning the almost sacrosanct position occupied by the IDF in Israeli society became more widespread during the Lebanon invasion, and continued during the *intifada* as questions of moral rectitude undermined the mantra of national security as justification for Israel's brutal response to violent—though for the most part nonlethal—expressions of Palestinian identity.[41] In this respect, the Oslo Accords were as much a product of the need to assuage increased tensions within Israeli society as a circumspect attempt to deal with the national aspirations of the Palestinians in the West Bank and Gaza; to paraphrase Robert Bowker, the accords were an attempt by Rabin's government on behalf of the state of Israel to seek security from itself.

Foreign-Policy Behavior

Israeli foreign-policy behavior is by no means a straightforward reaction to threat but is intimately shaped by identity, role, and the biases of the decisionmaking structure. This can be illustrated by reference to key Israeli decisions having intimate bearing on war and peace.

The 1982 Invasion of Lebanon

It was the permissive environment invoked by the need to ensure national security that allowed Ariel Sharon, as Israeli defense minister in 1982, to manipulate both cabinet opinion and Prime Minister Begin into authorizing Israel's invasion of Lebanon. Like Eshkol, Begin, despite his years as head of the Irgun Zvai Leumi during the British Mandate, had little direct expertise in strategic matters. This allowed Sharon, a controversial former general, a free hand in using violence in Lebanon to achieve a wider ideological end: the destruction of the PLO as a symbol of the national aspirations of the Palestinian people and the gradual ingestion of the occupied territories into Israel proper.[42] As Yaacov Vertzberger notes in his study of risk taking:

> Begin, Sharon and Eitan (the IDF chief of staff) saw the circumstances as auspicious for defeating the PLO and thus both settling an acute security problem and possibly winning in the long run the battle for *Eretz Yisrael* which was to them a matter of acute ideological, political and strategic importance. In fact, the same imperatives that drove their foreign and security policies also manifested themselves in a dynamic drive to settle the West Bank and, to a lesser degree the Gaza area and Golan Heights, so that giving up the territories, no matter

which political party was in power in the future, would have become practically impossible.[43]

It is of historical interest that in the year preceding Israel's invasion, Begin's own cabinet had proven decidedly lukewarm in its support for an extensive ground operation in Lebanon that would in effect be a "war of choice" against PLO forces. Preference was expressed instead for a more limited incursion that would clear Palestinian guerrillas away form Israel's northern border. Such concerns forced Sharon to seek cabinet approval for a more limited operation, while issuing orders to the Israeli General Staff to prepare for a more grandiose scheme. This plan called upon the IDF to attack and destroy Syrian forces in the Beqa' Valley, cut the Beirut-to-Damascus highway, and surround the Lebanese capital as a precursor to reestablishing Maronite hegemony throughout Lebanon.

As such, the cabinet remained ignorant of the war's larger aims when they approved the invasion of Lebanon as a response to the attempted assassination of the Israeli ambassador to the Court of St. James, Shlomo Argov, by a dissident Palestinian group on 3 June 1982. Indeed, Sharon had deliberately repressed a report by the head of AMAN, Major General Yehoshua Saguy, warning against a large-scale invasion of Lebanon, fearing it would expose the wider aims of "Operation Peace for Galilee" to the cabinet. As for Begin, his lack of military expertise in matters of grand strategy allowed Sharon to seduce the Israeli prime minister into accepting a plan whose broad sweep offered the chimera of tangible political/strategic gain without incurring heavy military costs.[44] The case of Sharon highlights how the structure of decisionmaking in Israel, particularly in crisis management, can amplify the policy recommendations and preferences of key individuals associated with national security.

Entering the Peace Process

It was Yitzhak Rabin's unique background that enabled him to use his position at the apex of government to exploit opportunities provided by the emergence of a more benign international and regional environment following the end of the Cold War. As defense minister at the beginning of the *intifada,* it had been Rabin who had encouraged soldiers to use "force, power and blows" in an attempt to reassert Israeli control over the occupied territories. Yet such recourse to violence did not reflect Rabin's view on the need for territorial compromise. Although dismissive of any return to Israel's pre-1967 borders, Rabin did concede the need to exchange land for peace when, speaking before a Labor Party convention in 1991, he declared his belief that Israel would have to relinquish control of "many kilometers" if regional peace were to be realized.[45] According to many analysts, the views of Rabin were influenced heavily by the deleterious impact that serving in the territories was having upon the morale of the IDF. The conclusion reached was that the very bastion of Israel's security was being undermined by occupying a land deemed essential for that self-same security.[46] Noted more for his pragmatism than his vision, the structure of decisionmaking nonetheless allowed Rabin to condone the Oslo process initiated by Deputy Foreign Minister Yossi Beilin and carried forward by Foreign Minister Shimon Peres.

Again, personality and personal diplomacy were, for the most part, the dominant variables in securing a peace agreement between Jordan and Israel. King Hussein and Yitzhak Rabin agreed on a detailed framework for a peace treaty in London on 19 May 1994 without the knowledge of Peres as foreign minister or key figures in the Israeli foreign ministry.[47]

Nowhere was the importance of personality more aptly demonstrated in Israeli decisionmaking than in Rabin's efforts to conclude a peace agreement with Damascus. Although the Golan Heights was long regarded as essential for the security of northern Israel, withdrawal back to the boundaries held by Tel Aviv on 4 June 1967 was a move Rabin was prepared to discuss, if not countenance openly, provided a "full peace" proved forthcoming from Damascus. Meaningful negotiations were held in Washington between January 1994 and April 1995, but an agreement was never finalized. Professor Itamar Rabinovich, appointed personally by Rabin as Israel's ambassador to Washington with a specific mandate to negotiate with his Syrian counterpart, has suggested that President al-Asad missed a window of opportunity to make peace, "not under the full terms that he would have wanted but under reasonable, acceptable conditions."[48] These "reasonable, acceptable conditions" included demilitarization of the Golan, early-warning stations, as well as the establishment of full diplomatic relations. It was in an effort to conclude agreement on the substantive security issues that Rabin dispatched the then Israeli chief of staff, Lieutenant General Ehud Barak, to conduct negotiations with his Syrian counterpart, Hikmat Shihabi. It was not until the death of Rabin that Shimon Peres, Israel's foreign minister, was informed by Rabinovich of what had been taking place in Washington.[49]

The Peace Process Under Stress

The way the hierarchical structure of foreign policymaking in Israel creates a permissive environment that affords strong leaders an opportunity to impose decisions and policies unencumbered by bureaucratic filters is also illustrated by the way Netanyahu sought to disengage Israel from the peace process. On assuming office in May 1996, Netanyahu, like his predecessors, moved quickly to appoint like-minded individuals to key posts within the prime minister's office, all of whom shared Netanyahu's antipathy toward the Oslo Accords: Avigdor Lieberman (director general of the prime minister's office), Danny Naveh (cabinet secretary), Uri Elitzur (cabinet adviser and board member of the Yesha council), Major General (Res) Meir Dagan (adviser to the prime minister's office on terrorism) and Dr. Dore Gold (foreign policy adviser and Israel's ambassador to the United Nations). At least in the early period of his office, Netanyahu's preference for close associates as policy advisers induced a "group think" mentality that appeared to negate objective analysis.[50] Such an approach was blamed for Netanyahu's failure to heed warnings issued by the heads of the security services concerning the high probability of violence erupting among Palestinians should Israel open the Hasmonean tunnel in Jerusalem, an archaeological excavation that linked the Jewish and Arab quarters of the Old City. Similarly, where both Rabin and Peres drew heavily on IDF and intelligence personnel to conduct negotiations with Arab interlocutors, Netanyahu preferred his own aides within the prime minister's office to conduct peace negotiations even though, as Uri Bar Joseph has pointed out, none had much experience in dealing with foreign affairs or security-related issues.[51]

The personalization of power continued under the troubled premiership of Ehud Barak. The former chief of staff made it clear that he intended to hold the portfolios of both prime minister and defense minister on assuming office. While Barak tried to introduce new momentum and policy innovation into the peace process, most notably with regard to Syria, his modus operandi still relied heavily on a massive reservoir of traditional conservatism that is Israel's culture of national security. Barak's decision to form a *minhelet shalom* (peace administration) within the prime minister's office, consisting of ex-generals to oversee negotiations with Syria, Lebanon, and the Palestine National Authority, is perhaps evidence of this particular cultural legacy.[52]

While Barak completed an Israeli withdrawal from south Lebanon in May 2000, his attempts to conclude full peace agreements with both the Syrians and Palestinians fell on barren ground. Indeed, the al-Aqsa *intifada* that erupted in October 2000 across Israel, the West Bank, and the Gaza Strip following the ill-conceived and insensitive visit of Ariel Sharon to the Temple Mount/al-Haram al-Sharif placed severe question marks over the future of the peace process and signaled the end of Barak's premiership. While he portrayed himself as the true inheritor of Rabin's ideals, it became apparent that Barak had not accepted the substantive shift that occurred in Rabin's thinking toward Israel's regional environment and, in particular, toward relations with the Palestinians. Indeed, despite signing the Sharm al-Shaykh agreement with PNA chairman Yassir Arafat on 5 September 1999, an agreement that was supposed to both clarify the Wye Accords and lead to further Israeli troop withdrawals from the West Bank, continued expansion of Israeli settlements over the Green Line did much to dampen the widespread hope that had met Barak's election in May 1999. Some critics blamed Barak's own personality for the apparent collapse of the peace process, his self-confidence being held responsible for his failure to consult fully with his own cabinet regarding the state of negotiations with both Syria and the Palestinians.[53]

Such character traits can only provide a partial explanation surrounding the impasse reached in Israel's relations with both the PNA and Damascus by 2001. Rather, the particular milieu that informed Barak's approach to the conduct of peace negotiations remained the legacy of a rather stratified view of national security that continues to prevail among key decisionmakers. In a biographical sketch of Barak written some ten months before the outbreak of the al-Aqsa *intifada,* Meron Benvenisti, a former deputy mayor of Jerusalem, noted somewhat prophetically:

> Anyone who hears Barak talk about "life in the Middle East, with its dangers of fundamentalism and terrorism," about the importance of the settlements in the territories for demarcating the country's borders, and about his considerations for setting permanent borders can only be astounded that this gifted individual has remained captive to such obsolete conceptions. He speaks and thinks as though he were engaged in demarcating the armistice lines of 1949, not in setting borders of peace as the successor of his mentor (Rabin), who denied that an "existential threat" is a decree of fate.[54]

Conclusion: The Past as Present?

On 13 July 1992, during the course of presenting his new government to the thirteenth Knesset, Prime Minister Yitzhak Rabin noted that "we are no longer an isolated nation and it is no longer true that the entire world is against us. We must rid ourselves of the feeling of isolation that has afflicted us for 50 years."[55] Israel has built bridges to the wider world, with the Oslo process opening doors for Tel Aviv to the Gulf states of Bahrain, Oman, and Qatar. The Jewish state rekindled old diplomatic ties with a plethora of African states that had previously been severed. Moreover, whatever its conceptual flaws, the Oslo process has seen Israel recognize formally the national aspirations of the Palestinian people. Indeed, there is substantial evidence to suggest that Israelis have begun to internalize the meaning of peace. Surveys have shown that not only do most Israelis believe that a Palestinian state will emerge, but, more importantly, that a majority, albeit small, believe that Palestinians actually deserve such a state.[56]

But whatever the changes in the political landscape of the Middle East, Israel's foreign policy remains conditioned by a realist agenda toward its immediate neighbors and marked by a hierarchical foreign-policy decisionmaking structure biased internally toward the politics, if not the cult, of national security. Israelis argue that it is an approach that has served them well. The establishment of a strong military, including the deliberate policy of nuclear ambiguity, has not only ensured Israel's continued survival in the Middle East, but its acceptance by much of the Arab world, however grudging, that it is a permanent fixture in the political constellation of the Middle East.

Yet Israel's foreign policy, particularly after 1967, has acted increasingly as a palliative to a normative debate regarding the direction of Israel's internal political identity, a debate entwined in the counter-claims of identity. To be a (religious) Jewish state or a (secular) state for the Jews remains a question Israelis have yet to address. Cohesion against the Other has provided a degree of unity and justified the vertical totem of national security around which Israeli society and its foreign policy came to be organized. The past as present? Perhaps, for like many of its regional neighbors, foreign policy has for Israel proven to be as much about assuaging potentially divisive debates over the internal boundaries of identity as about protecting and defining its external borders. But as perhaps the assassination of Premier Rabin demonstrated, only when horizontal bridges can be built among Israelis themselves can a broader conception of security inform Israel's foreign-policy agenda toward the wider Middle East.

Notes

1. Robert Bowker, *Beyond Peace: The Search for Security in the Middle East*, Boulder, CO: Lynne Rienner, 1996, p. 113.

2. Gad Barzilai, *Wars, Internal Conflicts, and Political Order,* Albany: State University of New York Press, 1996, pp. 3–24.

3. Ze'ev Schiff, "The Spectre of Civil War in Israel," *Middle East Journal* 39, no. 2, spring 1985, pp. 231–245.

4. See Alexander Wendt, "Anarchy Is What States Make of It: The Social Construction of Power Politics," *International Organisation* 46, no. 2, spring 1992, pp. 391–425.

5. Efraim Inbar, "Israel's Predicament in a New Strategic Environment," in Efraim Inbar and Gabriel Sheffer, eds., *The National Security of Small States in a Changing World,* London: Frank Cass, 1997, p. 156.

6. Yaacov Bar-Siman-Tov, "The United States and Israel Since 1948: A 'Special Relationship'?" *Diplomatic History* 22, no. 2, spring 1998, p. 231.

7. Ibid., pp. 252–257.

8. Sever Plocker, "The Israeli Revolution," *Yediot Aharanot,* 14 April 1995.

9. Alex Brummer, "A Plan for Picking Winners," *The Guardian,* 8 April 1999.

10. The cost of the Chetz (Arrow) program was estimated to be $1.6 billion, with the United States contributing two-thirds of the overall cost of research and development. See Amnon Barzilai, Yossi Verter, and Amos Harel, "Chetz Hits Virtual Target," *Ha'aretz,* 15 September 1998.

11. Shimon Peres, *Battling for Peace,* London: Wiedenfeld and Nicolson, 1995, p. 358.

12. Shlomo Gazit, "The Quiet Option," *Ha'aretz,* 19 August 1998.

13. David Rodman, "Regime Targetting: A Strategy for Israel," *Israel Affairs* 2, no. 1, autumn 1995, pp. 153–167.

14. Some Israeli commentators have voiced strong criticism of regime targeting, arguing that such tactics have often proved counterproductive, resulting in greater loss of life among Israelis as terrorist organizations seek to exact bloody revenge. See Zvi Barel, "Stop Preaching to the IDF," *Ha'aretz,* 12 January 2001.

15. P. R. Kumaraswamy, "India and Israel: Evolving Strategic Partnership," *BESA Security Studies Policy Paper,* no. 40, September 1998, pp. 3–33.

16. Neill Lochery, "Israel and Turkey: Deepening Ties and Strategic Implications, 1995–98," *Israel Affairs* 5, no. 1, autumn 1998, pp. 45–46.

17. David Makovsky and Daniel Sobelman, "PM Urges Turkey-Israel Defense Axis," *Ha'aretz,* 2 September 1998.

18. Amos Harel, "Swimming with the Dolphin," *Ha'aretz,* 28 October 1998.

19. Clive Jones, "Ideotheology: Dissonance and Discourse in the State of Israel," *Israel Affairs* 3, nos. 3 and 4, spring–summer 1997, pp. 28–46.

20. For a breakdown of Palestinian population figures, see Elia Zureik, *Palestinian Refugees and the Peace Process,* Washington, DC: Institute for Palestine Studies, 1996, p. 14.

21. Ilan Peleg, "The Peace Process and Israel's Political Kulturkampf," in Ilan Peleg, ed., *The Middle East Peace Process,* Albany: State University of New York Press, 1998, pp. 237–261.

22. Efraim Inbar, "Netanyahu Takes Over," *Israel Affairs* 4, no. 1, autumn 1997, pp. 39–42.

23. Efraim Inbar, "Attitudes Toward War in the Israeli Political Elite," *Middle East Journal* 44, no. 3, summer 1990, pp. 432–433.

24. Uri Ben-Eliezer, "Rethinking the Civil-Military Relations Paradigm: The Inverse Relation Between Militarism and Praetorianism Through the Example of Israel," *Comparative Political Studies* 30, no. 3, June 1997, p. 360.

25. Ibid., p. 367.

26. Ehud Sprinzak, "Revving Up an Idle Threat," *Ha'aretz*, 29 September 1998.

27. Michael Brecher, *The Foreign Policy System of Israel: Setting, Images, Process*, Oxford: Oxford University Press, 1997, p. 229.

28. Ibid., p. 232.

29. Ian Traynor, "Those Who Are Called," *The Guardian Weekend*, 10 December 1994.

30. Barzilai, *Wars, Internal Conflicts and Political Order*, p. 14.

31. For a full account of Israel's war aims, see Zeev Schiff and Ehud Ya'ari, *Israel's Lebanon War*, London: Allen & Unwin, 1985.

32. Stephen Krasner, *Defending the National Interest: Raw Materials, Investment and American Foreign Policy*, Princeton, NJ: Princeton University Press, 1978, p. 13.

33. Efraim Inbar, "Israeli National Security, 1973–96," *Begin-Sadat (BESA) Security and Policy Studies Paper*, no. 38, February 1998, p. 63.

34. Amy Wilentz, "Peace Warrior: Israel's Top Gun Becomes an Uneasy Politician," *New Yorker*, 20 May 1996, pp. 34–39.

35. Ahron Bregman and Jihan El-Tahri, *The Fifty Years War: Israel and the Arabs*, Harmondsworth: Penguin/BBC Books, 1998, pp. 51–59.

36. Daniel Ben Simon, "Ministry in Search of a Leader—But Has It Found One?" *Ha'aretz*, 16 October 1998.

37. For example, under the premiership of Netanyahu, Uzi Arad, foreign policy adviser in the prime minister's office, was charged with policy formulation toward the United States and Europe, Cabinet Secretary Danny Naveh and Yitzhak Molco with conducting negotiations with the Palestinians, Ariel Sharon (until October 1998) with relations with Jordan, and Trade Minister Natan Sharansky with relations with the states of the former Soviet Union. See Sarah Leibovich-Dar, "Left Out of the Loop," *Ha'aretz*, 11 September 1998.

38. Uri Bar Joseph, "A Bull in a China Shop: Netanyahu and Israel's Intelligence Community," *International Journal of Intelligence and Counter Intelligence* 11, no. 2, 1998, p. 162.

39. David Makovsky, "Government Approves National Security Council Concept," *Ha'aretz*, 8 March 1999.

40. See the booklet *The Four Mothers: Leaving Lebanon in Peace*, Nof Yam, Israel, 1999. The movement was established in February 1997 by four women who all had sons serving in the IDF in south Lebanon. It is an authentic grassroots organization that draws its support from across the political spectrum. In terms of gender, it represents something of a breakthrough in the traditional male-dominated arena of Israeli pressure-group politics. Many men, many ex-soldiers who have served in Lebanon, have become members, proclaiming loudly that they are proud to be "Four Mothers."

41. Don Peretz, *Intifada: The Palestinian Uprising*, London: Westview Press, 1990, pp. 119–162.

42. Shai Feldman and Heda Rechnitz-Kijner, *Deception, Consensus and War: Israel in Lebanon*, Tel Aviv: JCSS, Tel Aviv University/Westview Press, 1984, pp. 10–24.

43. Yaacov Y. I. Vertzberger, *Risk Taking and Decisionmaking: Foreign Military Intervention Decisions*, Stanford: Stanford University Press, 1998, pp. 363–364.

44. Ibid., pp. 365, 374.

45. Ian Black, "Israel's Divided Opposition Reaches Policy Compromise," *The Guardian*, 22 November 1991.

46. Martin Van Crevald, *The Sword and the Olive: A Critical History of the Israeli Defense Forces*, New York: Public Affairs, 1998, pp. 335–352.

47. David Horovitz, ed., *Yitzhak Rabin: Soldier of Peace*, London: Halban Publishers, 1996, p. 127.

48. For the full text of Rabinovich's comments, see Douglas Jehl, "Rabin Showed Willingness to Give Golan Back to Syria," *New York Times*, 29 August 1997.

49. Bregman and El-Tahri, *The Fifty Years War*, p. 267.

50. Uri Bar Joseph, "A Bull in a China Shop," p. 159.

51. Ibid., p. 164.

52. Akiva Eldar, "Barak to Create a 'Peace Team' Made Up of Top Ex-Generals," *Ha'aretz*, 10 June 1999; Patrick Cockburn, "Generals Will Take Charge of Israeli Peace Negotiations," *Independent*, 11 June 1999.

53. Yossi Klein Halevi, "The Flawed Savior," *Jerusalem Report* 11, no. 18, 1 January 2001, pp. 18–21.

54. Meron Benvenisti, "The Peace of the Generals," *Ha'aretz*, 9 December 1999.

55. For a full English translation of the speech, see "Rabin's Address to Knesset: Says He Is Willing to Visit Arab Capitals," *BBC Summary of World Broadcasts*, ME/1433 A/1, 15 July 1992.

56. Ephraim Yaar and Tamar Hermann, "The Peace Index/March 1999: After All, Most Believe the Palestinians Deserve a State," *Ha'aretz*, 5 April 1999. According to the survey carried out among 497 Israeli adults by the Tami Steinmetz Center for Peace Research at Tel Aviv University, 69 percent thought that a Palestinian state was inevitable while 56 percent believed that the Palestinian demand for a state was justified.

7

The Foreign Policy of Syria

Raymond Hinnebusch

The Syrian state began as a fragile artificial entity enjoying few power resources. It was both profoundly irredentist and a recurrent victim of stronger neighbors. Within twenty years it was transformed, under Hafiz al-Asad, into a regional middle power. No other Arab state has since proved so adept at exercising power out of proportion to its natural endowments or so resolute in ensuring that its interests could not be ignored.[1]

Foreign-Policy Determinants

Identity

Syria's foreign policy is rooted in both its Arab national identity and the frustration of the ambitions inherent in that identity. Syria has no history of prior statehood that might underlay a distinct (non-Arab) Syrian identity. Situated at a crossroads of the movement of peoples and religions, it is very religiously heterogeneous but also overwhelmingly Arabic-speaking. As such, secular Arab nationalism was its most plausible and potentially integrating identity. While Syria's Sunni Muslim majority came to naturally identify with Arabism, Syria's Christian and heterodox Islamic minorities—the Alawis, Druze, and Ismailis—also embraced an identity under which all Arabic-speakers, regardless of religion, were accepted as members of the polity. The relative success of Arabism as the dominant identity ensured that the foreign policy of independent Syria would be shaped by the ambitions of Arab nationalism.

Added to this was an enduring and profound irredentism issuing from the frustration of Syria's national aspirations by the Western imposition of the Middle East state system. A truncated Syrian state was subjected to French rule and detached from the rest of historic Syria (*bilad ash-sham*) by the creation of separate "mandates" in Palestine, Lebanon, and Jordan.[2] Thereafter, national identity, rather than attaching to the truncated Syrian entity, regarded as the artificial creation of imperialism, tended to focus on suprastate "imagined communities"— Greater Syria, Islam, and above all, the "Arab nation." Imperialism also sponsored the establishment of the state of Israel in Palestine and no Arab people, bar the Palestinians themselves, have found it more difficult to accept the legitimacy of Israel's creation at the expense of Arab Palestine. After these experiences, no Syrian political leader could gain credibility for a foreign policy that did not affirm Syria's membership in the wider Arab community and its pivotal role in defense of all-Arab causes, above all the struggle with Israel.

Syria's Arab identity and its frustrations issued in a foreign-policy role that, though altering over time, survived countless changes of leadership essentially intact: Syria saw itself as the "beating heart of Arabism." It was Syria that gave birth to Ba'thism, the movement that saw its mission as unifying the Arab states and is still the official ideology today. Syria has been the most consistent center of Arabist sentiment and actually surrendered its sovereignty—in the 1958 union with Egypt—in the name of Pan-Arabism. Since then, however, the gap between the Pan-Arab ideal and actual foreign-policy behavior has steadily widened. Ruling elites have tenaciously defended state sovereignty and, since the 1970s, public opinion, after forty years of statehood and repeated disappointments with unity experiments, came to view Pan-Arab unification projects as unrealistic.

By the late 1960s, Syrian irredentism was refocused on the struggle for Palestine. This climaxed in the effort of the radical wing of the Ba'th Party (1966–1970) to make Damascus the bastion of a war of liberation in Palestine and a Pan-Arab revolution that would sweep away pro-Western states. This, however, only brought on the 1967 defeat and the Israeli occupation of new Arab lands, including the Syrian Golan Heights. The struggle with Israel now had a specifically Syrian territorial dimension that intensified it, yet, in also focusing it on the recovery of the Golan, gradually transformed it from a battle of irreconcilable national aspirations to a resolvable contest over limited territory. That this territory was explicitly Syrian started to alter the meaning of Arabism from a cause for which Syria would sacrifice to a means to reach Syrian ends.

In spite of these alterations in identity, Syrians still perceived the Arab states to make up a nation with an overriding national interest that ought to govern their foreign policies. But Syrian leaders gave this less ambitious view of Arabism a distinctly Syro-centric twist: Syria claimed, as the most steadfast of the frontline states in the battle with Israel, to be defending Arab, not purely Syrian, interests. Particularly after Egypt relinquished its Pan-Arab role, Syrian leaders began to claim that the Arab national interest coincided with Syria's particular military-security needs.[3]

This view took on its sharpest thrust in Syria's relations with the former "fallen away" components of *bilad al-sham*—Jordan, the Palestinians, and above all, Lebanon—over which Syria, as the "parent state," came to presume special rights and responsibilities. As Seale points out, Syria perceived itself in a struggle with Israel over the Levant, in what amounted to a contest between "Greater Syria" and "Greater Israel"; it must be noted, however, that for most Syrians and their leaders there was no incompatibility between Pan-Arabism and "Greater Syria" since the latter was an integral part of the wider Arab nation and was not perceived as making up a distinct Syrian nation.[4]

The identification of Syrian interests with Pan-Arabism was no mere fiction. Had a purely Syria-centered policy been followed, Syria could, arguably, have reached a Sadat-like settlement with Israel over the Golan. But Syria's goals in the struggle with Israel, in particular the defense of Palestinian rights, coincided with wider Pan-Arab norms and without pan-Arab solidarity those goals could not be achieved.

Nevertheless, Syria's insistence on the priority of its own needs in the struggle with Israel was bound to end in conflict with other Arab powers at the expense of Arab solidarity. This was especially so when Syria violated conventional Pan-Arab norms in allying with Iran against Arab Iraq in the Iran-Iraq war (1980–1988) and in its conflicts with the Palestine Liberation Organization (PLO) in Lebanon. Moreover, by the 1990s, there was evidence that the national identity of Syrians was in transition toward a more distinctly Syrian identity. Long experience with truncated Syria as the habitual framework of normal politics and accumulated consciousness of the costs of bearing Syria's Pan-Arab mission had enervated Pan-Arab commitments. However, the major watershed in legitimating a certain narrowing of identity was the series of separate deals struck by Egypt, Jordan, and the PLO with Israel at Syria's expense. These generated a growing readiness to accept that Syria also had to put its own interests first. The persisting dilemma for Syria, however, was that the idea of an exclusively Syrian "nation," not essentially Arab, still held little credibility: whatever Syrian identity was, its content was Arab.

Geopolitics and the Balance of Power

A foreign policy is shaped not just by aspirations and frustrations, but equally by material realities. Syria's geopolitical location dictated an exceptional vulnerability and it normally faced an unfavorable regional power balance that necessarily tempered the wish to act on irredentist grievances. Syria's relatively small size and population provided a limited manpower base and little strategic depth or deterrence to invasion. Syria was unprotected by natural boundaries and exposed on all sides to countries that, at one time or another, constituted threats. Iraq, whether under Hashemite or Ba'thist leadership, had irredentist designs on Syria. Syria is one of only two Arab states that confronts two non-Arab neighbors. More powerful Turkey threatened intervention against Syrian radicalism in the 1950s, has held hostage Euphrates waters on which Syria depends, and in the 1990s entered an alignment with Israel that encircled Syria. Above all, Israel, Syria's main enemy, has enjoyed permanent military superiority. Syria's loss of the Golan Heights, its one natural defense against Israel, generated intense new security fears. Syria is also vulnerable to Israeli outflanking movements through Jordan and Lebanon. The disadvantageous regional balance of power has pushed Syria both to accept the reality of Israel and to seek the power to contain the Israeli threat.

If Syria is not to be a victim of neighboring powers, it must "power balance" against them through some combination of internal power mobilization and alliance formation. The drive to right the military imbalance with Israel was the dominant theme of Hafiz al-Asad's leadership. In this regard, Syria's location was also an asset, for, at the very heart of the Middle East, it enjoyed exceptional strategic importance. Its frontline position adjoining Israel gave it exceptional stature in the Arab world and made it pivotal to international efforts to resolve the Arab-Israeli conflict. Syria has also historically been a partner repeatedly sought by states such as Egypt, Iraq, and Saudi Arabia to balance rival power constellations. This geopolitical centrality gave Syria an importance that could be parlayed into resources and diplomatic support beyond its own borders.[5]

State Formation and Foreign-Policy Behavior

If identity and geopolitics defined the goals and challenges facing Syria's foreign policymakers, their ability to effectively pursue their goals varied widely according to Syria's level of state formation. Only as this advanced was Damascus able to conduct a foreign policy that changed Syria from a recurrent victim of its neighbors to a formidable actor in the region.

Syria as victim: Instability at home, vulnerability abroad. For the first quarter-century of its independent existence, Syria's foreign policy, the incoherent product of instability at home and weakness in the region, could not prevent the country from becoming the prize over which stronger states fought.

Pre-Ba'th Syria (1946–1963) was a classic penetrated state, rapidly destabilized by interlocking domestic opposition and external threats. The newly independent state's effort to consolidate public loyalties was fatally compromised when the precarious legitimacy won in the independence struggle was shattered by the loss of Palestine. President Quwatli's regime, buffeted by an aroused populace that raised volunteer forces to fight in Palestine, eventually committed its small regular army; but although it was able to seize and hold a few border slivers of Palestine, war profiteering and incompetence undermined its effort. After the Zionist victory, popular revulsion against a now discredited establishment threatened a breakdown of public order. The refusal of the beleaguered government, constrained by a nationally aroused public, to either sign a peace treaty with Israel or agree to the construction of a U.S.-sponsored oil pipeline from Saudi Arabia, inspired U.S. Central Intelligence Agency intrigue in the army, only the first episode of destabilizing Western meddling in Syrian politics. This encouraged Colonel Husni al-Za'im's 1949 coup d'etat, but after Za'im moved to meet U.S. demands, began peace negotiations with Israel, and otherwise generally alienated all political forces, he was himself soon overthrown.[6]

Syria's permeable artificial borders and Pan-Arab sentiment invited external penetration of Syrian politics: while the main opposition parties rejected the truncated Syrian state, rival Arab powers financed or armed Syrian clients and backed military coups in Syria. Hashemite ambitions to absorb Syria, such as King Abdullah's "Greater Syria" plan and Iraq's Fertile Crescent scheme, pushed President Quwatli into a defensive alignment with anti-Hashemite Egypt and Saudi Arabia.[7] Then, in the early 1950s, the People's Party (*hizb al-shab*), dominated by the rising Aleppo bourgeoisie that had been cut off from its historic markets in northern Iraq, came to power championing union with Iraq. Syrian sovereignty was preserved, not by popular attachment to the state, but by the resistance of the army to subordination to Iraqi command, Saudi financing of politicians against the project, nationalist opposition to absorption by a British-dominated monarchy, and Western discouragement of Iraq.[8]

By the mid-1950s, the failure of oligarchic-dominated political institutions to satisfy middle-class participatory demands and appease land-hungry peasants allowed radical antisystem parties—notably the Ba'th, Syrian Nationalist, and Communist Parties—to mobilize popular unrest. This was also expressed in military coups and countercoups that profoundly destabilized the state. Domestic instability coincided with perceptions of a rising threat from Israel as border skirmishes over the demilitarized zones escalated. Syria could not do without protective alignments, but Syrians were deeply divided between supporters of pro-Western Iraq, which advocated security through membership in the Western-sponsored Baghdad Pact, and followers of Egypt's Nasser, who opposed the pact in the name of a nonaligned Arab collective security. Since the fate of the Baghdad Pact was believed to turn on Syria's choice, a regional and international "struggle for Syria" took place (1954–1958). The mobilization of Syria's nationalist middle class swung the balance in favor of Egypt while Nasser's rising stature as a Pan-Arab hero, especially after the Suez war, weakened conservative pro-Western and pro-Iraqi politicians and strengthened those—above all, the Ba'th—aligned with Cairo. The result was the formation of Syria's 1956 pro-Egyptian, anti-imperialist National Front government. The West's sponsorship of several abortive conservative coups against it and a 1957 attempt to quarantine Syrian radicalism under the Eisenhower Doctrine, backed by Iraqi-sponsored subversion and Turkish threats, precipitated Soviet counterthreats against Turkey and a backlash of pro-Communist feeling inside Syria.[9]

It was this sense of interlocking external siege and internal polarization that led Ba'th leaders to seek salvation in a confederation with Egypt, thereby forcing their rivals to outbid them and unleashing an uncontrollable public demand for full union. Said one participant: "We followed the masses. The crowds were drunk. . . . Anyone at that hour who dared oppose unity—the people would tear their heads off." Syrian elites were swept into surrendering Syrian sovereignty to Nasser—the epitome, in the realist worldview, of state weakness and foreign-policy failure.[10]

The coup that brought the Ba'th Party to power in 1963 ushered in a new era of instability. The Ba'th regime had a narrow support base, owing to conflict with mass Nasserism (over failure of a 1963 unity project) and the opposition of the old oligarchs and Islamic rivals. On top of this, the regime was split between party patriarch Michel Aflaq, who still viewed Pan-Arab union as central to the party's national mission, and younger minority-dominated radicals more interested in a social "revolution in one country" than in sacrificing their power on the altar of Pan-Arabism. Foreign policy became a tool in their struggle, with each side forced to defend itself against the other by advocating greater militancy against Israel. These ideological and personal rivalries overlapped with sectarian divisions between Sunnis and the minorities long disproportionately represented in the party. As, in this and subsequent such struggles, Alawis increasingly won out, thereby disaffecting Syria's Sunni majority, the regime was put under pressure to prove its Arab-nationalist credentials.

The radical minority-dominated faction seized precarious power in a 1966 coup. Driven by ideological militancy and a search for legitimation through a revolutionary foreign policy, the radicals literally risked the Syrian state once again. Their aim of making Damascus the bastion of a war of Palestine liberation meant giving support to Palestinian *fedayeen* raids into Israel. This, however, ignored the unfavorable balance of power with Israel and thereby brought on the 1967 defeat and the Israeli occupation of Syria's Golan Heights.[11]

The loss of the war and the dominance of the post-1966 Syrian leadership by the Alawi minority alienated many Syrian Ba'thists who backed Aflaq's Pan-Arab leadership, now exiled in Ba'thist Iraq, which tried to subvert the Syrian regime. In the accompanying ideological war between Damascus and Baghdad, each regime tried to outbid the other in militancy toward Israel and Western imperialism.[12] Under these pressures, the regime again split over foreign policy, with the insistence of the radical leadership on a continuing high-risk challenge to Israel countered by the new realists clustered around Defense Minister Hafiz al-Asad. In 1970, Asad ousted the ideological radicals and set Syria on a new, more realist foreign-policy course that took account of Israel's military superiority. Syrian elites had learned the realist rules of the state system the hard way.[13]

Syria as actor: State consolidation under Asad. The consolidation of the Syrian regime under Asad was, in many ways, a product of Syria's beleaguered position in its external environment. The Ba'th state, the product of a nationalist party and an army radicalized by the conflict with Israel, developed, under Asad, into a huge national-security apparatus designed to confront Israel. The consolidation of the state was accompanied by the concentration of power in Asad's hands, and this, too, was driven by foreign-policy exigencies: it was accepted within the political elite as necessary to confront the gravest threat the country and regime had ever faced, a defeat and occupation brought on by the weakness and recklessness of a factionalized regime. Moreover, Asad's state building depended on external resources, that is, the Soviet arms with which he rebuilt the army and the Arab oil money by which the bureaucracy was expanded and the bourgeoisie co-opted.

Asad's consolidation of the Ba'th regime was marked by the concentration of power in a "presidential monarchy" achieved through a policy of balancing social forces. Under the radical Ba'thists who preceded Asad (1963–1970), the regime had achieved autonomy of the dominant classes by breaking their control over the means of production and mobilizing workers and peasants through the Ba'th Party. After 1970, Asad used the army to free himself from party ideological constraints; he built up his *jama'a*—a core of largely Alawi personal followers in the security apparatus—to enhance his autonomy of both army and party. At the same time, he appeased the private bourgeoisie through limited liberalization and fostered a state-dependent new bourgeoisie, generating a fourth leg of support to minimize dependence on the others. While elements of the Damascene Sunni bourgeoisie entered into tacit alliance with Alawi military elites at the top of the regime, the party and its auxiliaries incorporated a popular following at the base, particularly in the villages, Sunni as well as non-Sunni. Thus, Asad built a cross-sectarian coalition whose durability proved itself in defeating the major Islamic fundamentalist uprising of 1977–1982.

It was only as the state was stabilized and the regime attained relative internal cohesion that foreign policymakers achieved sufficient autonomy of domestic constraints to effectively adapt foreign policy to the changing geopolitical power balance. They were also now enabled to mobilize the capabilities needed to make Syria a player rather than a victim in the regional environment. The legitimacy of Asad's regime was largely built on its relative success in doing this.[14]

Foreign Policymaking

The Foreign-Policy Process

In the presidential monarchy he created, Asad enjoyed the widest latitude in foreign policymaking. At least initially, he tried to make policy by intra-elite consensus, rather than imposing a personal view. He seemed to take account of the ideological militancy of the Ba'th Party, yet was also prepared to be out in front of elite and party opinion. Both tendencies were apparent in key decisions during the 1970s. Thus, Kissinger noted in the disengagement negotiations after the 1973 war that in Syria, by contrast to Egypt where Sadat governed alone, the whole top political elite had to be present and convinced; but in the end it was Asad who accepted Kissinger's final proposal and dragged his reluctant lieutenants along with him. According to Dawisha, the 1976 intervention in Lebanon against the PLO was also taken by a collective leadership, but it is also clear that Asad overruled widespread dissent in the party and the army.[15] As Asad's preeminence was fully consolidated in the 1980s, foreign policymaking became ever more his reserved sphere, subject to no bureaucratic politics in which hawkish or dovish factions could veto his initiatives.[16]

Similarly, as the Ba'th regime was consolidated under Asad, public opinion ceased to be the *direct* constraint on foreign policymaking it had been when weak governments were regularly brought down over such issues. Asad took several unpopular foreign-policy positions, notably the 1976 intervention against the PLO in Lebanon, the alignment with Iran in the Iran-Iraq war, and the stand with the Western coalition against Iraq after its invasion of Kuwait. This is not to say that public opinion had no *indirect* effect. The regime had to take care not to irreparably damage its legitimacy, which ultimately rested on its claim to defend the Arab cause against Israel. As long as Asad could justify unpopular decisions as necessary to the long-term struggle with Israel, he evidently calculated that opposition could be contained. Such decisions, nevertheless, had domestic costs; arguably, the 1976 intervention against the Palestinians so damaged the regime's legitimacy that it was much more vulnerable to the Islamic rebellions of 1977–1982. And the bottom line was that no nationalist regime—especially an Alawi-dominated one—could, without grave risk, deviate from mainstream opinion in dealing with Israel. If Syria's government and public opinion could be said to approach a consensus on any issue, it was over Israel: while Syrians rejected its legitimacy, they nevertheless wanted a political settlement provided it was an honorable one entailing a comprehensive Israeli withdrawal from the occupied territories. This was the government position for decades.

Policy Implementation Capabilities

Asad's state building greatly enhanced his capacity to sustain and implement foreign-policy decisions.

Military capability. Syrian military power steadily expanded under Asad's rule. The 1967 defeat stimulated a massive rebuilding and professionalization of the armed forces, which paid off in improved performance during the 1973 war. Thereafter, Egypt's separate peace, leaving Syria facing Israel alone, and Israel's 1982 invasion of Lebanon set off further rounds of military buildup aimed at enough parity with Israel to constitute a deterrent and give backing to Syrian diplomacy.

By 1986, Syria had an enormous armed force for a state of its size: 5,000 tanks, 650 combat planes, 102 missile batteries, and over 500,000 men under arms. A Soviet-supplied long-range air umbrella and around 400 ballistic missiles, some chemically armed, gave Syria a new deterrent capability. Although Syria lacked a credible offensive capability, an Israeli attack on Syria was likely, given this balance of forces, to be very costly, with no guarantee that Syria could be defeated.[17] According to Evron, the Syrian buildup produced mutual deterrence that relatively stabilized the Syrian-Israeli military confrontation.[18] Syrian-Israeli rivalry was thereby largely diverted into political struggle over the conditions of a peace settlement. In these struggles, Syria's military deterrent meant that Asad did not have to bargain from weakness and it even allowed him to apply limited military pressure on Israel in southern Lebanon (via Hizbollah) at reasonable risk. Syria had to scramble, after the collapse of its Soviet arms supplier, to prevent the degradation of this deterrent.

Economic capabilities. Syria's turn to statist "socialism" from the late 1950s was, in good part, driven by the belief that a nationalist foreign policy could only be pursued by diluting economic dependency on the West. The displacement of the private bourgeoisie by the public sector realigned economic dependency toward the Soviet bloc and helped win Soviet aid and protection.

Under the Ba'th regime, a high degree of state control over the economy also allowed Asad to harness it to his foreign policy. In Syria's search for parity with Israel, as much as half of public expenditure was devoted to defense. Twenty percent of manpower served in the armed forces at its height in the 1980s. Military spending increased from $1.8 billion in 1977 to $5.4 billion in 1984. If one includes the value of arms imported on credit, Syria's military spending climbed to 30 percent of its gross domestic product.[19]

But Syria's slim economic base could not, alone, sustain its enormous military burden, which contributed to a permanent resource gap, forcing Syrian dependence on external aid and loans. According to

Clawson, from 1977 to 1988, Syria self-financed only 45 percent of imports, the remaining $42 billion being covered by grants and loans from the USSR ($23 billion), the Gulf Cooperation Council (GCC) states ($12 billion), Iran ($3 billion), and the West ($4 billion). In the late 1980s, however, external aid sharply declined: Arab aid may have fallen by one- to two-thirds of the $1.8 billion received in 1978.[20] Meanwhile, the Soviet military debt burgeoned and the heavy burden of military spending helped bring economic growth to a halt, forcing a leveling off of Syria's military buildup in the late 1980s.

Yet, although the economy was under maximum pressure, Asad refused to change his policies in Lebanon and his alliance with Iran to please his GCC donors. The potential constraints on foreign policy from the regime's economic dependency were eased by the diversification of Syria's donors and its ability to balance between rival Soviet/Eastern European, Western European, and Arab Gulf, Libyan, or Iranian sources of aid; foreign policies that alienated one donor might win rewards from another. Although Asad did occasionally exploit foreign policy to win economic relief—this was a factor in joining the anti-Iraq coalition—he had no record of taking decisions for economic reasons that would not otherwise have been taken on strategic grounds.[21]

Foreign-Policy Behavior

Foreign-Policy Strategy: A Rational Actor?

Asad's enhanced autonomy and capabilities permitted him to pursue policies approximating those that realists might expect of a "rational actor," notably the matching of ends and means, consistency, and the adaptation of strategies to the balance of power.

• *Limited goals.* Rationality was manifest in Asad's realist scaling-down of the highly revisionist goals deriving from Syria's identity to fit the constraints of geopolitics. Pre-Ba'th governments were too weak to contemplate either war or peace with Israel, while the Ba'th radicals were driven by a dangerous ideology of confronting Israel irrespective of the unfavorable balance of power. Asad replaced this policy with the still ambitious but more realistic goals of recovering the occupied lands, above all the Golan, and achieving Palestinian rights, notably in the West Bank and Gaza, as part of a comprehensive peace under UN Resolution 242.

The triumph of realism over revolutionary revisionism was evident in Asad's initial pivotal decisions: his opposition to the radicals' 1970 intervention in Jordan and his détente with the traditional pro-Western Arab states. The limited nature of Syria's aims in the struggle with Israel was evident in its conduct of the 1973 war: Syrian forces attacking into the Golan made no attempt, where they had the opportunity, of advancing into Israel itself, evidently not even having planned for such an eventuality.[22] Two decades later, Asad's stand in the 1990–1991 war against Iraq's invasion of Kuwait demonstrated a rather non-Ba'thist acceptance of the principle of state sovereignty. In short, far from being a Pan-Arab revolutionary, Asad pursued the limited and conventional goals prescribed by realism, namely, recovery of territorial losses and maintenance of a balance of power against threats.

• *Consistency.* Yet, Asad demonstrated great tenacity in pursuit of his scaled-down strategic goals by refusing to settle for less than full Israeli withdrawal to the 1967 lines. For a quarter-century he eschewed a separate settlement with Israel at the expense of the Palestinians. When the balance of forces did not permit achievement of a comprehensive peace, rather than concede principle, Asad preferred to work for a change in that balance, while actively obstructing schemes to draw other Arab parties into partial, separate settlements with Israel. When such vital interests were at stake, he was prepared to stand up to superior external power and proved to have a cool nerve not easily panicked. This was best illustrated by his risky obstruction of the 1983 Lebanese-Israeli accord at a time when Israeli and U.S. power was projected right on his "Lebanese doorstep."[23]

• *Strategic adaptability.* At the same time, Asad parlayed limited resources into a greater capacity to shape outcomes than would be expected from Syria's base of national power. He proved himself a master at mixing a variety of foreign-policy instruments—limited war, alliance formation, negotiations, obstruction—as conditions dictated. A realist who believed that military power was decisive in international politics, he matched his pragmatic scaling-down of Syria's objectives with a significant upgrading in its military capability, not only as a deterrent against Israel, but also to give his diplomacy credibility. Yet, ever cautious and preferring to husband his limited resources, he deployed the most economic and least risky means possible to attain his goals. This characteristic was most evident in his measured use of proxies in Lebanon.[24]

Because Syria alone lacked the resources to sustain his policy, Asad put a high priority on manipulating alliances, regardless of ideology, that would allow him to mobilize the resources of other states behind his goals: thus, he simultaneously sustained alliances with the conservative Arab oil states, the Soviet Union, and Islamic Iran.

Nor did Asad eschew diplomacy. Although extremely wary of the pitfalls of negotiating with Israel, he was ready to bargain when it could be done from a position of enough strength to win some advantage; otherwise, being a man of great patience, he preferred to wait until the balance of forces improved.[25]

• *Manipulating bipolarity.* Asad also used Syria's geopolitical centrality to mimic Nasser's balancing between the superpowers. The resources and protection needed to confront Israel made a superpower patron indispensable, and Asad proved adept in exploiting superpower rivalry to suit his ends.

Given U.S. backing of Israel, a close Soviet alignment was natural in a bipolar world. Soviet arms deliveries were key to Syria's relative success in the 1973 war and thereafter in the drive for parity. The Soviet Union's role as patron-protector had a crucial deterrent effect on Israel's freedom of action against Syria. In particular, Soviet support was pivotal in giving Asad the confidence to challenge Israeli and U.S. power in Lebanon after the 1982 Israeli invasion.[26]

At least from Damascus's point of view, the United States consistently biased the regional power balance in Israel's favor, not only by ensuring its military superiority but also by dividing the Arabs, notably in detaching Egypt from the anti-Israeli coalition. While relations with the United States were thus naturally and permanently uneasy, Asad nevertheless sought to exploit U.S. fears of Middle East instability to get pressure on Israel to withdraw from the occupied territories. Also, U.S. mediation more than once proved its value in keeping Syro-Israeli rivalry in Lebanon from escalating out of control. While for a period under Reagan the United States treated Syria as a Soviet surrogate to be punished, Asad exploited President George Bush's need for Syria in his anti-Saddam Gulf war coalition to appease the United States at a time when Soviet power was declining.[27]

Foreign-Policy Watersheds in the Struggle with Israel

From limited war to diplomacy (1970s). A realist, Asad was convinced Israel would never withdraw from the occupied territories unless military action upset the post-1967 status quo. The main thrust of his policy after coming to power in 1970 was, therefore, preparation for a conventional war to retake the Golan. Toward this end, the rebuilding of the shattered Syrian army had to be the first priority. He maintained Syria's close alliance with the USSR to secure arms. He put aside the radicals' ideological cold war and forged new alliances with the Arab oil states that secured the financing needed for a military buildup. Finally, he struck a strategic alliance with Sadat's Egypt, the most militarily powerful of the Arab states that shared Syria's interest in recovery of the occupied territories.[28]

Egypt and Syria went to war in 1973 to break the stalemate over the occupied territories. Although Syria failed to recover the Golan militarily, Syria and Egypt acquired enhanced political leverage from their credible challenge to the pro-Israeli status quo and from the Arab oil embargo. Asad sought to exploit this new leverage to get international pressure on Israel to withdraw from the occupied territories.

The first episode in this new strategy was Asad's acceptance of Henry Kissinger's mediation of the Golan Heights disengagement negotiations after the cease-fire. Weakened by Sadat's prior and unilateral first disengagement in the Sinai and the premature lifting of the oil embargo, Asad conducted a war of attrition on the front with Israel as part of a "fighting while talking" bargaining strategy. The resulting 1974 Golan disengagement agreement with Israel was seen as a first step in total Israeli withdrawal. However, Sadat's subsequent separate deals with Israel further undermined Syrian diplomatic leverage and shattered the Syro-Egyptian alliance needed to pressure Israel into a comprehensive settlement. In its place, Asad tried to build up a Levant bloc that would bring Syria, Lebanon, Jordan, and the Palestinians into Damascus's orbit, prevent separate dealing with Israel by them, and give Syria extra cards in the diplomatic maneuvering of the late 1970s.[29]

Tactical rejectionism (1980s). Once Sadat's separate peace with Israel exhausted the 1970s peace process, Asad aimed at preventing the legitimation of the Camp David process in the Arab world and sought to claim the Arab aid and support to which Syria was entitled as the main remaining frontline Arab state. This aid financed a military buildup aiming at parity with Israel: the threat of an Israel emboldened by the neutralization of its southern front had to be contained, while Asad believed that the resumption of peace negotiations depended on restoration of a more favorable Arab-Israeli power balance. In the meantime, Damascus would obstruct all attempts at partial or separate Israeli agreements with other states that tried to circumvent Syria. This "tactical rejectionism" aimed to demonstrate that if Syria could not achieve an Arab-Israeli peace to its liking, it could at least prevent others that damaged its interests or Arab rights: that seemed to be the lesson of Syria's role in the collapse of both the 1983 Lebanese-Israeli accord and of the 1985 Hussein-Arafat bid for negotiations with Israel under the Reagan Plan. But this rejectionism, combined with Syria's stand with Iran in the Iran-Iraq war, antagonized a multitude of Arab and Western powers and isolated Syria. Throughout much of the 1980s, therefore, Syria was largely lacking in the diplomatic leverage to advance its goals in the struggle with Israel.[30]

Asad's Regional Policy: Arabism or Syrian Reason of State?

Three key decisions could be held to demonstrate that, despite his rhetoric, Asad was prepared to violate Pan-Arab norms for Syrian state interests, much as Sadat had done. But each of them can be seen, from his point of view, to have served his wider Arab-nationalist strategy against Israel.

The Syrian intervention in Lebanon. Syria's 1976 intervention in the Lebanese civil war against the PLO was widely interpreted as serving Syrian reason of state, even a "Greater Syria" project. Certainly, this assault on the acknowledged representative of the Palestinian cause, the touchstone of Arabism, cost the regime considerable Arab-nationalist legitimacy. However, Asad's Lebanon strategy aimed to assemble an alternative Levant bloc against Israel as Egypt moved toward a separate peace with it; he used the civil war to insert Syria as arbiter and thereby draw Lebanon and the PLO into this sphere of influence. Lebanon was also a special danger spot because the civil war increased the risk of Israeli intervention, which Syria could not ignore.

Prior to its intervention, Syria had backed the Palestinians against a Maronite war of ethnic cleansing and then tried to broker an end to the civil war through reforms meant to appease each side: a mild redistribution of power in the Muslims' favor, and Palestinian respect for Lebanese sovereignty. But when the Lebanese Muslims and the PLO rejected these reforms in the name of a secular radical state and appeared intent on a military defeat of the Maronites, Syria forcefully intervened against them in mid-1976. Asad hoped to deter a Maronite alignment with Israel by demonstrating Syria's unwillingness to countenance a sectarian triumph over them. He also sought to prevent the emergence of a rejectionist Palestinian-dominated Lebanon, capable, in alignment with rejectionist Iraq, of upsetting Syria's peace diplomacy, and sponsoring guerrilla war against Israel. This could give Israel an excuse to intervene militarily, possibly to seize southern Lebanon and position itself to threaten Syria's soft western flank. Syria's intervention allowed Asad to station his army in the Beqa' Valley against this danger.

Furthermore, Lebanon was, given the PLO presence there, key to Asad's drive to control the Palestinian card: Syria's bargaining leverage in the Arab-Israeli conflict would be greatly enhanced if it enjoyed the capacity to veto any settlement of the Palestinian problem that left Syria out, or to overcome rejectionist Palestinian resistance to an acceptable settlement. Whoever controlled Lebanon was in a strong position to control the PLO. Interpreting Asad's intervention, as critics did, as a bid to break resistance to a separate Syrian peace with Israel at the expense of the Palestinians goes too far, however; although the intervention, in diminishing Palestinian power and demonstrating Syrian moderation to the United States and Israel, better positioned Asad for such a settlement, in continuing to insist on Palestinian rights and a comprehensive settlement, he passed up a chance to follow Sadat down the road of separate peace.[31]

The Iranian alliance. Asad's alignment with Iran against Arab Iraq in the Iran-Iraq war could be seen as serving regime interests in weakening a powerful neighbor run by a rival wing of the Ba'th Party at the expense of common Arab interests. But this decision, too, was ultimately driven by the struggle with Israel.

Syria was increasingly vulnerable in the face of superior Israeli power following Egypt's defection from its Syrian alliance after Camp David. The quick collapse of Syria's anti–Camp David alliance with Iraq, brought on by Saddam Hussein's 1979 seizure of sole power against pro-Syrian elements in the Iraqi Ba'th Party, left Asad doubly exposed. At the same time, the 1979 Islamic revolution was transforming Iran from an ally of Israel and the United States into a fiercely anti-Zionist state. Iran was now a potential Syrian ally whose strategic weight would be a valuable asset in the Arab-Israeli power balance.

When Iraq invaded Iran, Asad condemned it as the wrong war at the wrong time against the wrong enemy, rightly predicting that it would exhaust, divide, and divert the Arabs from the Israeli menace. He made his stand with Iran against Iraq. The value of the Iranian alliance proved itself after the 1982 Israeli invasion of Lebanon when the dramatic effectiveness of the Iranian-sponsored Islamic resistance to Israel helped foil a mortal threat to Syria. Nevertheless, sensitive to Arab opinion, Asad actively discouraged Iranian threats to Iraqi territory.[32]

Joining the Gulf war coalition. Asad's adhesion to the Western-led anti-Iraq coalition appeared to some pundits to be a cynical subordination of Arab nationalism to Syria's economic needs and rivalry with Iraq. However, Syria's strategy in the struggle with Israel permeated each of the many ostensibly separate considerations that went into this decision.

It is true that Syria had long depended on Saudi economic support that, Asad must have realized, would become all the more important as ties with the Eastern bloc slackened. If he failed to support the Saudis in their hour of need, Syria risked future loss of Saudi aid whether Riyadh was alienated or brought under Iraqi influence. The crisis was a perfect opportunity to revitalize the subsidy channel from the Gulf oil states that had dried up with the decline of oil prices. Saudi and Gulf support was, however, so indispensable to the maintenance of Syria's strategic position in the battle with Israel that economic and strategic factors became indistinguishable.

Likewise, Syrian-Iraqi rivalry must be put in the larger context of the Syrian-Israeli struggle. To be sure, Saddam Hussein was hostile and had an enormous army; but Saddam was preoccupied with his southern front and less a threat to Syria than heretofore. However, Iraq had been supporting General Aoun's challenge to Syria's position in Lebanon, which was pivotal to its standing in the conflict with Israel. Additionally, if Saddam succeeded in annexing Kuwait (and, by intimidating Saudi Arabia, in potentially wielding the oil weapon), he would be in a stronger position to claim Arab leadership in the conflict with Israel. Syria could not permit any other state to dictate decisions that could lead it into a war with Israel or entrap it in a peace settlement it found unacceptable.

Nevertheless, the political risk in joining the Western-led war coalition was high. Standing with the West against a fellow Arab nationalist state did serious damage to Syria's Pan-Arab legitimacy, an intangible but crucial asset from which Syria made its claim on the Arab support needed to sustain its policy toward Israel. The actions of the coalition also damaged Iraq, a major Arab power in the balance with Israel, but this might have happened regardless of what Syria did. On the other hand, joining the second Gulf war coalition enabled Syria to break out of the Arab isolation from its alignment with Iran. This put Syria back at the heart of a renewed Cairo-Damascus-Riyadh axis from which it could hope to orchestrate an all-Arab front on behalf of its struggle with Israel.

Ultimately, however, Syria's policy was most decisively shaped by the emerging breakdown of the bipolar world. By the 1990s, the withdrawal of the USSR as a reliable protector and arms supplier deprived Syria of a credible threat of war against Israel in the absence of an acceptable peace. How would hundreds of tanks lost in a new war be replaced or Israeli advances stopped without Soviet intervention? Without Soviet protection, Syria was also left dangerously vulnerable to Western animosity for its obstruction of the peace process in the 1980s and, particularly, for its alleged resort to terrorism, which Israel could exploit to justify an attack on it. A more long-range consideration was the threatened disappearance of the Eastern bloc as a source of markets, aid, and technology, and the consequent need to repair economic links to the West frayed during the 1980s over charges of Syrian support for terrorism.

An exposed Syria had no choice but to repair and diversify its international connections. In particular, Asad understood that he could not realize his goals in opposition to the remaining superpower. Syria's struggle with Israel would henceforth have to take a chiefly diplomatic form and that required détente with the United States, which alone had leverage over Israel. Asad needed to get the United States to accept Syria as the key to peace and stability in the Middle East and to recognize its legitimate interests in an equitable settlement with Israel.

The second Gulf war presented a golden opportunity to trade membership in the coalition—to the credibility of which Syria's nationalist credentials were arguably crucial—in return for U.S. acknowledgment of Syrian interests. Asad's gamble was that after the Iraqi occupation of Kuwait was resolved, the United States would have to fulfill promises to its Arab allies and resolve the Israeli occupation of Arab lands in a comparable way—on the basis of UN resolutions. In short, Syria saw Bush's "new world order" shaping up and wanted to influence it rather than become its victim.

Adhesion to the Gulf coalition also provided a valuable side benefit, namely, U.S. and Israeli tolerance of Asad's military intervention to defeat General Aoun's Iraqi-backed challenge to Syria's role in Lebanon. The establishment of hegemony in Lebanon would thereafter allow Asad to "play the Lebanon card" in inter-Arab and Arab-Israeli diplomacy. Being on the right side of the new world order reaped immediate strategic rewards.

By contrast to the primacy of external threats and opportunities in Asad's realpolitik, domestic constraints played remarkably little role.

Indeed, Syria's participation in the coalition seemed to underline, as no decision before, the regime's relative autonomy from domestic opinion, which was broadly pro-Iraq. In the end, however, regime legitimacy suffered remarkably little. Saddam's defeat and the destruction of Iraq showed what Asad had spared Syria.[33]

In summary, the apparent contradiction between Pan-Arab norms and Syrian behavior was resolved, at least from the viewpoint of Syrian decisionmakers, by the fact that Syria's power position in the conflict with Israel—at a time when Syria constituted the only Arab power still actively trying to contain Israeli power while refusing a separate peace at the expense of Palestinian rights—seemed to coincide with the Arab national interest.

Syria in the Post-Bipolar World

The new power balance. The new world order that emerged from the end of the Cold War and the second Gulf war was far less favorable to Syrian interests than the bipolar world in which Asad had so deftly exploited U.S.-Soviet rivalries. As he saw it, the balance of power had been upset with the collapse of bipolarity and the "main winners have been the Arabs' enemies."[34] Syria would have to blunt this threat by trying to maximize links to both friends and old enemies.

To be sure, Syria's entry into the Gulf coalition and the peace process had put U.S.-Syrian relations on a better footing. However, Washington's 1993 blocking of Syrian weapons acquisitions and its failure to remove Syria from its terrorism list kept Damascus uneasy about U.S. intentions. Securing access to arms after the fall of the Soviet Union was a first priority and Syria sought alternative sources in China and North Korea. Syria also acquired some high-quality equipment at cut-rate prices from the Eastern bloc and Russia evidently forgave much of Syria's military debt and resumed some arms and spare parts shipments on a commercial basis, though reputedly deferring to Israeli demands it restrain advanced-weapons deliveries. Syria preserved its Iranian alliance, which also gave it a partner in the development of an arms industry. Finally, during the Gulf war Syria reestablished damaged relations with Western Europe, which became Syria's main trading partner and source of economic aid in the post-bipolar era.

Syria also faced an enhanced threat on its northern border with Turkey. Syrian-Turkish relations were strained over historic Syrian resentment of Turkish annexation of Iskanderun (Alexandretta) and Turkish accusations of Syrian support for "terrorism" by Kurdistan Workers Party (PKK) guerrillas against Turkey. Disputes over Syrian rights to a share of the Euphrates water, whose flow Turkey used as political leverage over Damascus, were acrimonious. With rapid population growth, urban sprawl, and continuing vulnerability to drought putting massive pressure on Syria's limited water resources, Turkey's effort to dictate the distribution of Euphrates water was a grave security threat. Turkey's growing military accord with Israel spelled Turkish-Israeli encirclement, which Asad tried to balance by closer ties with Egypt and by reinforcing his alliance with Iran. This was the classic "checkerboard" power balancing typical of realist geopolitics. It did not, however, spare Syria the Turkish threats that forced Asad to end support for the PKK in 1998.

Syria in the peace process. Asad's entry into the Madrid peace process marked, not an abandonment of Syria's goals, but their pursuit by other means. As Shimon Peres put it, Asad conducted the peace process "just as one conducts a military campaign—slowly, patiently, directed by strategic and tactical considerations."[35] Asad aimed to maximize territorial recovery and minimize the "normalization of relations" and security concessions Israel expected in return.

Asad, however, had to make key concessions in order to enter the peace negotiations, specifically, conceding separate face-to-face negotiations rather than the joint Arab negotiating team on which he had long insisted. This made it impossible for Syria to coordinate a bargaining position with Jordan and the PLO. When the PLO opted for the Oslo Accord, Syria forfeited any pretense of wielding the Palestine card in dealing with Israel; but it was also relieved of the responsibility to make its own recovery of the Golan contingent on the satisfaction of Palestinian rights. Thereafter, Syria negotiated for the Golan alone.

In these negotiations, Syrian diplomacy displayed a new flexibility. Israel's 1993 admission that the Golan was Syrian territory stimulated Syria to break the deadlock over whether Israeli commitment to withdrawal or Syrian acceptance of peace had to come first. Syrian negotiator Muwaffaq al-Allaf put forth a formula under which the more land Israel conceded the more peace it could have, and Israel responded that the depth of withdrawal would correspond to the scope of peace. Asad agreed that a settlement would result in the establishment of "normal relations." He also agreed to leapfrog a formal resolution of the core land-for-peace issue and negotiate the security arrangements on which agreement would have to be reached if Israel were to withdraw from the Golan. In these negotiations, Syria conceded asymmetrical demilitarized zones on the border with Israel. The negotiations stalled over an Israeli demand for a surveillance station on Mount Hermon, which Asad took as an affront to Syrian sovereignty, and with the 1996 Likud election victory, the opportunity for a settlement was missed. Its brief revival after the 1999 election of Ehud Barak foundered on conflicts over control of Golan water resources and Israel's insistence on adjusting the pre-1967 boundary around Lake Tiberias to its advantage. The positions of the two parties were, however, closer than ever before and an agreement remained perfectly possible in the future.[36]

Contrary to the claims of some pundits,[37] Syrian domestic politics was no insurmountable obstacle to reaching a political settlement with Israel as long as it could plausibly be presented as equitable. Syria's behavior in the negotiations was shaped by what Israel was willing to concede and what Asad believed the power balance would allow him to achieve, and very little by Syrian domestic politics. The Alawi security barons, confident of retaining their dominant position in the postpeace downsized army and security forces, did not overtly oppose a settlement, while the Syrian bourgeoisie, ambivalent about the consequences of a peace agreement for business, did not push for one. The economic consequences of peace neither attracted nor repelled the regime sufficiently to be a decisive factor in its policy. Syrian public opinion defined only the broad—but by no means unchangeable—boundaries of what Syria could accept. Crucially, it did not deter pursuit of the less-than-comprehensive settlement that appeared in the cards after Oslo: the separate Palestinian and Jordanian deals with Israel at Syria's expense convinced Syrians the government had to give priority to Syria's interest in recovery of the Golan. Asad lamented: "What can we do since the others have left us and gone forward?"[38] There was intense war-weariness among Syrians, a desire to divert resources from the military, and, especially among the bourgeoisie, a new perception of opportunities in economic relations with the West. But the sort of settlement that seemed possible—one that returned the Golan but failed to more than very partially satisfy Palestinian rights—would be no legitimacy windfall for the regime. Failure to reach a settlement, however, seemed no better an option and the sooner the conflict was resolved, the sooner Syria could concentrate on its domestic problems.

The smooth succession of Bashar al-Asad to the presidency in June 2000, with much of the incumbent elite united behind the new leader, put to rest fears his father's death would unleash a new era of instability.

Bashar was seen as a liberalizer in domestic affairs, which implied increased opening to the West. He quickly sought improved regional relations, notably with Jordan and Iraq. However, his foreign-policy advisers were members of the old guard and neither he nor they could afford to squander the legitimacy with which his father's insistence on an honorable peace had endowed the regime. As such, they could not easily make concessions to Israel that his father had refused. Continuity, more than change, therefore, seemed to be the order of the day.

Conclusion: Syria in the International System

The international system literally constituted the Syrian state. It is impossible to understand the durability of Syria's foreign-policy goals without appreciation of how Syria's Arab identity and domestic politics kept alive deep-seated irredentist protest at the mutilation of *bilad ash-sham* and the fragmentation of the Arab world under imperialism. The Ba'thist state was literally a product of Arab nationalist reaction to this, while the centrality of Arabism to the legitimacy of the state ensured its precepts would drive and constrain policymaking.

The 1967 war disaster was, however, a watershed in tempering Syria's irredentism and socializing it into the rules of the international system. The defeat was both a consequence of Syria's failure to conform to the realist survival rules of a state system and a precipitant of the major changes needed for its survival in this system. Severe threat levels and the high cost of ideological policies led to the rise of a realist leadership that defined more limited goals and pursued them within the constraints of the power balance. The new realist elite also undertook the state formation that gave it the autonomy at home and the military capability to implement a realist agenda. At the same time, state formation was itself dependent on the regime's ability to extract resources—arms and oil money—from the international system.

The end of the Cold War arguably marked another comparable deterioration in Syria's foreign-policy environment. Hafiz al-Asad only grudgingly adapted to this new era of globalization. Yet, in his attempt to reach a peace settlement with Israel, he began a process that, should it reach fruition, is likely to precipitate major changes in a state built to fight Israel. The ascension to power of his son, Bashar, a more liberal leader seemingly more at ease with the West, could mark a new beginning in Syria's international relations and domestic policy. But, no less than his father, Bashar will have to struggle to reconcile Syria's

Arab identity with the constraints imposed by a hostile international environment.

Notes

1. Alasdair Drysdale and Raymond Hinnebusch, *Syria and the Middle East Peace Process*, New York: Council on Foreign Relations Press, 1991, pp. 1–9.

2. A. L. Tibawi, *A Modern History of Syria*, London: Macmillan, 1969; Zeine N. Zeine, *The Struggle for Arab Independence*, Beirut: Khayats, 1960.

3. Raymond Hinnebusch, "Revisionist Dreams, Realist Strategies: The Foreign Policy of Syria," in Bahgat Korany and Ali E. Hillal Dessouki, eds., *The Foreign Policies of Arab States: The Challenge of Change*, Boulder, CO: Westview Press, 1991, p. 378.

4. Patrick Seale, *Asad: The Struggle for the Middle East*, Berkeley: University of California Press, 1988, pp. 349–350; Patrick Seale, "La Syrie et le processus de paix," *Politique Etrangere* 57, no. 4, winter 1992, pp. 788–789.

5. Drysdale and Hinnebusch, *Syria and the Middle East Peace Process*, pp. 1–3.

6. Patrick Seale, *The Struggle for Syria: A Study in Post-War Arab Politics, 1945–1958*, London: Oxford University Press and RIIA, 1965, pp. 37–63; Andrew Rathmell, *Secret War in the Middle East: The Covert Struggle for Syria, 1949–61*, London: I. B. Taurus, 1995, pp. 22–61.

7. Seale, *The Struggle for Syria*, pp. 5–15; Malik Mufti, *Sovereign Creations: Pan-Arabism and Political Order in Syria and Iraq*, Ithaca and London: Cornell University Press, 1995, pp. 43–59; Bruce Maddy-Weitzman, *The Crystallization of the Arab State System, 1945–1954*, Syracuse, NY: Syracuse University Press, 1993, pp. 15, 41–43.

8. Maddy-Weitzman, *The Crystallization of the Arab State System*, pp. 105–114, 143–174; Seale, *The Struggle for Syria*, pp. 73–117; Mufti, *Sovereign Creations*, pp. 49–54.

9. Seale, *The Struggle for Syria*, pp. 164–306; Mufti, *Sovereign Creations*, pp. 65–81.

10. Seale, *The Struggle for Syria*, pp. 307–326; Mufti, *Sovereign Creations*, pp. 82–98; Mustafa Kamil as-Sayyid, "The Rise and Fall of the United Arab Republic," in Michael Hudson, ed., *Middle East Dilemmas: The Politics and Economics of Arab Integration*, London and New York: I. B. Tauris, 1999, pp. 109–127.

11. Avraham Ben Tzur, "The Neo-Ba'th Party of Syria," *Journal of Contemporary History* 3, no. 3, 1968, pp. 161–181; Avner Yaniv, "Syria and Israel: The Politics of Escalation," in Moshe Ma'oz and Avner Yaniv, *Syria Under Assad*, London: Croom Helm, 1986, pp. 157–178; Eric Rouleau, "The Syrian Enigma: What Is the Ba'th?" *New Left Review*, no. 45, 1967, pp. 53–65.

12. Eberhard Kienle, *Ba'th Against Ba'th*. London: I. B. Taurus, 1990.

13. Malcolm Kerr, "Hafiz al-Asad and the Changing Patterns of Syrian Politics," *International Journal* 28, no. 4, 1975, pp. 689–707; Tabitha Petran, *Syria*, London: Benn, 1972, pp. 194–257.

14. Seale, *Asad,* p. 492; Moshe Ma'oz, "Syria Under Hafiz al-Asad: New Domestic and Foreign Policies," in *Jerusalem Papers on Peace Problems,* Jerusalem: Hebrew University of Jerusalem, pp. 5–29; Moshe Ma'oz, "Hafiz al-Asad: A Political Profile," *Jerusalem Quarterly* 8, summer, pp. 16–31; Mufti, *Sovereign Creations,* pp. 231–252.

15. Adeed Dawisha, "Syria's Intervention in Lebanon, 1975–1976," *Jerusalem Journal of International Relations* 3, nos. 2–3, 1978, pp. 245–264; Adeed Dawisha, *Syria and the Lebanese Crisis,* London: Macmillan, 1980; Edward Sheehan, "How Kissinger Did It: Step by Step in the Middle East," *Foreign Policy,* no. 22, spring 1976.

16. Seale, *Asad,* pp. 340–344.

17. Zeev Ma'oz, "The Evolution of Syrian Power, 1948–1984," in Moshe Ma'oz and Avner Yaniv, *Syria Under Assad,* London: Croom Helm, 1986, pp. 72–76; Aharon Levron, "Syria's Military Strength and Capability," *Middle East Review* 14, no. 3, spring 1987.

18. Yair Evron, *War and Intervention in Lebanon: The Syrian-Israeli Deterrence Dialogue,* Baltimore: Johns Hopkins University Press, 1987.

19. Patrick Clawson, *Unaffordable Ambitions: Syria's Military Buildup and Economic Crisis,* Washington, DC: Washington Institute for Near East Policy, 1989, pp. 10–11, 18.

20. Ibid., pp. 14–18.

21. David Waldner, "More Than Meets the Eye: Economic Influence on Contemporary Syrian Foreign Policy," *Middle East Insight* 11, no. 4, May–June 1995; Zuheir Diab, "Have Syria and Israel Opted for Peace?" *Middle East Policy* 3, no. 2, 1994, p. 87.

22. Charles Wakebridge, "The Syrian Side of the Hill," *Military Review* 56, February 1976, pp. 20–30; Moshe Ma'oz, *Asad, the Sphinx of Damascus: A Political Biography,* New York: Grove Weidenfeld, 1988, p. 90.

23. Seale, *Asad,* p. 494.

24. Ma'oz, "Hafiz al-Asad"; Seale, *Asad,* pp. 366–420.

25. Sheehan, "How Kissinger Did It."

26. Helena Cobban, *The Superpowers and the Syrian-Israeli Conflict,* New York: Praeger, The Washington Papers, no. 149, 1991, pp. 112–138; Drysdale and Hinnebusch, *Syria and the Middle East Peace Process,* pp. 149–174; Pedro Ramet, *The Soviet-Syrian Relationship Since 1955: A Troubled Alliance,* Boulder, CO: Westview Press, 1990.

27. Drysdale and Hinnebusch, *Syria and the Middle East Peace Process,* pp. 174–199; Ma'oz, *Asad, the Sphinx of Damascus,* pp. 135–148; Talcott Seeyle, "Syria and the Peace Process," *Middle East Policy* 2, no. 2, 1993, pp. 104–109.

28. Seale, *Asad,* pp. 185–225; Kerr, "Hafiz al-Asad."

29. Seale, *Asad,* pp. 226–266; Ma'oz, *Asad, the Sphinx of Damascus,* pp. 113–134; Sheehan, "How Kissinger Did It."

30. Seale, *Asad,* pp. 267–315, 344–349.

31. Raymond Hinnebusch, "Syrian Policy in Lebanon and the Palestinians," *Arab Studies Quarterly* 8, no. 1, winter 1986, pp. 1–20; Elie Chalala, "Syrian Policy in Lebanon: 1976–1984: Moderate Goals and Pragmatic Means," *Journal of Arab Affairs* 4, no. 1, spring 1985, pp. 67–87; Adeed Dawisha,

"Syria's Intervention in Lebanon, 1975–1976," *Jerusalem Journal of International Relations* 3, nos. 2–3, 1978, pp. 245–264; Adeed Dawisha, *Syria and the Lebanese Crisis,* London: Macmillan, 1980; Adeed Dawisha, "Syria in Lebanon: Asad's Vietnam?" *Foreign Policy,* no. 33, winter 1978–1979; Adeed Dawisha, "The Motives of Syrian Involvement in Lebanon," *Middle East Journal* 38, no. 2, 1984, pp. 228–234.

32. Yair Hirschfeld, "The Odd Couple: Baathist Syria and Khomeini's Iraq," in Moshe Ma'oz and Avner Yaniv, *Syria Under Assad,* London: Croom Helm, 1986, pp. 105–124; Elie Chalala, "Syria's Support of Iran in the Gulf War: The Role of Structural Change and the Emergence of a Relatively Strong State," *Journal of Arab Affairs* 7, no. 2, 1988, pp. 107–120; Christian Marschall, "Syria-Iran: A Strategic Alliance," *Orient* (Oplanden) 33, no. 2, 1992, pp. 433–445; Anoushiravan Ehteshami and Raymond Hinnebusch, *Syria and Iran: Middle Powers in a Penetrated Regional System,* London: Routledge, 1997, pp. 87–115; Seale, *Asad,* pp. 351–365, 368–420, 396–397.

33. Eberhard Kienle, "Syria, the Kuwait War and the New World Order," in Tareq Ismael and Jacqueline Ismael, eds., *The Gulf War and the New World Order,* Gainsville: University Press of Florida, 1994, pp. 384–385, 392–393; Zuheir Diab, "Have Syria and Israel Opted for Peace?" *Middle East Policy* 3, no. 2, pp. 82–83; Raymond Hinnebusch, "Syria's Role in the Gulf War Coalition," in A. Bennett, J. Lepgold, and D. Unger, eds., *Friends in Need: Burden Sharing in the Gulf War,* New York: St. Martin's Press, 1997, pp. 219–239; Neil Quilliam, *Syria and the New World Order,* Reading, England: Ithaca Press, 1999, pp. 155–174; Ehteshami and Hinnebusch, *Syria and Iran,* pp. 78–83; Ghayth Armanazi, "Syrian Foreign Policy at the Crossroads," in Youssef Choneri, ed., *State and Society in Syria and Lebanon,* Exeter: University of Exeter Press, 1993.

34. *Middle East Mirror,* 1 April 1992, p. 13.

35. *BBC Summary of World Broadcasts,* 3 August 1993.

36. Raymond Hinnebusch, "Does Syria Want Peace? Syrian Policy in the Syrian-Israeli Peace Negotiations," *Journal of Palestine Studies* 26, no. 1, 1996; Muhammed Muslih, "Dateline Damascus: Asad Is Ready," *Foreign Policy,* no. 96, fall 1994, pp. 145–163; James Moore, "Israel-Syria: So Close and Yet So Far," *Middle East Policy* 3, no. 3, 1994, pp. 60–82; Patrick Seale, "Asad's Regional Strategy and the Challenge from Netanyahu," *Journal of Palestine Studies* 26, no. 1, autumn 1996; Helena Cobban, *The Israeli-Syrian Peace Talks: 1991–96 and Beyond,* Washington, DC: U.S. Institute of Peace Press, 1999.

37. Daniel Pipes, *Syria Beyond the Peace Process,* Washington, DC: Washington Institute for Near East Policy, 1996.

38. *The Middle East,* September 1995, p. 8.

8

The Foreign Policy of Iraq

Charles Tripp

War has dominated Iraqi politics and policymaking for the past twenty years. It has been the result of Saddam Hussein's foreign policies and has also shaped the strategies designed to deal with its unexpected and unwelcome consequences. This catastrophic series of events, precipitated by a state that had hitherto been remarkably cautious in its foreign initiatives, has caused a number of theories to be advanced to explain Iraq's behavior. These have ranged from the personality of Saddam Hussein himself to the structural determinants of Iraqi history. There are epistemological problems at both ends of the spectrum. Nevertheless, it is clearly important to understand the degree to which Iraqi state policies during the past few decades have been shaped both by the constraints under which Iraqi leaders must operate and by the choices their own cognitive environment has presented to them.

As a way into this problem, the intention of this chapter is to problematize the state of Iraq as a unit of analysis and as an international actor. In this approach, the state will be viewed as a project always on its way to realization, stressing its emergence as an imaginative as well as a material construct. In the Iraqi case, the state has been and remains not simply an engine of power, but also a terrain of contestation. The competing narratives associated with this process have been visible in the political struggles that have in turn shaped Iraqi foreign-policy initiatives. By focusing on the multiple character of the Iraqi state it may be possible, therefore, to better understand the ways in which domestic politics have shaped Iraq's relations beyond its frontiers. In particular, the central importance of symbolic politics in the shaping of a state's strategies will be emphasized. However, it is also recognized that it is the interactions between these imaginative priorities with calculations about available resources and regional opportunities that produce the distinctive patterns of a state's foreign policy.

Foreign-Policy Determinants

As a state and a state actor, Iraq embodies competing narratives, some of which are dominant at any particular time, others having been subordinated or even incongruously incorporated into the mythical and material constructs of the ruling regime. It is these that influence the behavior of Iraq in its region and in the world beyond, often in contrasting and sometimes contradictory ways. As with many states of Asia and Africa, created by the empires of the European powers, there is an intimate relationship between these multiple aspects of the state as it presents itself to the world and as it interacts with its associated society. Questions of identity, hierarchy, status, and dependency are all aspects of the Iraqi state in both its guises (as international and domestic actor), and the resonance of each within the other has been a marked feature of the politics of all Iraqi governments.

This study of Iraqi foreign policy under Saddam Hussein will highlight a number of aspects of the Iraqi state that capture the contested and ongoing process not only of policy formation, but also of state definition. They are of particular relevance in understanding foreign policy, since they all bear heavily on the ways in which Iraqis have perceived and acted upon the world beyond their country's borders. In the first place, the genesis of the state of Iraq as a British imperial creation in 1920 has given rise to a distinct set of preoccupations that have affected Iraq's foreign policy in a number of ways, visible not only during the past thirty years but also at other moments of the state's history.

Identity and Domestic Politics

A key aspect of the Iraqi state as a controversial project still being realized is the unresolved question of Iraq's identity as a political community. With no history of prior statehood, Iraq was invented after World War I by Great Britain by combining the territories of three former Ottoman provinces. The new state contained a population of considerable ethnic and religious diversity: Sunni Arabs (20–22 percent) dominated Baghdad and the northwest of the country; Kurds (18–20 percent) were concentrated in the mountains of the northeast; meanwhile, the south was overwhelmingly populated by Shi'a Arabs who formed the majority of Iraq's inhabitants (55–60 percent).

Ever since its foundation, the question of whether Iraq is primarily a nation-state or an Arab state within the larger Arab nation has been fiercely contested. It has the capacity to rouse conflicting passions among different sections of the population, and any attempt to resolve it definitively one way or the other has generally presaged the downfall of the Iraqi government responsible. Although Sunni Arabs have been consistently more enamored of Pan-Arabism than any other group in Iraq, their hold on the power of the state has tended to reinforce their determination to guard it against any other claimants, Arab or not.

In addition, Kurdish rejection of any attempt to categorize the Iraqi state as an Arab state has led to armed rebellion and has also contributed to the downfall of successive Iraqi governments. The Ba'thist attempt to square this circle by declaring in 1970 that Iraq was a state of two nations—one Arab and one Kurdish—did little to resolve this question, as the repeated Kurdish rebellions of the last thirty years have demonstrated.[1] As far as Iraq's Shi'a majority is concerned, the response to Iraq's projection primarily as an Arab state has been mixed: on the one hand, a section of lay Shi'a embraced Pan-Arabism, believing that it would put them on an equal footing with their Sunni Arab compatriots; on the other hand, those Shi'a who remained closer to the spiritual leadership of the community mistrusted the Sunni undertones of Pan-Arabism and were repelled by a secular ideology that made a sharp separation between them and the majority of their cosectarians in Iran.

Yet the projection of an Iraqi state nationalism has been equally problematic. Quite apart from the tenuous hold that such an identity may have on the imaginations of the vast majority of Iraqis when contrasted to other, more congenial social identities, there has been a conspicuous absence of the equality that would give such a notion a chance of acceptance as an ordering principle in people's lives. Whether as Kurd or Shi'a, or indeed as a Sunni Arab outside the favored circles of the intimates of the regime, it has become clear that the often declared importance of Iraqi nationalism does not confer on all Iraqis equal rights. In such circumstances, the Iraqi nationalist identity of the state comes no closer to realization and becomes instead a possible area of contestation, pitting those who control the state as an apparatus of power against large numbers of their compatriots, who are often asking for no more than to be treated as equals in terms of rights and access to resources.

Geopolitics

Another consequence of the problematic genesis of Iraq as a state has been its existential insecurity, particularly over its territorial integrity. The defiant rhetoric of Iraqi governments often conceals a deeper fear that what the great powers created, they may one day decide to dismantle, indicating an awareness of the vulnerability of Iraq in a world not of its own making. Saddam Hussein's determined appropriation of the histories of Mesopotamian civilizations can be seen as a way of banishing his fear that Iraq, like many countries in the Middle East, is little more than lines drawn on a map that may be erased or altered at the whim of the great powers.[2] This has lent an added sharpness to border disputes with Iraq's neighbors, often made more bitter by the Iraqi belief that they have benefited at the expense of Iraq by colluding with the very powers that have given Iraq a conditional license to exist. Since the 1930s, this has crystallized around boundary disputes with Iran and Kuwait—disputes that found their most violent expression in the Iraqi invasions of those countries in 1980 and 1990, respectively.

Economics: Oil and Dependency

A final aspect of Iraq as a state is its aspiration to economic sovereignty, entitling it to control the resources within its territory and safeguard the interests deriving from the foundations of the Iraqi economy. That economy has been based on two major sectors, agriculture and oil, with the latter far outstripping the former in terms of revenues and importance by the early 1970s. With the increase in the importance of oil and the vast resources it unlocked for those who controlled the Iraqi state at the time, the Iraqi government's sense of vulnerability on this front increased proportionately.

Successive Iraqi governments' struggles with the British-dominated consortium of the Iraq Petroleum Company (IPC) have entered into Iraqi nationalist historiography. Portrayed as a fight against imperialism and an assertion of Iraq's sovereign control of its own resources, the eventual nationalization of the IPC in 1972 by the Ba'thist regime has been part of the present government's legitimation myth.[3] With the massive oil price rises of the 1970s and the associated rise in Iraq's revenues, it appeared that Iraq was indeed dictating the terms under which it engaged with the global economic system.[4] However, the 1980s and the 1990s were not so kind and increased the already sharply tuned sense of insecurity of the Iraqi government. With the imposition of economic sanctions in 1990 and the only partial lifting of the restrictions on the sale of Iraqi oil after 1996, the situation of Iraq as a sovereign economic actor changed dramatically.

Foreign Policymaking

In the context of foreign policymaking, a further aspect of the state must be discussed. Any state can be understood as a regime of power and in Iraq that regime has been marked by a structured inequality that has had notable consequences for the way power is organized, for the processes of decisionmaking, and for the attitudes of those in power toward the excluded majority. To some degree, the hierarchies of status and power and the culture that surrounds them reflect the fault lines of Iraqi society, where the "Other" is denoted by alien ethnic, sectarian, or tribal affiliation. But they also reflect the ways in which the resources at the disposal of those who command the state have been used to maintain important differentials. Systems of co-optation and repression have been established that make provisional even the access of those who imagined themselves safely within the circles of the privileged.[5]

The core of the regime of Saddam Hussein—and in some respects, although differently ordered, of most of the regimes that have dominated the history of the Iraqi state—has been a small circle of men, often related through family or clan bonds, whose trust in one another has been tested through forty years or more of conspiracy in and out of office. Their command of the security and intelligence services has been paralleled by their command of the economic resources of the state, giving them unmatched power to suppress dissent and to co-opt potential supporters. This has been the basis of the Dawlat al-Mukhabirat (secret service state) and the centrality of the Ahl al-Thiqa (the "trusted people" within it). It has sustained networks of neopatrimonial control that proved to be extraordinarily resilient during the last two decades of the twentieth century. Saddam Hussein has been the commanding presence at the center of this regime and has manipulated it with skill and ruthlessness. However, his strategies have been successful largely because of the complicity of significant numbers of Iraqis and because of the imaginative congeniality of such a system of governance, even to those who can only aspire to be included in its benefits.[6]

The significance of this aspect of the state for the shaping of foreign policy is twofold. In the first place, there is a sense in which all those beyond the "community of trust" at the heart of power are regarded as "foreigners." In this respect, "foreign policy" could be said to start at the boundaries of the presidential compound in Baghdad or outside those areas of Takrit associated with Saddam Hussein's clan. This is in part because the majority of Iraqis are seen in some sense as alien and possibly hostile, beyond the bounds of trust, although they may be susceptible to inducements and brought into alliances. It is also because many of them, as individuals or as members of suspect communities, are thought to be peculiarly amenable to the machinations of outside powers, whether regional or from beyond the region. Under this reading, therefore, they are always potentially ready to act as the instruments of foreign intervention in Iraqi affairs.[7]

The second significant aspect is the effect of this structure when it comes to understanding the world beyond the boundaries of Iraq, where different rules apply and the game cannot be so easily shaped to suit the wishes of those at the center of the state in Iraq. For those who dominate the heart of the regime, their direct experience of the outside world is limited and their impressions of it largely colored by the ruthless view of politics that has served them so well inside Iraq itself. In a world where all players are by definition alien, the Iraqi regime has formed an unsentimental and largely predatory view of its international environment. In such a context, force and fear, but also enticement and material inducement, have their parts to play. Potential predators can be bought off, as well as deterred and crushed. This reading has sometimes proved to be accurate enough as a basis for policy, but has also contributed to Iraq's major foreign-policy disasters of the past twenty years—most obviously in the decisions to go to war in 1980 and 1990, when Saddam Hussein and his closest advisers made such catastrophic miscalculations about the consequences.

The world views of those in power at any given moment will, of course, be a product of Iraqi history and of their particular part in it. This is no less the case for Saddam Hussein and his circle. His provincial origins, his relative ignorance of the outside world, his experience of Egypt during the heyday of Nasserism, as well as the prejudices he shows vis-à-vis other communities in Iraq—all these have played a part in his views of Iraq's international environment. In some respects, this means that the various strands are conflated. The determination to enhance the status of Iraq cannot easily be disentangled from Saddam Hussein's quest to promote his own status. The more successful his autocracy, the more he has identified his person with that of the state. Consequently, the search for the ever elusive grail of "Arab leadership" may spring less from some considered ideological position based upon

Arab-nationalist principles than from his conviction that it is in this arena that he and Iraq will be judged and must make their mark. This is the community of esteem that has meaning for him and those who do not share these goals put themselves beyond the pale, meriting in his view appropriate treatment.[8]

Such views carry great weight in a system where he is so all-powerful. Furthermore, they are reinforced by the fact that, with one or two notable exceptions, those closest to him in the hierarchy come from Saddam Hussein's own social milieu. Many of them, indeed, are members of the extended clan networks of his largely Takriti tribal grouping, the al-Bu Nasir.[9] These networks have helped to keep Saddam Hussein in power, but have proved to be peculiarly limited when offering advice on foreign policy. There seems rarely to have been an input of counterarguments, even when external developments were placing in jeopardy the whole enterprise. In their public utterances, Saddam Hussein's circle of intimates have never departed from the general views or tone adopted by their leader. This is not simply through prudence. There are strong grounds for believing that men such as Taha Yassin Ramadhan, Izzet Ibrahim al-Duri, Ali Hassan al-Majid, Abd al-Jabbar Shanshal, and Saddam Hussein's half-brothers see the world much as he does.

The only possible exception to this is Tariq Aziz, Saddam Hussein's long-serving principal foreign-policy adviser. However, he is an exception in part because he is an outsider. He comes from the Christian minority in Iraq and is therefore not politically threatening in any sense. However, as an outsider he has evidently been unable or unwilling to give advice that would go against the judgments of Saddam Hussein himself. As others have discovered to their cost, this is a risky business in the restricted circles of Iraqi elite politics. Beyond the narrow elite at the heart of power, there is a body of skillful and worldly Iraqi diplomats and advisers who are called upon to devise and explain Iraqi tactics. They have no significant input into foreign-policy strategy and suffer under the disability that the more cosmopolitan they appear, the more suspect they can seem to their political superiors. This makes them vulnerable to the political placemen and the various competing Iraqi intelligence agencies whose informants are so ubiquitous within the Iraqi foreign ministry and its establishments.

Thus, at the heart of power and of decisionmaking in Iraq lies the self-confirming myopia of a successful autocracy. Based on their manipulation of Iraqi politics, these men have tended to "read" foreign states as mirror images of Iraq, misleading as this has proved to be. By suppressing all those narratives of the Iraqi state that would otherwise trouble or challenge his hold on power, Saddam Hussein has restricted Iraq's foreign-policy options, subordinating all to the question of his political survival. It has served him well, but it has taken a terrible human toll on the Iraqi population, leading them into two disastrous wars the price of which they are continuing to pay.

Foreign-Policy Behavior

The multiple facets of the Iraqi state and the narratives that have competed for dominance within the arena of Iraqi politics have shaped Iraqi policies toward the region and toward the wider world. Filtered through the perilously restricted circles at the heart of the Iraqi regime, this has created some of the distinctive features of Iraqi foreign policy during the past three decades or so. The following section will examine the ways in which the major themes outlined above have contributed to this distinctive pattern. In particular, given the record of the past few decades and the present predicament of Iraq, the readiness of the Iraqi government to use military force as a major foreign-policy instrument will be examined.

State Identity

Nowhere has the fragmentary and contested nature of Iraq as a state been more marked than in the question of the identity of Iraq itself. Constructed in 1920 out of three provinces of the Ottoman Empire that had never shared a common history as a political community, the Iraqi state encompassed a large number of communities that looked with suspicion upon the others and often had greater affinities with peoples beyond the newly drawn borders of Iraq itself. This diverse social underpinning has not only contributed to the instabilities and insecurities of Iraqi domestic politics, but has also had a significant effect on the ordering of Iraq's foreign relations, especially insofar as the region surrounding Iraq is concerned. Historically, the sympathies of the various groups that make up the society of Iraq have tended to go in different directions as far as regional alliances and enmities are concerned. However, even where there would seem to be a "natural affinity" between a section of the Iraqi population and a neighboring state, there have been ambiguities and ambivalence, caused by forces pulling in different directions.

The championing of Pan-Arabism and broadly defined "Arab issues" is a case in point. Often associated with the ruling circles from the

minority Sunni Arab population that have dominated the Iraqi state
since its formation, the assertion of Iraq's Arab identity has tended historically to direct the Iraqi state's attention and energies in foreign policy toward the rest of the Arab world and, more particularly, toward
Syria, Jordan, Palestine, and Egypt. With the seizure of power by the
Ba'th Party in 1968, such a direction might have been automatically assumed. However, while it was certainly true that the Ba'thist regime
made much of its claim to champion distinctively Arab causes, the consequences of doing so brought problems. In the first place, there was the
challenge of the unification of Arab states, particularly when a fellow
Ba'thist regime was in power in Damascus. Yet the Iraqi state, as an apparatus of power, was not to be yielded easily to the control of others by
the small conspiratorial group that had seized it in the name of
Ba'thism, regardless of the Pan-Arab credentials of others. The brief
and dismal experience of the Ba'thist regime, which lasted for only ten
months in 1963, had convinced Hasan al-Bakr and Saddam Hussein that
any attempt to pursue Pan-Arabism as a mechanism for greater integration with other Arab states would be disastrous for their own hold on
power. On the contrary, they, like their predecessors in government, had
a real interest in preserving the state since it was the chief guarantor of
their privileges.[10]

The language of Pan-Arabism remains a key element in the self-
legitimation of the present regime, and the Arab world—broadly defined—remains the primary arena of Iraqi foreign policy. However,
despite the important symbolism of such an arena, the thrust of the policy itself is largely driven by the determination to ensure the dominance
of the Iraqi state or to ensure that the resources of the other Arab states
are made available to the rulers of Iraq. In this regard, Saddam Hussein's policies have taken two principal directions. One has been on the
Arab-Israeli question and the other has been centered on Iraq's relations
with the Gulf states.

As far as the former is concerned, it has been noticeable that despite
much rhetorical radicalism, Iraq's actions in this sphere have been
rather limited. Small, dissenting groups of Palestinians have been sponsored from time to time and, during the war for Kuwait, Iraq launched
some missiles against Israel in a largely symbolic show of defiance.
These actions bear out the impression that the Iraqi government's principal engagement with the Arab-Israeli conflict has been demonstrative.
It has been intended to emphasize the virtue of its own stated position
as a means either of showing up other Arab states or of proclaiming its
solidarity with them.[11]

Thus, the period prior to the Iran-Iraq war was characterized by the Iraqi government's gradual assertion of a leadership role for Iraq in the Arab world, exploiting the opening created by Egypt's ostracism in the wake of its 1979 treaty with Israel. Once it became clear that the war was going to be longer and more costly than Saddam Hussein had calculated, or than the resources of the Iraqi state could match, Pan-Arab solidarity was invoked principally to enlist the economic resources of the Arab Gulf states for Iraq's war effort—a war effort that was portrayed as fearlessly undertaken by the state of Iraq on behalf of the Arab world as a whole. Ever mindful of the potency of the touchstone of Pan-Arab obligations—the Arab-Israeli conflict—Saddam Hussein went to some lengths to argue that the war with Iran was an aspect of that conflict as well.[12]

However, Iraq's relations with the neighboring Arab states of the Gulf had always been uneasy, caused by the weight and dominance of the Iraqi state as a player in Gulf politics. Thus, the Gulf states were willing to support Iraq's war effort because of the critical nature of the situation after 1982, but they were not willing to include Iraq in the Gulf Cooperation Council. The Iraqi government resented its exclusion and when the war with Iran ended that resentment showed itself in an increasingly threatening form. The Arab Gulf states' insistence on Iraq's repayment of the massive sums owed to them by Iraq led Saddam Hussein to turn on them, accusing them not only of stabbing Iraq in the back, but also of betraying the Arabs as a whole.

In 1990, although it was an attack on a fellow Arab state, the invasion of Kuwait was represented by the Iraqi government as part of a legitimate Pan-Arab venture, rectifying a wrong that had been done not simply to the people and state of Iraq, but to the Arabs as a nation. This unlikely claim found an echo of sympathy among the disenfranchised and poor across the Arab world, but was dismissed by the majority of Arab states' governments.[13] The Iraqi assumption that its fellow Arab governments would endorse its action against Kuwait, or at the very least, would seek to resolve the crisis collectively as an "Arab issue," proved to be wholly mistaken as the events of 1990–1991 demonstrated.

Saddam Hussein has been equally contemptuous of the Arab states' reactions to the plight of Iraq during the years following the imposition of international economic sanctions in 1990. Having championed his own regime and having placed its interests above all else, it is ironic that he seemed surprised that Iraq is viewed less as an Arab state than as a "Saddamist" state. Certainly there has been unease and disquiet throughout the Arab world, both at popular and government levels, about the plight of the Iraqi people under sanctions. However, their expressions of sympathy have not amounted to decisive, concerted action to have the sanctions lifted—nor is it probable in the present configuration of world power that any such action could have a hope of succeeding. Nor has the Iraqi handling of relations with the major Arab states helped to build any effective consensus. On the contrary, as the Cairo foreign ministers' summit of January 1999 demonstrated, Saddam Hussein had succeeded in alienating even those governments that might otherwise have been sympathetic to the plight of Iraq.[14]

A further foreign-policy complication arising from the unsettled identity of Iraq has been due to the distinctive and troubling linkages between aspects of the fragmentation of Iraqi society and Iraq's regional environment. This has increased the insecurity of an already restrictive government, focusing their fears in particular on the cross-border alliances and loyalties that various sections of the population are assumed to have. Most obviously, the question of the role of the Kurds in the Iraqi state has long influenced Iraqi policies toward Turkey and Iran. Equally, currents among the Shi'i population of Iraq have had an impact on Iraqi relations with Iran, both before and, with renewed intensity, after the establishment of the Islamic Republic of Iran.

As far as the Kurds are concerned, when viewed from Baghdad, they have always constituted a potentially disaffected population that, although far from united, has presented many opportunities for outside powers to play mischievous roles in Iraq's affairs. Given the history of the Kurds' relations with the central government, this view has a good deal to support it. During the 1970s, when the government of Hasan al-Bakr and Saddam Hussein was feeling particularly beleaguered, the Kurdish rebellion led by Mustafa Barzani provided Iran, the United States, and even Israel with the opportunity to play a part in weakening the Iraqi government. Iran emerged with the territorial and prestige gains of the Algiers Treaty of 1975 and the United States had the satisfaction of seeing Iraq apparently accepting its subordinate place in the regional balance of power.[15] Meanwhile, the Kurds themselves paid the price of being used as an instrument in a game dominated by forces more powerful than they. This did little to reconcile their leadership to the status quo. Instead, they bided their time, waiting for the next opportunity when the particular configuration of regional forces would allow them to challenge their subordination to the central government in Baghdad.[16]

With the outbreak of the war between Iran and Iraq in 1980, the cycle was repeated and Kurdish forces rose in rebellion once more, actively assisted by Iran or simply profiting from the distraction and weakness of the central government forces. The situation was further complicated by the escalating violence of the Kurdish insurrection led by the Kurdistan Workers Party across the border in Turkey. By the mid-1980s, the Iraqi government had lost control of much of the Kurdish region, providing an opportunity for Turkey and Iran to actively intervene in the northeast of the country. For the Iraqi government, the prosecution of the war on the southern front was the most pressing immediate security question and the Kurdish issue could be deferred until the military situation allowed the government to act. When that happened, the Iraqi government was able to implement the devastating operation known as Al-Anfal to break the cycle once and for all, as they imagined, of the twin dangers of Kurdish insurrection and of foreign intervention. This involved not simply hunting down and executing the Kurdish *peshmerga* guerrillas, but also the annihilation of all villages in a thirty-kilometer-wide strip along the Iranian and Turkish frontiers, with corresponding loss of life and massive population transfers.[17]

Despite the devastation of Al-Anfal, the Kurdish uprising in the spring of 1991, following the Iraqi defeat in Kuwait, showed that the old cycle of Kurdish exploitation of Iraqi government weakness was still operating. However, the vigorous and ruthless central government retaliation and the flight of some 2 million Kurds fearing retribution impelled the allied coalition states to intervene. "Safe havens" were established initially and then the protection of the leading powers of the coalition was extended across most of the Kurdish region of Iraq. This has faced the Iraqi government with a form of Kurdish autonomy and of unparalleled direct foreign intervention. In some respects, of course, it is a direct, ongoing consequence of the Iraqi defeat in the war for Kuwait. The fact that the situation persists as it does is due to the unresolved "problem of Iraq" that still faces the UN Security Council and particularly, in its present form, the United States.

However, the situation in Kurdistan may also partly be seen as resulting from a new configuration of priorities in international relations following the end of the Cold War. Allied intervention on behalf of the Kurds in 1991 was due to a belief in London and Washington that the humanitarian disaster unfolding would tarnish their carefully cultivated images as victors in the Gulf war in the name of a "new world order." This led to the establishment of de facto autonomy for the major part of the Kurdish region under allied protection, giving concrete expression within Iraq to two intermittent preoccupations of the post–Cold War world: privileging human rights over concerns for state sovereignty and seeking actively to promote democracy, even at the expense of the power of sovereign governments. Given the changing priorities of the great powers that have posed as champions of these ideals, the divisions among the Kurdish parties, and the imperviousness of the central government in Iraq, these themes have not been effectively or single-mindedly pursued. However, the persistence of this situation during the past decade would suggest that any future government in Baghdad may find it difficult to reassert its control in this region, even when, in most other respects, it is able to exercise full sovereignty once again.

More generally, this also introduces the possibility that the ethnic and sectarian rifts that have marked the troubled history of Iraq may be providing a link with the emerging norms of the dominant international order, which are qualitatively different from those that have gone before. The realist concerns of the Iraqi government that Kurdish or Shi'a politics provide leverage for regional power-plays may be supplemented by the normative concerns of the international order regarding the rights of these people and the duty of the international community to intervene. In some respects, this could be a more threatening development for the regime of power that constitutes the state of Iraq than the cross-border linkages and subversive rebellions with which it is quite well equipped to deal.

State Territory

Cross-border links raise the equally important question of another legacy of the imperial European state system to Iraq—the symbolic weight and the material delineation of the territorial frontiers of the state. In both of Iraq's recent wars, territorial or boundary issues have been invoked: in the case of Iran it was the frontier in the Shatt al-Arab; in the case of Kuwait, an initial border question was conflated into the claim that the whole territory of Kuwait rightfully belonged to Iraq. Other issues were involved in these wars, but it is worth looking briefly at the question of territory, both because of the role that the safeguarding of territorial integrity must play in shaping the foreign policy of any state and because of the particular symbolic resonance it has had in the politics of Iraq.

In both cases, the Shatt al-Arab and the territory of Kuwait, Saddam Hussein invoked a number of powerful themes in the symbolic history of Iraq. Iraq was portrayed as a victim of the malign intentions of the great powers, aided and abetted by their local clients that harbored equally malign intentions toward Iraq. Thus, Iraq's abrogation in 1980 of the 1975 Algiers Treaty (settling the Iran-Iraq frontier in the Shatt al-Arab in Iran's favor—by comparison with the 1937 settlement) was portrayed as its rejection of an unjust frontier imposed on Iraq by the military might of Iran in the mid-1970s, backed by the hostile power of the United States.[18] In the case of Kuwait, the very existence of the state was attributed to the evil intentions of Great Britain, which had unjustly separated "this part and branch, Kuwait, [from] the whole, origin and source, Iraq" in order, allegedly, to restrict and control Iraqi access to the waters of the Gulf and to deprive Iraq of Kuwait's oil reserves.[19]

Saddam Hussein was appealing to a certain nationalist mythology concerning the "rightful" frontiers of the territorial state of Iraq. However, this does not explain why he chose to portray these territorial issues as reasons to go to war. More relevantly, in both 1980 and 1990 Saddam Hussein was facing crises of authority within Iraq, not primarily among the public at large, where the language of Iraq's territorial integrity might have had some appeal, but among those better placed in the regime and the armed forces to affect his prospects of political survival.

In 1979 Saddam Hussein had pushed aside his elderly relative Hasan al-Bakr and made himself president of Iraq. The accompanying purges in party and state indicated that he was aware of opposition to his rise to power. He also knew that he was personally vulnerable on the concessions made in the 1975 Algiers Treaty. In 1980, the redrawing of the frontier along the Shatt al-Arab, therefore, was to be the symbol both of Iraq's humbling of the new regime in Tehran and of Saddam Hussein's supreme leadership of Iraq, championing the territorial integrity and independence of the state of which he was now president.[20]

It can be argued that the territoriality of the Iraqi state did constitute an important issue in the decision to use war as an instrument of policy. The seizure of Iranian territory was expected to wring concessions from the Iranian government and these concessions were, in large part, to be expressed in territorial terms through adjustments to the Iran-Iraq border in the Shatt al-Arab. Territorial concessions were to be the token of Iran's submission and of Iraq's ascendancy and, with it, the leadership of Saddam Hussein. In this case, therefore, the material and the symbolic aspects of the state and of its power are deeply intertwined. One was not being used simply as a pretext for the other. On the contrary, the materiality of territory could have no meaning unless it were assigned one within the symbolic universe of those before whom Saddam Hussein was performing his role as head of state.

It can also be plausibly argued that similar considerations came into play in relation to the Iraqi invasion and annexation of Kuwait. The Iraqi claim to Kuwait had been a long-standing one, surfacing at moments when the government of Iraq tried to rally Iraqi nationalist sentiment and—as importantly—when it wanted to give expression to its resentment and rejection of a regional order dictated by outside powers that appeared to disadvantage Iraq. This was the case under King Ghazi in the 1930s and under Brigadier Abd al-Karim Qassim in the 1960s.[21] In some respects, this also applies to Saddam Hussein's revival of the claim in the 1990s. This does not mean that he was acting under a kind of myth-driven determinism. There was nothing inevitable about the assertion of the claim. However, when the claim was made it had a certain resonance among the Iraqis in general and a significant plausibility among the officers and officials who were expected to do Saddam Hussein's bidding.

Of course, the plausibility of the claim did not depend solely on its ideational appeal. Its assertion was intended to bring with it a number of significant material advantages, in particular the appropriation of Kuwait's oil wealth, or the pledging of an equivalent sum by those, especially the government of Saudi Arabia, who were initially intimidated by the invasion. The economic resources were meant to resolve the crisis of Iraq's near-bankruptcy in 1990, taking some of the pressure off Saddam Hussein as disillusionment set in following the trumpeted "victory" against Iran in 1988. Here the parallel with the invasion of Iran is marked. Saddam Hussein was evidently under pressure domestically from the very circles that posed the greatest danger to his position: the threat of invasion by Iran had been removed, but it was followed by the emerging discontent and loss of confidence in Saddam Hussein's leadership that had been developing in the officer corps in particular during the war.[22] He had to fear, therefore, that, as in 1980, there were people well placed in the circles of the regime who might be tempted by his ebbing authority to mount a challenge based on his proven incompetence on the economic front and on the continuing absence of any kind of satisfactory settlement with Iran.

The invasion and subsequent annexation of Kuwait were intended therefore as strategies to reinforce the authority of Saddam Hussein, as much as they were instrumental moves calculated to yield territorial and economic concessions. Material resources can be tokens of the assertion of symbolic claims, appropriate to the dominant discourses defining the state's power under Saddam Hussein. However, the elimination of a sovereign member of the United Nations was self-defeating. It may have made sense within the universe of the Iraqi regime, but it violated all international norms so comprehensively that it helped to cement a formidable international coalition against Iraq.

This would suggest, again, that when the center is beset by crisis Iraqi foreign policy and its government's calculations about the use of force are shaped by a set of beliefs and values that emanate from very local perceptions of advantage, opportunity, and threat. In the face of these, views informed by concerns more appropriate to steering Iraq as a state through the normative and regulatory framework set by the dominant powers of the international order carry less weight. Whether one impulse or another shapes Iraqi policies at any particular time depends upon which aspect of the state itself is to the fore, which narrative highlighted in the continuing effort to define the nature of the Iraqi state.

It was for this reason that, faced by military defeat, all claim to Kuwait could be so blithely renounced by Saddam Hussein. "The eternal union" was rapidly dissolved when it seemed that the center of power in Iraq itself was going to suffer directly and devastatingly as a result of Iraq's assertion of its claims. The recognition of Kuwaiti sovereignty that eventually followed in 1994 and Iraq's reluctant acceptance of the newly demarcated Iraq-Kuwait border was due to the calculation that Iraq's compliance with this norm of international behavior would be instrumental in ending the sanctions regime and rehabilitating Iraq into the international community. As it turned out, this was a vain hope, given the veto of any such possibility by the United States and its allies. Thus, territory and control over territory can be ceded when it suits or when something more important is at stake. However, there are moments when it becomes an important focus of state policymaking, precisely because of the implications it may have—at that moment—for those who lead the state.

State Autonomy and State Dependence

Violations of Iraq's territorial sovereignty have redoubled Iraqis' awareness of their country's vulnerability in a world dominated by great powers. This domination has been part of successive Iraqi governments' perceptions of the possibilities open to them. The development of the Axis challenge to British power in the Middle East during World War II encouraged one faction in Iraqi politics to seek a patron in Germany—with disastrous results.[23] The Cold War provided further opportunities for Iraqi governments to align themselves with one side or another and thus exercised a distinctive influence on the policies of Iraqi governments, insofar as regional alignments and arms supplies were concerned.[24] The government of Saddam Hussein played the game suggested by these rules with some skill during the 1970s.

Saddam Hussein saw the Cold War principally as a means of allowing Iraq to enhance its strategic value to both sides, while advancing

his own interests as the emerging dictator. Thus, the USSR was cultivated in the 1970s for a variety of reasons, domestic as well as regional.
In this event, the USSR proved to be something of a disappointment,
forcing Saddam Hussein to conclude the painful and humiliating Algiers
Treaty with Iran in 1975, rather than risk a war he knew Iraq could not
win.[25] However, the oil price rises of the 1970s allowed Iraq to escape
from the zero-sum game suggested by Cold War logic. With vast oil reserves and proportionately great revenues to spend, Iraq could cultivate
both East and West, becoming beholden to neither, but attractive to both.

Saddam Hussein also realized that, after the establishment of the
Islamic Republic in 1979, Iran too had escaped from the logic of the
Cold War, although for rather different reasons, given the slogan "Neither East nor West" used repeatedly by the revolutionary regime in
Tehran. It can plausibly be argued that this led him to believe in 1980
that it would be possible and profitable to launch a short, decisive war
against Iran. As was soon apparent, that war became something very different and much more dangerous than Saddam Hussein had originally
planned. However, the very scale of Iraq's plight after the tide of battle
turned in 1982 was exploited by him not simply to cement domestic support for his otherwise little-loved regime, but also to use the resources of
both the USSR and the United States and their allies to extricate Iraq
from the consequences of his 1980 decision to go to war. In large measure, Saddam Hussein was successful, at least insofar as the immediate
objective of thwarting Iran's military objectives was concerned.[26]

Iraq enlisted the United States and other allied forces to check
Iran's attempts to wage economic warfare in the waters of the Gulf
while the Iraqi air force continued its increasingly effective attacks on
the Iranian oil industry. In this, Iraq was greatly helped both by the sale
of French military aircraft, and generally by the ease with which it could
purchase military equipment from both Soviet and Western sources. It
was during this period that Iraqi foreign policy seemed to have been
marked by a determination to increase, rather than decrease, its dependence on outside powers. Saddam Hussein calculated that only by doing
so would he have access to the economic and military resources needed
to defeat Iran. He also had another, related purpose that this strategy
clearly facilitated: the building up of Iraq's nuclear, chemical, and biological warfare capacity, together with the missile delivery systems that
would make this so formidable an arsenal.[27]

During the 1980s, Iraqi war strategy and its foreign policy were
founded, therefore, on the apparently paradoxical principle of increasing dependence in the short term to achieve immediate objectives that

would enhance Iraq's independence in the longer term. While the war with Iran raged and Iran itself appeared inimical to both East and West, Iraq's strategy seemed to work. It acquired, developed, and used some of its nonconventional arsenal with apparent ease and impunity.[28] The strict controls on proliferation that had been, by and large, a feature of the Cold War were decaying—as was the logic of the Cold War itself during the late 1980s as the power of the USSR waned by comparison with that of the United States. This worked to Iraq's advantage at the time.

The war had, however, underlined Iraq's vulnerability in a number of areas, most notably in the key sector of oil production. First, Iraq's oil installations were open to physical destruction by the enemy. Second, its oil export routes were also vulnerable to hostile action, either in the waters of the Gulf, or in the trans-Syria pipeline. More insidious, however, was the steady decline in the price of oil during the 1980s. This devalued the oil that Iraq did succeed in exporting and greatly diminished the creditworthiness of the state.[29] Although the oil-price collapse was largely caused by the forces at work in the global economy that meant that the supply of oil far outstripped demand, the Iraqi government chose to see this as partly due to the greed and malice of its fellow OPEC members, especially its neighbors in the Gulf. The critical nature of this situation was brought home to Saddam Hussein at the end of the war against Iran.

It was then that the Iraqi leadership discovered to its dismay that it no longer had the kind of leverage it had enjoyed when its very existence was threatened and when some elements of great-power competition still persisted. On the contrary, during 1989–1990 the Iraqi government experienced with mounting panic the situation of debtor nations in a world dominated by unforgiving creditors. They were no longer impressed by a government that appeared steadfast and heroic, and saw it instead as brutal and incompetent. Meanwhile, the value of oil fell steadily while the interest on the Iraqi debt accumulated. The dependence of Iraq on the scant goodwill of others was underlined by the simultaneous threat to bar Iraq from further loans and to penalize the Iraqi state for its government's many human-rights abuses.[30] Having claimed to have won the war against Iran, Saddam Hussein now found everything, including his own position, placed in jeopardy.

Indeed, it could be said that the scale of the debt had already changed Iraq's position as a sovereign state during the 1980s. During those years, the Iraqi government scarcely had full control over its economy. The illusion of control existed because of the terms and size of the loans and the extent of Iraq's oil reserves, which acted as tempting collateral and also gave the Iraqi government the impression that this would always grant it great room for maneuver. The closing down in 1990 of a number of credit channels and the determination of some states—especially the oil-rich ones of the Gulf—to demand repayment of their loans created a crisis. However, the vulnerability of the Gulf states also suggested a solution. In 1990 Kuwait became the target of an attempt by Saddam Hussein to regain the sovereign powers of decision on economic matters that had been lost to an array of foreign banks, companies, and governments. He decided to seize the initiative, using the major resource—military might—over which Iraq still had autonomous control to create a crisis that would, he believed at the time, work to his advantage.

Saddam Hussein thought that Iraq's move would oblige the regional states and their external allies, particularly the United States, to find a solution not simply to the crisis of the invasion, but also to the pressures that had driven Iraq to make so radical a move. However, as in 1980, Saddam Hussein had grossly miscalculated, failing to predict the reactions of most of the parties directly affected. Faced by antagonism not only from the United States but also from the United Nations and the Arab League, the whole strategy unraveled, culminating in the defeat of the Iraqi forces and their flight from Kuwait in February 1991.

Adjustment to a post–Cold War world of unipolarity has proved to be difficult for Iraq. Occasionally during the crisis following the invasion of Kuwait, Saddam Hussein acted as if the old certainties of the Cold War still applied. However, if anything, the attitude of the USSR at the time and the few resources, diplomatic or otherwise, it was able or willing to expend on behalf of Iraq, graphically illustrated the collapse of the old order. During the long aftermath of the Kuwait war, with Iraq crippled by a punitive sanctions regime and by intrusive inspections of its military establishment, there were attempts by the Iraqi government to revive elements of the global competition between Washington and Moscow. However, the balance of power had altered so greatly that there never was much hope of Iraq using this to escape from the consequences of challenging the dominant global order. The subordination of Iraqi sovereignty to the desiderata of the U.S.-led Western alliance, and thus of the UN Security Council, currently leaves the Iraqi government with little room for maneuver.

What movement it could initiate was generally confined to provoking crises over the intrusive weapons inspections set up by the UN Security Council in 1991 under the auspices of UNSCOM.[31] The brinkmanship and the occasional military operation against Iraq that this strategy provoked had the twofold effect of causing rifts between the

United States and some of the other permanent members of the UN Security Council, and of leading many to question the effectiveness of such a form of inspection. As Saddam Hussein repeatedly made plain, the only solution to which Iraq was willing to agree was one that would restore full sovereignty over Iraq's economic resources and military establishment to the Iraqi government itself. However, as the previous decade has shown, this may be a policy goal of the Iraqi regime, but it has few instruments with which to achieve it. This gap, caused by the disparity between aspiration and achievement, has been a marked feature of Iraqi foreign policy—as it has of the foreign policies of large numbers of weak, Third World states.

Possibly hoping that cultivation of Russia, China, and France would cause a dramatic change in UN Security Council attitudes, Iraq paraded the real economic hardships of the population as a way of building up international pressure to have sanctions lifted without having to comply on the question of weapons of mass destruction. Given the advanced state of research and development within the country, Iraq would almost certainly be able to retain a nonconventional weapons capability, even if every last physical component of these programs had been handed over for inspection and destruction by UNSCOM. It seems, therefore, that the key consideration here has been the avoidance of the symbolic act of abject surrender, principally for reasons of the domestic authority of the regime and of Saddam Hussein himself. Yet the price paid by the Iraqi people and by the Iraqi state for this maintenance of a symbolic facade of defiance has been devastating.[32]

Much the same could be said of the reluctance of the Iraqi government to accept any of the early proposals made by the UN Security Council to alleviate the hardships of the Iraqi people caused by the economic sanctions. As early as 1991–1992, the United Nations had proposed that Iraq should be allowed to use a proportion of its earnings from a limited sale of oil to import goods that would meet the basic health and nutritional needs of the Iraqi people. This was rejected by Saddam Hussein on the grounds that the restrictions placed by the UN on the use of the funds, as well as on the distribution of imported goods, were unwarranted infringements of Iraqi sovereignty. Yet the material advantages, not simply for ordinary Iraqis but also for the regime itself, seemed self-evident.

Apparently more important for the Iraqi government, however, were two considerations, one instrumental and one symbolic. Instrumentally, Saddam Hussein calculated that Iraqi acceptance of such measures would tend to perpetuate the sanctions regime since it would undermine the growing humanitarian concerns that he hoped would lead to the sanctions' removal. There was also the fear that Iraq's agreement would be taken to represent its government's acquiescence in the punitive sanctions imposed upon it. This was thought to be as dangerous symbolically for the authority of Saddam Hussein as the implied loss of control of the funds, especially when a proportion of these funds was to be earmarked for the Kuwaiti victims of the Iraqi occupation and for the de facto, and unrecognized, autonomous Kurdish region in the north of Iraq.[33]

Yet a few years later, in 1996, the Iraqi government accepted UN Security Council Resolution 986, which allowed Iraq to sell $2 billion worth of oil every six months to import necessities for its population—and imposed conditions apparently as stringent as those Iraq had earlier rejected. Symbolically, the deal was as humiliating as those that had been offered previously. However, there had been some changes in Baghdad that seem to have altered Saddam Hussein's view of the merits of acceptance. Financially, the five years of sanctions, with the prospect of no end in sight, was taking its toll of the Iraqi economy as a whole and thus of the leadership's ability to deliver the kind of resources required to cement the adherence of those who had an expectation of being part of the favored network of clients on which it is based.

Equally important, in terms of the government's perception of the situation, the obstacles in the way of lifting sanctions seemed insuperable: the powers that Iraq had cultivated at the UN appeared unable to make headway against the intransigence of the United States and the United Kingdom, in particular; the dramatic revelations of Iraq's concealed weapons' programs caused by the defection of Saddam Hussein's son-in-law, Hussein Kamil, in 1995 had done nothing to persuade UNSCOM that Iraq had now yielded all its secrets. Rather the contrary. It may also have been realized that with such sums becoming available and with the scale of the distribution system it would entail, there were also greater chances of the government being able to turn the scheme to its own advantage.

It could be argued, therefore, that the expected material benefits, not simply for the small circle of the government but also for the expanding circles of those whose support or complicity guarantee the reproduction of the system of government itself, outweighed the symbolic humiliation of the loss of sovereignty. This could lead one to the conclusion that, in the last analysis, self-interest defined largely in economic terms plays the most important role in policy formation. Alternatively, and more plausibly, it could be argued that such considerations are always important, but not always equally so.

On a symbolic level, there may be moments in the history of the Iraqi state when considerations of sovereignty and the symbolic humiliation of accepting limitations on that sovereignty are uppermost in the minds of the decisionmakers, due partly to what is happening elsewhere in the world, but also to the mood or feeling within the Ahl al-Thiqa. Equally, it is possible to argue that the symbolism of formal state sovereignty, associated with the Western model and imagination of the sovereign state, is not necessarily the most important consideration at certain times. This is not because it is displaced by purely material considerations, but because of a rather different symbolic repertoire that engages the imaginations and loyalties of those at the heart of power, shaped by more meaningful ideas of status, differentiation, and the proper uses of power that come out of a local history, both ideational and material.

Conclusion

The purpose of arguing that the foreign policy of Iraq can best be understood by examining the state of Iraq itself, has been to draw attention to its multiple, unfinished, and contested nature. These aspects of the state both problematize it as an international actor and help to bring out the ongoing process of the interaction between the project being realized within Iraq's boundaries and developments in the international system of states. This chapter has focused on the period of Saddam Hussein's dominance of the Iraqi state not only because of its contemporary relevance, but also because the thirty years or so that have witnessed his imprint upon Iraqi state policy have brought out some of the key narratives associated with Iraqi foreign-policy formulation.

From a certain perspective, the peculiar situation of the Iraqi state in 2001, poised between ostracism and reintegration into the international system of states, can be argued to be a consequence of some of Saddam Hussein's foreign-policy decisions. Here, the aspect of the state as a regime of power, encapsulating a significant moment in the ideational and structural ordering of distinctively Iraqi politics under Saddam Hussein, helps to explain why certain decisions were taken—and especially why force was used with such detrimental effects not simply for the region, but also for Iraq and the Iraqis.

In this regard, although the role of Saddam Hussein is clearly central, it is by no means the only factor that must be taken into account to explain the distinctive patterns of Iraqi foreign policy under his direction. Rather, these emerge out of the processes of interaction between moral universes (norms, values, legitimacy) and material possibilities (oil, arms, economic structures) that have allowed a figure such as Saddam Hussein not only to rise to control the state, but to succeed in maintaining that control for nearly thirty years. As in any state, neither the moral nor the material aspects of Iraqi politics are wholly confined to Iraq itself. On the contrary, they have also been shaped by narratives developed beyond the borders of the state and beyond the control of any given Iraqi regime. Nevertheless, their interaction has helped to produce the distinctive field of Iraqi politics, and it is this that must be negotiated by those seeking to give reality to Iraq as a state actor.

These processes will continue beyond the demise of the present Iraqi regime, giving future governments of Iraq a set of possibilities, depending upon their origins and their relationship with the associated society of Iraqis. However, as always, these possibilities will not provide a free range of choices, open to the whim of whosoever rules Iraq, even if he or they rule the state in as autocratic a manner as Saddam Hussein. Like him, they will have to cope with the structural and imaginative legacies of the foregoing years of Iraqi state existence, favoring possibly contrasting, possibly very similar aspects of the Iraqi state's multiple nature. Again like him, they will have to deal from within these interwoven features of Iraqi politics with a regional and a global environment that is also in flux, with certain preoccupations and forces more in evidence than others. The future direction of Iraqi foreign policy will owe much, in terms of substance and form, not simply to the distinctive legacies of Saddam Hussein's Iraq, but also to the legacies of an Iraq that could produce Saddam Hussein's regime. In attempting to follow a particular path, any Iraqi government will also have to take into account the fact that the developments of the past twenty or so years have altered the boundaries of the kinds of relationship that the state of Iraq, however characterized, will be able to construct with its region and with the wider international community.

Notes

1. David McDowall, *A Modern History of the Kurds*, London: I. B. Tauris, 1996, pp. 327–340; Edmund Ghareeb, *The Kurdish Question in Iraq*, Syracuse: Syracuse University Press, 1981, pp. 87–103.

2. Saddam Husain, *Al-Mu'allafat al-Kamila*, vol. 15 (1986–1987). Baghdad: Dar al-Shu'un al-Thaqafiyya al-'Amma, 1987–1990, p. 295.

3. Edith Penrose and Ernest Penrose, *Iraq: International Relations and National Development*, London: Ernest Benn, 1978, pp. 381–420; *The 1968*

Revolution in Iraq—Experience and Prospects (Political report of the 8th Congress of the Arab Ba'th Socialist Party in Iraq, January 1974), London: Ithaca Press, 1979, pp. 49–60.

4. Iraq's oil revenues during the 1970s rose from $1.022 billion (1972) to $6.506 billion (1974) to $9.114 billion (1976) to $10.850 billion (1978) to $21.289 billion (1979) to $26.136 billion (1980). See Eliyahu Kanovsky, "Economic Implications for the Region and the World Oil Market," in Efraim Karsh, ed., *The Iran-Iraq War: Impact and Implications,* London: Macmillan, 1987, pp. 234–235.

5. See Charles Tripp, *A History of Iraq,* Cambridge: Cambridge University Press, 2000.

6. Samir Al-Khalil, *The Republic of Fear,* London: Hutchinson Radius, 1989, pp. 3–45, 73–109.

7. Husain, *Al-Mu'allafat al-Kamila,* vol. 5 (1979–1980), pp. 417–428; British Broadcasting Corporation—Summary of World Broadcasts—Middle East and Africa (BBC/SWB/ME), Iraqi News Agency (INA) dispatch of 9 April 1980, 11 April 1980, pp. A/1–2.

8. Husain, *Al-Mu'allafat al-Kamila,* vol. 18 (1988–1989), pp. 365–371; Ofra Bengio, *Saddam's Word—Political Discourse in Iraq,* New York and Oxford: Oxford University Press, 1998, pp. 79–82, 154–155; Charles Tripp, "Symbol and Strategy in the War for Kuwait," in Wolfgang F. Danspeckgruber and Charles Tripp, eds., *The Iraqi Aggression Against Kuwait*, Boulder, CO: Westview Press, 1996, pp. 23–29.

9. Amatzia Baram, *Building Towards Crisis: Saddam Husayn's Strategy for Survival,* Washington, DC: WINEP, 1998, pp. 7–36.

10. Hanna Batatu, *The Old Social Classes and the Revolutionary Movements of Iraq,* Princeton, NJ: Princeton University Press, 1978, pp. 1003–1026.

11. The Al-Aqsa *intifada* of 2000 mobilized Arab opinion in support of Palestine and provided an opportunity for the Iraqi government to proclaim its solidarity with a common "Arab cause," allowing Iraq to be invited to the Arab Summit meeting in Cairo in October 2000—the first time Iraq had been invited to attend such a summit since its occupation of Kuwait in 1990.

12. Husain, *Al-Mu'allafat al-Kamila,* vol. 6 (1980), pp. 278–282, and vol. 7 (1981), pp. 325–339; Saddam Husain's speech, reported by INA on 4 October 1981, BBC/SWB/ME, 6 October 1981, p. A-12.

13. Ann Mosely Lesch, "Contrasting Reactions to the Persian Gulf Crisis: Egypt, Syria, Jordan and the Palestinians," *Middle East Journal* 45, no. 1, 1991, pp. 30–50; Maha Azzam, "The Gulf Crisis: Perceptions in the Muslim World," *International Affairs* 67, no. 3, 1991, pp. 473–485.

14. This was a summit dominated by reactions to the U.S. and British military attack on Iraq in Operation Desert Fox of December 1998. Saddam Hussein called on the Arabs to rise up and overthrow their "charlatan" rulers, Iraqi satellite TV, 5 January 1999, BBC/SWB/ME, 7 January 1999 (MED 4-8); see also the comments by Iraqi minister of foreign affairs Sa'id al-Sahhaf, as reported by Iraqi radio, 13 January 1999, BBC/SWB/ME, 15 January 1999 (MED 3-4), and reports on the Arab foreign ministers' summit in Cairo on 24 January 1999, BBC/SWB/ME, 26 January 1999 (MED 1-3).

15. At Saddam Hussein's initiative, Iraq had signed this treaty with Iran as a means of ending Iranian support for the Kurdish rebellion, which collapsed as

soon as Iran sealed its frontier. The tangible price Iraq paid was to cede sovereignty to Iran in the Shatt al-Arab waterway, redrawing the frontier between the two states along the Thalweg (median line of the deepest channel). Less tangibly, there was the general acknowledgment of Iran's military and regional supremacy.

16. McDowall, *Modern History of the Kurds,* pp. 337–340; I. C. Vanly, "Le Kurdistan d'Irak," in Gérard Chaliand, ed., *Les Kurdes et le Kurdistan,* Paris: Francois Maspéro, 1978, pp. 272–302.

17. Human Rights Watch/Middle East, *Iraq's Crime of Genocide: The Anfal Campaign Against the Kurds,* New Haven, CT: Yale University Press, 1995.

18. Husain, *Al-Mu'allafat al-Kamila,* vol. 6 (1980), pp. 247–260.

19. Iraq's RCC statement, Republic of Iraq Radio, 8 August 1990, BBC/SWB/ME, 10 August 1990, pp. A/1–3.

20. Shahram Chubin and Charles Tripp, *Iran and Iraq at War,* London: I. B. Tauris, 1988, pp. 26–30.

21. Richard Schofield, *Kuwait and Iraq: Historical Claims and Territorial Disputes,* London: RIIA, 1991, pp. 74–110.

22. Charles Tripp, "The Iran-Iraq War and the Iraqi State," in Derek Hopwood, Habib Ishow, and Thomas Koszinowski, eds., *Iraq: Power and Society,* Reading, England: Ithaca Press, 1993, pp. 91–116.

23. The attempt by the government of Rashid Ali al-Kailani to enlist the support of the Axis powers in its defiance of Great Britain led to the British invasion and military occupation of Iraq in May 1941.

24. Charles Tripp, "Iraq," in Yezid Sayigh and Avi Shlaim, eds., *The Cold War and the Middle East,* Oxford: Oxford University Press, 1997, pp. 186–189, 194–196, 199–202.

25. Ibid., pp. 202–206; Marion Farouk-Sluglett and Peter Sluglett, *Iraq Since 1958,* London: I. B. Tauris, 1990, pp. 140–160.

26. See Martin S. Navias and E. R. Hooton, *Tanker Wars: The Assault on Merchant Shipping During the Iran-Iraq Crisis 1980–1988,* London: I. B. Tauris, 1996; also Thomas McNaugher, "Walking Tightropes in the Gulf," pp. 171–199, and Robert Litwak, "The Soviet Union and the Iran-Iraq War," pp. 200–214, both in Efraim Karsh, ed., *The Iran-Iraq War—Impact and Implications,* London: Macmillan, 1989.

27. See Tim Trevan, *Saddam's Secrets,* London: HarperCollins, 1999; Anthony Cordesman and Ahmad Hashim, *Iraq—Sanctions and Beyond,* Boulder, CO: Westview Press, 1997, pp. 290–343.

28. Anthony Cordesman, *The Iran-Iraq War and Western Security 1984–1987,* London: Jane's Publishing Co., 1987, pp. 19, 63–64; Dilip Hiro, *The Longest War,* London: Grafton Books, 1989, pp. 200–207.

29. Iraq's oil revenues fell from $26.1 billion (1980) to $6.9 billion (1986), rising to $11 billion (1988). Iraq's total oil revenue for the period 1980–1988 was $104.1 billion. By contrast, Iraq's military expenditure alone during the same period has been estimated at $177.6 billion—see Abbas Alnasrawi, *The Economy of Iraq,* Westport, CT: Greenwood Press, 1994, p. 93; Kamran Mofid, *The Economic Consequences of the Gulf War,* London: Routledge, 1990, pp. 120–142.

30. Lawrence Freedman and Efraim Karsh, *The Gulf Conflict 1990–1991,* London: Faber & Faber, 1993, pp. 19–41.

31. UNSCOM was the United Nations Special Commission established by the secretary-general of the United Nations following UN Security Council Resolution 687 (April 1991) to oversee and implement the destruction of Iraq's chemical, biological, and nuclear weapons capabilities, as well as its long-range missiles. It ceased operation in 1998 following Iraq's refusal to cooperate in the aftermath of Operation Desert Fox.

32. Sarah Graham-Brown, *Sanctioning Saddam: The Politics of Intervention in Iraq,* London: I. B. Tauris, 1999, pp. 179–190.

33. Ibid., pp. 70–83.

9

The Foreign Policy of Saudi Arabia

F. Gregory Gause III

S audi Arabia is an unconventional power. It is militarily weak compared to its regional neighbors. Its population, of which one-quarter are noncitizen foreign workers, is dwarfed by that of Egypt, Turkey, or Iran. In terms of citizen population, it is not even the largest state on the Arabian Peninsula, where Yemen rivals it in size. Yet it has the largest economy, in terms of total gross domestic product, in the Arab world, and is exceeded in the Middle East only by Turkey. It is the world's largest producer and largest exporter of oil, and sits atop one-quarter of the known oil reserves of the entire world. It is also home to the two holiest cities in Islam, Mecca and Medina, and therefore claims a special leadership role in the Muslim world.

The crosscurrents in Saudi foreign policy are best understood by keeping in mind the fundamental goals of Saudi foreign policy: to protect the country from foreign domination and/or invasion and to safeguard the domestic stability of the Al Saud regime.[1] Saudi foreign policy is one tool among many used to secure the ruling elite and build the Saudi state. But the pursuit of these goals is rarely direct and clear-cut, because Saudi foreign policy must operate on various levels simultaneously: (1) the international level, dominated by the Saudi strategic alliance with the United States and the Saudi role as an oil power; (2) the Middle East regional level, where Saudi Arabia plays a balancing game among larger and more powerful neighbors; and (3) the Arabian Peninsula level, where Saudi Arabia asserts a hegemonic role vis-à-vis Yemen and its smaller monarchical neighbors.

Policies that seem unambiguously beneficial for the Saudis at one level can present problems for them at other levels. Their alliance with the United States has been of great benefit militarily and economically, but has also exposed them to regional attack and domestic criticism.

Their leading role in the world oil market has brought wealth and international status, but also subjected them to intense regional and international pressures. Their self-conscious assertion that they are the "most Islamic" of the Muslim countries has been an important element of their domestic legitimation and regional stance, but has also opened them up to criticism from rival claimants to leadership in the Arab and Muslim worlds. It is the management of these contradictions that gives Saudi foreign policy its normally cautious character, as the Saudi leadership seeks to reconcile competing pressures. It is those instances where reconciliation is not possible, where the Saudis are forced to make unambiguous choices, that illuminate the guiding principles of Saudi foreign policy.

Foreign-Policy Determinants

The International System

Saudi Arabia is integrated into the world economic and strategic system largely through its role as a major world oil producer. In March 1999 Saudi Arabia produced 12.3 percent of the world's oil and was the largest producer and exporter of oil in the world.[2] As of 1998, it possessed 24.8 percent of the world's known oil reserves, more than double those of any other country.[3] It also has the world's most flexible oil-production profile, able to increase production by approximately 2 million barrels per day practically overnight. This allows it to act as "swing producer" with a unique ability to moderate oil prices. Oil revenues allow it to be a major importer of military hardware. Oil is the basis of the strategic relationship between Saudi Arabia and the United States, which has developed into a tightly woven web of economic, political, and military ties.

These close ties with the United States have led some analysts to depict Saudi Arabia's role in the international system as one of classical dependence.[4] In this view, Saudi Arabia has very little autonomy in terms of its foreign- and economic-policy choices. It is forced to follow the lead of the United States because its economic and political stability is dependent upon U.S. support and goodwill.

The record of Saudi foreign policy depicts a more complex picture. Saudi Arabia played a major role in the formation of OPEC in 1960; closed the U.S. airbase in Dhahran in 1961; embargoed oil shipments to the United States in 1973–1974; took control of ARAMCO (the

Arabian-American Oil Company, the consortium of U.S. oil companies that developed the Saudi oil industry) in the 1970s; played a leading role in efforts to manipulate the world oil market, at times to U.S. disadvantage, over the past three decades; refused to support the Camp David Accords in the late 1970s; and refused on a number of occasions after 1991 to allow the United States to use Saudi facilities for attacks on Iraq. In fact, within the context of their close relationship with the United States, the Saudis have retained a fair amount of autonomy.

Saudi Arabia's integration into the world economic and strategic system is better understood in terms of asymmetric interdependence, rather than dependence. The size of its oil reserves, the volume of its oil production, and its ability to alter levels of production all make Saudi Arabia a player, and not simply a playing field, in the world economy. Saudi Arabia has been able to use that leverage to further its foreign-policy goals of preserving the state's independence and the regime's stability.[5] Saudi Arabia's vast oil reserves drew U.S. oil companies to the kingdom; they in turn helped to develop the capacities of the nascent Saudi state in the 1940s and 1950s. Oil made Saudi Arabia a strategic asset for the United States, helping to guarantee the security of the kingdom against external threats. Saudi decisions that helped drive the price of oil up in the 1970s brought the regime untold wealth, which it used to consolidate the regime domestically.

The particularities of oil as a commodity increase the Saudi state's leverage, both domestically and internationally. Revenues from the sale of oil accrue directly to the government, not to private actors within the country. This revenue has given the state the dominant role in the economy, which the Saudi rulers have used to consolidate themselves domestically.[6] The direct control by the state over oil decisions, particularly since the 1970s when the Saudis developed the technical capacity to actually control the industry, gives the Saudi rulers more power in their dealings with other international actors. They do not need to negotiate with other domestic actors to make decisions on oil, and foreign actors cannot develop alliances with domestic Saudi actors in an effort to bypass the Saudi government on oil questions.

Because of its oil wealth, Saudi Arabia has been an attractive strategic partner for the United States. Washington helped build and supply the Saudi armed forces in their formative years, has been the major supplier of high-technology weaponry to Saudi Arabia since the oil wealth of the 1970s, and has provided an unofficial (there is no defense treaty between Saudi Arabia and the United States) guarantee of Saudi security against outside attack. In exchange, Saudi Arabia generally followed the U.S. line on diplomatic, political, and strategic issues at the global level in the Cold War, using its oil wealth to aid other pro-U.S. regimes in the Middle East and support anticommunist forces around the world (e.g., Afghanistan and Nicaragua). From the 1980s, and particularly after the Iraqi invasion of Kuwait in 1990, it opened its military facilities for use by U.S. naval and air forces. However, it has not completely followed the Washington line on regional issues, particularly on Arab-Israeli questions. As discussed below, the U.S. connection has at times conflicted with Saudi security interests at the regional level.

While oil is the primary avenue through which Saudi Arabia is integrated into the international economic and strategic system, Riyadh also plays an important role in another arena of the international system—the loosely affiliated group of Muslim states.

The Regional System

Saudi Arabia and the Middle East. In the larger Middle East region, Saudi Arabia is a militarily weak state that seeks to preserve its independence and autonomy by preventing the emergence of regional hegemons. Conversely, in the Arabian Peninsula, Saudi Arabia claims a hegemonic role, asserting the right to be the dominant foreign partner for Yemen and the smaller monarchical states that with it make up the Gulf Cooperation Council (GCC).[7]

Saudi foreign policy in the region is complicated by the importance in the Middle East of the transnational political identities of Arabism and Islam. Because of the mobilizational capability of political movements that spring from these identities, Saudi calculations of power and threat in the region are more complicated than classical balance-of-power theories would indicate. The Saudis have to react not just to shifts in military and economic strength within the region, but also to purely political threats that call into question their domestic legitimacy and security. Foreign leaders who claim the mantle of Arabism or Islam can appeal directly to Saudi citizens, over the heads of the Saudi regime, to pressure their rulers or rise up against them. Moreover, because of the importance of Arabist and Islamist feelings among the Saudi population, encouraged to some extent by the government itself, Riyadh risks domestic reactions if it is seen as deviating too far from the Arab-nationalist and/or Islamist consensus on issues concerning Israel and relations with the United States.

The threats posed by these transnational ideologies to Saudi security and regime stability have come from a variety of sources over time. From the 1920s through the early 1950s, it was the Hashemite monarchs of Iraq and (Trans)Jordan. The Hashemites had ruled in the Hijaz until their defeat by the Al Sa'ud in 1926 and maintained contacts with Hijazis for decades thereafter.[8] Arab unity plans proposed by the Hashemites were opposed by Saudi Arabia not just to balance Hashemite power regionally, but also to prevent the Hashemites from being able to threaten Saudi control domestically. The Saudis opposed the Arab unity movement of Gamal Abdul Nasser in the late 1950s and the 1960s for similar reasons. Nasser's successes not only increased Egyptian power in the conventional sense, but also appealed directly to Saudi citizens sympathetic to his brand of Arab nationalism.[9] The Iranian revolution of 1979 was not simply a regional challenge for Saudi Arabia, but also a domestic challenge, as Ayatollah Khomeini castigated monarchies in general as un-Islamic and the Shi'a minority in Saudi Arabia's oil-rich eastern province responded to his calls with protests and demonstrations.[10] Saddam Hussein raised both Arab-nationalist and Islamist banners during the second Gulf war of 1990–1991 to delegitimate the Saudi regime and encourage Saudi citizens to rebel against their government.

The dual nature of the threats the Saudis face—conventional power and ideological appeal—at times have complicated their foreign-policy choices. When faced with situations where conventional power measures would dictate one kind of balancing policy, and regime security considerations would dictate another, Riyadh has tended to balance against the potential source of domestic threat and support the more conventionally "powerful" but not obviously threatening actor in regional disputes.

Transnational Arabist and Islamist sentiments also limit Saudi freedom of maneuver, blocking foreign-policy moves that might seem natural from a purely balancing perspective. Israel would have been an ideal alliance partner for Saudi Arabia against Hashemite and Nasserist unity plans, against the Islamic revolution in Iran, and against Saddam Hussein. However, the Saudis have felt unable to have any kind of public relationship with Israel, because of the potential domestic and regional reactions. They even refused, in 1979, to support the Egyptian-Israeli peace treaty, despite pressure from the United States and their close relationship with Egyptian president Sadat. For the same reasons, until the Gulf war, Saudi Arabia attempted to avoid overt identification with U.S. military plans in the region, preferring to keep U.S. forces "over the horizon."

It would be a mistake to see transnational political identities in the Middle East as nothing but a threat to the Saudi regime. Riyadh has been able to use its status as a leader of the Muslim world to advance its foreign-policy goals. When confronting Nasserist Pan-Arabism in the 1960s, Saudi Arabia asserted that the organizing principle of regional politics should be Islam, not Arabism, trying to draw into the regional mix friendly non-Arab states like the shah's Iran and Turkey. It was a Saudi initiative that established the Islamic Conference Organization in 1969. The Saudis also maintained ties with Islamist opposition groups, such as the Egyptian Muslim Brotherhood, as a means of pressuring other Arab governments and extending their influence. Such transnational ties were hardly guarantees of support for Saudi positions, as many of these same Islamist groups condemned Saudi policy during the Gulf war of 1990–1991.[11] However, Riyadh has consistently sought out ties with Islamist political groups across the Arab and Muslim worlds, both for practical political influence and to affect the debate in the Muslim world over the meaning of Islam in political life.

Saudi Arabia and the Arabian Peninsula. While Saudi Arabia plays a complicated balancing role in the Middle East region as a whole, its behavior in the Arabian Peninsula is guided by a simple operating principle—deny any other power a position of substantial influence. To this end, Riyadh has endeavored to be the dominant foreign partner for the smaller monarchical states that border it to the east and southeast (Kuwait, Bahrain, Qatar, the United Arab Emirates, and Oman) and for Yemen. The Saudi leadership sees the rest of the peninsula as its natural sphere of influence. Were it not for the power of the British Empire in these coastal areas in the early decades of the twentieth century, many Saudis believe that they would be ruling over the entire peninsula today.

Saudi Arabia has been largely successfully in asserting its dominant role among the monarchies of the peninsula. Institutionally, that dominance is expressed in the GCC, formed in 1981. In the face of the security threats posed by the Iranian revolution and the Iran-Iraq war, the smaller monarchies accepted what many of them had for years resisted—formal acknowledgment of Riyadh's leadership role.[12] During periods of peace and relative stability in the Gulf, the smaller monarchies are more likely to attempt to assert their independence, but their overall place within the Saudi orbit is not questioned.

Yemen has been harder for the Saudis to bring to heel. The unification of Yemen, in 1990, created a rival to Saudi Arabia in terms of population.

Since the revolutions in North and South Yemen of the 1960s, Yemeni states have been republics, setting up an inevitable atmosphere of distrust in dealing with the Saudi monarchy. Both North and South Yemen sought foreign patrons to balance against Saudi influence.[13] After unification, Yemen maintained cordial relations with Iraq and refused to join the Saudi-brokered Arab coalition opposing the 1990 invasion of Kuwait. While the Saudis have maintained important avenues of influence in Yemen, in terms of financial aid to Yemeni governments and political ties to Yemeni tribes and personalities, they were unable to prevent unification in 1990 or to effectively support the secessionist efforts of former South Yemeni leaders in the brief 1994 Yemeni civil war. The Saudis now have a cordial if wary relationship with united Yemen.[14] The Saudi-Yemeni agreement of June 2000 to define and demarcate their contested border, if it holds, will eliminate a major bone of contention in the relationship.

State Formation and Domestic Politics

The modern state of Saudi Arabia was built by conquest. It consists of four geographical areas that had rarely, since the time of the Prophet Muhammad, been united under one rule. The patrimony of the Al Saud family was Najd, central Arabia, the heartland of the Saudi empires built in the eighteenth and nineteenth centuries by earlier generations of the family. At the turn of the twentieth century, the founder of the modern kingdom, Abd al-Aziz ibn Abd al-Rahman Al Saud, known in the West as Ibn Saud, began to reassert his family's control of Najd, completing its consolidation after World War I. Earlier, in 1913, he had expanded his realm to the east by taking al-Ahsa, now the Eastern Province. Al-Ahsa gave Abd al-Aziz access to the Persian/Arabian Gulf and, in later years, an even more important economic boon. The area is the heart of the Saudi oil industry, the richest oil patch in the world. But with these economic benefits came a new complication for his rule. There is a significant Shi'i Muslim minority in al-Ahsa, which now comprises between 5 percent and 10 percent of the total Saudi citizen population.

In 1926, Abd al-Aziz completed the conquest of the Hijaz, the western coast of Arabia bordering the Red Sea, then under the control of the Hashemite dynasty. Bringing the Hijaz under his control contributed enormously to Abd al-Aziz's prestige, as he became the protector of the holy cities of Mecca and Medina, and to his meager treasury, as he could collect the tax levied on pilgrims. He rounded off his territorial expansion in 1932 with the acquisition of Asir, the mountainous area in the southwest corner of the kingdom, in a short war with the imam of Yemen.[15]

The four geographical areas of the Saudi state retain strong senses of regional identity. The potentially fractious nature of this new political construct made the Saudis particularly worried about regional powers meddling in their domestic affairs, be it Hashemite Jordan or Iraq in Hijaz, Yemen in Asir, Iran with their fellow Shi'a in al-Ahsa, or Nasser's Egypt with restive Arab nationalists throughout the kingdom. It also made them acutely aware of the need to balance the influence of the great powers interested in Arabia, whether it be a relationship with Great Britain to balance the Ottomans at the beginning of the century or a relationship with the United States to balance Britain at mid-century.

Creating and maintaining the new state required political and financial resources beyond those readily available to Abd al-Aziz. He needed to forge a political movement to support him. He found it by drawing on the long historical association between the Al Saud and the puritanical, reformist Islamist strain known in the West as "Wahhabism." In the eighteenth century, one of Abd al-Aziz's forebears, the ruler of a small Najdi oasis town, had struck an alliance with Muhammad ibn Abd al-Wahhab, a zealous Arabian preacher who sought to purge Islam of modern accretions and return to the pristine faith of the prophet's time. The Wahhabi message allowed the Al Saud to mobilize support outside of their immediate environs, and build a major Arabian empire. Abd al-Aziz revived the Wahhabi movement, gaining tribal support across Najd and greatly expanding the size of his armed forces. Wahhabi clerics acted as judges and administrators in his newly conquered territories. Spreading the *da'wa* (call to proselytization) of Muhammad ibn Abd al-Wahhab provided the ideological justification for the expansion of Saudi rule.[16] Even today, the Wahhabi religious establishment is an important constituency of and support for the Saudi regime, controlling large parts of the religious, judicial, and educational bureaucracies in the kingdom.[17]

Wahhabism was a mixed blessing, however, for Saudi state builders. As an ideology, it was not particularly appealing for many of Abd al-Aziz's new subjects. It was anathema to the Shi'a of al-Ahsa, because Muhammad ibn Abd al-Wahhab considered Shi'a little better than unbelievers. Many Hijazis, accustomed to more liberal social mores, chafed under the puritanism of the Wahhabi interpretation of Islam. The Wahhabis themselves created problems. In 1929, Abd al-Aziz had to mobilize loyal forces from the Najdi towns and tribes to defeat rebellious Wahhabis who wanted to attack British-protected Iraq and Transjordan. Since the Gulf war, Islamic groups have formed the most serious and organized element of domestic political opposition to the Saudi regime. The four Saudi citizens executed for blowing up a U.S. military training mission office in Riyadh in November 1995 were, in their ideological motivations, the direct successors of these earlier rebels.[18]

Money was another problem as Abd al-Aziz sought to knit together his disparate realms into a unified and pacified state. The distribution of benefits, through patron-client ties, was a major element in his strategy for keeping his realm together, but his needs always seemed to exceed his assets. In 1933 Abd al-Aziz granted the California Standard Oil Company (now Chevron) a concession to explore for and produce oil, in exchange for an immediate cash payment in gold and royalties on future production. The deciding factor in choosing California Standard over other oil companies seems to have been its willingness to provide money up front to the cash-strapped monarch.[19] California Standard later brought in the Texas Oil Company (Texaco), and then Standard Oil of New Jersey (Exxon) and Socony-Vacuum (Mobil), to develop and market Saudi oil, forming the Arabian-American Oil Company (ARAMCO).[20]

ARAMCO became the vehicle through which the nascent Saudi government funded its operations. It also provided a number of other services to the Saudi regime over the decades, building roads and a railroad, providing the first modern educational facility in the Eastern Province, serving as lender of last (and frequently first) resort, and acting as the international legal adviser to the government.[21] The increasing U.S. economic stake in the kingdom eventually led the U.S. government to take a more active interest in events in Saudi Arabia. During World War II, with pilgrimage traffic essentially halted and oil development suspended, U.S. Lend-Lease funds helped to maintain Abd al-Aziz's treasury.[22]

With the development of steady oil income in the 1950s, and the huge jump in that income in the 1970s, the Al Saud were able to build the administrative structure of a modern state—centralized military, police, judicial, health, and educational bureaucracies—and to provide their citizens with an increasing array of benefits. Oil money came to supplement, and then to supplant, Wahhabism as the glue that keeps the Saudi realm together. While regional particularities and identities persist in Saudi Arabia, and integrating the Shi'a minority into national politics remains an unfinished task, it is interesting to note that the most serious opposition in the 1990s to the Saudi regime was not based on regional identity. To a great extent, the Saudi state-building project that oil revenue made possible has eliminated regionalism as a threat to the integrity and security of the kingdom.

Oil money allowed the Saudi state to develop a particular relationship with its society. For decades, the basis of state-society relations has been the provision of goods and services by the state to society, with little but political loyalty expected in return. The consequences for politics of the rentier character of the Saudi state are much debated.[23] For Saudi foreign policy, two important consequences emerge. First, Saudi oil policy has to provide the government with the money necessary to support the system of social services, government employment, and security spending that undergirds the regime. Oil still accounts for approximately 90 percent of the kingdom's yearly export earnings and 75 percent of its government revenue.[24] As oil prices have declined from their historic peaks in the early 1980s, and as the Saudi population has grown, the government's fiscal situation has become more precarious. Saudi oil policy has thus regained the central role it held in the 1930s and 1940s for regime security as the vital source of revenue for the government.

The second important consequence of Saudi Arabia's rentier bargain relates to security. Citizens have come to expect the government to defend the state without requiring military service of them. Saudi Arabia is the only major Middle Eastern country that does not require military service of its young men. Experience with several attempted Arab-nationalist military coups in the 1960s undermined the regime's confidence in the likely political reliability of a large military. Residual suspicions of Hijazis and Shi'ites add to the regime's reluctance to expand the size of the Saudi military. While its defense budget dwarfs those of its neighbors, the total Saudi armed forces number fewer than 200,000, much lower than other regional states with similar or smaller populations.[25]

Two characteristics of Saudi foreign policy flow from this unwillingness to mobilize the Saudi citizenry for military purposes. First, the Saudi reliance on security ties with the United States is heightened. Second, the Saudis are less able to assert themselves in the regional politics of the Middle East. Much of the Saudi "caution" and balancing proclivities discussed earlier can be traced to Saudi Arabia's military weakness compared with its neighbors.

Foreign-Policy Role

If the rhetoric of Saudi leaders is taken at face value, we would have to conclude that Islam defines the role of Saudi Arabia in the world. As host of the annual Muslim pilgrimage to Mecca, Saudi Arabia receives (in recent years) approximately 1 million pilgrims from across the Muslim world every year. The organization of the *hajj* by itself imbeds the kingdom in an important and practical web of relations with other Muslim countries.[26] Mirroring the central role that Islam plays in the Saudi regime's domestic legitimation formula, Riyadh has also asserted for itself a leading political role among Muslim states. Saudi Arabia played the major role in the formation of the Organization of the Islamic Conference, the international organization of the world's Muslim countries, and contributes the largest share to its budget. It is headquarters for, and the major financier of, Islamic nongovernmental organizations such as the Muslim World League and the World League of Muslim Youth. The Saudi government has used its oil wealth to support Muslim charities and causes across the world, from mosque building in the Philippines to, at various times, Islamic political groups across the Arab and Muslim worlds.[27]

That leadership role in the Muslim world, as interpreted by the Saudis, requires very little in the way of actual leadership, however. The Muslim countries as a group are too geographically dispersed and politically disparate to have a common political agenda, and Saudi Arabia has been able by and large to define for itself just what an "Islamic" foreign policy is.[28] Saudi Arabia's conception of its Islamic leadership role is perfectly compatible with its strong ties to the United States, something that more radical Muslim thinkers would see as completely incompatible. Their leadership role does not challenge the existing international status quo, seeking only better treatment for individual Muslims and for Muslim states within that status quo.[29]

This is not to argue that the Saudis' conception of their role in the Muslim world is unimportant in their foreign policy. As discussed above, it has been both a tool used by Riyadh and a constraint on its behavior, particularly in dealing with Israel and the United States. It complicates their relations with Iran, which since the Islamic revolution of 1979 has challenged the Saudis' right to define the proper relationship between Islam and politics at the international level. It can open up the regime to criticism domestically, as was the case during and immediately after the Gulf war, from groups that see Saudi foreign policy as deviating from Islamic standards.[30] But the Saudi leadership's conception of their role as a leader of the Muslim world has never created significant tension with the basic goals of Saudi foreign policy: state independence and regime security.

Saudi role conception in other arenas does not involve assertions of leadership. The Saudis naturally see themselves as part of the larger Arab world, but view Arab unity as solidarity and cooperation among the existing Arab states. Similarly, in the oil field, the Saudis have generally been reluctant to assert a leadership role in OPEC, even though they are the organization's largest oil producer. They are willing to work outside the OPEC framework to achieve their ends in the world oil market, as Saudi negotiations with other major producers, both in and out of OPEC, in the late 1990s indicate.[31] But they always bring agreements made outside of OPEC to the formal OPEC forum for approval. The leadership they assert in the oil area remains, with some exceptions, that of quiet consensus building and deal making, not that of risky public stands and open confrontations.

Foreign Policymaking

The key decisionmaking body on foreign policy in Saudi Arabia is that group of senior members of the Al Saud family who, by reason of their official position or their standing within the family, decide all major issues of policy. When there is a strong king, as in the days of Abd al-Aziz or Faysal (1964–1975), decisionmaking on foreign policy is concentrated in his hands. When the king is not a forceful personality, the decisionmaking circle widens. People outside the ruling family play important roles as advisers, but the key decisions are made within the Al Saud.[32] For example, in the meeting in August 1990 when the Saudi decision to invite U.S. forces to the kingdom was made (or, at least, announced to the United States), there were approximately eight Saudis in the room, of whom at least five (and probably more) were members of the ruling family.[33]

The dominance of the ruling family in foreign policy means that the decisionmaking process will not follow neatly constructed rational-bureaucratic lines. It is generally believed, for example, that major princes have particular responsibilities for relations with specific countries—Crown Prince Abdallah with Syria, Prince Sultan with Yemen. There is a fluidity to the decisionmaking process that depends more upon the dynamics of intrafamily politics than upon neatly defined bureaucratic lines of responsibility.

This intertwining of foreign policy and ruling-family relationships means that disputes and differences in one area will inevitably spill over into the other. The clearest example was the struggle for power between then King Saud and then Crown Prince Faysal in the late 1950s and early 1960s. During the struggle, Saudi policy toward the Nasserist Pan-Arab challenge oscillated between confrontation and appeasement, as the contenders sought to use foreign-policy issues against one another. It was not until Faysal became king in 1964 that a consistent line was reestablished.[34] No such serious a split has occurred, at least publicly, in the ruling family recently. If such splits do reappear, they are sure to affect the content and conduct of Saudi foreign policy.

Observers of the kingdom debate the importance of the religious establishment in policymaking, some contending that it has an effective veto and others arguing that its power is greatly attenuated from earlier days.[35] In the field of foreign policy, the latter interpretation seems closer to the truth. The Saudi regime looks to the religious leaders to validate and approve important decisions in the area of foreign policy. King Fahd, for example, sought *fatwas* from Shaykh Abd al-Aziz bin Baz, the senior Muslim cleric in the kingdom, to justify both his invitation of U.S. forces to the kingdom and the initiation of hostilities against Iraq.[36] It does not appear that the king asked the men of religion for their permission before acting. There is also no case in recorded Saudi history where a foreign-policy decision or initiative was rescinded or dropped because of publicly expressed disapproval by the *ulama*.

If the religious establishment influences, but does not have a decisive voice in, foreign policy, the same might be said for the Saudi Consultative Council. Established in 1992, the council is an appointed body commissioned with the task of advising the government on issues of the day.[37] The council has a foreign-affairs committee, and Foreign Minister Saud al-Faysal has appeared before it to set out the general lines of the kingdom's foreign policy.[38] As of yet, it is not clear that the council has had much influence on specific foreign-policy decisions, but its role could grow if the institution as a whole begins to play a larger role in Saudi politics.

In terms of foreign-policy implementation, the tools at the disposal of Saudi leaders to get their way in the world are much more limited than they were in the 1970s and 1980s. The Saudis had in the 1970s and 1980s huge sums of money with which to achieve their foreign-policy aims. At the same time, the Saudis had a great deal of discretion in their oil policy—to raise or lower production as they saw fit to influence prices—because they could weather temporary decreases in their oil revenue much more easily than other states. Now, the Saudis no longer have the financial cushion to fund a major foreign-policy/military initiative like Desert Storm. Foreign aid money is much more limited. The Saudis also have less freedom to maneuver on oil policy because of their immediate revenue needs. They cannot afford to push prices down for a sustained period (as they did in late 1985–1986), in an effort to discipline other producers and reassert their market dominance. Nor can they afford to sacrifice market share to try to sustain price (as they did from 1982 until early 1985).[39]

In terms of the personnel actually implementing Saudi foreign policy, an enormous change took place during the twentieth century. In the early decades of the Saudi state, Saudi diplomats and foreign-policy advisers were routinely recruited from other Arab countries. With the development of the Saudi educational system, the kingdom's foreign service has been completely "Saudi-ized," and is generally acknowledged as a very competent and professional group of diplomats playing an increasing role in international organizations and on the world stage.

Foreign-Policy Behavior

The continuities in Saudi foreign policy have been highlighted throughout this chapter: strong ties with the United States, a sophisticated balancing strategy in Middle East regional politics, an overriding concern with regime security, and state independence/autonomy as the goals of foreign policy. During "normal" periods, these continuities are not in conflict. The Saudis can maintain their Washington connection, balance in the region, and use both foreign and oil policy to help sustain the regime domestically. But at certain crucial historical junctures, these goals have come into conflict. Reviewing these episodes will illuminate how the Saudis reconcile contradictions in their foreign policy.

In dealing with Egyptian president Gamal Abdul Nasser in the late 1950s and early 1960s, the Saudis faced just such a conflict. Nasser's popularity in the Arab world, including within Saudi Arabia, made it risky for Riyadh to actively oppose him. However, his growing power in the region, particularly after the 1958 Egyptian-Syrian union, and his increasingly anti-U.S. stance made him threatening to the Saudi rulers. After supporting a disastrous, publicly exposed attempt to assassinate Nasser in 1957, the Saudis attempted to appease him, going so far as to refuse to renew the U.S. lease on Dhahran airfield in 1961.[40] When Egyptian forces landed in North Yemen in 1962 and Nasser began to aim his propaganda and subversive efforts against the Al Saud regime, Riyadh abandoned appeasement. The Saudis aided the royalist forces in the Yemeni civil war, renewed military cooperation with the United States and Great Britain, opposed Nasser diplomatically in the Arab world, and cracked down on Arab-nationalist activity domestically.

Riyadh reacted much differently to the emergence of a strong Arab axis between Egypt and Syria in the early 1970s. When these two states went to war with Israel in 1973, King Faysal put at risk his close ties with the United States to support them, declaring an embargo on Saudi oil shipments to the United States and cuts in Saudi oil production. The difference in this case is that the new leaders of Egypt and Syria, Anwar Sadat and Hafiz al-Asad, abandoned the anti-Saudi rhetoric and policies of their predecessors. Maintaining this shift in inter-Arab politics, which greatly strengthened the domestic stability of the Saudi regime, was seen by Riyadh as worth risking a confrontation with the United States. Quickly after the 1973 Arab-Israeli war, the Saudis restored their close ties with the United States.

The Egyptian-Israeli peace treaty and the Iranian revolution, occurring almost contemporaneously in 1979, presented the Saudis with another hard choice.[41] The United States, which had proved powerless to help the shah of Iran against his domestic opponents, pushed Riyadh to support Egypt and the new treaty. Iraq and Syria, leading a solid Arab bloc, urged the Saudis to join them in cutting ties to Egypt and opposing the treaty. Meanwhile, the Iranian revolution had stirred up Islamic political activity throughout the region, including in Saudi Arabia itself. The Saudi leadership, split internally, eventually decided that the risk of Arab and Islamic criticism, both regionally and domestically, was too great to support the treaty. Riyadh cut ties with Egypt, its strongest regional ally, and rebuffed the United States, its superpower patron.

Relations with the United States got back on track when the Saudis were faced with a new strategic challenge, the Iran-Iraq war of 1980. The Saudis then confronted a difficult choice in regional politics. They opted, however reluctantly, to back an increasingly powerful Iraq at the outset of that war because of the open calls from revolutionary Iran for Saudi Muslims to make their own revolution against the Al Saud. In 1990, the combined military and ideological threat posed by Saddam Hussein's invasion of Kuwait led the Saudis to overcome past hesitations about the domestic and regional consequences of their ties to the United States and publicly invite U.S. military forces into the kingdom.

Conclusion

The episodes outlined above, where the Saudis had to make difficult choices among competing foreign-policy goals, highlight some enduring

patterns in Saudi foreign policy. First and foremost, domestic regime security is the paramount objective of the Saudi government. When foreign
powers directly challenge the legitimacy of Saudi rule and pose direct
military threats, the Saudis will take significant risks to oppose them and
call upon the United States for support. When regional powers emerge
that do not overtly threaten the Saudi regime, Riyadh will move to accommodate them, even at the risk of complicating its relations with the
United States. As soon as possible after these episodes, Riyadh worked
to repair the breach with Washington, an important indication of the
long-term interest the Saudis have in their connection with the United
States. But that interest is always tempered by a reluctance, except in the
most dire circumstances, to be too closely identified with the United
States, for fear of stirring up regional and domestic opposition.

This tension for the Saudis between the centrality of their Washington ties and the needs of domestic regime security will not disappear.
The attacks by Saudi opposition groups on U.S. military facilities in the
kingdom in 1995 and 1996 highlight the continuing sensitivity of the
issue domestically. After the September 11 events, the Saudis found
themselves caught between domestic pressures and U.S. demands to
support the "war on terrorism" and were perceived in Washington to
equivocate. Oil policy could become another issue around which this
tension is manifested. Given Saudi Arabia's revenue needs, it has
worked in recent years to push oil prices up. The United States, whose
economic boom in the 1990s was partially attributable to low energy
costs, could turn to Saudi Arabia for help in restraining prices, and find
the Saudis reluctant to comply.

Notes

1. The two leading works on Saudi foreign policy stress the centrality of
state and regime security interests. See Ghassan Salamah, *Al-siyasa al-khari-
jiyya al-sa'udiyya munkh 'am 1945 (Saudi Foreign Policy Since 1945)*, Beirut:
Ma'had al-'inma' al-'arabi, 1980, p. 31; and Nadav Safran, *Saudi Arabia:
Ceaseless Quest for Security,* Cambridge: Harvard University Press, 1985, p. 3.
This assessment of the goals of Saudi foreign policy is echoed by Jacob Gold-
berg, *The Foreign Policy of Saudi Arabia: The Formative Years, 1902–1918,*
Cambridge: Harvard University Press, 1986, p. 183; and by James Piscatori,
"Islamic Values and National Interest: The Foreign Policy of Saudi Arabia," in
Adeed Dawisha, ed., *Islam in Foreign Policy,* Cambridge: Cambridge Univer-
sity Press, 1983, pp. 51–52.

2. U.S. Department of Energy, Energy Information Agency, "Monthly Energy Review." Available on-line: <www.tonto.eia.doe.gov/mer>.

3. BP Amoco, *Statistical Review of World Energy 1999*. Available on-line: <www.bpamoco.com/worldenergy>.

4. See, for example, Helen Lackner, *A House Built on Sand: A Political Economy of Saudi Arabia*, London: Ithaca Press, 1978; and Fred Halliday, *Arabia Without Sultans*, New York: Vintage Press, 1974. Even Salamah concludes that Saudi oil policy is directed at base at serving U.S. interests, *Al-siyasa al-kharijiyya al-sa'udiyya*, pp. 425–426.

5. The critique of the dependency argument is strongly made by Robert Vitalis, "The Closing of the Arabian Oil Frontier," *Middle East Report*, no. 204, July–September 1997, pp. 15–21.

6. A large literature has developed around the general issue of how oil wealth affects politics. See, for example, Giacomo Luciani, *The Arab State*, London: Routledge, 1990; Jill Crystal, *Oil and Politics in the Gulf*, Cambridge: Cambridge University Press, 1990; and Kiren Aziz Chaudhry, *The Price of Wealth*, Ithaca: Cornell University Press, 1997.

7. This distinction between Saudi behavior in the larger regional system and on the peninsula is highlighted by Salamah, *Al-siyasa al-kharijiyya al-sa'udiyya*, pp. 23–24, chapters 8–10.

8. Yehoshua Porath, *In Search of Arab Unity, 1930–1945*, London: Frank Cass, 1986, pp. 20, 27; Avi Shlaim, *Collusion Across the Jordan*, New York: Columbia University Press, 1988, pp. 90, 552, 566.

9. Safran, *Saudi Arabia*, pp. 77–112.

10. Joseph Kostiner, "Shi'i Unrest in the Gulf," in Martin Kramer, ed., *Shi'ism, Resistance and Revolution*, Boulder, CO: Westview Press, 1987; David E. Long, "The Impact of the Iranian Revolution on the Arabian Peninsula and the Gulf States," in John L. Esposito, ed., *The Iranian Revolution: Its Global Impact*, Miami: Florida International University Press, 1990.

11. See James Piscatori, ed., *Islamic Fundamentalisms and the Gulf Crisis*. Boston: American Academy of Arts and Sciences, 1991.

12. Michael Barnett and F. Gregory Gause III, "Caravans in Opposite Directions: Society, State and the Development of Community in the Gulf Cooperation Council," in Emmanuel Adler and Michael Barnett, eds., *Security Communities*. Cambridge: Cambridge University Press, 1998.

13. F. Gregory Gause III, *Saudi-Yemeni Relations: Domestic Structures and Foreign Influence*, New York: Columbia University Press, 1990.

14. Jamal S. Al-Suweidi, ed., *The Yemeni War of 1994: Causes and Consequences*, Abu Dhabi: Emirates Center for Strategic Studies and Research, 1995.

15. On the development of the modern Saudi state, see Christine Moss Helms, *The Cohesion of Saudi Arabia*, Baltimore: Johns Hopkins University Press, 1981; Gary Troeller, *The Birth of Saudi Arabia*, London: Frank Cass, 1976; Joseph Kostiner, *The Making of Saudi Arabia*, New York: Oxford University Press, 1993.

16. The importance of "Wahhabism" as the ideological basis for the development of Abd al-Aziz's state is emphasized by Turki al-Hamad in "Tawhid al-jazira al-'arabiyya: dur al-'idiyulujiyya wa al-tanthim fi tahtim al bunya al-'ijtimayiyya al-'iqtisadiyya al-mu'iqa lil-wahda" ("The Unification of the Arabian Peninsula: The Role of Ideology and Organization in Overcoming the Socio-Economic Structure Preventing Unity"), *Al-mustaqbal al-'arabi* 93, November 1986, pp. 28–40.

17. Ayman al-Yassini, *Religion and State in the Kingdom of Saudi Arabia,* Boulder, CO: Westview Press, 1985.

18. On contemporary Islamist opposition in Saudi Arabia, see Mamoun Fandy, *Saudi Arabia and the Politics of Dissent,* New York: St. Martin's Press, 1999.

19. Anthony Cave Brown, *Oil, God and Gold: The Story of Aramco and the Saudi Kings,* Boston: Houghton Mifflin, 1999, chapter 2.

20. On the formation of ARAMCO and the U.S. government's role in its founding and operations, see Irvine H Anderson, *Aramco, the United States and Saudi Arabia,* Princeton, NJ: Princeton University Press, 1981; and, for a more popular account of ARAMCO's history in Saudi Arabia, see Cave Brown, *Oil, God and Gold.*

21. The mixed record of ARAMCO in the development of the Saudi state is thoroughly explored in Robert Vitalis, *America's Kingdom,* forthcoming.

22. Safran, *Saudi Arabia,* p. 61.

23. For an argument that oil wealth weakened the Saudi state, see Chaudhry, *The Price of Wealth.* A similar argument is made more generally for all oil states in Terry Lynn Karl, *The Paradox of Plenty: Oil Booms and Petro-States,* Berkeley: University of California Press, 1997.

24. In 1996, crude petroleum and petroleum products accounted for 90.6 percent of Saudi Arabia's exports; in the same year, oil revenue accounted for 75.9 percent of government revenue. Ministry of Planning, Kingdom of Saudi Arabia, "Achievements of the Development Plans 1390–1418 (1970–1998)," 16th issue, Riyadh, Saudi Arabia, table 30, table 4.

25. International Institute for Strategic Studies, *The Military Balance, 1998–99,* pp. 123–145.

26. David E. Long, *The Hajj Today,* Albany: State University of New York Press, 1979.

27. The best discussion of the role of Islam in Saudi foreign policy continues to be James Piscatori, "Islamic Values and National Interest: The Foreign Policy of Saudi Arabia," in Adeed Dawisha, *Islam in Foreign Policy,* Cambridge: Cambridge University Press and RIIA, 1983, pp. 33–53. On the organizational expressions of Saudi policy toward Islam, see also al-Yassini, *Religion and State,* pp. 72–73.

28. Piscatori, "Islamic Values and National Interest."

29. James Piscatori, *Islam in a World of Nation-States,* Cambridge: Cambridge University Press, 1986, pp. 69–74 and chapter 4.

30. F. Gregory Gause III, *Oil Monarchies,* New York: Council on Foreign Relations Press, 1994, pp. 35–37.

31. *Petroleum Intelligence Weekly,* 30 March 1998, 22 March 1999.

32. This is the consensus of opinion among those who have written about Saudi foreign policy. See Safran, *Saudi Arabia,* pp. 217–220; Salamah, *Al-siyasa al-kharijiyya al-sa'udiyya,* pp. 74–84; William Quandt, *Saudi Arabia in the 1980s,* Washington, DC: The Brookings Institution, 1981, pp. 76–89.

33. Saudi attendees at the meeting are reported in Bob Woodward, *The Commanders,* New York: Simon & Schuster, 1991, p. 266, as "half a dozen key members of his government and the royal family" besides the king, listing the crown prince (Abdallah ibn Abd al-Aziz), the foreign minister (Saud al-Faysal), the deputy defense minister (Mit'ab ibn Abd al-Aziz), and the ambassador to

the United States (Bandar ibn Sultan). It is inconceivable that such a meeting could be held without the presence of the defense minister, Sultan ibn Abd al-Aziz, as well.

34. Safran, *Saudi Arabia,* pp. 81–103.

35. For examples of the first line of thought, see Joseph Kechichian, "The Role of the Ulama in the Politics of an Islamic State: The Case of Saudi Arabia," *International Journal of Middle East Studies* 18, no. 1, February 1986, pp. 53–71; for the second line of thought, see al-Yassini, *Religion and State,* chapters 3 and 4.

36. The first was published in *al-Sharq al-Awsat* (London), 21 August 1990, p. 4. The second was reported in the *New York Times,* 20 January 1991, p. 18.

37. Gause, *Oil Monarchies,* pp. 108–109.

38. Personal interviews with members of the Consultative Council, Riyadh, May 1999.

39. Ian Skeet, *OPEC: Twenty-Five Years of Prices and Politics,* Cambridge: Cambridge University Press, 1988, chapters 11–12.

40. Safran, *Saudi Arabia,* p. 92.

41. Salamah, *Al-siyasa al-kharijiyya al-sa'udiyya,* identifies 1979 as a serious crisis in U.S.-Saudi relations, pp. 253–264.

10

The Foreign Policy of Libya

Tim Niblock

Since the Mu'ammur al-Qadhafi regime came to power in 1969, Libya has pursued one of the most engaged and outgoing foreign policies of the Arab world. Unlike the foreign policies of many Arab countries over the decades of the 1970s–1990s, Libyan foreign policy has sought actively to reshape the dimensions of international politics that affect the countries of the Arab and Islamic worlds and of Africa. In the pursuit of this policy and in defense of the regime's own domestic interests, moreover, it has been prepared to flout the conventions of international relations and diplomacy that are maintained in the wider international system. The Libyan state has, at times, involved itself in "international terrorism," providing support for organizations or operations that strike (whether directly or indirectly) at those who oppose the regime's objectives. The targets of such actions have been the major Western powers, regional governments that are unsympathetic to the Libyan regime's transformationist vision, and Libyan opponents of the regime abroad.

Libyan foreign policy has, it will be contended in this chapter, been shaped more by a mind-set than by clearly defined interests or ideological objectives. That mind-set has been that the freedom and well-being of Arabs (and, in a wider and perhaps less intense context, Muslims and Africans) can only be assured through a radical promotion of their interests and their independence against the outside world. There has been an assumption that the outside world, especially the major Western powers and Israel, will always be seeking to subvert that freedom and well-being, and to harm the interests of Arabs, Muslims, and Africans so as to further their own interests. A preparedness to be confrontational in the defense of Arab, Muslim, and African interests, therefore, is integral to the mind-set.

Not surprisingly, the confrontational approach that the Libyan regime has tended to take toward the Western powers and Israel has encouraged these states themselves to adopt a confrontational approach to Libya. Libya, perceived (correctly, from the viewpoint of Western powers) as a threat to Western interests and Western-purveyed stability in the Middle East and Africa, has found itself subject to Western measures of restriction and retaliation. The Libyan regime's expectation that Western powers are prepared to damage the interests of Arab states in defense of their own interests, therefore, has been realized. Libya has found itself the target of more Western governmental hostility than any other Arab country with the exception of Iraq.

Foreign-Policy Determinants

The durable factors affecting Libyan foreign policy are clearly those that are not specific to the present regime but which exerted an influence under the monarchy also. The manner in which different regimes respond to the same factor will, of course, vary.

There are three durable factors that have been of critical importance in setting the parameters of Libyan foreign policy. The first is the country's economic base. Oil exports began in 1961, and by 1963 oil revenues made up 98.3 percent of the country's exports. Although the proportion of exports accounted for by oil has fluctuated over time, it has since 1963 not fallen below 90 percent.[1] The Libyan state, therefore, is a distributive state rather than a production state, deriving its income from the sale of a commodity and not from the extraction of taxes from its population.[2] The vast revenues from oil exports that have accrued directly to the state, coupled with the country's relatively small population, have meant that Libya's economic structure is comparable to that of the oil-producing states of the Arabian Peninsula. Although the Libyan state may create structures that enable popular participation, the balance of state-society power is such that decisionmakers (whether in foreign policy or any other field) can insulate themselves against pressures from different socioeconomic groupings—provided the all-important oil exports are maintained.

The economy's oil base raises a dilemma for Libyan policymakers that is faced by other states with a similar resource base. On the one hand, the substantial resources accruing to the state constitute a powerful instrument that can be used in the pursuit of an active and outgoing foreign policy—aimed at promoting the interests and the ideological objectives of the state. On the other hand, the resources create vulnerability, making the state the target of regional or international aggressors that covet the resources. States with this resource base, therefore, have often sought to establish a close and protective relationship with such great powers as have an interest in keeping the existing regime in power.

The Libyan monarchy, up to its overthrow in 1969, followed a similar course of foreign policy to that of the oil-producing states of the Arabian Peninsula: conscious of its vulnerability, it looked toward a close relationship with the Western powers to protect it from what it perceived as the threat of communism on the global stage, and the threat of Nasserist radicalism on the regional stage.[3] Since the present regime, under Mu'ammur al-Qadhafi, came to power, foreign policy has been framed more around the strengths flowing from the country's oil resources, using the revenues to promote the radical transformationist vision of the regime at the regional and international levels. There has no doubt also been an appreciation of vulnerability, which is perhaps reflected in the regime's tendency to assume that the Western powers are always conspiring against the regime. This appreciation, however, has not restrained the regime from undertaking policies that inevitably increase that vulnerability by giving external powers (usually the major Western powers) reason to seek to undermine the regime. The relationship that developed with the Soviet Union in the early 1970s, despite the antipathy shown by al-Qadhafi to Soviet ideology, reflected the need to counter the threat posed by Western powers.

The second durable factor has stemmed from the manner in which culture and geography have interacted in Libya. Geographically, the country does not cohere well: the eight hundred kilometers of semi-desert that separate the main population centers of Tripolitania from those of Cyrenaica, and the even longer distances separating both of these from the population centers of Fezzan, have created strong and distinct regional identities in the different parts of the country. Tripolitania was historically oriented toward the parts of North Africa to the west of Libya; Cyrenaica had strong links with Egypt; and Fezzan was linked into the wider Saharan belt of Africa. Nonetheless, the peoples of the area shared a common Arab culture, and that culture formed the basis on which the modern Libyan state could create a sense of common identity among the different population groups. This undertaking, however, held a paradox: the emphasis on common Arab culture linked the country's population groupings not only to one another but also to the wider Arab world, drawing the country into wider Arab concerns—not only those specific to Libya.

Under the Libyan monarchy, there was an ambivalent attitude toward Arabism. On the one hand, Libya's Arab identity needed to be given emphasis, for the reasons outlined above. On the other hand, regional Arabist radicalism was seen as the major threat to the regime. The monarchy looked toward Britain and the United States to underpin its security, and the presence of British and U.S. bases in the country bore witness to the strength of that security relationship. Yet Libya also needed to play an active role in the Arab League and to show support for other Arab countries when the latter came into conflict with one or more of Libya's Western allies, as occurred during the Suez crisis and at the time of the 1967 Arab-Israeli war. The expansion of the Libyan educational infrastructure required the recruitment of teachers from other Arab countries (which effectively meant Egypt, which could best supply the trained manpower), yet the regime also needed to curb any political influences coming from that quarter.

Since al-Qadhafi came to power, the commitment to Arab nationalism has been integral, not only to the ideological framework espoused by the regime, but also to its claim to legitimacy.[4] A critical element in the justification for the takeover of power in 1969 was the contention that the monarchy had been suppressing Libya's Arab identity, and that the new regime would reassert that identity. The Arab identity meshes in, moreover, with a wider Islamic identity: Islam and Arabism are seen as closely interlinked forces.[5] The pursuit of Arabism, therefore, is not simply an aspect of the state's foreign policy, but is crucial to the basis on which the regime is built. Even the greater emphasis that came to be given to Libya's relations with other African states after 1998 provides, paradoxically, further evidence of the centrality of the Arab dimension. The justification for the new emphasis on Africa was phrased in terms of Libya's Arab objectives: the expression of disappointment at the failure of fellow-Arab countries to measure up to Libya's expectations of collective Arab activity, the assertion that the closer relations with African countries would serve Arab interests, and the assurance that Libya would resume its close involvement with Arab countries once these countries had followed Africa's example of showing resistance to external pressures.[6]

The third durable factor is Libya's geographic/strategic location. Whether through positive involvement or by reaction, Libya is bound by virtue of its location to have to respond to developments in three different milieus: those of the Arab world, Africa, and the Mediterranean. Of particular importance here has been the relationship with its western neighbor, Egypt. The latter's regional importance (which has impinged on all three of the above-mentioned milieus) has inevitably set the context for Libya's own regional roles. As has already been indicated, the Libyan monarchy's foreign policy was significantly affected by the perception that Nasser's Egypt constituted a threat. The pattern of post-1969 foreign policy was also crucially influenced by the relationship with Egypt. It will be shown below that the al-Qadhafi regime's changing perception of Egypt (initially viewed as a role model, but by the mid-1970s deemed to be serving the interests of Western imperialism) conditioned and shaped the changes in Libya's overall foreign policy.

Foreign Policymaking

The focus here will be exclusively on the period since September 1969, when Mu'ammur al-Qadhafi and his colleagues from the Free Officers movement took over power.

The Structure of the al-Qadhafi Regime

The al-Qadhafi regime is headed by the charismatic leader who governs through several instruments, including the military, the bureaucracy, links to tribal elites, and a set of unique political institutions through which the regime attempts to consult with the public in order to incorporate popular support and legitimize its power.

Formal political authority in Libya since the Declaration of the Authority of the People on 2 March 1977 has resided in a structure of people's congresses. The roles and powers of the congresses are outlined in al-Qadhafi's *Green Book*.[7] Basic people's congresses, now constituted in units referred to as *mahallat* (localities), form the foundation of the Jamahiri structure. At the beginning of 1999 there were 375 such congresses in existence,[8] covering the whole of the country's population. Each locality has a people's committee, responsible to the congress, exercising an administrative role within the commune. Similar congresses and committees, consisting of individuals delegated by the basic people's congresses and committees and by the professional associations and unions, operate at the level of the provinces/municipalities (*sha'a-biyat*, of which there were twenty-six in 1999). At the national level, formal authority rests with the General People's Congress. The members of the latter are described as carrying delegated instructions from the lower-level congresses and associations, rather than exercising a wider role of representation. National executive/administrative powers reside with the General People's Committee, which is responsible to the General People's Congress. Al-Qadhafi currently holds no position within this formal structure of authority.

The intention that the General People's Committee should be tightly bound by the guidelines of policy laid down by the General People's Congress is given expression by the titles carried by the members of the committee. Although the committee plays the role of a cabinet or council of ministers, its members carry the title of secretary rather than minister. What would in most other countries be the minister of foreign affairs, therefore, is the secretary for foreign liaison, and the government department that he heads is the Secretariat for Foreign Liaison.

The formal structure of authority outlined above, however, does not accurately reflect the realities of power and influence. This is made clear in the regime's own political texts. The final sentence in part 1 of al-Qadhafi's *Green Book* reads: "Theoretically, this is genuine democracy. But realistically, the strong always rule, that is, the stronger part in society is the one which rules."[9] To gain a more realistic picture of the actual processes whereby power is exercised, reference must be made to the volumes of commentaries on the *Green Book*, and to the speeches of al-Qadhafi that are compiled in the *Sijil al-Qawmi* (*The National Register*).[10]

In the documents referred to above, the popular congresses still constitute the basis of legitimate authority, but the development of policy depends crucially on two other elements: the "leader of the revolution" (al-Qadhafi) and the revolutionary committees (first formed in 1977, but not publicly announced until 1979). The former is described as shaping the political debate in the congresses and committees through his political speeches (*al-khitab al-siyasi*). The latter hold responsibility for inciting the masses to exercise authority, practicing revolutionary supervision, agitating the popular congresses, directing the popular committees and the secretariats of congresses to "the right path," and protecting, defending, and propagating the revolution.[11] In this perspective, the close relationship between the leader and the revolutionary committees provides much of the dynamic of practical politics. No doubt this perspective leaves out some other dimensions of actual political power, but it does represent a broadly realistic picture of the political structure—especially during the late 1970s and the 1980s.

Outside of the officially acknowledged political structure, the influence of some other pillars of political power and influence require some mention. Three are of significance. First, individuals in the most senior positions in the military and security organizations, forming part of the inner circle around al-Qadhafi, are clearly able to have an impact on policy. Second, the administrative machinery, coming under the General People's Committee, has the technical and professional expertise needed for policies to be realized. This machinery is described in the literature as simply an instrument for implementing policies determined by the General People's Committee, but in practice the power to implement cannot be separated from the power to decide. Third, the tribal elite, although deliberately sidelined in political terms during the 1970s and 1980s, retained some informal influence within the political structure. Since 1993, the elite has been given a formal role in managing and controlling the population through the institution of the "popular social leadership." The latter has involved the formation, in every part of the country, of groups composed of "respected national leaders," responsible for countering corruption, spreading revolutionary culture, and resolving local conflicts.

The Foreign-Policy Process

Al-Qadhafi's role and ideology. Consistent with the pattern just outlined, al-Qadhafi has clearly been the central figure in the framing of Libyan foreign policy. No major decision is likely to be taken unless it has been specifically approved by him. He has also set the operational style of Libyan foreign policy. On issues that are of significance, he deals directly with foreign governments and representatives, issues the main policy pronouncements and statements, and determines the form and timing of foreign-policy initiatives. His individual approach and inclinations clearly determine which particular national and international causes the Libyan government chooses to support, encompassing such diverse struggles as those involving the rights of black and native Americans, the republican movement in northern Ireland, and Kurdish rights to self-determination.[12]

The ideological framework espoused by al-Qadhafi, therefore, is of critical importance in the framing of Libyan foreign policy. It is these ideological conceptions that underpin the mind-set of Libyan foreign policy outlined above: a blend of anti-imperialism, Arab nationalism, and Islamic radicalism.[13] The link between nation and religion provides a thread drawing the three elements together, as religion is seen as forming a central element in the definition of national identity. In al-Qadhafi's view, the significance of national identity is such that state systems that are not based on a national identity will not survive: "When the political structure embraces more than one nation, its map will be torn up by each nation gaining independence under the emblem of nationalism. Thus, the maps of the empires which the world has witnessed have been torn up because they were made up of a number of nations."[14]

The Palestine issue has been crucially important in al-Qadhafi's Arab nationalism.[15] It has constituted the pole around which his Arabism has revolved, creating the most urgent and immediate grounds for Arab unity. Al-Qadhafi's attitudes toward other countries, both within and outside the Arab world, have been shaped and conditioned by the positions adopted by their governments on the issue of Palestine.

The very strength of al-Qadhafi's commitment to Arab nationalism has in practice complicated and often damaged his relations with other Arab states. The failure of other Arab states to share his particular Arab-nationalist vision, their unwillingness to join with Libya in pursuing a confrontationalist line with external powers that are supporting Israel, and their lack of solidarity with Libya when the country has been under pressure from external powers (as when Libya was subject to UN sanctions), all provide the basis for a feeling of betrayal—not just of a rational difference in policy. The result can be bitter confrontations with other Arab states, including on occasion Libyan support for movements committed to overthrowing the regimes concerned. The strength of al-Qadhafi's association with Arabism also explains, as mentioned above, his turn toward Africa in 1998. Publicly praising the preparedness of African countries to resist pressures from Western imperialism is, in part, intended to mobilize Arab opinion against what al-Qadhafi regards as the supine international position adopted by Arab governments.[16]

Other foreign policy actors. Despite al-Qadhafi's centrality in the making of Libyan foreign policy, there are other individuals and groupings that can at times affect its outcome. These will be listed here in terms of their closeness to the center of the policymaking process. First, there is an inner circle of influential individuals (generally known in Libya as the *rijal al-khaimah*) with whom al-Qadhafi discusses and develops his policy positions. While in the early years these individuals were largely members of the Free Officers organization, from the mid-1970s more were drawn from the ranks of the "revolutionary youth." The latter were the activists of the younger generation to whom al-Qadhafi appealed so as to bring about the social and economic transformation that he sought, and who formed the leadership of the revolutionary committees that developed after 1977. Although the role of the revolutionary committees has been restricted since 1988, the old leadership remains integral to the inner circle. Of increasing importance in more recent years have been

members of al-Qadhafi's family, especially those occupying senior positions in the security services. The central value around which the inner
circle revolves is that of loyalty—a value that binds al-Qadhafi to others, as well as binding others to him. Al-Qadhafi has needed, therefore,
to ensure that actions he takes do not run counter to his loyalties to the
inner circle. The possibility of his handing over to foreign governments
individuals within the inner circle for trial for crimes in which they are
suspected of implication, for example, has never been a practicable
proposition: it would destroy the basis on which the system rests.

Second, the Liaison Committee of the Revolutionary Committees
(the central leadership of the revolutionary committees) has played a
key role both in the formulation of policy and at times in its implementation. This has been made possible by its direct links into the inner circle, as mentioned above. Although the role of revolutionary committees
in guiding and controlling popular opinion has been reduced, the central
leadership has remained strong. The Liaison Committee has its own
structure for the conduct of foreign relations, independent of that of the
foreign ministry. Libya's militancy on the international stage during the
early and mid-1980s, which saw Libya providing support for a wide
range of organizations committed to radical and often violent change in
other countries, was carried forward by the revolutionary committees
and not by the Secretariat for Foreign Liaison—except to the extent that
the latter was for a time itself used by and controlled by the revolutionary committees.

Third, the role of the Secretariat for Foreign Liaison has been significant, but subsidiary. The secretaries have not usually formed part of the
inner circle, and have therefore often not played a key part in the shaping of policy. Nonetheless, the expertise of the secretariat has been important in ensuring that Libya's policies are effective—whether in galva-
nizing opinion in other Arab and African governments to oppose
measures taken against Libya by the Western powers, or in pursuing legal
and UN channels to challenge the legitimacy of the actions taken by
Western powers. When the secretary for foreign liaison has been strong,
the secretariat has been able to limit the ability of the Liaison Committee
for the Revolutionary Committees from pursuing independent activities.

The role of the basic people's congresses and the General People's
Congress in the making of foreign policy has never been more than a legitimizing one. The congress has been used to give the stamp of popular authority to decisions that have effectively already been taken. An
example of this occurred in December 1998 when al-Qadhafi submitted
to the basic people's congresses the decision as to whether Libya should

accept the handing over of the two citizens accused of the Lockerbie bombing, in accordance with the proposals put forward by the British and U.S. governments the previous August.[17]

Foreign-Policy Behavior

While the values, political processes and institutions, and resource and environmental parameters discussed above have provided the framework within which Libyan foreign policymaking has been carried forward since 1969, an understanding of Libya's changing relationships with other countries over this period requires a focus on three specific elements in the domestic and international environments. These "conditioning elements," as they will be referred to here, are the changing dynamics of Libya's domestic politics, the policies that great powers (especially the Western powers) pursue toward Libya, and developments in the regional politics of the Middle East, with particular respect to the Palestine issue and how other Arab countries (especially Egypt) are handling that issue. Each of the phases in Libyan foreign relations covered below has a character of its own, set by the impact and interaction of the conditioning elements over the period concerned.

1969 to 1973

Over the first four years after the revolution, the new regime was engaged in establishing a basis for Libya's domestic and international politics consistent with its own ideological perceptions. Both domestically and internationally, this involved strong emphasis being placed on Arab-nationalist objectives, contrasting the authentic Arabism of the new regime with the pro-Western client status of the monarchy. As Egypt carried the greatest political weight among Arab countries, despite the defeat of 1967, Libya's alignment with Egypt was stressed. While Nasser was alive, through to September 1970, the alignment was emotional as well as pragmatic; when Sadat took over the Egyptian presidency, it became more simply pragmatic. Strong support was expressed for the Palestinian cause, and practical support was offered to the more militant Palestinian organizations. Arab countries that were deemed not to be supporting the Palestinian cause were fiercely condemned.[18]

The attitude adopted toward the major Western powers was confrontational, insofar as the assertion of the new regime's objectives ran counter to established Western interests in Libya and the wider region. The military presence in Libya of the United States and Britain, at the

Wheelus and el-Adam military bases, was brought to an end. The Libyan state played an active role in restructuring its involvement with its own oil sector, and with the oil industry internationally: the major part of Libyan oil production came under state ownership, and Libya was among the most militant of the oil-producing states in bringing about the major rises in the price of oil in the early 1970s.

Despite the confrontational position that Libya adopted toward the Western powers, the relationship itself was not characterized solely by confrontation. This was largely because there was some determination on the side of the Western governments to seek means of conciliating and cooperating with the new regime. There were two reasons for this. First, it was noted that the new regime was even more suspicious and hostile toward the Soviet Union than it was toward the West. The hope existed, therefore, that Libya would resist the general trend for Arab radicalism to align itself with the Soviet Union. Second, despite the nationalization of Western oil interests in Libya, there remained substantial economic gains for Western companies, given that the regime was engaged in intensive economic development. The latter was fueled not only by the new regime's ambitious development plans but also by the sharply rising sums available from Libya's oil sales.[19]

Notwithstanding the radicalism of the new regime's ideology and the militancy with which it pursued these objectives (providing support at this time for some organizations that directly struck at individual Western governments, such as the Irish Republican Army), Libya therefore retained a relationship with the United States and most European countries that involved significant elements of cooperation: diplomatic relations were in place, arms and some strategic commodities were being sold to Libya, and there was substantial commercial exchange.[20]

1973 to 1977

This period saw relations between Libya and the Western world, and some Arab countries, become increasingly antagonistic. Changes were occurring over these years in Libyan domestic politics. There was a gradual move away from the pattern of formal political organization centered around a single party, the Arab Socialist Union (copied from the Egyptian model), toward one based on popular committees.[21] This, however, was not of great significance to the change in the tenor of the country's foreign relationships. It was more a reflection of the changing relationship with Egypt than a cause of it.

The causes of change came from the two other conditioning elements. Of greatest importance were developments in the regional environment, with particular regard to the Arab-Israeli issue and to the manner in which President Sadat of Egypt was handling it. In the early 1970s, despite the element of rivalry between Sadat and al-Qadhafi (who both saw themselves as inheriting the mantle of Nasser), Egypt and Libya had moved toward unity—as represented by their common membership (with Syria) of the Federation of Arab Republics, formed in 1971, and the merger agreement between the two countries that was signed in 1972. In the course of 1973, however, Sadat was developing a strategy aimed to bring the United States into the peacemaking process in the Middle East, and began to distance himself from al-Qadhafi's activities and objectives.[22]

To al-Qadhafi's dismay, he found himself excluded from the planning and coordination that led up to the 1973 October war, and was sidelined in the negotiations that followed.[23] The limited operation that Sadat envisaged for the 1973 war, aimed primarily at moving forward the process toward negotiations leading to the withdrawal of Israeli troops from the Sinai and a resolution of the Arab-Israeli issue on the basis of Security Council Resolution 242 (which Libya rejected), was not one to which al-Qadhafi would in any case have given his support. In the aftermath of the war, as Sadat negotiated the two disengagement agreements that took Israeli troops back from the vicinity of the Suez Canal, the Libyan government became an active supporter of the rejectionist grouping, which saw the path that Sadat had taken as a sellout of the Arab cause. The relationship with Egypt became increasingly embittered, to the extent that in July 1977 the two countries fought a brief border war when Egyptian troops launched an attack on Libyan forces along the frontier.

The second cause for change was the revised attitude that Western powers, in particular the United States, began to adopt toward Libya. This was brought about by a lessening confidence that Libya would play a role in countering Soviet influence in the Middle East. There was also the realization that Libya was active in seeking to undermine the line of policy that the United States was encouraging Sadat to take on Arab-Israeli matters. The value of the regime to the Western powers was thus diminishing, and there was correspondingly less preparedness to accept with equanimity Libya's support for organizations within the area that were regarded as being involved in international terrorism. While the latter activities increased over this period, as will be pointed out below, they were targeted mainly at those Middle Eastern states that opposed Libyan policy than at the Western powers directly.[24]

As a result of the two dimensions just discussed, Libya played an increasingly disruptive role within the region between 1973 and 1977.

Destabilizing policies were pursued toward a number of regional states that were pursuing policies the Libyan regime regarded as pro-Western or betraying traditional Arab objectives on the Palestine issue. Support was given to opposition groupings in Tunisia and Morocco, assassination campaigns were launched against some prominent Egyptians, and extensive support was given to the more extreme Palestinian rejectionist groupings, especially the Popular Front for the Liberation of Palestine (general command) and the Abu Nidal grouping.[25]

1977 to 1981

Over the years 1977–1981, Libyan foreign policy was marked by some contradictory tendencies. Developments on the domestic level tended toward an intensification of militant confrontation with the Western powers and their allies (in and outside the Arab world). This dynamic came not so much from the Declaration of People's Authority in January 1977, which formalized the transfer of power to the people's committees, as from the establishment of the revolutionary committees in the same year.[26] The latter would in due course concern themselves with matters that inevitably drew Libya into conflictual relations with other countries, such as the elimination of Libyan opponents of the regime abroad, the spread of the ideas of Libyan popular power to other countries, and the taking control of Libyan embassies abroad (which became Libyan "people's offices"). A new dimension had come into the making of foreign policy, closely linked to al-Qadhafi but with a spontaneous militancy that created its own dynamics.

Nonetheless, Libya's international stance during this period was in fact less confrontational, both in its relationship with most other Arab countries and in its relationship with the Western powers, than over the previous phase. This is explained, first, by the turn taken by regional developments. President Sadat's visit to Jerusalem in November 1977, and the subsequent September 1978 Camp David agreements, meant that Libya was now no longer isolated in its confrontation with Egypt. There was a trend toward "unifying Arab ranks," bringing all Arab countries besides Egypt into a common position to oppose Egypt's bilateral negotiations and settlement with Israel. It was now Egypt that was regionally isolated, while Libya was welcomed into the consensus of Arab states critical of Egypt. Libya now had a strong interest in avoiding confrontation with other Arab states and working toward a resolution of the disputed issues.

Over these years, therefore, despite the militancy of the revolutionary committees, Libya was in general not engaged in activities that sought to undermine existing regimes within the Arab world. Good relations were established at this time with a number of states that had previously been subject to periodic denunciation from Tripoli, in particular the Kingdom of Saudi Arabia and some of Libya's neighbors in North Africa. The period was, however, not entirely without conflict in this arena: in 1980, the Tunisian government accused Libya of supporting an armed uprising in Gafsa (in southern Tunisia). As there were also indications of Algerian involvement in the uprising, however, the dynamics that led to Libya's involvement in this incident (if indeed there was such) remain unclear.[27]

The second reason for Libya's less confrontational stance in the arena between 1977 and 1981 relates to Jimmy Carter's assumption of the U.S. presidency in January 1977. Carter became president with a human-rights agenda that identified Libya as a major transgressor on human rights and supporter of international terrorism, and a commitment to maintain a distance from Libya until it improved its human-rights record. After Sadat's visit to Jerusalem, moreover, Libya was actively and militantly opposing the bilateral approach to Arab-Israeli peaceful settlement, which was now central to U.S. policy in the region.[28] This suggested that the antagonism between the two countries was likely to increase. Yet in practice President Carter's tendency toward a problem-solving and, where possible, nonconfrontational approach to international relations ensured that this did not happen. Libya exerted substantial (albeit not consistent) efforts during Carter's presidency to persuade U.S. opinionmakers and decisionmakers that Libya should be taken seriously and was committed to working within the framework of international law. The Libyan government disavowed international terrorism,[29] discontinued support for the Irish Republican Army, sought to mobilize favorable opinion within the United States by inviting U.S. delegations to visit the country (including Billy Carter, the president's brother), and made donations to some U.S. academic institutions.[30] In late 1979 and early 1980 there were secret talks between Libyan and U.S. officials, including Secretary of State Cyrus Vance, to explore the possibilities of cooperation.[31]

The period of Carter's presidency opened the way for Libya to move away from confrontation and to create a better international understanding of its aims and objectives, and there was some evidence that Libya was responding to this. Paradoxically, however, Carter's handling of Libya was to be a source of undoing for his presidency. It was one of the factors that reduced his credibility with U.S. public opinion, contributing to the image of U.S. weakness in the face of radicalism that undermined his run at reelection in 1980. The image of the president's brother, Billy Carter, visiting Tripoli and speaking favorably of a regime that was inimical to U.S. interests in the region, intent on destroying U.S. attempts to resolve the Palestine issue through the framework created by Egypt and Israel at Camp David, and that had entered into military cooperation with the Soviet Union, did substantial damage to the president himself.

1981 to 1989

Over most of the decade of the 1980s, Libya was lodged in a confrontational posture vis-à-vis much of the international system. Relations with the major Western powers (to varying degrees, depending on the power), a number of Arab and African countries, and some countries elsewhere in the world (such as the Philippines, due to Libya's links with Muslim separatists in the country) were tense and antagonistic. The conditioning element that brought this new phase in Libya's foreign relations into being was a new determination on the part of the U.S. government to confront Libya's radicalism and its Soviet links, which was followed in due course by similar policies being adopted by other Western powers. Although the new trend in policy began under Carter, associated with Carter's concern over the weakening of the U.S. position in the Middle East after the Iranian revolution and the Soviet engagement in Afghanistan, the major change occurred after Ronald Reagan took over the presidency in January 1981. From the outset of his presidency, Reagan was intent on curbing what he saw as Libya's destabilizing role within the region and in the wider international system. On the day after his inauguration, he presided over a meeting of the National Security Council, where Libya was one of the main issues under discussion. It was decided that Libya would be challenged and controlled, possibly paving the way for al-Qadhafi's downfall.[32]

The Libyan reaction to the new U.S. stance itself buttressed the move toward a more intense confrontation. There was a reversion to the practice of supporting radical organizations that used violence to pursue their aims (from the Irish Republican Army to the Abu Nidal organization), and Libya became increasingly and actively antipathetic to those Arab and African governments that maintained close links with the United States.[33] This trend was encouraged, and to some extent made possible, by the development in Libyan domestic politics that was covered in the previous section: the militant role that the revolutionary committees were playing, both within Libya and abroad. The latter came to constitute not only the inspiration behind Libya's destabilizing international policies but also the instrument through which they were carried out.

Much of the 1980s, therefore, was spent in open military and diplomatic confrontation with the United States. The confrontation was most overt in the clashes between the U.S. Navy and Libyan air and sea forces in the Gulf of Sirte, where the U.S. insistence on its right to navigation was met by Libya's assertion that the waters fell within its own territorial sovereignty. Attempts by European countries to maintain their own (usually profitable) relationships with Libya were undermined by the combination of U.S. pressure and Libyan militancy. Britain, for example, was able to maintain a strong economic relationship with Libya, and a substantial diplomatic presence there, until 1984. Relations were severed, however, following the shooting of Yvonne Fletcher outside the Libyan people's bureau in London, apparently from a shot fired from within the bureau. The European Community was eventually persuaded to impose diplomatic sanctions on Libya in April 1986, in the wake of the U.S. air strikes on Libya. Libyan diplomatic representation in European Community countries was cut, and the representation of European countries in Libya was reduced to a minimal level.[34]

1989 to 1999

At the end of the 1980s, domestic developments within Libya, and regional developments within the Middle East, appeared to lay the basis for Libya to establish more settled relations with the Western world and with regional states. Domestically, al-Qadhafi took measures in the course of 1988 and 1989 to restrain the role of the revolutionary committees. At the fourteenth session of the General People's Congress, held in Ras al-Unuf in March 1998, al-Qadhafi criticized the excesses of the committees and called for their role to be controlled and limited. The congress duly passed a resolution to this effect. The committees remained in existence, but they were no longer able to wield such direct authority over the population. In the international arena, they began to lose the ability to play an independent role. The spillover of domestic militancy into foreign adventures, therefore, was gradually coming to an end. There were other indications that the domestic scene was beginning to change: a measure of economic liberalization was introduced, a substantial number of political prisoners were released, and freedom of travel was granted.[35]

At the regional level, there was also change. The ending of the Iran-Iraq war, the outbreak of the Palestinian *intifada,* and the prospect of a lessening in the Soviet Union's ability to support regional allies had created a trend toward more harmonious inter-Arab relationships. Libya followed this trend, establishing cooperative relations with most other Arab governments, including that of Egypt. President Mubarak of Egypt visited Libya during 1989, helping to allay Western suspicions that Libya was producing chemical weapons at al-Rabta. In an interview with the Egyptian magazine *Al-Musawwar,* al-Qadhafi indicated that Libya would terminate its support for "groups which sought to achieve their aims by using acts of terrorism and that had harmed their cause."[36] Tunisia was offered a share in the oil production of the continental shelf between the two countries, and some of the border controls on the land frontier were removed to facilitate trade. Following the Iraqi occupation of Kuwait in August 1990, the Libyan government initially adopted a position that was not far divorced from that of the Western powers: the Iraqi action was denounced and support was given to measures through the United Nations to seek the withdrawal of Iraqi forces. This, however, was to change later, after demonstrations in Libya attacked Western military involvement and called for support for Iraq.[37]

The basis that seemed to be developing for Libya to play a less confrontational role in the international system, however, was not to have the effects that might have been envisaged. The most crucial factor that shaped Libya's foreign relations over the ten years following 1989 was the Western reaction to the bombing of PanAm flight 103 in November 1988, leading to the loss of 250 lives when the plane crashed on the Scottish town of Lockerbie, and the bombing of UTA flight 772, which crashed in Niger in September 1989. The issue of Libyan responsibility for these bombings will not be dealt with here in depth, but the impact of the bombings must be covered as it set the context for the whole of Libya's foreign relations through the 1990s.

The new stage in Libya's foreign relations did not begin immediately after the Lockerbie bombing. For the first two years after Lockerbie, the predominant belief in Western security circles was that the bombing had been carried out by a radical Palestinian group, with the support of Syria and Iran. The first public indication that the finger of suspicion was pointing at Libya came in press reports in early October 1990.[38] The grounds for suspicion rested on the discovery by French investigators that the mechanism used to trigger the explosion on PanAm flight 103 was of the same type as that used on UTA flight 772, and the existence of considerable evidence that there had been Libyan involvement in the latter. The discovery of evidence implicating Libya came at a convenient time for the U.S. and British governments: they were at the time seeking to ensure Syrian and Iranian support for the coalition that sought to enforce Iraqi withdrawal from occupied Kuwait. Any indication that new action might be taken against these countries as a result of their involvement in international terrorism would have critically undermined their objective.

In July 1991, French investigating magistrates announced that evidence had been found implicating two Libyan nationals in the bombing of PanAm flight 103. A U.S.-British declaration in November 1991 called for the handing over by Libya of the two accused. Libya rejected this on the grounds that the declaration carried an assumption of guilt and of Libyan governmental complicity—an assumption that would prejudice any fair trial. The Libyan refusal led to the orchestration by the United States, Britain, and France of UN resolutions that imposed sanctions on Libya for its failure to hand over the suspects. Libya, meanwhile, maintained that a trial of the suspects could be held under international supervision in Libya, provided the evidence against the two accused was made available. UN Security Council Resolution 748, passed on 31 March 1992, imposed sanctions against air links between Libya and the rest of the world, and Resolution 883, passed on 11 November 1993, froze Libyan assets abroad and also forbade the sale to Libya of equipment used in the downstream processing of oil.[39]

Over the seven years that followed the initial imposition of sanctions on Libya, all aspects of Libya's foreign relations were affected by the sanctions. The focus of Libya's foreign policy came to rest on mobilizing international support against the sanctions, such that international relationships were shaped by the attitudes that other states adopted on the issue of sanctions. The Libyan government could have saved itself the substantial difficulties that followed by handing over the two accused before the sanctions were imposed, yet having set itself against taking this line of action it did achieve some success. Over the years that followed, it won considerable support from African and Arab countries for its contention that any trial of the suspects should be held outside Britain or the United States. The British-U.S. proposals of August 1998, which envisaged a trial in the Netherlands under Scottish law and ultimately led to the suspension of sanctions in April 1999, were in part an outcome of the success that Libya had achieved. The conviction in 2001 of one of the two accused Libyans in this trial did not raise any prospect of the reimposition of UN sanctions. While Libya's relations with European Union countries continued to improve rapidly, those with the United States remained problematic.

Conclusion

While Libyan foreign policy has often been described by Western observers as unpredictable, irrational, and "maverick,"[40] it has in fact stemmed from a mind-set that has remained broadly consistent over the past thirty years. Such criticism as may be appropriate, indeed, may be more usefully directed to whether the consistency has been useful. More could perhaps have been gained if Libyan foreign policy had shown greater flexibility in responding to changing regional and global realities. Nor are there grounds for the accusation of irrationality. Foreign policy has responded, within the framework of the mind-set and the accompanying ideology, to the three conditioning elements of domestic politics, regional developments, and the policies of external powers. The most relevant criticism here is that the regime failed to realize the extent to which the achievement of its ideological objectives was being undermined by the means used to pursue them. To a significant extent, the means used have damaged the regime's ability to defend effectively the interests and sovereignty of Libyans, Arabs, and Africans—the key goal it has sought to pursue in its foreign policy.

Notes

1. Figures on Libyan oil revenues and exports can be found in the quarterly reports on the country produced by the Economist Intelligence Unit (EIU), *Libya: Country Profile,* London: EIU.

2. An excellent discussion of the character of Libya's distributive state is to be found in Dirk Vandewalle, *Libya Since Independence: Oil and State-Building,* London: I. B. Tauris, 1998.

3. An account of Libyan foreign policy in the monarchical phase can be found in Mansour Al-Shukry, "Continuity and Breakdown: The Role of Leadership in Libya's Relations with Britain (1951–1984)," unpublished Ph.D. dissertation, University of Manchester, 1996, part 1.

4. For the significance of Libya's policies aimed at Arab unity since 1969, see Younis Lahwej, "Ideology and Power in Libyan-American Relations from the Revolution to the Lockerbie Affair," unpublished Ph.D. dissertation, University of Reading, 1998, chapter 4.

5. The linkage between Arabism and Islam is deeply rooted in popular attitudes, as well as those of the regime. See Amal Obeidi, "Political Culture in Libya: A Case Study of Political Attitudes of University Students," unpublished Ph.D. dissertation, University of Durham, 1996, chapter 9.

6. For an example of al-Qadhafi's continuing assertion of Arabism, reference may be made to reports of the speeches he made during his visit to Egypt

in mid-March 1999. See Jamahariya News Agency, *Weekly News Bulletin*, 19 March 1999.

7. Mu'ammur al-Qadhafi, *The Green Book (Part One): The Solution of the Problem of Democracy,* Tripoli: Public Enterprise for Publishing, n.d.

8. Information from interviews carried out by the researcher in Tripoli, January 1999.

9. Al-Qadhafi, *The Green Book,* p. 40.

10. *Al-Sijil al-Qawmi: Bayanat wa Khutab wa Ahadith Mu'ammar al-Qadhafi,* Tripoli: Centre for the Study of the Green Book, 1969–1995.

11. H. Mattes, "The Rise and Fall of the Revolutionary Committees," in Dirk Vandewalle, ed., *Qadhafi's Libya, 1969–1994,* Basingstoke, England: Macmillan, 1995, p. 94.

12. One of the occasions when al-Qadhafi asserted the Kurdish right to self-determination was during the visit of Turkish prime minister Necmettin Erbakan to Libya in October 1996. Al-Qadhafi told the prime minister that "the state of Kurdistan should take its place under the Middle Eastern sun." *Guardian,* 7 October 1996.

13. A discussion of the values underlying al-Qadhafi's foreign policy can be found in Muhammed Arab, "The Effect of the Leader's Belief System on Foreign Policy: The Case of Libya," unpublished Ph.D. dissertation, Florida State University, 1988.

14. Mu'ammur al-Qadhafi, *The Green Book (Part Three): The Social Basis of the Third Universal Theory,* Tripoli: Public Enterprise for Publishing, n.d., p. 88.

15. An early expression of this dimension can be found in an address delivered by al-Qadhafi two weeks after his regime took power. He stated: "Arab unity is the decisive historical answer to the challenges of both imperialism and Zionism. It is the safe base and the solid land from which the great masses of the Arab people will surge forward to liberate the holy and emancipate what the enemy has usurped through aggression." See National Cultural Centre, *Address Delivered by Col. Mu'ammar al-Qadhafi,* 16 September 1969.

16. For an appreciation of this point, reference should be made to the speeches that al-Qadhafi made during his visit to Egypt in March 1999. There is, here, a repetition of the threats facing the Arab world from Zionism and from other external forces, and the assertion that "the unity of the Arab nation is the only option for its salvation from its present state of fragmentation and dismemberment." See J.A.N.A., *Weekly News Bulletin from the Jamahariya News Agency* (London Office), 12 March 1999.

17. *Guardian,* 16 December 1998.

18. An overview of foreign-policy developments in this period can be found in Ministry of Information and Culture, *Aspects of the First of September Revolution,* Tripoli: n.p., n.d.

19. An account of these developments is given in Mahmoud El-Warfally, *Imagery and Ideology in US Policy Toward Libya, 1969–82,* Pittsburgh: University of Pittsburgh Press, 1988, chapter 3.

20. Ibid., pp. 67–72.

21. See Vandewalle, *Libya Since Independence,* chapter 4.

22. For the dynamics of the changing relationship with Egypt, see David Blundy and Andrew Lycett, *Qaddafi and the Libyan Revolution,* London: Corgi, 1988, chapter 6.

23. Al-Qadhafi's own views on the development of relations with Egypt and the link with the Palestine issue more broadly are found in Mirella Bianco, *Gadafi: Voice from the Desert,* London: Longmans, 1975, part 3. The book is based on interviews with al-Qadhafi.

24. See El-Warfally, *Imagery and Ideology,* pp. 85–93.

25. See Mary-Jane Deeb, *Libya's Foreign Policy in North Africa.* Boulder, CO: Westview Press, 1991, chapter 5.

26. Mattes, "The Rise and Fall," pp. 90–95.

27. The Algerian involvement was reported in *Le Monde,* 31 January 1980. One factor that caused tension between Libya and Tunisia was the rejection by Tunisia of al-Qadhafi's proposal that the two countries should join with Algeria in a federal union, put forward in June 1978. See Deeb, *Libya's Foreign Policy,* p. 127. Al-Qadhafi strongly rebutted the allegations of Libyan involvement.

28. The different concerns of the Carter administration find expression in a letter that the U.S. State Department sent to Senator Jacob Javits in April 1977, stating that Libya had "actively assisted a number of different terrorist groups and individuals, including the Palestinian 'rejectionist' factions." See *Facts on File, 1977: Weekly World Digest,* Waterloo, IA: Waterloo Publications Library, p. 380.

29. In the early part of 1978, Libya signed three international conventions on airplane hijacking.

30. See El-Warfally, *Imagery and Ideology,* pp. 112–113.

31. B. Davis, *Qaddafi, Terrorism and the U.S. Attack on Libya,* New York: Praeger, 1990, p. 37.

32. Ibid., p. 39. When U.S.-Libyan relations had reached their most conflictual, early in 1986, there were a number of reports in U.S. newspapers that revealed the content of the early discussions in the U.S. administration over Libya. See, for example, *Washington Post,* 14 January 1986. See also the U.S. State Department's own account of the developments over Libya: U.S. Department of State, *Libya Under Qadhafi: A Pattern of Aggression,* Washington, DC: Bureau of Political Affairs, 1986.

33. An account of these developments can be found in Edward Haley, *U.S.-Libyan Relations,* New York: Praeger, 1984.

34. Davis, *Qaddafi, Terrorism and the U.S.,* pp. 159–165.

35. The elements of political and economic liberalization are covered in Lahwej, "Ideology and Power," pp. 351–354, and Vandewalle, *Qadhafi's Libya,* chapters 4 and 9.

36. *Al-Musawwar,* 25 October 1989.

37. See Lahwej, "Ideology and Power," pp. 354–357.

38. See *Guardian,* 10 October 1990.

39. United Nations, S/RES/748, 31 March 1992, and S/RES/883, 11 November 1993.

40. A notable exception to such assessments of Libyan foreign policy is Ronald St. John, *Qaddafi's World Design,* London: Saqi Books, 1987, which emphasizes elements of consistency in the pattern of foreign-policy behavior.

11

The Foreign Policy of Tunisia

Emma C. Murphy

Tunisia's foreign-policy goals have been modest, its techniques eminently practical and realistic, and its results undramatic, though very beneficial to the country in terms of economic assistance. Given Tunisia's small size, limited resources, and military vulnerability, Presidents Bourguiba and Ben Ali have managed to establish a respectable position for Tunisia in world affairs.[1]

Foreign-Policy Determinants

Geopolitics: Location, Location, Location

Tunisia is a small state in terms of its territory, population, and military apparatus. This, together with its specific location and history, have combined to make Tunisians constantly aware of their own vulnerability to the ambitions of external powers and foreign policy is therefore inevitably geared toward minimizing this vulnerability.

Since ancient times, Tunisia has been subject to one invasion after another. The Carthaginians, Romans, Vandals, Byzantines, Arabs, Ottomans, and French all coveted Tunisia as a strategically valuable vehicle for their own ambitions. The country sits reaching out into the Mediterranean, far enough westward to be accessible to Europe, but close enough to the Middle East to identify with the peoples and issues of western Asia. It has historically also been a gateway from Africa to these two arenas. The central location is not matched, however, by geographic or resource strength. Beyond the sea lies the European continent, from whence came the most recent wave of occupiers. Today, more than ever, Tunisians are aware of the economic might of that continent, and its continuing ability to assert itself over Tunisia to the latter's disadvantage. As Europe develops and asserts its own collective foreign policies, backed by military capabilities in the Mediterranean, Tunisia must keep one eye always to the north. The other eye must inevitably be focused primarily on the more immediate neighborhood. Algeria, Morocco, and Libya all have regional, if deeply varying, ambitions and all are actually or potentially more powerful than Tunisia. The rivalry between them, and particularly between Morocco and Algeria, is a constant factor in Tunisia's perceptions of its own interests and policy requirements.

The Maghrebi dimension overlaps with Tunisia's membership in the community of Arab states. Powerful Egypt and turbulent Sudan lie to Tunisia's east. Beyond them lie the Mashreq and the Persian Gulf, the conflicts and rivalries of which have a habit of drawing in Arab states further afield. The strategic importance of the Middle East and North Africa (MENA) region, and the vast hydrocarbon deposits that lie within it, have also invited international interest that Tunisia has had to take account of in its own foreign policymaking. While Tunisia's African identity and the economic potential of that continent have not incited much international interest and have therefore taken a relative back seat in Tunisian foreign policymaking, Islam has in recent years become more of an issue in domestic politics with a spillover effect for foreign policy.

In sum, geography makes Tunisia vulnerable to the interests of both regional, intracontinental, and international powers. One may ask, however, what particular resources are located in Tunisia that either stimulate those interests, or enable Tunisia to withstand them.

Economic Imperatives

Tunisia is not overendowed with natural resources. Although it has moderate hydrocarbon deposits, water is in short supply in much of the country. Without the finances or technology to make the most of what it has, agriculture is subject to climatic variations and these can include both floods and droughts. The tourist potential is good and has generally been carefully developed, but perhaps Tunisia's greatest resource is its manpower. The population may be relatively small (9 million) but it is one of the best-educated in the MENA region, lives longer, and enjoys better health.

With this combination of resources, Tunisia's economy has enjoyed mixed fortunes since independence. The young state had few natural advantages. Industry had been sadly neglected under French rule, while agriculture and mining had been dominated by colonial interests. The administrative system was left without sufficient trained manpower and public utilities were in urgent need of investment. The country's first president, Habib Bourguiba, worked hard to combine the strategic need to establish state control over utilities and vital productive resources, with maintaining a liberal economic policy that would stimulate private-sector activity. The weakness of the domestic bourgeoisie, however, inclined the state to take an ever more active role in management and ownership of economic assets, while reliance on French technical aid was a necessary (if not particularly liked) way of funding public services such as education.

After a short but fairly miserable experiment with socialism in the late 1960s, efforts to liberalize the economy in the 1970s in pursuit of export-led growth foundered on resistance from trade unions, party hard-liners, and the state bureaucracy. Existing import-substitution industries were unable to stimulate growth due to weak domestic demand (resulting from low agricultural wages and high urban unemployment), capital- rather than labor-intensive foreign investments, and an inability to compete in international markets. The resulting deteriorating balance-of-payments profile was temporarily ameliorated by a combination of hydrocarbon export revenues, foreign borrowing, and labor remittances. In the 1980s, all three sources of income began to dry up due to declining oil prices, diminishing debt credibility and rising debt-servicing costs, and reduced demand for Tunisian labor in Libya and the Gulf. Added to this were the negative impact on tourism of regional security problems and a series of severe droughts necessitating increased food imports. Early efforts to stabilize the economy and reduce consumption through austerity measures were deeply unpopular and the regime lacked the political will to pursue them effectively. By 1986 the regime was forced to resort to an International Monetary Fund–sponsored stabilization program and announced plans for structural reforms, including privatization. It was to fall on the country's second president, Zine el Abidine Ben Ali, to actually implement these measures and to secure the political stability that would make that implementation effective. The subsequent economic liberalization program has been the linchpin of government policy since 1987. Both domestic political and foreign policies have been structured to service requirements for a stable domestic, regional, and international environment that will allow Tunisia to exploit the maximum of economic opportunities with the least political resistance.

It is important to note that Tunisia's economic-reform policies have been relatively successful. Real economic growth has recently averaged over 5 percent a year. Gross domestic product per capita is on a par with the European periphery, the public-sector deficit is below 3 percent a year, inflation below 4 percent, modest foreign direct investment flows have been attracted, foreign debt is basically under control and the international credit standing restored, exports have been diversified, trade liberalized, prices and markets deregulated, and a significant part of the public sector either reformed or privatized. The stock market, after an initial boom-and-bust cycle, started steady growth, and the financial sector has been slowly reformed. While the negative effects of reform can still be felt in high unemployment rates (probably well above the official figures of around 15 percent), higher and more widespread taxes, weaker labor protection, rapid price rises that are not included in official statistics (especially for housing), and subsidy removals, the government has worked hard to target social transfers more specifically. Its claims that only 6 percent of the population live in poverty may be optimistic, but it is true that the widespread pauperization of victims of economic reform has been avoided.[2]

In short, Tunisia is considered by international financial agencies and creditors alike to be a model of successful economic reform, a position the regime is determined not to jeopardize and one that is based on a foreign policy that prioritizes economic trading and investment interests over ideological affiliations.

Identity: Bourguiba and the Roots of Tunisian Pragmatism

If a single word were needed to describe the approach that has been consistently pursued under both Tunisian presidents, it would be *pragmatism*. It draws its origins from the vision for Tunisia held by Bourguiba, which was based on his understanding of the Tunisian identity. Reflecting his own personal preferences and experiences, foreign policy under his rule was unmistakably secularist, modernizing, westward-looking, and realist.

For Bourguiba, the French legacy was almost as much a part of the Tunisian identity as was Arabness. As a student in France, he had absorbed a romantic imagery of nationalism, justice, equality, and humanism that he believed to be at the root of French civilization. As Derek Hopwood put it, "He had acquired from his stay in Paris an undying affection for France, bourgeois, reformist, lay France, and he wanted to instill those values into Arab Muslim Tunisia."[3] French civilization could offer the values and strategies needed for modernization; the synthesis of Tunisian and French culture could provide the means for social regeneration and evolution. He acknowledged that, while he had happily assimilated aspects of French identity, the transformation would not be as easy for a whole society. He knew that he could not hurry Tunisians through the process or force upon them too many cultural adoptions from the former colonial power. Nonetheless, he strove where possible to retain and develop strong cordial relations with France and to ameliorate lingering resentments from the colonial era.

This was not always easy to do. His first real foreign-policy crisis arose ironically over neighboring Algeria's struggle for independence from France. Despite Bourguiba's preference for maintaining good relations with France, nationalist pressures forced him to offer refuge to Algerian fighters, provoking France into bombing the Tunisian village of Sakiet Sidi Yousef. Bourguiba was enraged by the eighty deaths that resulted and immediately demanded that France evacuate its remaining troops from their military base at Bizerte. The French refused and in July 1961, after complaints to the UN failed to resolve the matter, Bourguiba ordered his own soldiers to retake the base. The attack was a dismal failure, with as many as five thousand Tunisians being killed, and Bourguiba found cold comfort in the thought that he had established Tunisia's Arab-nationalist credentials. It was to be another two years before relations with France began to recover when the last French forces were finally removed from Bizerte. Even then, arguments over Tunisian nationalization of French settler–held properties soured relations and interrupted promised French financial aid to the young state. Further problems arose as the European Common Market began to raise trade barriers against Tunisian exports in the mid-1960s. Nonetheless, the weight of shared history and culture, as well as trade, labor migration, and financial assistance, was to sustain a special relationship that has lasted to this day.

Bourguiba also viewed Tunisia as having a unique identity among the Arab states. While others in the region were expressing their nationalism through a specifically Arab prism, Tunisia, according to Bourguiba, was unable to separate this identity from the many others that had been absorbed from the various conquering forces. According to him, these had given Tunisia a greater propensity for openness to the outside. The country had less difficulty in accommodating itself to relations with the West, and was generally less constrained in its external relations. Unlike many of his Arab-nationalist allies, Bourguiba thus had no problem in developing his relations with the United States. He had personally recognized the importance of the United States early on in his efforts to win independence from France. During the occupation by Axis powers, he had called on Tunisians to unreservedly support the Allies and in 1946 he had embarked on a "hand-shaking" visit to New York and Washington, much to the chagrin of France and the embarrassment of the United States, but nonetheless staking his claim to U.S. friendship. The rewards came quickly. When France suspended financial and material assistance to Tunisia during the Bizerte crisis, an Anglo-U.S. alliance filled the gap. In 1961 Bourguiba embarked on a tour of English-speaking countries that included making an address to the U.S. Congress, where he was warmly welcomed by President Kennedy. This friendship with Washington was ultimately to come under pressure from Arab quarters. Tunisians were themselves uncomfortable with U.S. support for Israel (especially when Israel invaded Lebanon in 1978 and 1982) and with its war in Vietnam, and outraged by the U.S. raid on Libya in 1986. Nonetheless, the incentive of U.S. military aid to help buttress Tunisia against possible Algerian or Libyan territorial ambitions proved sufficient to keep the regime closely aligned to Washington.

Arab states often found Bourguiba's diplomacy disconcerting. While politics dominated their international agendas from early in their independent lives, Bourguiba quickly determined that political economy should guide Tunisia's policies. Realism and enlightened self-interest predominated over any ideological persuasion and the Ministry of National Economy frequently had as much input into foreign affairs as the ministry directly responsible. For that reason above all, Tunisia opted to politically align itself with the West rather than the East during the Cold War. The still vigorous pursuit of cooperation with Eastern-bloc countries was never on the basis of ideological affinity but rather on the coattails of mutual advantage. Agreements with Yugoslavia, Poland, Bulgaria, Rumania, Czechoslovakia, and the Soviet Union were intended to improve trading possibilities and enlarge Tunisian options, not to indicate a political preference. Likewise Bourguiba's son was to tell the UN General Assembly in 1965 that, with regard to China:

> Whatever the reservations which a number of us may feel about certain actions of the People's Republic of China, whatever some of us may feel about her international behaviour, it is nevertheless high time to allow this country, which is playing a big role in the world and which has acceded to the status of a nuclear power, to take the place due to her among the member states. It is obvious that the absence of the People's Republic of China deprives us of the valuable contribution this

country might make to the consolidation of peace and security in the world.[4]

Thus Bourguiba sought not to balance East and West but rather to extract the maximum possible from both, thereby reducing Tunisia's dependency on either. Even the pro-Western political alignment was as much about the latter's ability to contribute to Tunisia's modernization as it was about any congruence of values or aspirations.

Even so, Bourguiba could not escape entirely his regional obligations, nor did he wish to. Tunisian diplomacy worked on the basis that the country lay at the center of four concentric circles: the Maghreb, the Arab World, Africa, and the underdeveloped world. He viewed greater Maghreb unity as a moral vision, although he believed it should be established through economic collaboration rather than political or ideological means: "If we succeed in rationalising and organising our production, our outlets and our development in a coherent way, we shall have taken a great step towards Maghreb unity."[5]

Tunisia's Destour Party attended the 1958 Tangier meeting of independence parties, which first developed a common postindependence strategy for development and achievement of unity, but the program was abandoned when Morocco and Algeria fell out over the borders inherited from the colonial division. In 1964 the Permanent Consultative Maghrebi Committee was formed, including Libya, Tunisia, Morocco, and Algeria, but following the 1969 revolution in Libya, al-Qadhafi tried to forge unity arrangements with Egypt and Sudan, unnerving Maghrebi neighbors with his realignment eastward toward the Arab heartland and effectively dividing the Maghreb.

Oddly enough, in 1974, after an extremely brief one-to-one meeting with the young revolutionary al-Qadhafi, Bourguiba announced a new union between the two countries, much to the horror of most of his ministers, including Prime Minister Hedi Nouira. The agreement, written on a piece of hotel notepaper, made Bourguiba the president of a government almost all of whose ministers would be Libyans. There were serious doubts as to whether the agreement was constitutional or not, and Bourguiba's own conviction that this was his finest moment was countered by the fear of his subordinates that he was being led astray by the grand visions of the young Libyan leader. The union failed to materialize, and by 1983 a new initiative led by Chadli ben Jedid of Algeria was drawing Tunisia into a Union de Concorde et de Fraternité, later to include Mauritania, while Libya and Morocco responded with an unlikely alliance in 1985. Morocco and Algeria were by now deeply at odds over the future of the western Sahara and, whatever dreams of Maghreb unity Bourguiba might have had, the reality was that the region was dominated by stronger states than his own with deeply held grievances against one another.

Bourguiba's Tunisia also had an ambiguous relationship with the wider Arab world. Prior to independence, the country was under the spell of Nasser's Egypt, and Bourguiba was eager that he should be seen as a committed and competent Arab nationalist. He was unable to reconcile himself, however, to Nasser's geopolitical visions for the region, especially when it came to Arab policies toward Israel and Nasserist conceptions of Pan-Arab unity. In February 1965, he proclaimed that, while Israel was a danger, even a catastrophe for the Arabs, "the negative attitude of the Arab leaders has no effect but that of strengthening the status quo."[6] He criticized Nasser's aggressive rhetoric, arguing that negotiating with Israel would be more productive for the Arabs, managing thereby to endear himself to the West while engendering hostility toward his government in the Arab world. What he argued was his realism was also reflected in his attitude toward Arab unity. Again he rejected Nasser's grandiose visions, arguing that:

> The only justification we find for unity is that of facilitating economic and social advancement in countries that have attained different stages of development but which, by their solidarity and their co-operation, might become mutually complementary and back each other up. . . . We think the only way of initiating co-operation between us is that of free discussion on the basis of the mutual respect of national sovereignties.[7]

He was to come similarly into conflict with Nasser over their respective positions in Africa. Tunisia's priority was to support African struggles for independence (for example, intervening in the Congo, and cutting off diplomatic relations with Southern Rhodesia in 1965). With pragmatism again in mind, Bourguiba initiated efforts to develop francophonic African cooperation through an economic organization. His efforts to develop hinterland markets for Tunisian goods would in theory unite black and white Africa. Nasser was meanwhile making his own bid for leadership through the Afro-Asian Peoples' Solidarity Conference, which first met in Cairo in 1957. The organization was fiercely anti-Western, was sponsored by the Soviet Union, and was viewed by Bourguiba as an attempt by Nasser to turn the Maghreb into little more than a political appendage to the Arab East. Bourguiba found some sympathy among sub-Saharan Africans, who were willing to go along with the pro-independence rhetoric, but who found the violent denunciations of Israel and the United States less relevant to their own, Pan-African, positions. The rivalry between Bourguiba and Nasser led the former to boycott sessions of the Arab League and the latter to denounce him for it as a lackey of the West.

One of the principal reasons for Bourguiba's reluctance to be drawn into Nasser's orbit was his conviction that Tunisia's best interests lay in developing globally good relations, dealing as comfortably with the developed world as with the underdeveloped. Since military and political alliances would, in the Cold War epoch, reduce a nation's capacity for making friends, they were to be avoided and pragmatic neutrality pursued as often as possible. International organizations such as the United Nations were therefore viewed as a positive force, providing small states with a voice and some degree of protection in international affairs.

Although foreign policy under Bourguiba was very much a reflection of Bourguiba himself, it nonetheless found a deep resonance in a Tunisian identity that saw itself as pragmatic, adaptable, moderate, and modernizing. It was not set off course by popular Arab-nationalist sentiments, but rather incorporated the latter into a more profound Tunisian-nationalist whole. The brief experiment with socialism did not include any ideological commitments to the Eastern bloc and moves such as the agreement for unity with Libya were aberrations. Bourguiba's own self-belief and his desire for personal greatness were generally pursued through realism rather than rhetoric, and his personal charisma enabled him to lead his country down a nonaligned path that was frequently unpopular with his neighbors but equally did not enslave Tunisia to the agendas of others. Through his control over the party and his popular appeal, he managed to constantly tone down the demands of party leftists, internationalists, and Arab nationalists and sustain a continuity in Tunisian diplomacy that won him respect from both East and West.

Foreign Policymaking

State Formation: Power Consolidation Under Ben Ali

The essence of this approach has not altered under the current president, Zine el Abidine Ben Ali, despite sea changes in the regional and international environments on the one hand, and the domestic political and economic challenges faced by the regime on the other. The commitment to economic liberalization has led Ben Ali's foreign-policy agenda, but the regime's ability to pursue this has been largely due to a reconstruction of political structures under the new president.

When Ben Ali came to power through a constitutional coup in November 1987, his first task was to resolve the domestic political crises that had accumulated during the last fifteen years of Bourguiba's rule. The former president had concentrated power in his own hands and, as president-for-life, had been unwilling to allow a clear path for the succession to emerge. He first built up, then systematically demolished, the political reputations of potential successors, leaving those around him constantly nervous of political commitments and unwilling to stick their necks out on policies or issues. He had equally allowed an inflated bureaucracy and arrogant Parti Socialiste Destourien (PSD) to become consumed by their own self-interest and self-perpetuation. The PSD had lost touch with grassroots members, had been corrupted by its own abuse of patronage, and had come ideologically adrift in its efforts to reject both the socialism of Ahmed Ben Salah and the liberalism of Ahmad Mestiri. An unwillingness on the part of the regime to deal decisively with the developing economic crisis, and its ultimate resort to the army to quell the riots and disturbances of 1978 and 1984, demonstrated the immobilism and stagnation that now characterized Tunisian politics. It was this political impasse, and the lack of public confidence in the system (illustrated by growing support for the Islamist movement and an increasing willingness on the part of secular opposition groups to express their dissatisfaction by taking to the streets) that confronted Ben Ali upon his assumption to power.

Ben Ali initially attempted to reconstruct the corporatist consensus of the early postindependence days by drawing government and opposition, as well as national organizations, trade unions, and lobby groups, into a National Pact. The pact, which was agreed upon in 1988, revives a social contract whereby support for the regime and the broad direction of its economic and social policies is exchanged for commitments to political liberalization, democratization, and inclusiveness in the structure of power. The regime has legalized a number of opposition parties (although not those such as the Islamists who might challenge the nature of the state itself or the general direction of policy), introduced limited opposition representation into the National Assembly and Municipal Councils, engaged in numerous consultation processes with interest groups and opposition parties, encouraged associationalism (albeit under strict state sponsorship), and generally tried to appear to be introducing a gradual and circumspect process of political reform. More ominously, real challenges to the regime have been curtailed through the very limitations of those reforms and, in the case of direct critics, through repression, arrest, detention, and the abuse of human rights. The bottom line is that popular participation is welcomed and some degree of tolerance for engagement in dialogue is encouraged, but that genuine efforts to reduce the overall hegemony of the regime or to challenge its policy priorities are not to be allowed.

Meanwhile, the ruling PSD has been reformed and restructured into the Rassemblement Constitutionnel Démocratique (RCD). A massive recruitment drive based on promises for more internal and national democracy enabled the regime to alter the base of the party, to remove party diehards from senior positions and replace them with imposed technocrats and military/security personnel who were loyal to either the person or the policies of the president. Today the party remains hegemonic within the political system but is subservient to, rather than the power base of, the president. This gives Ben Ali considerably more room to maneuver than his predecessor had. In effect, he has managed to achieve relative autonomy for the state in a way that proved ultimately beyond the capacity of Bourguiba. To do so he has relied on the alliance of pro–economic reform technocrats, an emerging business elite, and the military and security personnel with whom he has a shared history. Bourguiba, in contrast, relied on his own personal charisma and his position as the patrimonial figurehead of the populist, nationalist party.

Ben Ali has also taken advantage of Tunisia's large middle class and the prevailing unwillingness to abandon political moderacy and stability in favor of faster or more radical political reform. In his fight with the Islamists, he only had to point to the spiraling civil war in Algeria as an example of what uncontrolled democratization and premature political transformation could lead to. He, on the other hand, offered a combination of political stability (long a treasured social virtue) and economic opportunity. Privatizations on the *bourse* (stock exchange), for example, offered opportunities for small savers, while various incentives were offered for small businesses. The downside—of regularized taxation, increasing prices (especially of property), and job insecurity— were pressures that could generally be absorbed by the middle classes in a way that would have been more difficult for a country with a larger lower-income population.

Ben Ali has also taken specific actions to increase the power of the presidency and thus his own direct role in policymaking. Tactics have included drawing opposition politicians into the cabinet, abolishing the post of party director (thereby removing any party official from the cabinet), introducing new legislation that prevents ministers from simultaneously holding National Assembly seats, and getting himself elected as president of the RCD. One might also argue that the gradual enlargement of the National Assembly, and the introduction of guaranteed opposition minorities within it, have also weakened the RCD's ability to contain or influence the president, who has effectively been raised above party politics.

Leadership and the Policymaking Process

The leadership is in many ways the key to foreign policymaking. Under Ben Ali, as with Bourguiba, foreign policymaking, much as with other aspects of policy, remains essentially the privilege of the president. Officially, the Ministry of Foreign Affairs acts as an instrument to implement a general orientation determined by the president, under advice from both the ministry and officials of other departments. The ministry may prepare concept papers and present policy options to the president, but it is for him to make decisions on both general direction and specific policies. The petitions of lobby groups, such as businesspeople, opposition groups, and the like, may guide him, but it is he who personally is the ultimate policymaker. He is not, however, at least in theory, wholly unaccountable. Foreign policy is regularly discussed in the parliament, which includes a guaranteed minimum of opposition representation. Each year the prime minister must present the government's program for the year, including foreign-policy aspects. The parliament may alternatively request the foreign minister to appear before a special session to answer questions and hear opinions. A Political and Foreign Affairs Commission (which currently has more opposition representatives than the RCD) may likewise debate policy and send recommendations to the president via the minister and all debates are recorded in the *Official Gazette* for public consideration. It should be noted, however, that the parliament cannot veto policy, or make it, only debate it and make recommendations. And, despite the activities of a very competent and professional diplomatic corps and foreign ministry, the reality is that the president determines foreign policy. For all the constitutional arrangements that should act as checks and balances, it is the individual who has the ultimate "yea or nay" and who selects priorities in policymaking.

This has become even more true of Ben Ali than it was of Bourguiba. While Bourguiba's personal imprint was perhaps more colorful, Ben Ali has (as was pointed out earlier) achieved a greater degree of autonomy from the RCD and more important interest groups such as the

UGTT[8] or UGAT.[9] In addition, while Bourguiba was guided largely by a general political and strategic pragmatism, Ben Ali's policy is motivated to a much more focused degree on achieving economic goals. Domestic stability and regional security are required not just for their own sakes, but because Ben Ali does not see an economic future for Tunisia without them. Integration into the global economic system on as advantageous terms as possible is the key to his approach to foreign policy-making and the most powerful lobbies in Tunisia when it comes to foreign policymaking are therefore not surprisingly the representatives of the new entrepreneurial class (among them many of Ben Ali's own extended family). In the meantime, those more determinedly political or ideological voices (such as Arab nationalists and leftists) who had some credibility in the postindependence era have been almost entirely marginalized as their priorities are seen as increasingly irrelevant for a modern future.

That is not to say that Ben Ali is able to act wholly independently of public opinion or the National Assembly itself. Indeed, he has tried to steer a political course that reassures public opinion that Tunisian, Arab, and Muslim sensibilities are all being taken into consideration, even as the direction of policy is distinctly pro-Western and toward integration in a global economic culture. A good example of this was the Tunisian response to the Iraqi invasion of Kuwait and the subsequent U.S.-led effort to expel the invading force. Initially, the Tunisian government was deeply critical of the Iraqi invasion, in line with its own desire to see international law and the protection of small states upheld. As the United States moved troops to the region, public opinion turned against this position and Ben Ali altered his public statements to be less hostile to Saddam Hussein and more concerned about the Western presence in the Gulf. (He also used the occasion to make clear his own annoyance at past Saudi and Kuwaiti financial support for the Tunisian Islamists.) Finally, he replaced Foreign Minister Ismail Khelil with the pro-Ba'thist Habib Boulares. However, the debate in Tunisia was tightly controlled, not least since Rachid Ghannouchi attempted to use the opportunities presented by the Gulf war to incite Islamist demonstrations against the government.[10] More importantly, perhaps, the government quickly recognized that the war was having severe adverse effects on Tunisia's economy. As well as an immediate loss of export markets in Kuwait and Iraq, Tunisia lost investment funds from an irate and cash-strapped Kuwait worth nearly $200 million, tourist revenues, and U.S. aid. The cost of imposing sanctions mounted to $700 million by the end of 1990 alone.[11] Boulares, whose Arab-nationalist rhetoric was now proving to be a financial liability, was replaced in turn by the more pragmatic and pro-Western Habib Ben Yahia. Meanwhile, press attacks on the Western alliance were met by newspaper seizures and the arrest of editors. Islamist-led demonstrations met a fierce response and it was soon clear that, while the government has sympathies with the pro-Iraqi sentiments of the population, it would not allow Tunisia's own interests to suffer for the sake of ideological gestures.

Foreign-Policy Behavior

Tunisia in the International System

If Ben Ali has altered the domestic inputs into foreign policy, he has also had to take account of changes in the regional and international environments. The end of the Cold War affected Tunisia less directly than it did those Arab states and players who had in any way sided with the Soviet Union. Relations with the United States were not diminished since military aid to Tunisia was still considered important for ensuring stability in the Maghreb, not least given the continued and unpredictable rule of al-Qadhafi in Libya (which fell neatly into the category of "rogue state" in the "new world order"). The civil war in Algeria threatened the rise to power of an Islamist regime, not too far away from the Sudanese Islamist-backed military regime. All in all, the stability of Tunisia, and its protection from both domestic and regional threats, was considered sufficient a priority to sustain U.S. commitments.

Tunisia did have to operate, however, within an Arab subsystem, some parts of which had been rocked by the withdrawal of Soviet sponsorship. It was hoped by the United States that moderate Tunisia, with its revived Arab nationalist credentials, could play a part in the region's acceptance of first the Madrid and then the Oslo peace processes. On the other hand, Tunisian society was not immune to the wave of anger and frustration that swept the region as the U.S.-led coalition forces moved into the Persian Gulf. Tunisians are as conscious as any Arabs that the "new world order" is one that subordinates the peoples of the less developed world to specifically U.S. global interests. Thus, the government has insisted time and again on the ever more important role of the United Nations in defending international law, even at the expense of U.S. interests. The 1998 Kosovo crisis was a case in point. Despite obvious Muslim sympathy with the Albanian Kosovars, Tunisians were unimpressed by the NATO assault on Serbia, coming as it did without any UN mandate.

If only one superpower remains active in the MENA subsystem— that is, the United States—Europe is working hard to be a runner-up. Despite reservations over what he sees as Europe's soft line on Islamic terrorists, Ben Ali has been adamant that Tunisia's future depends on advancing relations with Europe. This is not least since the European Union (EU) accounts for around 75 percent of Tunisia's trade, with France by far the largest partner. The EU Association Agreement, ratified in January 1998, has formalized this relationship and committed both sides (but Tunisia to the greater extent) to deeper relations in the future. This is not the place to give a detailed report on the agreement and its contents. However, in terms of Tunisian policy, several points should be noted.

First, Tunisia is eager to diversify its links *within* Europe. Currently the bulk of its trade is with France, Germany, and Italy. It would like to see wider European interest in Tunisia, not least since the negotiation of the agricultural aspects of the deal are yet to be completed. In this, Tunisia needs to dilute the influence of those European states with which it competes, especially in terms of olive oil production (i.e., Italy, Spain, Portugal, and to some extent Greece). Much to the chagrin of the French, Tunisia also seeks to dispel international perceptions that it is destined to fall forever into the francophone sphere of influence. Efforts to increase the use of the English language have been partly directed toward this end and, while French economic assistance is still welcome, Tunisia wishes to portray itself as "open for business" to a much wider clientele.

Second, Tunisia is deeply conscious of the myriad of potential problems that can arrive from issues of migrant labor from the south to the north of the Mediterranean. While Europe would like to stem the flow, Tunisia can only provide the domestic employment necessary to do so through speedy economic growth, for which it needs EU investment, trade, and assistance. There is therefore a mutual interest in securing economic growth in Tunisia (as well as Algeria, Morocco, and elsewhere in the Middle East).

Tunisia hopes that those parts of the association agreement that relate to political cooperation can help to raise Tunisia's footing in its negotiations with the EU to that of equal rather than junior partner. Its efforts to revive Arab Maghreb Union and Arab cooperation are also partly designed to strengthen both its own hand, and those of its neighbors, in discussions with the EU and to secure better terms and a higher status overall. Partnership with the EU has also raised U.S. interest, giving that relationship a new edge as Tunisia demonstrates that it has an alternative major international partner. The United States has since stepped up its own economic initiatives toward North Africa.

The agreement contains many risks. Not only is it predicted that as many as one-third of Tunisian firms will be run out of business by new European competition,[12] but there are further concerns that North African countries are being forced prematurely into direct competition with one another for European markets, preventing rationalization of the Maghrebi market and fragmenting the subregion as a whole. Moreover, the EU has, on occasion, seen fit to actually assert the political conditionalities of the agreement. In May 1996 the European Parliament adopted a resolution condemning Tunisia's human-rights record and its persecution of the opposition. This was seen as outright interference in Tunisian domestic affairs, yet the government nonetheless felt compelled to release some significant opposition figures from detention. It has even been argued that the agreement serves little purpose other than to reassure EU states that immigration can be controlled and both EU and undemocratic Arab ruling regimes that Islamic extremism can be collectively fought.[13] In Tunisia's case, however, the failure of European countries to adequately control or extradite Islamist figures was a source of tension in bilateral relations, although slightly less so at the end of the 1990s. Ben Ali fiercely criticized governments such as those of Britain and France. He said in 1994: "In the name of freedom and democracy, you are giving asylum to the enemies of freedom and democracy."[14] His efforts began to bear fruit in 1995 when the French government began rounding up and arresting suspected Islamic activists of the Front Islamique Tunisien (an al-Nahda splinter group). Rachid Ghannouchi (the former leader of al-Nahda) has remained free, although exiled in the United Kingdom.

With Europe being insufficiently cooperative, Ben Ali has turned to his regional neighbors for assistance in combating the Islamist threat. He has worked hard to promote inter-Arab cooperation in curbing what he has called "Islamic terrorism," and a Tunisian proposal for a code of conduct was adopted by the Islamic Conference Organization meeting in Casablanca in December 1994. Under Ben Ali's urging, the Arab League adopted a similar code obliging states to refrain from sponsoring Islamic terrorist groups in any way.

The Regional Dimension

In analyzing regional determinants of Tunisian foreign policymaking, one must remember that Tunisia's own regional status is unclear, or at least multifaceted. One might comfortably define three priority regional identities that feed into the process: those of the Maghreb, of the Arab world, and of the southern periphery of Europe. Tunisians are also conscious of their African regional status but since that offers fewer economic opportunities or political pressures, it is less important to Tunisian policy and therefore not covered below.

The potential for a cross-border Islamist challenge to the Tunisian regime in the late 1980s reinforced existing concerns over subregional disputes between its larger and stronger neighbors. Mary-Jane Deeb has argued, correctly, that historically, attempts at Maghrebi unity or merger over the years have had more to do with Moroccan, Algerian, and to some extent Libyan efforts to draw weaker subregional states under their own influence in the rivalry between themselves.[15] Put another way, "when Algerian-Libyan relations are on the upswing, relations with Tunisia tend to decline, and vice versa."[16] Tunisia, as a relatively small state with a small army, and in view of its experiences, sees various dangers lurking amongst its neighbors. However, neither Morocco, Algeria, or Libya was in a particularly strong position by the end of the 1980s. The Algerian regime was struggling to get a grip on its own political and economic crises and, while tensions over the western Sahara rumbled on between Morocco and Algeria, both states could sense potential danger for their European markets as the wall between East and West came down. Like Tunisia, they were both engaged in structural reform programs that would ultimately rely upon European trade and investment, at least in the medium term.

The shared alarm of the three states at these threatening developments in Europe inspired a new effort at coordination and integration, resulting in 1989 in the creation of the Arab Maghreb Union (AMU), which also included Libya and Mauritania. Despite the signing of a series of agreements and the establishment of a number of institutions, the union never really developed into anything substantive. Ironically, given the objective of free movement of labor between the countries, the main achievements of the union were in the realms of security collaboration. Rather than collectively negotiating their economic relations with Europe, the member states peeled off into independent bilateral negotiations, with Morocco and Tunisia not surprisingly being better able to define their positions and being more attractive as partners for Europe, given their political stability and advancing economic reform programs, than war-torn Algeria. Tunisia remains committed to the AMU, however. The small size of its own domestic market is an impediment to foreign and domestic investors alike, and the potential for a larger subregional market with no barriers to trade and with integrated transport and financial facilities is profoundly appealing. Hence in 1999 there was a renewed diplomatic effort on the part of Ben Ali to revive the union. This may also have been in part due to his desire to see Tunisia protected from the domineering tendencies of either Morocco or Algeria as the western Sahara conflict seemed near to resolution and Algeria ready to emerge from the diversions of its internal strife. Tunisia signed a free-trade-zone accord with Morocco in March 2000 and will be eager to extend this to Algeria and to Libya, especially as the lifting of sanctions on Libya offered new possibilities for intraregional economic activity. Tunisian relations with Libya, which have long been strained (not least by Tunisian official observation of the international sanctions regime), may benefit from Libya's own determination to combat internal Islamic resistance. Libya is particularly important to Tunisia: it is currently Tunisia's single largest MENA export market and the two countries have signed a number of agreements to facilitate the delivery of Libyan energy to the Tunisian market.

In sum, a functioning AMU could offer Tunisia protection from the political rivalries of its larger neighbors, but only if Libya and Mauritania are also members, if serious economic commitments between the members are followed through, and if common economic linkages with Egypt can be fostered. It is worth pointing out, however, that Tunisia is not putting all its eggs in one basket. It has concentrated in recent years on signing bilateral free-trade agreements with Morocco, Egypt, and Jordan and cooperation agreements with Lebanon, Mauritania, and Libya. While multilateral efforts such as the Arab League Free Trade Area or the MENA economic process are desirable, they have proved clearly subject to political sabotage and are unlikely to yield significant benefits in the short to medium term.

That is not to say that Ben Ali undervalues the significance of the MENA region to Tunisian interests. One aspect of Bourguiba's legacy for Tunisia was the country's moderate and pragmatic approach toward peace between Israel and the Arabs. However, by offering sanctuary to the Palestine Liberation Organization (PLO) in 1982, Bourguiba somewhat ameliorated criticism that he was too soft on Israel. His condition that the PLO presence in Tunis should remain civilianized, combined with the absence of a Palestinian refugee population, helped to avert the kind of domestic impact of the Palestinian relocation that had occurred in Jordan and Lebanon. In fact, the extended PLO family became deeply unpopular in Tunis, pushing up property prices, squeezing Tunisians out of the more fashionable areas of the city, and generally being considered flashy with other people's money. Tunisians were nonetheless outraged when Israel attacked a PLO house in the suburbs of Tunis in 1985, and when they assassinated PLO leader Abu Jihad in 1988. In short, while Tunisians' popular sentiment was sympathetic to the plight of the Palestinians as a whole, it was not radical enough to undermine the extension of governmental pragmatism toward the conflict as a whole. The government's welcome of the Oslo Accords of 1993 consequently met with little criticism other than from remaining Islamist fringes. Indeed, the government went

out of its way to show its support for the peace agreement. It has invited delegations of Tunisian-born Jews to visit Tunisia, encouraged tourism of Israelis to Tunisia, hosted conferences with Tunisian Jews in Paris at UNESCO, and held major events in Washington in 1993 around the theme of Jewish culture in Tunisia. . . . On the day of the signing of the Oslo II agreements, the Tunisian Foreign Minister, Habib Bin Yahya, agreed to speak on Israeli television, the first time ever by any high-ranking Tunisian official. He stated, "to the Tunisian-born Jewish community, [I wish] to tell them that Tunisia, the land of peace, which stood for dialogue and moderation, is playing the same role and is committed to achievement of peace, a comprehensive peace and the sooner the better, because I think time is of the essence for everybody."[17]

Tunisia anticipated early economic benefits from the Oslo peace process and the following efforts towards MENA economic cooperation and integration. It was one of the first Arab states to abandon the Arab boycott and to establish low-level diplomatic relations with Tel Aviv. Israel was allowed to open a trade mission in Tunis, although since the accommodation provided was in a hotel there was always an intimation that continued relations depended on advances in the peace process. In fact, when the process stalled under Israeli prime minister Netanyahu, the Israeli representative was discretely advised to withdraw and Tunisia put further economic ties on hold. Tunisia still attended the controversial Doha Economic Summit but President Ben Ali made strong statements condemning the continued Israeli policies of settlement, economic closure, and political repression of the occupied territories as "cowardly" and "abominable."[18] In the event, when the al-Aqsa uprising began in September 2000, Tunisia cut off diplomatic relations entirely. Thus, with MENA development on hold, Tunisia has moved ahead instead with the Arab League Free Trade Area and bilateral agreements, the latter of which is more likely to bear fruit than the former. It has not restricted itself to the Arab world, however, working simultaneously on developing ties with Turkey in an effort to promote both economic cooperation and Mediterranean security.

As Guido de Marco stated, the Mediterranean region emerged from the Cold War "very poorly equipped to deal with its regional problems."[19] Yet the Mediterranean has been bordered by severe conflicts in recent years. There have been military flare-ups or stand-offs between Turkey and Syria, in the Balkans, between Turkey and Greece, between Israel and Lebanon, within Algeria, and effectively between Israel and the Palestinians. Tunisia has been an enthusiastic participant in a number of initiatives to promote Mediterranean security, as usual seeing its interests as lying more in collective security and common action and less in the politics of identity and confrontation.

Conclusion

In summation, we can see elements of both alteration and continuity in Tunisian foreign policy and policymaking during the decades since independence. Continuity has been evident in the generally pragmatic and nonideological thrust of policy, in the prioritizing of development and modernization-friendly international relations, and in the primacy of the presidential figure in determining the specifics of policy. Change has been evident in the domestic configuration of power that enables the president to do so. It can also be seen in the subtleties of policy. In order to achieve the same goals, policies under Ben Ali have had to be adjusted to new international, regional, and domestic conditions. While he has himself managed to alter the domestic influences on his foreign policymaking to the extent of increasing presidential autonomy in policymaking, Ben Ali has been less able to alter the objective international environment in which he must make that policy. Therefore, he must adapt policy to it.

Change at the international level has coincided with efforts to resolve the domestic economic crisis of the 1980s in the form of Tunisian participation in the process of globalization. Efforts to increase Tunisian economic independence under Bourguiba have necessarily been replaced by a clear choice in favor of global integration. Foreign policy now serves the search for ever wider markets, for foreign investment, and for connectedness to international communication systems that standardize rather than recognize cultural alternatives. Inevitably, this comes into conflict with domestic public fears of new forms of cultural and economic imperialism. The United States and Europe are seen as both the source of career-enhancing education and employment, and the producers of the most desirable consumer goods, while at the same time representing colonialism in both old and new forms. The regime has clearly made its choice in favor of globalization, but in order to preserve its own stability and legitimacy it has simultaneously sought to reassure the population with a rhetoric that speaks of a Tunisian way of achieving economic growth. This accounts for the observation by Mary-Jane Deeb and Ellen Laipson that there has been a change in policy direction under Ben Ali, in line with a perceived repositioning of public opinion, in favor of the country's African, Arab, and Mediterranean identity and away from explicit pro-Westernism.

According to this view, Tunisia today is rediscovering its Arab and Islamic heritage, one that was repressed to a certain degree under Bourguiba's modern secularist philosophy. Ben Ali has thus adapted his foreign policy in its public articulation to a new Tunisian self-image, all the while maintaining the important political and material links to key Western countries.[20]

As with Bourguiba, Ben Ali's policy has been principally a balancing act between two poles of interest. On the one hand, strong relations with the West—with the United States and the EU in particular—are considered essential for economic and military security. On the other, the Arab Maghrebi dimension to Tunisia's geographic and social identity draws it into commitments that might at times run counter to the pro-Western alignment.

Both Bourguiba and Ben Ali have attempted to reconcile these poles rather than choose between them. Bourguiba perhaps seemed more often to forfeit Arab and Islamic identities for economic development strategies. Ben Ali, in contrast, has tried to appear more sensible to the advantages of belonging to the Maghreb and the Arab worlds. In reality, however, the substance of Ben Ali's policymaking has been to prioritize long-term economic and security needs over and above his people's sensibilities. That is not to charge him with insincerity in his policies to relink Tunisia to the mainstream MENA region. There are still real efforts being made to breathe life into Arab and Maghrebi organizations and institutions, and the state has gone out of the way to establish its own Muslim credentials (even as it has ruthlessly annihilated the Islamist challenge). However, the reality has been that Tunisia's security and economic future lies in its wider international profile. Therefore, regional initiatives and the rhetorical profile of the regime are not allowed to interfere with larger and more profitable agendas. If there have been changes in foreign policymaking under Ben Ali, they are not substantively to do with redirecting the Tunisian focus away from the West, but rather altering the nature of that focus to lay even greater emphasis on the economic opportunities that exist, serving most particularly a Tunisian entrepreneurial class eager to engage in globalized patterns of economic activity. This policy is formulated by a president who has located himself (and his family) firmly within that class, and who has subordinated domestic ideological agendas to an economic future that he believes is the only realistic option available if Tunisia is not to be a victim but a survivor of unstoppable global economic processes. He has altered domestic political structures to enable him to pursue these objectives and, while he may be less colorful than his predecessor, he may well yet prove to be more successful in attaining them than Bourguiba was in achieving his.

Notes

1. David Long and Bernard Reich, *The Government and Politics of the Middle East and North Africa,* Boulder, CO: Westview Press, 1995, p. 444.

2. For statistical data on Tunisia's economy, see various issues of *North Africa Monitor,* London, Business Monitor International.

3. Derek Hopwood, *Habib Bourguiba of Tunisia: The Tragedy of Longevity,* Hampshire, England: Macmillan, 1992, p. 142.

4. Pierre Rossi, *Bourguiba's Tunisia,* Tunis: Editions Kahia, 1967, p. 191.

5. Ibid., p. 184.

6. Ibid., p. 185.

7. Memorandum addressed to the Third Arab Summit meeting held at Casablanca on 13 September 1965.

8. Union Générale des Travailleurs Tunisiens.

9. Union Générale des Agriculteurs Tunisiens.

10. Mohamed Elhachmi Hamdi, *The Politicisation of Islam: A Case Study of Tunisia,* Oxford: Westview Press, 1998, p. 70.

11. Economist Intelligence Unit, *Country Report: Tunisia, Malta,* no. 1, 1991, p. 11.

12. *Middle East Economic Digest,* 19 May 1995.

13. Béchir Chourou, "The Free-Trade Agreement Between Tunisia and the European Union," *The Journal of North African Studies* 3, no. 1, 1998, pp. 25–56.

14. Ben Ali interview in *Le Figaro* 28, 1994.

15. Mary-Jane Deeb, "Inter-Maghrebi Relations Since 1969: A Study of the Modalities of Unions and Mergers," *Middle East Journal* 43, no. 1, winter 1989.

16. Richard B. Parker, *North Africa: Regional Tensions and Strategic Concerns.* New York: Praeger, 1984, p. 60.

17. Mary-Jane Deeb, "North Africa in the Nineties," in Robert O. Freedman, ed., *The Middle East and the Peace Process: The Impact of the Oslo Accords,* Gainsville: University Press of Florida, 1998, pp. 293–315.

18. *North Africa Monitor,* July 1998, p. 7.

19. Guido de Marco, "Inaugural Speech at the II Inter-Parliamentary Conference on Security and Co-operation in the Mediterranean," quoted in Fred Tanner, "An Emerging Security Agenda for the Mediterranean," *Mediterranean Politics* 1, no. 3, winter 1996, pp. 279–294.

20. Mary-Jane Deeb and Ellen Laipson, "Tunisian Foreign Policy," in I. W. Zartman, ed., *Tunisia: The Political Economy of Reform,* Boulder, CO: Lynne Rienner, 1991, p. 235.

12

The Foreign Policy of Yemen

Fred Halliday

Yemen has occupied an apparently marginal place in the international relations of the modern Middle East, a status equally evident in the relative lack of attention it receives in the comparative literature on the region. While there exists a significant body of case-study work on the country in international relations, politics, and other disciplines, comparative analysis of the region, as much by Middle Eastern as by nonregional specialists, tends to ignore it.[1] This is partly a function of its geographical remoteness, on the southwest corner of the Arabian Peninsula, and partly a result of the difficulties of working on what is a turbulent and at times unwelcoming subject. Yet the importance of Yemen in the modern Middle East needs little restatement: North Yemen was, after 1918, the first independent Arab country and has continued, both before and after its unification with South Yemen in 1990, to play an independent foreign role; during the 1960s and 1970s the two Yemens were, in their respective alignments with East and West, and with radical and conservative Arab states, embroiled in the Arab cold war. In an Arab world concerned since 1918 with the issue of unity, the unification of Yemen in 1990 is the only case of such a merger being completed and sustained. A country of over 17 million people, it ranks in population with the middle range of Middle Eastern states, roughly equal to Morocco, Sudan, and Iraq.

For the comparative student, Yemen offers an important case study of both the interactions of international, regional, and domestic forces in policy formation, and also of the shifting force of ideologies and influences—from the rival claims of Ottoman and British colonialism in the early part of the twentieth century, through Arab nationalisms in the 1950s and 1960s, Soviet-style Marxism in the 1970s, and more recently,

257

neoliberalism on the one hand and radical Islamism on the other. Yemenis like to joke that when Adam returned to earth he found everything changed and unrecognizable, except Yemen, which he recognized at once. The opposite is also to a considerable extent true: Yemen, in both its impact on regional politics as a whole, and in the impact on it of external factors, has changed continuously during the post-1918 period. It may have more surprises, welcome and unwelcome, in store.

The particular history of Yemen has certainly shaped it in a way that makes it comparable with, but also distinct from, other Arab states. In three respects it is broadly comparable to the majority of other Arab states. First, foreign policymaking has for most of modern history been the preserve of a small authoritarian elite, if not, as in North Yemen since 1978, of one individual, the president.[2] Such elites, and individuals, have had to pay attention to other factors—popular sentiment, external constraints, and economic opportunities. But the study of the formation of contemporary foreign policy is, first and foremost, that of the decisions of President Ali Abdullah Salih. Second, Yemeni politics, domestic and international, have reflected the attractions and pressures of Arab politics as a whole: for North Yemen after 1918, this was above all a matter of resisting the pressure of its increasingly powerful and often belligerent neighbor, Saudi Arabia, and for both North and South this involved, from the 1950s onward, responding to the rise of Arab nationalism. The history of Yemeni politics is, to a considerable degree, that of the pressures—interstate, ideological, transnational—of shifting currents within the Arab world. Third, Yemen is economically weak, its trade in substantial deficit, and its ability to attract foreign investment meager: the international political economy of Yemen is, therefore, one of dependency, and maneuver.

On the other hand, there are several factors that mark Yemen off from the majority of its fellow Arab states. First is geographic location: while Yemen is most definitely part of the historic Arab world, it also has connections, of many centuries, with the Horn of Africa. The peoples, scripts, and cultures of Ethiopia and Eritrea are marked by ancient South Arabian influences; in modern times, strategic balances between flows of people and weapons across the Red Sea have been as important as any others as far as Yemen is concerned. An official of the Yemeni foreign ministry told me in the mid-1990s that they spent as much of the day dealing with the pressures of refugees from Somalia as on regional issues. The explosion of fighting between Eritrea and Yemen over the disputed Hanish Islands in 1996 underlines this connection. Second, Yemeni politics and international relations have throughout the modern period been dominated by one issue above all, that of unity: the division of Yemen in the course of the pre-1918 period into an Ottoman-dominated North and a British-dominated South produced, after the withdrawal of the two colonial powers (in 1918 and 1967 respectively), two Yemeni states—the northern Yemeni Arab Republic and the southern People's Democratic Republic of Yemen.[3] The concern of politicians, state officials, and political movements with unity has tended to overshadow all other concerns, and, given the disputes that have continued since then, has continued to do so after 1990.[4] Third, Yemeni foreign policy, and politics in general, have reflected the character of the Yemeni states: a centralized pro-Soviet regime in the South, up to 1990, pursued one kind of foreign policy, while a decentralized, unstable, and easily penetrated North took an alternative option in style and orientation. Since the unification of the two Yemens in 1990 has led, in broad terms, to the assimilation of the South into the North, it is the Northern pattern, in which fragmentation and a plurality of armed power centers has increased, that has prevailed, and that must merit the main attention in this analysis. Finally, the political and geographic formation of Yemen has given it a particular form of nationalism, one that combines more conventional hostility to extraregional powers (Ottomans in the north, British and later Americans in the south) with hostility toward another, fellow Arab, state, namely Saudi Arabia. The depth of antagonism toward Saudi Arabia is a constant in Yemeni politics, one that successive leaders, in North and South, have sought to use and to direct, even as they have endeavored, when opportunity arises, to find accommodations with their Wahhabi neighbor.

Foreign-Policy Determinants

Within all three contexts in which it found itself—the global or international, the regional or inter-Arab, and within the Arabian Peninsula itself—Yemen was consistently in a broadly dependent position, more influenced than influencing, more prey to external forces than able to act upon them. Yet for all the pressures that outside states and transnational forces have exerted upon Yemen, they have failed, repeatedly, to mold Yemen to their will. Yemen has been, therefore, in a dependent, but recalcitrant, relation to the external environment in which it has found itself. This can be shown by reference to five elements in the external environment that have affected it.

Colonialism

The decisive formative influence in the delimitation of two Yemeni states, and on the form of state they immediately inherited upon independence, was that of external colonialism. While Yemen as a whole had seen a succession of relatively extensive states, fragmentation of the country preceded the advent of colonial powers: in this sense, nationalist historiography, claiming division as a direct result of colonialism, is overstated. The Turks had been present in what became the North in the sixteenth century and returned in the nineteenth century, partly in response to growing British influence. The British, for their part, occupied the port of Aden in 1839 as a colony, and then, gradually, and in response to the Ottoman presence, extended a looser protectorate system over the hinterland. By the eve of World War I, a delimitation had occurred between North and South, creating a line that was to prevail until the unification of 1990.

The departure of the Turks from the North reflected both local and international factors: Yemeni resistance was strong prior to World War I and the imams were granted a form of autonomy in the Treaty of Da'an of 1911: Yemen was notorious in Turkish army lore as the site of losses—"Yemen, Bloody Yemen," as the Turkish soldiers' song went. But the defeat of the Ottomans in World War I compounded this and led to the independence of the North in 1918. From then until 1962, the North was ruled by the Zaydi imams: the country was isolated, having diplomatic relations with almost no country, and no economic development occurred. The Turkish legacy, in addition to the territorial delimitation, was to be found in a rudimentary administrative and legal system.

In the South, the British retained control, and, in response to the rise of Italian influence across the Red Sea in the 1930s, extended the protectorate system into the western and eastern Aden protectorates. By the 1960s, the territory that was bequeathed to the nationalist government was complete, albeit with ill-defined frontiers with Saudi Arabia and with Oman. British influence in the South extended to the armed forces, the political system, and education: the rise of a nationalist movement in the 1950s and 1960s was to challenge, but not entirely overcome, this colonial legacy. When the South became independent in 1967, two postcolonial entities—Ottoman and British—confronted each other across a boundary line delineated in 1913.

An overall assessment of the character of this colonial domination would have to conclude that, while the overall expansion of both colonial states was strongly economic, and located within a world-historical context of growing maritime and territorial acquisition, the particular impact on Yemen was less economic than territorial-administrative. Neither power developed the economy, with the exception of the British port at Aden, nor was local policy dictated by evident financial or economic factors. The Yemens were the objects of a preemptive, strategic colonialism that subjugated them without leading them to any significant economic or social development. This was exploitation of the periphery in its purest form.

The Cold War

Cold War rivalry between the Western and Soviet blocs had an intermittent, but significant, impact on the Arabian Peninsula. The USSR had sought, in the 1920s, to outflank the British and find allies in the peninsula—it was the first state to recognize Saudi Arabia, and it had relations with the imam of Yemen as well. But these ties did not mature or even last, and it was only with the rise of Arab nationalism in the 1950s that Moscow began, once again, to court the imams. With the advent of the Yemeni Arab Republic in 1962, the USSR became the main arms supplier, mainly via Egypt, of Sana'a, a position it was to preserve even as political relations worsened in the 1970s. The independence of the South, by contrast, and above all the advent of the Marxist left to power in June 1969, gave Moscow its strongest ally in the Arab world, an alliance that was to endure until the decomposition of both regimes in the late 1980s.[5]

The result of this Soviet entry into the Yemeni arena, combined with British presence in the South up to 1967, and the U.S. presence in Saudi Arabia, was to superimpose on the Yemeni division a Cold War character: unlike Germany, China, and Korea, where division was itself the result of the Cold War, that of Yemen preceded the post-1945 rivalry. But this did not prevent the kind of confrontation seen in these other cases. The Soviet military, economic, and political influence in the South grew, while in the North Saudi and U.S. influence increased. North and South Yemen supported armed opposition within each other's territories. Wars between the two Yemeni states, in 1972 and 1979, had a Cold War character, the latter being seen in the West as a result of a wider Soviet offensive at the time.[6] The Anglo-Ottoman line of 1913 therefore became, from the late 1960s until the decline of international tensions in the late 1980s, a Cold War frontier.

Saudi Arabia

The independence of North Yemen after 1918, and the British position in South Yemen, were challenged in the 1920s by the rise of a new expansionist power, the armies of Ibn Saud. There can be little doubt that, in their initial period, the Wahhabis intended to conquer the whole of the Arabian Peninsula and to subject its heterogeneous, albeit Muslim, peoples to their Wahhabi interpretation of the Muslim religion. Maps and designs of Saudi Arabia for sale in the kingdom to this day include Yemen as part of the national territory. This aspiration entailed a clash not only with British colonialism, entrenched along the coastline from Aden to Kuwait, but also with indigenous rulers: the king of Asir, the sultan of Muscat, the imam of Yemen, the sultans of the South Arabian protectorates, the emir of Kuwait. Asir was, in the end, wholly absorbed, while two-thirds of Kuwait were also annexed. Yemen proved more difficult: war followed in 1934. As a result, in the Treaty of Taif of 1934 Yemen ceded, initially for twenty years, the three provinces of Asir, Jizan, and Najran; henceforth, these were to be a source of nationalist resentment in Yemen—*al-'aradh al-mahtalla* (the occupied lands), which popular sentiment, but not an ineffective state, demanded be returned. Settlement of the border with the North did not, however, lead to a resolution of relations with the British in the South: while no clashes occurred and no war ensued, the border remained in large measure unclear. This imprecision was to be inherited by the People's Democratic Republic of Yemen (PDRY), with border incidents in 1969 symbolizing a wider conflict and uncertainty.

Relations between the two Yemens and Saudi Arabia remained controversial throughout the post-1945 period. With the outbreak of the North Yemeni revolution of September 1962, Saudi Arabia was drawn into support of the royalist forces, which it sustained until the peace settlement of 1970. Thereafter, Saudi money, arms, and influence continued to affect the northern tribes, who, despite their adherence to Zaydi Shi'ism, were socially and politically linked to Saudi Arabia; it was widely believed that Saudi policy on Yemen was made not in Riyadh, but by the governor of Najran. Through manipulation of tribes, and occasional clashes on the frontier, Saudi Arabia was able to influence Yemen, even as it sought for influence at the center. The independence of the South, bringing a centralized Marxist regime to power, precluded any direct Saudi influence there. Relations remained tense until the exchange of diplomatic relations in 1976, following on the end of Aden's support for the guerrilla war in the Dhofar province of Oman.

By the late 1970s, therefore, it appeared as if the most difficult period in Saudi-Yemeni relations had come to an end: a pro-Saudi president, Ali Abdullah Salih, was in power in the North, and the ambitions of the revolutionary regime in the South had been tamed. But this was far from being the end of the story. In the first place, Saudi support for the Zaydi tribes in the North, and later for the *al-tajammu' al-yamani l'il-islah,* the Yemeni reform grouping of Shaykh Abdullah al-Ahmar, led to resentment within Yemeni public opinion. In time, Ali Abdullah Salih came to distance himself from Saudi Arabia and to criticize its influence. Second, popular resentment at Saudi Arabia grew as a result of transnational integration of the poorer Yemen into a then-richer Saudi Arabia: hundreds of thousands of Yemenis worked as migrant laborers in Saudi Arabia, where they were granted autonomic residence under the 1934 treaty, but treated badly in many respects. Meanwhile, the disparity in income between the oil-rich kingdom and Yemen was evident to all.

The culmination of this conflict came in 1990 following the Iraqi occupation of Kuwait. Yemen, while condemning the Iraqi action, refused to support sanctions, or military action, against Iraq. In Saudi eyes this amounted to support for the Iraqi occupation. Sentiment in Yemen was mainly supportive of Iraq. The Saudis' anxiety was that they were trapped by an international pincer movement involving Iraq, Jordan, and Yemen. It was alleged that Yemeni shopkeepers in Saudi Arabia had put up pictures of Saddam Hussein, anticipating the arrival of Iraqi troops. Saudi Arabia proceeded to punish Yemen: all official aid was cut off, and hundreds of thousands of Yemenis were expelled. The action would appear to have reflected a longer-term policy of reducing the presence of foreign, particularly Arab, residents in the country, but it also had a vindictive dimension, following the Kuwaiti crisis. Relations between the two countries, at the official and popular levels, had reached the lowest point since 1934.

The persistence of tensions at official and unofficial levels reflects several factors. One is the fact that Yemen is a society easily penetrated by outside forces. Saudi payments to tribal leaders, to political leaders (often the same as tribal leaders), and to state officials have been a factor for decades. Goods, guns, money, and people have easily crossed the vague frontier. At the Yemeni popular level, there is a sense of Saudi hostility and unwillingness to give Yemen its due place. On the Saudi side, there is a sense of Yemen as unreliable and dangerous, as a potential source of weapons and ideas designed to undermine the kingdom. After 1990 there was much contempt for *al-shawish al-saghir,* the "little sergeant," as the Yemeni president was termed.

All of this was overshadowed by the continuing issue of the border, the largest undefined border in the world.[7] While negotiations were under way since 1995, progress was, until June 2000, limited. Yemen recognized Saudi control of the three provinces taken in 1934, though even this must, in Saudi eyes, have been provisional. But Saudi Arabia put pressure on Western oil companies not to prospect in disputed territorial waters, border clashes continued, and there was a spate of smuggling and insecurity in border regions. Over all this hung the Yemeni fear that, one day, Saudi Arabia, which would like to lessen its vulnerability in the Persian Gulf, would push through to the sea via Hadramaut, or encourage Hadrami secession, and so cut off part of Yemeni territory. The political consequence of this fear was immense. Resentment at Saudi Arabia remains the deepest and most enduring of popular attitudes in Yemen, more than resentment of past colonialisms, of Israel, or of other hegemonic powers.

This inter-Arab rivalry is evident, as it is in some other Arab states, by the uses made of the pre-Islamic past. For Yemenis it is, implicitly, insulting to be told that all that came before Islam is a period of ignorance, or *jahiliya*, the orthodox Muslim position. Before Islam, Yemen was the site of settled civilizations—those of Himyar, Saba (or Sheba), and Marib. In Yemen nationalisms there is an implicit superiority to the bedouin of other parts of the Arabian Peninsula. Hence the invocation, at moments of tension, of "Sons of Himyar and Saba," and until 1990 the national emblem was the Pillars of Bilqis, Bilqis being the Queen of Sheba. Beyond specific issues—border definition, financial subsidies, disagreements on international issues—this remains a substantial issue within Yemen. That Saudi Arabia appeared not to be in any hurry to resolve the issue, and was happy to keep Yemen poor and weak, and, so Yemenis argued, divided, only added to the resentment.

Arab Nationalism

The price of North Yemen's early independence, and of its insulation from the mainstream of Arab politics, was that it remained, longer than many other Arab states, outside the realm of influence of Arab nationalism. An autarkic imamate in the North, and a fragmented colonial structure in the South, precluded active participation in the struggles that beset the Arab world from 1918 onward. Yet, even in the interwar period, Yemeni politics was not immune to external influences. In the North, intellectuals and army officers were aware of the rise of Arab-nationalist issues—unity, Palestine, modernization—and a broad opposition, the Free Yemenis (*al-yamaniin al-ahrar*), developed from the 1930s onward.[8] In 1948, in a combination of insurrection from below and military coup from above, an unsuccessful attempt was made to overthrow the imamate. In the ensuing decade and a half, Imam Ahmad himself sought to maintain the insulation of the country even as he accommodated to the prevailing winds by forming tactical alliances with the United Arab Republic of Nasser, and with Russia and China: presenting himself as an anti-imperialist, against the British in the South, he championed Yemeni, and Arab, unity. It was only in 1962, upon the death of Imam Ahmad, that a nationalist group within the officer corps, trained in Egypt and Iraq, overthrew the imam, and proclaimed the Yemeni Arab Republic.

The form of nationalism in the North was, therefore, shaped by the Arab climate of the times, but had a particular Yemeni character, focusing on the twin goals of overthrowing despotism within and achieving unity, with the South, without. In the British-ruled South, by contrast, the nationalist currents were of a more orthodox anticolonial and anti-imperialist kind. Again, there had in earlier decades been considerable Islamic and nationalist activity in the Hadramaut, in part because of the influence of the Hadrami diaspora in the East Indies on the homeland.[9] From the 1940s onward this began to affect Aden—first in relatively liberal calls for constitutional government and then, with the growth of a substantial trade-union movement in the port and service industries, in a more radical Nasserist direction. From 1956 onward, Arab nationalism, of both Nasserist and Ba'thist variants, was strong in the South, and in 1963 this was to break into armed resistance against the British.

By 1965, however, the armed movement around the Movement of Arab Nationalists (MAN) had split into a more conciliatory faction backed by Egypt, the Front for the Liberation of Occupied South Yemen (FLOSY), and a more radical "Marxist-Leninist" tendency, the National Liberation Front (NLF). This split reflected both a specifically Yemeni process—one of disillusion with Egypt's conciliatory policy in North Yemen—and the radicalization of the MAN among Lebanese and Palestinians. The result was a new, autonomous, radical nationalism that denounced the petty bourgeois character of Egypt and the Ba'thist regimes of Syria and Iraq. In the denouement accompanying the British withdrawal in 1967, it was the more radical NLF that prevailed. The one country in which the radicalized Arab nationalism that had been brewing since the 1950s came to power was, therefore, in South Yemen.

The legacy of this Arab nationalism was to shape Yemeni politics and foreign policy in the ensuing decades. The North retained some of the trappings, and alignments, of the nationalism of the 1960s, the ideology of its ruling General People's Congress (founded in 1984) being a diluted Nasserism, its model of state, to be discussed below, a form of nationalist military regime. In the conflicts that divided the Arab world in the late 1980s, North Yemen tended to side with the more radical nationalist camp, opposing reconciliation with Israel and maintaining friendly relations with Iraq. The South sought to distance itself from the Arab-nationalist mainstream, and had difficult relations with both Egypt and Iraq: in 1980 Aden put on trial a group of people accused of being part of a pro-Iraqi conspiracy. Only with Syria did it maintain a reasonably steady relationship, in part because of the presence within the Yemen Socialist Party (YSP) of a former pro-Syrian Ba'thist group, Hizb al-Tali'a.

The PDRY saw its nationalism as one that dictated not reconciliation with other Arab regimes, but a resolute struggle against those who had betrayed its popular potential; it therefore gave voice, more than any other Arab state, to the radicalism of a broadly Marxist kind that had emerged around the 1967 Arab-Israeli war. Thus in 1970 it opposed the entry of the Sultanate of Oman into the Arab League, and the UN, on the grounds that this state was controlled by the British. In 1971 it was virtually the only Muslim state to recognize Bangladesh, breaking what was otherwise a general solidarity with Pakistan. In regard to Palestine it sought, for the first decade after independence, to back the radical former MAN factions, the Popular Front and the Popular Democratic Front, not al-Fatah. In the Horn of Africa, it backed the revolutionary regime in Ethiopia after 1974 against what was widely seen as an "Arab" cause, that of Eritrea.

Yet even the PDRY could not, indefinitely, defy the course of change in the Arab world. From 1976 onward it had official and increasingly cordial relations with Saudi Arabia. In 1982, seven years after the defeat of the Dhofar revolt, it exchanged diplomatic relations with Oman. In the same year, relations with North Yemen were normalized. When, after the dispersal of Palestinian forces from Beirut, they became the hosts for thousands of Palestinian fighters and officials, both Yemeni states were drawn into the Palestinian cause more as supporters of unity, and of conciliation between factions, than as patrons of one guerrilla group or another.

Throughout this relation of Yemeni politics to Arab nationalism, the process of adaptation was evidenced in the use by Yemeni political forces of broader trends, ideas, and alignments within the Arab world for their own purposes. Yemen could not ignore the Arab ideological and strategic context, but given the force of local political currents and the distance of Yemen from the centers of Middle Eastern conflict, it was able to use these for its own purposes. Thus two brands of Arab nationalism served, in Yemeni guise, to legitimate the two states that emerged from the 1960s. The Yemeni unity that almost all forces in Yemen espoused was a reflection, with all its illusions and hegemonic subtexts, of the Arab-nationalist commitment to unity in the 1950s and 1960s. Later, in the 1980s, each sought to align itself with new, evanescent, coalitions—South Yemen with a Libyan-Ethiopian alliance, North Yemen with the Arab Cooperation Council. Later still, a united Yemen was to seek, with equally little substance, admission to the Gulf Cooperation Council (GCC). The final stages of this intersection of Yemeni with inter-Arab politics were to break with traditional forms of patronage: in the civil war of 1994, the divisions that had formed over the Iraqi invasion of Kuwait were expressed in the Yemeni case by the alignment of Iraq and much of Arab-nationalist opinion with the North, in what was presented as a struggle against *infisaliin,* or secessionists, while the South was to receive support, ineffectual as it transpired, from its former antinationalist foes in the GCC, notably Saudi Arabia and Abu Dhabi.

Transnational Economic Factors

Yemen appears, at first sight, to be largely insulated from the broader structures of international trade and production. Neither in the British colonial period, nor since independence, has it been the object of major foreign settlement or investment. Its low per capita income has rendered its ability to import insignificant compared to Middle Eastern states with larger populations or oil-rich governments. Yet this apparent insulation is misleading. The autarky visited upon North Yemen in the period after 1918 contrasts with an earlier period of considerable commercial interaction with the outside world, based above all on the export of coffee, via the port of Mokka. The economic history of the North over recent centuries is one not of gradual integration with the world market, but of a disengagement, a tendency to autarky brought on by changes in world demand and domestic political considerations alike. An export-oriented economy, based on coffee, has been replaced by an isolated and, later, dependent economy reliant on external rents. A parallel story applies to the South. If British interest in Yemen was primarily strategic, this very conception of strategy was driven by broad concerns about the security of trade routes and of markets and colonies further east. It was this that led to the initial colonization of Aden, to the later territorial expansion into the hinterland, and to the development of Aden as a major military and commercial port in the 1950s and 1960s.

If the precise political economy of British colonialism remains to be written, its general contours are clear. This integration of Aden with the Indian Ocean trading system, and of Hadramaut with the East Indies, was gradually undermined by the independence of states and the ending of the colonial commercial links that had knit these states together.[10]

In one respect, however, both Yemeni states continued to be linked to the world market, and that is through emigration. Up to 1 million Yemenis worked in Saudi Arabia and other Gulf states, including a large number from the South. From the 1970s, the remittances these workers sent home came to have a decisive role in the balance of payments of both countries and in the formation of their two societies. At the same time, both Yemeni states sought rent from elsewhere—from Arab states, from the Soviet Union and its allies, from the UN, and from the West. The amounts of money achieved were modest, but helped sustain the states of North and South. For the North there was an added bonus from 1984 onward as oil production began near Marib and, later, elsewhere. While the total output of Yemen in the 1980s was not, in comparative terms, large (as much as 400,000 barrels a year, bringing in from $700 million to $1 billion), this was another welcome source of revenue for the northern state. In the meantime, with the advent of Gorbachev to power in the USSR, the Soviet commitment to aiding the PDRY was declining. Unification in 1990 was to produce contradictory consequences for the finances of the Sana'a regime: on the one hand, the expulsion by Saudi Arabia of Yemeni citizens and the severing by Saudi Arabia and Kuwait of financial support cost Yemen dearly—equivalent to up to one-third of the gross domestic product by one estimate. On the other hand, Yemen, which kept its ties to Washington open, was able to secure loans and other support from the World Bank and the International Monetary Fund (IMF) in the 1990s. For Yemen, political economy was decisive, but conservative: as in other peninsula states, there was no transparency in state finances. External rents from oil or international financial institutions served only to sustain the state rather than to develop the economy as a whole.

Foreign Policymaking

State Formation

The defining feature of the Yemeni state in the 1990s, and one that marks it off from all other Arab and Middle Eastern counterparts, is its administrative and coercive weakness, its lack of control of a fragmented society where tribal formations, possessed of an independent political and military capacity, constitute much of the countryside outside the major cities. In the whole region, only Afghanistan bears comparison, in part for the same reason, namely the lack of a colonial period in which a centralized, modern, state could be established.

This distinctive pattern of state-society relations is, evidently, a product of Yemen's history. In the South a relatively strong state did emerge, first through the creation of a Federation of South Arabia under British rule, and then, after 1967, through the centralization of power in the hands of the NLF/YSP. Tribes were disarmed, a national economy and legal system were created, and a unified political authority was established. The foreign policy of the PDRY was, therefore, one of a centralized state conducting its external relations with an eye to the consolidation of its own power: hence the shifting emphasis on export of revolution, up to the mid-1970s, and the continued alliance, until it was no longer possible at the end of the 1980s, with the Soviet bloc. Ideological preference, and the need to preserve its independence vis-à-vis the North and Saudi Arabia, produced the most radical of all Arab foreign policies.

Yet even here domestic divisions played their role. From its foundation in 1965 through to the unification with the North in 1990, the NLF/YSP was riven by factionalism, both between elements originally from North Yemen and those from the South and between different southern factions themselves. These were largely internally generated—a result of personal, factional, tribal, and regional divisions—but external alignments such as those between Russia and China and between different factions of the Arab left also played their role. The factional disputes of 1969 and 1978 were relatively contained, even as they served to isolate the PDRY from the Arab world. That of 1986 marked the beginning of the end for the regime, and greatly weakened it vis-à-vis both the North and its supporters in the Soviet bloc.

The state in the North was of a very different character. The minimal state maintained by the imams was, in conditions of autarky, sufficient to keep the outside world at bay and to sustain an elementary foreign policy. The revolution of 1962 brought North Yemen into direct contact with the outside world, and led to a series of dramatic confrontations, not only with those opposed to it, in Saudi Arabia and, to a lesser extent, the United States, but also with its Arab-nationalist allies, notably Egypt. As was seen in other cases where apparently weak and porous Third World states were able to manipulate more powerful patrons who had come to assist them with troops (e.g., Vietnam and the

United States, Afghanistan and the USSR), the Sana'a regime resisted Egyptian pressures, even as it appeared to comply. The most dramatic crisis came in 1967, when, following the Egyptian defeat in the June war, Nasser decided to withdraw his forces and, at the Khartoum conference, to seek a compromise with Saudi Arabia. Yemeni president Sallal protested, and was, in the end, removed.[11]

Any discussion of policy formation has to give special attention to successive leaders. The Republic of Yemen has had five presidents since the revolution of 1962: Abdullah al-Sallal (1962–1967), Qadi Abd al-Rahman al-Iryani (1967–1974), Ibrahim al-Hamdi (1974–1977), Ahmad al-Ghashmi (1977–1978), and Ali Abdullah Salih (1978–). Each has, with varying degrees of effectiveness, controlled foreign policy. Foreign policy under President Ali Abdullah Salih has reflected the strengths and weaknesses of his position. In general terms, decisions on foreign policy are taken by the president and his close associates; these latter include an overt element, the civilian politicians who have served in successive Yemeni governments ever since the revolution of 1962, and a less visible component, those relatives and tribal associates of the president on whom his domestic power base rests. The former provide the prime ministers, foreign ministers, and economic specialists charged with managing the country's affairs. The latter staff key military and intelligence units and, as members of the president's family, enjoy special access to funds and shares in commercial activities of the kind enjoyed by the relatives of other Arab heads of state.[12] As elsewhere, the president's son, Ahmad, is being groomed for succession.

Domestic Political Forces

The general direction and the key decisions in Yemeni foreign policy have, therefore, been taken by the president, as have the major decisions on other major questions, notably unification, the economy, and relations with other political forces in the country. In this, unified Yemen is similar to other Arab states. Yet there are important differences that must qualify any picture of a simple, monolithic, political structure. In the first place, the particular character of state-society relations has placed great power in the hands of tribal forces, and above all in those of the main alternative focus of political power in North Yemen, Shaykh Abdullah al-Ahmar bin Hussein, leader of the Hashid federation. A figure of importance in Yemeni politics since the time of the civil war, Shaykh Abdullah became in the 1990s the leader of *al-tajammu' al-yamani l'il-islah,* the Yemeni Reform Grouping, a coalition of tribal, merchant, and

Islamist groups. Islah was not of the most militant Islamist kind—it copied some of the social program of other Islamists, but avoided the anti-Western rhetoric of most others, and sought an accommodation with the president, sometimes within coalitions and sometimes in opposition. Shaykh Abdullah, however, had long had an independent relationship with Saudi Arabia, and was seen in Yemen as being a conduit of finance and political influence from Riyadh. The foreign relations of the president were, therefore, paralleled by those of Shaykh Abdullah. On a small scale, this fragmentation of power was repeated many times over—in the North and, after 1990, in the South, tribal and other leaders established independent links to Saudi Arabia, with whom they bargained, as did the president, for financial and other support.

Elements of Civil Society

This fragmented state-society relationship has been compounded by the persistence within Yemen, before and after unification, of elements of civil society, that is, of social and civil forces independent of the state and of the traditional tribal centers of power. These included a diverse press that, despite repeated state interventions, continued to be published; a number of professional and trade-union organizations; and, beyond all of this, a strong and argumentative public opinion.

No political force, including the president, could afford to ignore this element of Yemeni society. While largely confined to the literate, urban milieu, the power of society stretched further through radio, informal family links, and the presence in the countryside of a considerable informed opinion. Thus on such patriotic issues as Saudi Arabia and Eritrea, or on the sensitive question of relations with the United States, the president had to be careful to keep public opinion on his side. His decision in 1990 to give qualified support to Iraq reflected a reading, accurate as it transpired, of the balance of public opinion on this issue. No political leader, even in the most dictatorial country such as Syria or Iraq, could entirely ignore public opinion; in the Yemeni case, the pressure was arguably stronger, and reflected that very diversity of Yemeni society that, in other respects, weakened the cohesion of foreign-policy decisionmaking.

Foreign-Policy Behavior

The unification of May 1990, followed by an increasingly tense transition period up to 1994, and ended by the seventy days' war of April to

July 1994, produced for the first time in modern history a united Yemeni state.[13] Much, if not most, of the energy put into foreign policy in this period, and throughout the 1990s, consisted in mobilizing external backing for the consolidation of the president's rule, against the opposition in the south and the numerous fissiparous forces that continued to operate within the united country. This involved, on the one hand, the isolation insofar as was possible of opposition elements from external backing, and, on the other, the mobilization of resources from outside to consolidate the president's rule. In this, President Ali Abdullah Salih was, on the whole, successful, but not without certain difficulties. A survey of certain key moments in Yemeni external relations in the 1990s may make this pattern of external maneuvering more evident.

The Unification Agreement of 1990

Mention has already been made of how changes in the external environment contributed, on both sides, to the decision of the two Yemeni leaderships to proclaim unity in 1990. Decreasing Soviet support for the PDRY, on the one hand, and a more relaxed international context, on the other, encouraged both leaderships to proceed. While the issue had been under discussion for decades, and a draft constitution had existed as early as 1981, it was only in November 1989, when the Northern president was in Aden to celebrate the twenty-second anniversary of the British withdrawal, that he and President al-Bidh announced, suddenly, the program of unification.

This was, in the first place, something that was greeted with almost universal support in North and South. Perhaps the respective peoples shared their leaders' views about the economic benefits that would follow. A strong element was, however, the belief that this would strengthen Yemen vis-à-vis the outside world. Yemen had, it was argued, set the Arab world on the path of effective unity: the unification of the two Yemens would lead to a wider unity. Here echoes of an earlier Arab nationalism could be heard. It was equally believed that this would strengthen Yemen against Saudi Arabia. The unity announcement was made at a time when hopes were high, not only in Yemen but also in international oil circles, about Yemen's oil production potential. A unified, rich Yemen would be able to stand up to Saudi Arabia.

There was, moreover, an element of encouragement for this process from another Arab state where nationalist and unificationist ideas were still strong and that had, as a result of shared animosity to the oil-producing states, an interest in Yemen and its unity, namely Iraq. No outsider can say what the role of Saddam Hussein was in the unification agreement, be it in terms of offers of financial support or in broader political and diplomatic encouragement. It would appear that he had, from 1988, encouraged Ali al-Bidh, the YSP secretary-general, to proceed along this path. Certainly Iraq warmly welcomed the announcement. It was linked with the North through the four-state Arab Cooperation Council and saw Yemen as a future ally in the region. This Iraqi component, together with the changing, more permissive external environment and the patriotic enthusiasm released by the unification process, gave to this inter-Yemeni merger a broader, international character.

Yemen and the Kuwait Crisis

The crisis that broke over the Arab world on 2 August 1990 had particular, dramatic consequences for Yemeni unification. The formal unification of the country had taken place less than four months before, and the political forces in the country were feeling their way. Opinion within Yemen was also divided on how to respond to the crisis. Undoubtedly, the majority of Yemenis sympathized with Iraq: despite Saudi and Kuwaiti financial assistance to Yemen over the years, there was widespread resentment at the attitude of the oil-producing states to poorer Yemen. This was, most certainly, compounded when soon after the start of the crisis Saudi Arabia expelled over eight hundred thousand people of Yemeni descent from its territory, and severed all official aid, thereby not only depriving Yemen of financial flows but also landing it with a major resettlement problem. But there were those who took a different position. Within the foreign ministry itself, the officials who had to react on the morning of the crisis did not endorse the Iraqi action: they were overruled later in the day. For those political forces who were opposed to President Ali Abdullah Salih, the Iraqi invasion was not welcome; while many YSP leaders backed Iraq, some of the YSP in the south and some secular and left-wing opposition forces in the north, notably the Yemeni unionist group *al-tajammu' wahdawi al-yamani* of Umar al-Jawi, were, on historic grounds, hostile to Iraq. They feared what a stronger Iraqi presence, in conjunction with the president's own predilections, could do.

For Ali Abdullah Salih, there does not, however, appear to have been much doubt as to Yemen's stance: while it condemned the Iraqi invasion, and called for a withdrawal, Yemen consistently opposed sanctions and military action against Iraq. This might not have attracted such international attention if it had not been for the fact that Yemen was, at that time, occupying a seat in the UN Security Council. It was one of the fifteen states that decided on action by the international body. From August 1990 to March 1991 Yemen was, therefore, in an exposed position, earning in the process the animosity of the Arab oil producers (diplomatic relations with Kuwait were only restored in 1999) and of the United States. U.S. secretary of state James Baker noted after its representative had opposed Security Council Resolution 678, allowing the use of force to oust Iraq from Kuwait, that Yemen's permanent representative Abdullah al-Ashtal had "just enjoyed about $200 to $250 million worth of applause" for his stance.[14]

Expensive or not, and within a realist perspective of calculating national interest, irrational, the Yemeni decision can be explained by several factors.[15] First, the president and his advisers may well have felt, and rightly so, that there was a distinction between condoning or endorsing an act of aggression and resisting calls for military action to reverse it: this was, after all, the position of most Western states with regard to Israeli occupation of land after 1967 or the Turkish occupation of northern Cyprus. There was an element of victimization here, as there was, subsequently, in the differential treatment handed out to Yemen, which remained a semi-outcast for years, and the other Arab leader who had taken a similar stance, King Hussein of Jordan—his disloyalty was quickly forgotten. Second, the Yemenis, like others in the Arab world, may have calculated that Saddam Hussein would win. This was the belief of many Palestinians and indeed of some of Iraq's opponents. There were, however, other factors, internal to Yemen, that may have contributed to the outcome. One was the historic connection, possibly reinforced over the unification a few months before, between the president and Iraq: he was said to model himself, in a milder form, on Saddam, Iraqis provided assistance in military and security training, and Iraq had provided decisive help against internal opponents and the South, in the early consolidation of the president's rule after 1978. A second domestic consideration was the sense the president had that, precisely because of the divisions in Yemeni public opinion, he could use the Kuwait crisis to isolate his opponents, painting them as enemies of Arab unity and pawns of the Saudis and the United States. Finally, as the president rightly saw, the stance he took was, despite the costs to Yemen, popular in the country; indeed he could, to a degree, now blame the shortcomings of unity on precisely those whom most Yemenis saw as responsible for their ills—the Saudis, the other GCC countries, and the West. Thus *domestic* calculation may have overridden what was, in its own terms, an act of *international* irrationality.

The War of 1994

The crisis that engulfed Yemen in 1994, as the two components of the unified state fell into open war, was one with manifold international dimensions.[16] No outside power intervened directly in the war, nor, despite repeated claims by both sides on this score, were outside states mainly responsible for the outbreak of the conflict between North and South. During the course of the crisis, there was considerable diplomatic activity to prevent the war, and much speculation about possible recognition of the new Southern state, the Democratic Republic of Yemen, proclaimed at the end of May. In the end, however, no such diplomatic change occurred: the world outside, Arab and non-Arab, continued to recognize the government in Sana'a and therefore to maintain the status quo that had prevailed prior to the outbreak of hostilities.

International factors were, however, significant in a number of respects. First, the isolation of Yemen from part of the Arab world, and from the West, following the Kuwait crisis was only gradually overcome. The growing tension in Yemen from late 1992 onward led to renewed difficulties abroad: the YSP appeared to have the support of some of the Arab oil producers, and it was after a visit to the United States in the summer of 1993 that Vice President Ali al-Bidh broke formal contact with the president and took up residence in Aden. In the ensuing months, as both sides prepared for a possible armed conflict, the still separate military apparatuses of North and South purchased, and received, weapons from their respective patrons. The conflict was, therefore, internationalized well prior to the president's launching of his offensive against the South in April 1994.

The growing tensions inside the country did lead a number of outside states to offer mediation. Jordan hosted one such meeting in Amman in February, Oman another in Salala. In the days prior to the outbreak of fighting, a U.S. envoy, Robert Pelletreau, visited Sana'a to talk with the president. The latter's strategy was, however, not to respond to such mediation attempts: Ali Abdullah prepared for war on the ground, one that took his YSP opponents by surprise, and used a semblance of cooperation with external mediators to win legitimacy, and above all to ward off recognition of a separate Southern regime. The Northern argument was straightforward: the Southerners had started the war by their illegal attempt to secede.

This was the strategy the North pursued once the war began: at no point did Sana'a denounce external powers, other than Saudi Arabia, and the policy of Yemeni diplomats was to continue an apparently cooperative dialogue with the United Nations and other interested parties. In such a dialogue, Sana'a presented itself as the aggrieved party, the victim of a secessionist movement by the South, to which it, as a sovereign state, had to respond. When on two occasions the Yemen war came to the UN Security Council, which passed resolutions calling for a cease-fire, Sana'a appeared to cooperate, even as it pressed on with its offensive in the South. It had no doubt learned from other cases—Bosnia and, before that, Lebanon—how to play along with cease-fires called by international bodies while laying the ground for further activities.

This strategy was, in broad terms, successful. In the eyes of most Northern Yemenis, and much of the Arab world, the Southerners were seen as *infisaliin* (secessionists) acting at the behest of outside forces, and trying to divide an Arab nation. The supporters of the South were themselves caught off guard. Saudi Arabia had supplied large amounts of weapons to the YSP in the preceding months, estimated by some to total $2 billion in value. The Saudi ambassador to the United States, Prince Bandar bin Sultan, had argued, in Washington and Riyadh, that the South would prevail. But as the course of the war ground on, Saudi Arabia appeared to lose faith in the ability of the South to hold out, and in the end no diplomatic recognition was offered. The story with other GCC states was similar: Oman was concerned at the war, and allowed a businessman of Yemeni origin, Ahmad Farid, to send trucks and weapons into Yemen; the United Arab Emirates was reportedly most keen to extend recognition, Qatar the least. Had the South held out longer this might have been the case, but within six weeks of the proclamation of the Democratic Republic of Yemen, on 27 May, the Northern forces had entered Aden. Northern diplomatic stalling, combined with the situation on the ground, ensured that neither the Arab states nor the UN, nor the West, were willing to go out on a limb for the South. This was a signal success for the president's foreign as well as domestic policy.

Foreign Policy After 1994: A Qualified Normalization

The foreign policy of Yemen after 1994 was determined by the need the regime felt to overcome the crises of 1990 and 1994, and to increase the flow of financial support into the country. Relations with the Arab states and the West gradually improved, and by the end of the decade the overt damage of the 1990–1994 period had been overcome. The first Yemeni ambassador to Kuwait since 1990 took office in July 1999. A final settlement of the boundary with Oman was agreed on. Relations with Saudi Arabia also improved, if slowly: Ali Abdullah Salih was again invited to Riyadh and in 1995 a Memorandum of Understanding on the solution of the boundary was reached. This covered the area adjacent to the three provinces ceded in 1934. In June 2000, following a visit by Crown Prince Abdullah to Sana'a, an overall agreement on the border was drafted. Hopes were raised that this could lead to an overall settlement of the issue. Relations with the West also improved somewhat: ambassadors returned to post, and in 1997 President Salih paid official visits to Britain and France. As part of the policy of keeping reasonable relations with the United States, Yemen also agreed to participate in the multilateral regional talks stipulated after the Madrid and Oslo agreements. President Salih attended the Taba antiterrorism conference in 1996, and Prime Minister al-Iryani addressed the pro-Israeli Washington Institute for Near East Policy in 1998. In 1997 Yemen entered into a new military relationship with the United States, via Central Command: U.S. ships began to refuel at Aden, and Yemeni officials were trained on U.S. soil. This had obvious political benefits for Yemen, but such an opening ended abruptly on 12 October 2000 when anti-U.S. guerrillas attacked the *USS Cole* in Aden harbor, killing seventeen and wounding thirty-nine U.S. seamen.

This graduated improvement in relations with the outside world did not, however, mean that all was going well. Despite the 1995 memorandum and the 2000 border settlement, the oldest problem of all, relations with Saudi Arabia, remained. Up to June 2000, clashes along the border continued, there was no resolution of the status of the Yemenis expelled in 1990, and Saudi Arabia intervened to prevent Western oil companies from exploring in disputed territorial waters. Even after that border settlement, there was little love lost between the leadership of the two states: the Yemenis resented Saudi arrogance, the Saudis did not forget 1990. Relations with the Arab world, and the West, were made more complex by the emergence of a new problem, that of accusations about Yemen harboring Islamist terrorists of Yemeni or other origin. Considering the conditions of Yemen, it was not surprising that armed individuals and groups from elsewhere should be based there: what was less clear was the role of the Yemeni government in all this—the appearance of opposition to such groups contrasted with the known history of Sana'a using Islamist groups to fight the YSP, before and after 1994. Certain Arab states, notably Egypt and Saudi Arabia, were critical of Yemen in this regard, and the United States also saw Yemen as a candidate for its "terrorism" list. The improvement that began in U.S.-Yemeni relations in 1997 ended abruptly with the *USS Cole* incident. Britain also became involved when, in late 1998, in a complex set of events, British tourists were murdered by local tribesmen linked to an Islamist group, and six Britons of Arab and Pakistani origin were charged by the Yemenis with complicity in terrorism.

An even more dramatic new development, unexpected by most, was the outbreak of hostilities between Yemen and newly independent Eritrea: in 1995 Eritrean forces seized a set of islands in the Red Sea whose status was unclear, and inflicted a defeat on Yemen. This caused great resentment in Yemen, and the president was seen as having failed to defend the national territory. Eritrea was widely believed to be acting at the behest of Saudi Arabia or Israel, but also to be responding to support given by one of the more militant leaders of Islah, al-Zindani, to Sudan, at that time embroiled in conflict with Eritrea and with Egypt. Yemen had no choice but to agree to arbitration by the Permanent Court at The Hague and settlement was found in October 1998, to which both sides assented. But, perceived as it was within a broader context of inter-Arab tension, and having the domestic repercussions that it did, the conflict with Eritrea presented a particular challenge to the standing of the Sana'a state.

This uneasy connection between domestic and foreign policy was evident in two other respects. One was criticism from abroad of Yemen's political and human-rights record. Both Amnesty International and Human Rights Watch published critical reports on Yemen, stressing, as was pertinent, the gap between the appearance of cooperation on Sana'a's part and the reality of noncompliance.[17] Such criticisms were amplified by the opposition, which sustained an international campaign of criticism: in 1997, on the eve of a possible vote critical of Yemen in the European Parliament, al-Iryani, with French support, flew to Strasbourg to offer a compromise.

At the same time, the government sought, throughout the 1990s, to obtain sources of foreign finance. Oil continued to produce some revenue, but in neither the quantity of output nor the price per barrel anticipated at the time of unification in 1989–1990. Some foreign aid was forthcoming, on a bilateral and multilateral basis, but Yemen had to accept the new constraints of structural adjustment and good governance, pressures that created their own domestic tensions and subjected the politics of Yemen to international scrutiny. The state's response was to proclaim that, while Yemen was not a full democracy, it was on the way to democracy; international observers were invited to monitor elections. The new millennium began with Yemen, and Ali Abdullah Salih in particular, continuing the complex balancing act that they had sustained for so long, guiding foreign policy in a direction that would strengthen domestic support, and seeking to use foreign relations to bolster the state's position at home.

Conclusion

The determining context of Yemen's place in the international system has, throughout the modern period, been shaped by one factor above all: its weakness vis-à-vis the states and the structural forces acting on it. Yemeni states prior to and subsequent to unification have sought, through external policies, not only to preserve their independence, but to use such policies both to bolster their position vis-à-vis more powerful neighbors, and, before 1990, each other, and to use external linkages, military and financial, to compensate for the weaknesses of the state at home. Without either a strong state or significant natural resources, Yemeni states have faced a particular set of challenges that they have sought to resolve by adjustments in foreign policy. The balancing act required by such policies has, however, been made more difficult precisely because of the fragmented character of Yemeni society itself, be this on tribal, confessional, or political grounds. The success of Ali Abdullah Salih was, in the face of great uncertainties at home and broad, to remain in power for over two decades and to preside over the forcible unification of his country. The failure was that this was purchased at the expense of much suffering, lost opportunities, and conflict within Yemen, and with a continued set of tensions with the outside world. In a group of states that would include Lebanon and Palestine, Yemen has conducted its foreign policy from a position of structural weakness and domestic fragmentation. It would seem that only a significant change within the political and economic systems of the country would bring this precarious record to an end.

Notes

1. For case studies of foreign policy, see F. Gregory Gause, *Saudi-Yemeni Relations: Domestic Structures and Foreign Influence,* New York: Columbia University Press, 1990; Fred Halliday, *Revolution and Foreign Policy: The Case of South Yemen 1967–1987,* Cambridge: Cambridge University Press, 1990; Ahmed Noman Kassim Almadhagi, *Yemen and the United States: A Study of a Small Power and Super-State Relationship 1962–1994,* London: I. B. Tauris, 1996; Abdeldayem Mubariz, "Foreign Policy Making in the Yemen Arab Republic During the Republican-Royalist War 1962–1970: A Study of Four

Major Decisions," Ph.D. dissertation, London School of Economics, Department of International Relations, 1991. For general political analysis, see Robert W. Stookey, *Yemen: The Politics of the Yemen Arab Republic,* Boulder, CO: Westview Press, 1978; John Peterson, *Yemen: The Search for a Modern State,* Baltimore: Johns Hopkins University Press, 1982. For North Yemen, see Robert Burrowes, *The Yemen Arab Republic: The Politics of Development 1962–1986,* Boulder, CO: Westview Press, 1986. For South Yemen, see Halliday, *Revolution and Foreign Policy,* and Helen Lackner, *PDR Yemen: Outpost of Socialist Development in Arabia,* London: Ithaca Press, 1986.

2. Mubariz, "Foreign Policy Making."

3. Called variously Aden, South Arabia, and the South Arabian Protectorates under British rule, the area was first known as the People's Republic of South Yemen and then, in 1970, as the People's Democratic Republic of Yemen. For convenience, the latter term, PDRY, is used for the whole period 1967–1990.

4. I have discussed this in *Revolution and Foreign Policy,* chapter 4, and in "The Formation of Yemeni Nationalism," in James Jankowski and Israel Gershoni, eds., *Rethinking Nationalism in the Arab Middle East,* New York: Columbia University Press, 1997, reprinted in Fred Halliday, *Nation and Religion in the Middle East,* London: Saqi, 1999.

5. Halliday, *Revolution and Foreign Policy,* chapter 6; Mark Katz, *Russia and Arabia: Soviet Foreign Policy Towards the Arabian Peninsula,* Baltimore: Johns Hopkins University Press, 1986; Stephen Page, *The Soviet Union and the Yemens: Influence in Asymmetrical Relationships,* New York: Praeger, 1985; Christian Scheider, *Der südliche Jemen und die Sowjetunion: Grossmachengagement und politische Radikalisierung in der Dritten Welt,* Hamburg: Deutsches Orient-Institut, 1989.

6. Halliday, *Revolution and Foreign Policy,* chapter 3.

7. For analysis, see Richard Schofield, "The Last Missing Fence in the Desert: The Saudi-Yemeni Boundary," in G. Joffé, M. J. Hachemi, and E. W. Watkins, eds., *Yemen Today: Crisis and Solutions,* London: Caravel, 1997.

8. J. Leigh Douglas, *The Free Yemeni Movement 1935–1962,* Beirut: American University of Beirut, 1987.

9. U. Freitag and G. Clarence-Smith, *Hadramami Traders, Scholars and Statesmen in the Indian Ocean 1750s–1960s.* Leiden, Netherlands: Brill, 1997.

10. I am grateful to Christian Lekon, research student at the London School of Economics, for guidance on these matters. His thesis on Hadramaut 18 traces the evolution of British strategy from the 1840s to 1967.

11. For discussion, see Mubariz, "Foreign Policy Making," chapter 5.

12. On decisionmaking under Sallal and al-Iryani, see Mubariz, "Foreign Policy Making."

13. For this period, see Robert Burrowes, "The Republic of Yemen: The Politics of Unification and Civil War, 1989–1995," in Michael Hudson, ed., *Middle East Dilemmas: The Politics and Economics of Arab Integration,* London: I. B. Tauris, 1998; Fred Halliday, "The Third Inter-Yemeni War and Its Consequences," *Asian Affairs,* June 1995; Michael Hudson, "Bipolarity, Rational Calculation and War in Yemen," *Arab Studies Journal,* no. 3, 1995; Joseph Kostiner, *Yemen: The Tortuous Quest for Unity, 1990–1994,* London: Pinter, 1996.

14. James Baker, *The Politics of Diplomacy: Revolution, War and Peace 1989–1992,* New York: G. P. Putnam's, 1995, pp. 326–327.

15. Abdullah al-Ashtal, "Eventually There Can Only Be an Arab Solution," *Middle East Report* 21:2, no. 169, March–April 1991. For statements by Yemeni leaders, see BBC, *Summary of World Broadcasts,* part 4, passim, e.g., "President Salih on Reasons for 'Failure' of Arab Summit," ME/0842/A/6-8, 14 August 1990.

16. See Mark Katz, "External Powers and the Yemeni War," in Jamal al-Suwaidi, ed., *The Yemeni War of 1994: Causes and Consequences,* London: Saqi Books, 1995.

17. Amnesty International data, 1997 and 1999.

13

The Foreign Policy of Iran

Anoushiravan Ehteshami

At least since the early 1970s, Iran has been regarded as an important regional player; prior to that it had managed to accumulate considerable strategic value as a weighty pawn in the Cold War chessboard that straddled much of Asia and Europe. But it was the 1979 Islamic revolution that made Iran stand out on the international scene; after the overthrow of the shah by a coalition of Islamist, liberal, and radical forces, Iran emerged on the international scene as a defiant, fiercely independent, proactively religious, and nonaligned power. Since then, as James Piscatori has noted, there has rarely been a period that "Iran escaped the attention of the world's foreign offices, press, and academic experts on the Middle East and Islam."[1] Piscatori's observations have continued to hold true; dramatic developments in Iran and notable adjustments to its international relations since the late 1980s have ensured that Iran remains the country to watch and, for other actors in the international system, a growing force to reckon with. Calculations about the Islamic Republic, therefore, have been on the domestic and foreign-policy agendas of most regional actors and key international players, to the point that Iran watching has now been turned into a profitable little cottage industry.

Regionally, no country could afford to ignore the impact of the Iranian revolution and the Islamic Republic on its national security. The Iranian revolution disrupted the regional order and also ended the slowly emerging alliance of moderate forces in the Middle East. But as Halliday demonstrates, the revolution also made Iran a factor in the domestic politics of the superpowers: "for the USA . . . Iran provoked the greatest crises of the Carter and Reagan administrations . . . within the USSR Iran was not only an issue of dispute within the foreign policy making apparatus but also contributed to exaggerated Soviet leadership perceptions of an Islamic challenge."[2]

However, despite its revolutionary zeal and a reputation for non-conformity and defiance since the revolution, it can be argued that revolutionary Iran has always been a "rational actor" in the classic realist mold. Even some of its excesses can be seen as calculated risks or opportunist responses to difficult situations. Looking back at the post-Khomeini era, one cannot help but be struck by how "normal," largely nonaggressive, and pragmatic Iran's foreign policy has been since 1989. The roots of this transformation in Iran's international relations must be found in Iran itself, but it also has much to do with Tehran's calculations about its standing in a changed regional and international environment since the end of the Cold War. So much so that Iran is now fully engaged in the international system and is playing the more assertive role expected of a regional middle power in the Middle East and North Africa.

Foreign-Policy Determinants

Geopolitics: Between Autonomy and Ambition

The Iranian state, once the plaything of rival foreign forces, was transformed under the Pahlavi dynasty in the twentieth century into a significant regional power, albeit one frequently acting as a surrogate for Western interests. Since the Islamic revolution, Iran's power assets have been deployed in defense of regional autonomy from the West, even though in economic terms Iran never managed to distance itself from the capitalist world order, nor develop a truly independent economic base.

Geography has played a key part in informing Iran's foreign policy for centuries. An ancient landmass empire on the Eurasian crossroads, the modern state's regional ambitions extend to much of western Asia. In Iran's case, geography has acted as a single force with two countervailing tendencies. On the one hand, it has facilitated the spread of Persian influence in Asia, and on the other it has exposed Iran to great-power rivalries and the diplomatic machinations of out-of-area states. Historically, fears and perceptions of foreign interference have formed the basis of Iranian nationalism.[3] Iranian nationalism, furthermore, has for generations been intertwined with the issue of ensuring Iran's territorial integrity, which in turn has created what Fuller calls "an intensely

Irano-centric" view of the world. As he says, in this land "history itself is in part a product of classical geopolitical factors."[4] Geopolitics, therefore, has had, and continues to have, a special place in Iran's role conception, and as such must be given a special place in any analysis of Iranian foreign policy. Over time, then, a combination of factors—geography; the need to secure the country's territorial integrity; adverse historical experiences; competition with other empires (such as the Ottoman Empire); meddling in Iran's internal affairs by Western/Eastern powers such as Russia, Britain, and the United States; and the country's resource endowment—have come together to give geopolitics and an acute awareness of the weight of history a special place in determining Iranian foreign policy.

Iran's historical impotence in the face of foreign influence has left a deep and seemingly permanent scar on the Iranian psyche, which has also been guiding elite thinking for many decades. An almost obsessive preoccupation with outside interference in Iran's internal affairs has made Iranians wary of big-power involvement in the area, but at the same time the perception among most Iranians that Iran has been able to overcome outside pressures has allowed for the rise of a condition that I call "the arrogance of nonsubmission." Ayatollah Khomeini's celebrated phrase, "America cannot do anything," which is plastered all over Iranian towns and cities, is a good example of this tendency.[5] The above "condition" or tendency has given rise to a sense of exaggerated importance of Iran and a rather misplaced belief in the infallibility of the state, which has on more than one occasion led Iranian policymakers to make serious miscalculations not only about their own country's power and abilities, but also about the power as well as the motives of their adversaries.

Iranian perceptions of their environment and historical fears of outside interference were partly responsible for the evolution of the "negative balance" doctrine that at times formed the basis of Iran's pre- and postrevolution foreign policy.[6] The same views have also informed the fierce struggle in Iranians for both political and economic independence (esteqlal) from foreign powers. Thus, one of the main battle cries of the revolution was "Esteqlal, Azadi: Jomhouri Eslami" ("Independence, Freedom: Islamic Republic"), purposefully placing independence as the precondition for the long-cherished goal of freedom. Thus, the attainment of full sovereignty and control over Iran's destiny has for many decades been both a popular and elite sentiment.

Another, equally significant, revolutionary slogan was "Khod kafaye" ("Self-Sufficiency"), referring to the country's deep desire to reduce its economic dependence on Western powers and outside economic forces. Both left and right have argued for many years that it is economic independence that will deliver political independence and not vice versa. Thus, successive governments in Iran pursued an import-substitution strategy with vigor; by the mid-1970s, and despite the presence of a powerful private sector, the state was already the biggest economic actor in the country. For both practical and ideological reasons, state control and ownership of the economy reached new heights after the revolution.[7]

For the Iranian elite, pre- and postrevolution, economic power and independence of action in economic terms have been seen as the precursors to political independence and regional influence. Despite this desire, for the first half of the twentieth century Iran was in substantial receipt of foreign economic and military aid, largely from the United States. The situation was to change in the second half of the 1960s, when Iran began to accumulate capital from oil rent at an accelerated pace and developed an awareness of its own economic potential, a learning process that was to reach its zenith in the 1970s, thanks to the rapid increase in the price of oil. The shah's ambition to modernize Iran by the end of the twentieth century reflects the importance of a sound economic base as a precondition for the rise of Iran. Apparently, oil wealth was to magically transform Iran into a great regional military and global economic power. The emphasis during this period was on the rapid expansion of the domestic economy and the broadening of the country's industrial and manufacturing base through an intensive import-substitution industrialization strategy. Foreign capital and expertise were viewed as the necessary evils for the realization of this mission. In many analysts' eyes, on the other hand, the shah had reduced Iran to a semiperiphery country with a comprador bourgeoisie that was deeply dependent on the metropolis.[8]

Identity and Role: Iran as an Islamic Actor

The drive toward regional supremacy has long been a feature of Iranian foreign policy. Derived from Iran's long history and its geography, Iran sees itself as uniquely qualified to determine, at the very least, the destiny of the Gulf subregion. Furthermore, it sees itself as one of only a handful of "natural" states in the Middle East, which by virtue of being an old and territorially established civilization (based around the notion of "Iran-zamin") can and should have influence beyond its borders. Mohammad Reza Shah's long reign is full of evidence of this tendency

in Iranian elite thinking after 1953, particularly so in the 1970s.[9] Throughout the latter decade Iran tried to become the Gulf region's premier military power and aimed to become the main pillar of the Western security
system in the Middle East—to resume, as the shah himself put it, Iran's
"historic responsibilities."[10]

Since 1979, where geopolitics has mattered, Iran has added a religious dimension to its power-projection ability. Over time this new factor has formed a new layer over the deeply felt territorial nationalism of
the state. Since the revolution, then, Islamic issues have emerged to affect Iran's regional profile and its policies toward many of its neighbors.
Iran's postrevolution posture has also been affected by what could be
called the geopolitics of Islam. In the first instance, Tehran's messianic
Shi'ism of the early 1980s posed a direct challenge to the regional status quo and the political integrity of Iran's Arab neighbors. In making
explicit its demand to speak in the name of Islam, Tehran's revolutionary leadership caused noticeable tensions in the country's relations with
Saudi Arabia and other influential Islamic actors in the Muslim world as
it tried to "export the revolution." The Iranian leadership's call for
Islamic uprisings may have found sympathetic ears in many Arab and
Muslim societies in the 1980s, but this call also reinforced Arab elite
suspicions of Iranian intentions and encouraged their attempt to contain
Iranian influence. The "blockage" really only began clearing toward the
end of the 1980s, thanks to several developments: the end of the Iran-
Iraq war, the rise of a more pragmatic leadership in Iran, the growing
importance of oil politics, the Kuwait crisis, and Iran's post–Cold War
bridge-building regional strategy.

At the same time, Iran's stand vis-à-vis the Soviet occupation of
Afghanistan and Moscow's treatment of its own Muslim population
added a new religious dimension to the Cold War–based Iranian-Soviet
relations. Additionally, implicit and explicit support for the growing
number of Islamist movements in Afghanistan and elsewhere in the
Middle East became a fixture of Iranian foreign policy in its interstate
and substate interactions.

In the 1990s and beyond, despite its more integrationist and nonideological foreign policy, nonetheless Tehran has tried to keep pace
with the politicized Islamic groups in the Arab world and has been active in showing support for the following movements: the Hizbollah in
Lebanon, the Front Islamique du Salut (FIS) in Algeria, the Turabi
regime in Sudan, Hamas and Islamic Jihad in Palestine, the Muslim
Brotherhood in Jordan, the al-Nahda Party in Tunisia, and the Jihad
group in Egypt. Further afield, Tehran has been quite content to allow

itself to be portrayed as a supporter of Islamist movements of all denominations. The support given to the Islamic Moro National Liberation Front movement in the Philippines in the 1980s and to the Bosnian Muslims in the 1990s are good examples of this Iranian strategy. One can deduce from Tehran's behavior that the country's overt use of Islam, or at least Islamic symbols, remains a feature of its role conception. Islam's place in its formulation of policy and strategic aims has caused serious rifts in—and continues to complicate—Tehran's relations with a number of the Sunni-dominated, largely secular-led, Arab states around it.

The Economic Factor

The primacy of hydrocarbons. Oil had always been an important factor in the making of modern Iran, but the mad rush of the 1970s to modernize Iranian society and industrialize the economy increased the country's dependence on its hydrocarbon resources. Over a very short period of time the economics and politics of oil began to influence the foreign-policy and national-security strategy of the country. At the same time, this heavy reliance on oil wealth as the main pillar of Iran's grand strategy increased the country's vulnerability to outside forces and international economic pressures. Oil wealth, in short, had become both the salvation and the curse for the country's modernizing elites; as the shah himself was to acknowledge, it was in the end its Achilles' heel.[11]

The Islamic Republic inherited the peculiarities of Iran's oil-based socioeconomic system and its oil-related place in the international economic division of labor. While in the first few years after the revolution the new elite did try to tinker with the economy and Iran's trading system, the war with Iraq effectively put a stop to any opportunities to redirect the economy away from its heavy reliance on oil wealth and thus ended any prospects of Iran changing its relationship with the international capitalist system. Iran's inability to leave the system or change Iran's position within it meant that eventually the theocracy too would have to behave according to the rules set by the Pahlavi regime—and more to the point, to those regulating the international capitalist system. Iran's place in the international division of labor as a supplier of hydrocarbons did not change, but what did change was Iran's place in the system as an emerging newly industrializing country (NIC). The revolution and Iran's postrevolution international posture effectively ended this Iranian ambition; the end of its Western alliances froze the national capital–foreign capital ties that had been emerging since the late 1960s and starved Iran of the essential inputs for the diversification of the economy and the expansion of its industrial base. In historic terms, Iran was off the boat that it and South Korea had caught from the mid-1960s.

In net terms, the negative effect of these developments was twofold. On the one hand, the interdependencies that were created by developments in the oil industry in the 1970s between Iran's rentier economy and international capitalism remained intact. On the other hand, the overthrow of the shah and the Islamic Republic's new priorities effectively checked any national drive to turn the country into a regional capitalist center, into a successful NIC. Iran was, to paraphrase Rafipoor, to leave that capital-driven, materialist rat race—for a little while at least.[12]

Export or die. Under Ayatollah Khomeini's influence, Iran had acquired a large degree of freedom in its foreign policymaking and in exerting its influence in the region. The freedom to act "independently" of outside powers, of course, had been one of the main aims of the revolution, but in regard to policymaking this newly cherished freedom was reinforced by the clerics' domination of the long-autonomous Iranian state, founded as it had been on its monopoly of income from the country's hydrocarbon resources. Not surprisingly, oil and the drive to secure maximum return for its sale soon became the political-economy prism through which the Islamists viewed the world as well. Eventually, they too had learned that low oil prices meant economic weakness in an oil-dependent country like Iran. They therefore had to find ways of boosting oil income, which they started doing as early as 1988 through cooperation with other regional oil producers, to many of whom Tehran had been extremely offensive during its war with Iraq.

But the Islamist leadership also learned, just as the shah had, that oil income in itself is not a panacea for Iran's economic and social ills. As many of its leaders were to acknowledge, there were to be no quick-fix solutions to the Islamic Republic's problems.[13] The leadership, therefore, even before Ayatollah Khomeini's demise, had come to accept the need for economic and administrative reform.

After the end of the Iran-Iraq war, significant sections of the revolutionary elite begun arguing that Iran's economic problems, caused by the difficulties and policy mistakes of the 1980s, necessitated an overhaul of the economy. This line was championed by Iran's first executive president, Hojjatoleslam Rafsanjani. The crisis was indeed serious and multifaceted: negative growth, high unemployment, low productivity and underutilization of capacity, shortages of investment capital, high import dependency, managerial weaknesses, substantial loss-making enterprises under state control, a ballooning public sector, and lack of confidence in government policy.[14] In the absence of foreign investment and other immediately available and accessible resources, Iran's many economic difficulties merely reinforced the country's dependence on oil and the need to generate investment capital, technology, and industrial expertise from the West.

Growing general understanding at home of Iran's vulnerabilities strengthened the hand of President Rafsanjani and his allies in dealing with the hard-liners, and enabled the president to continue with the conciliatory foreign-policy line that he had championed. The bottom line for him was that outside assistance was essential for the reconstruction of the country. The remedies of the new Rafsanjani administration resembled an International Monetary Fund–type economic reform strategy that preached liberalization and deregulation as the necessary tools for the restructuring of the economy.[15]

Focusing more closely on the political economy of foreign policy, the major impact on Iranian foreign policy of its economic predicament in many ways resembled developments in Algeria, where, as Korany has demonstrated, the increasing role of oil in the economy caused an "economisation of foreign policy."[16] In Iran's case, by the late 1980s, the same priorities that had preoccupied the shah's last decade had reemerged to dominate the economic and political agenda of Iran's post-Khomeini leadership. The talk again was of attracting direct foreign investment, establishment of foreign-trade zones, and deeper economic relations with the West. Some at home feared that Iran was in danger of returning to the bosom of the West, despite its long struggle to free itself of direct outside interference in its domestic affairs and the fact that its revolutionary leadership had managed to behave much more independently of outside powers and pressures than at any time in Iran's modern history.

The lasting impression of post-1945 Iranian foreign policy must be that oil has enhanced the country's capabilities and its potential to influence developments around it. Furthermore, global dependence on this commodity gave the Pahlavi political elite opportunities to forge close alliances with outside powers and enabled it to build a substantial military capability in the 1970s and pursue with impunity ambitious political objectives in the Middle East and beyond. But the same commodity also imposed many restrictions on the freedom of the state and made it more dependent on oil rent and on outside forces and much more vulnerable to systemic changes. The more it relied on hydrocarbons to free itself from poverty and lack of control over the country's destiny and its desperate inability to influence developments in the regional and international systems, the more it became vulnerable to pressures outside of its control, and ultimately the more economic considerations began to dominate its foreign policy. So while Iran has been able to mobilize domestic resources in the service of its foreign policy, the heavy reliance on hydrocarbons has influenced developments and the evolution of Iranian domestic and foreign arenas in ways not altogether expected by the elite.

With the above in mind, it was not too surprising that the political upshot of the oil price–induced economic crisis of the 1990s has been the reiteration of the need to behave nonideologically and seek cooperation with Iran's neighbors (particularly the oil exporters of the Persian Gulf) and trading partners (mainly the European Union and Japan). The latter, resisting the Clinton administration's "dual containment" strategy, chose to reschedule some of Iran's debt and used Iran's economic weakness to acquire more political leverage—albeit for business considerations—with Tehran. As a consequence, Iran today maintains good relations with the components of the "Western camp"; it has close economic and growing political links with the European Union, it has developed extensive links with Egypt, and has been busy developing a very close politico-economic "partnership" with Saudi Arabia.

Foreign Policymaking

Leadership and Factionalism

For much of the 1980s, with the Iran-Iraq war as its strategic backdrop, foreign-policy issues were addressed by Ayatollah Khomeini himself, and at key junctures it was his office that made and implemented policy. But various factions and centers of power within the clerical establishment took advantage of many opportunities to advance their own interests and to implement their own foreign agendas. This was particularly visible in relation to the Arab world. The radicals were in constant search of the vehicles for exporting the Islamic revolution and concluding alliances with Islamist movements in the region. To this end, in the early 1980s the radical groups cultivated such movements in Iraq, Kuwait, Bahrain, Saudi Arabia, Afghanistan, and, of course, Lebanon, among other places. In the first decade of the republic, the struggle between the so-called moderates or pragmatists and the radicals was a determinant element of the policy process.

Factionalism and institutional competition was, from the beginning, an important feature of the postrevolution Iranian political system. The factions themselves are rather fluid, and as they are normally comprised of a variety of tendencies and blocs built around powerful personalities, they tend to act as "fronts" and as such do not always function as a single entity.[17] So, in the 1980s, the presence of such personalities as Ayatollah Hossein Ali Montazeri and Hojjatoleslams Mehdi Karrubi, Sadeq Khalkhali, Mohammad Khoinia, and Ali Akbar Mohtashemi ensured that the radical agenda would dominate, the "Iran-gate" deals with Israel and the United States notwithstanding. Between 1990 and 1997, of course, the position of individuals such as Mohtashemi had been gradually weakening, most decisively with the accession of the pragmatist Hojjatoleslam Hashemi Rafsanjani to the presidency; Karrubi and Khoinia later resurfaced as loyal allies of Khatami and supporters of his reforms.

With the emergence, between 1989 and 1997, of a triple alliance between Ayatollahs Khamenei and Mohammad Yazdi (the head of the judiciary at the time), and President Rafsanjani, the radical/populist factions suffered a decline in their political fortunes, although several influential individuals, such as Ayatollah Ahmad Jannati, continued to object to many of President Rafsanjani's reformist initiatives and fan the coals of populism.

The first three personalities were instrumental in formulation of the republic's new priorities in the 1990s. The *faqih,* Ayatollah Khamenei, proved to be a close ally of Rafsanjani and largely a supporter of many of his administration's policies. Ayatollah Khamenei is an opponent of the radical factions in the Islamic Republic but is himself a "conservative" in Iranian political terms, favoring a reasonable distance between Iran and the West and opposing any Westernization of Iranian society.[18] To prevent "corruption" of Muslim Iran, he frequently speaks against foreign investment in Iran and against measures that might facilitate a cultural invasion of the country by the U.S.-led Western powers. Such perceptions have had an impact on Tehran's foreign policy, but not enough to dislodge or derail the pragmatic foreign-policy orientation Rafsanjani espoused.

Executive Institutional Consolidation

Since August 1989 and the constitutional reforms of that year, a "presidential center" has been created at the heart of the executive power structure of the republic.[19] The constitutional reforms also brought into being a National Security Council (NSC), controlled by the president and his staff. This body has become the nerve center of policymaking in Iran and the key body where foreign policy is debated. The president, thus, has since 1989 taken the main responsibility for foreign policy-making and has been allowed to use his new powers to formulate and direct Iran's international relations. Under the reformed constitution, the foreign minister reports directly to the president, who heads the council of ministers. Thus, implementation of foreign-policy initiatives through the foreign ministry is also monitored through the president's office. However, although the presidential office has emerged as the main foreign-policymaking organ of the state, the president's foreign-policy decisions are not made in isolation from other power centers.

The *faqih* is the individual whose support is crucial in implementation of foreign-policy decisions. The *faqih*'s position and support is normally arrived at in the formulation stage of policies: through his personal representative on the NSC, he follows and conveys his views to this decisionmaking body. When controversial decisions have to be made, therefore, the fact that the *faqih* has been involved, albeit indirectly, in the policy formulation means that he can and does make public statements in endorsement of decisions, thus providing justification for the president's foreign-policy initiatives and diffusing direct criticism of his administration. Despite differences between Khamenei and Rafsanjani (largely over personalities in official positions and appointing of their own allies to key government posts) and a certain degree of institutional competition between their offices, the president and the *faqih* managed to work closely enough to ensure the isolation of their opponents in regional, national, and institutional power centers.

The foreign ministry's role in the policy process, including that of the foreign minister, must not be ignored, however. The former Iranian foreign minister, Ali Akbar Velayati, was one of the world's longest-serving foreign ministers and the Iranian cabinet's longest-serving member, having been a member of the government since December 1981. His presence assured continuity in the policy-implementation process. Over the years he was able to place pragmatists in key ministry positions, and by keeping close ties with both President Rafsanjani and Ayatollah Khamenei he managed to reserve himself a place at the power table. His power in the ministry, however, was not unlimited, nor did it remain unchecked. Interestingly, he was one of the key ministers to lose his job in Khatami's cabinet. Since 1997 he has been acting as the *faqih*'s adviser on foreign affairs, at times trying to influence the decisions of President Khatami's foreign minister, Dr. Kamal Kharazi.

Kharazi too is a seasoned politician and core elite member, having been around since the very beginning of the establishment of the Islamic Republic. He was one of the founding members of the Supreme Defense Council set up in 1980. He is well known for his moderate line and has been pushing for better relations between Iran and its Arab and non-Arab neighbors.

The consolidation of the presidency and NSC has not, however, ended intra-elite power politics in the system. Indeed, given the absence or weakness of a political-party system, both informal and policy-based consultative circles or coalitions have formed to fill the vacuum at various levels of decisionmaking. These have included the Militant Clerics Society (once "radical," now in the proreform camp); the "conservative" Combatant Clergy Association; the "pragmatic" Servants of Construction; and the Mojahedin-e Islam, once radical but later in the reformist camp. In one sense, these perform some of the functions of parties, namely, aggregating factions into broader alternative policy "platforms," hence limiting the corrosive impact of factional rivalries on the system. On the other hand, the traditional factions have capitalized on such circles to influence policy and the circles have tended to sharpen the broader ideological divisions in the republic.

Before 1997, the deliberate process of marginalization of the leftist-radical forces had resulted in the decline of their influence over foreign policy. The presidency, during and since the Rafsanjani period, is the key foreign policymaker, and both post-Khomeini presidents have favored Iran's integration into the international system and improved relations with the outside world. But the triumph of the moderates neither eliminated the radicals altogether nor indeed ended factionalist tendencies in the republic. In fact, no sooner had the radicals been marginalized than another caucus emerged to block the pragmatists. This time, the opposing faction, dubbed the "conservatives," gave almost unreserved support to Rafsanjani's economic reform policies, but adopted a strong line against the state's liberalization of social policy. On foreign policy, the conservatives objected to the administration's efforts to rebuild bridges with the West and remained suspicious of moves that would undermine the influence of the clergy and of Islam in society, but they were not prepared to support the call of the radical forces for a return to the policies of the 1980s. For much of the 1990s, the conservatives were the most powerful political force in the country, dominating the Majlis and the bureaucracy. They have remained the main institutional opponents of Khatami's brand of politics, and have actively objected to many of his domestic policies. On foreign policy, too, they are active, opposing his gestures toward the United States and the West in general, but also with regard to Iran's rapid rapprochement with its neighbors.

The Role of Legislature, Press, and Public Opinion

While the legislature is constitutionally barred from interfering in the executive's foreign-policymaking process, the Majlis does discuss foreign-policy issues. Indeed, the institutional ties between the Majlis and the executive have been so intimate that Hojjatoleslam Hassan Rouhani, a long-standing deputy Majlis speaker, has served as the secretary of the NSC and as Ayatollah Khamenei's representative on the body. Furthermore, Majlis deputies try to influence the direction of foreign policy through the power of the Majlis' own committees and frequent contacts with foreign dignitaries. The Majlis can play an active part in foreign-policy thinking and the floor of the Majlis and its Foreign Affairs Committee are avenues for the deputies' pronouncements on foreign-policy matters. Majlis deputies have the power to seek clarification from ministers and detailed written responses relating to domestic and foreign policies of the executive body, and through these mechanisms the deputies can influence foreign-policy decisions. The Majlis can monitor foreign-policy developments through other avenues as well since the government is required to obtain the Majlis' approval for entering into any "international treaties, memorandums of understanding, contracts and agreements" with other states and parties. This constitutional clause gives the Majlis the authority to critique the administration's overseas initiatives.

The tribune of the Majlis offers the deputies a unique opportunity to challenge presidential initiatives and policies by influencing public opinion, itself an important factor in the foreign-policymaking process, through their speeches, interviews, and writings in the national press. Although it may not always pay off, influencing public opinion is the traditional method of putting pressure on the executive to revise or continue to pursue a particular policy, and partly explains the remarkably open nature of political debate in Iran.

The place of the Council of Guardians in foreign policymaking is not as direct as that of the Majlis. The Council of Guardians' formal role in this context is to ensure that the administration's foreign-policy initiatives do not contravene the constitution. Where the Council of Guardians does make judgments, these are mainly of technical nature and largely deal with the republic's bilateral agreements with other countries.

Another important factor influencing Iranian foreign policy today is public opinion, which is shaped by open debate in the press and disseminated by a relatively free and large media machinery. Numerous newspapers and periodicals discuss and get involved in their discussions virtually all the core opinionmakers from within the political establishment, as well as increasingly influential individuals from the world of academia and slowly emerging semi-independent think tanks. To put the importance of the printed media in perspective, as Table 13.1 indicates, there were in 2000 some sixteen daily newspapers in circulation and another six important weeklies, a couple of biweeklies, and three important political monthlies engaged in debate with each other, the public, and the political establishment.

Table 13.1 Key Regular Iranian Publications and Their Political Affiliations

Name	Affiliation	Frequency
Aftab-e Emrouz	Reformist, pro-Khatami	Daily
Akhbar-e Eqtesad	Reformist, pro-Khatami	Daily
Kayhan	Extreme Right	Daily
Resalat	Traditional Right	Daily
Salaam	Old Left, pro-Khatami	Daily
Sobh-e Emruz	Modern Left, pro-Khatami	Daily[a]
Khordad	Technocrat, pro-Khatami	Daily[a]
Neshat	Nationalist-religious, pro-Khatami	Daily
Hamshahri	Technocrat, pro-Khatami	Daily
Iran	Technocrat, pro-Khatami	Daily
Ettela'at	Pro-Khatami	Daily
Abrar	Traditional Right	Daily
Zan	Technocrat, pro-Khatami	Daily
Kar-o Kargar	Pro-Khatami, Left-leaning	Daily
Jebhe	Extreme Right	Daily
Jomhuri Eslami	Religious fundamentalist	Daily
Javan	Pro-Right faction	Daily
Entekhab	Pro-Right faction	Daily
Jahan-e Islam	Old Left	Daily
Afarinesh	Traditional Right	Daily
Arzeshha	Pro-Left	Weekly
Jaam	Traditional Right	Weekly
Payam-e Hajar	Nationalist-religious	Weekly
Mosharekat	Pro-Khatami	Weekly
Tavana	Pro-Khatami	Weekly
Asr-e Ma	Modern Left	Biweekly
Iran-e Farda	Pro-Reform, Old National Front	Monthly
Ya Lesarat al Hussein	Extreme Right	Monthly
Paym-e Emruz	Nationalist-democratic	Monthly

Source: Tavana, no. 34, 3 May 1999, and other national sources.
Note: a. Closed down in 1999.

Foreign-Policy Behavior

Regional Policy

Broadly speaking, five phases can be observed in the regional policy of Iran since the revolution. Each phase is indicative of and a product of the changing priorities of the regime at home, reactions to internal developments, and, to a lesser degree, of the balance of forces within the Iranian political elite.

The first phase is identified as the *consolidation* stage. This phase was accompanied by the gradual entrenchment of the clerics in power and a rejection of the status quo in the Middle East. During this period (1979–1981), the power struggle between the "liberals" (such as Bazargan and Bani Sadr) and the more radical clerical forces (Maktabis) was in full swing, and the reference to "consolidation" is intended to highlight: (1) the emergence of a post-Pahlavi foreign-policy outlook, and (2) the domination of the Maktabis in the government machinery by the end of this period. In these early years of the republic, the differences among the clerical forces had not crystallized into competing factions and thus they tended to adopt a more or less common position on the power struggle with the more liberal and secularist nonclerical forces.

The essence of the consolidation phase thus was to develop an alternative, Islamic, foreign policy for Iran and for it to seek to effectively change the regional balance of power in favor of the Islamist and radical forces. An important aspect of this strategy was the rejection of Western and Communist-bloc alliances in the Middle East.[20] Efforts to "export the revolution" and the U.S. hostage crisis of the early 1980s were indicative of this trend.

The second, *rejectionist* phase (1981–1988) was largely coterminous with the Iran-Iraq war, during which Iran was isolated, locked in mortal combat with Saddamist Iraq, and at odds with many of its neighbors and former friends. Iran's isolation was partly due to the pro-Iraq line of the moderate Arab forces, who had during this period been totally alienated by Tehran, and partly a result of the hard line Tehran was taking in international forums. Regionally, by 1987 Iran was at odds with Iraq, Kuwait, Saudi Arabia, Sudan, Egypt, Israel, Jordan, Morocco, Tunisia, North Yemen, and Afghanistan. It could only count Syria as its ally and South Yemen and Libya as friendly countries. Although it maintained normal relations with three other countries (Algeria, Pakistan, and Turkey), two of them non-Arab, neither of these countries had developed strategic ties with the Islamic Republic.

A review of Iran's regional policy in the 1980s reveals a multidimensional effort aimed at overcoming its isolation in the Middle East and penetrating areas hitherto closed to Tehran. In the Persian Gulf subregion, Tehran was following a three-pronged strategy to (1) defeat Iraq militarily, (2) drive a wedge between Baghdad and the Gulf Arab states, and (3) cultivate a constituency for itself among the Gulf Arab peoples (particularly the Shi'a population) at the same time as subverting the most vulnerable regimes among the traditional monarchies.

With its non-Arab neighbors, particularly Pakistan and Turkey, Tehran sought to maintain cordial relations, never really Islamizing the basis of its relations with these states. The post-1979 situation in Afghanistan, however, provided Iran's new rulers not only with an opportunity to reassert their traditional authority among the Afghanis, but also enabled Tehran to ride the Islamist revival in that country and carve for itself a new basis of activity in Soviet-occupied (and post-Soviet) Afghanistan.

In the Levant, Tehran was seeking to deepen its newly found alliance with Syria while also capitalizing on the politicization of the Shi'i community in Lebanon, in addition to attempting to form a broad constituency among this confession in that country. The creation of Hizbollah and Tehran's ability to deploy armed revolutionaries among the Shi'i strongholds were the main achievements of Iran's Lebanon policy. The importance of Lebanon to Tehran was also to be found in geopolitical factors, as Lebanon offered it the opportunity to jump over Iraq and reach a wider constituency within the Arab world.[21]

The second aspect of Tehran's Levant strategy focused on the Arab-Israeli conflict. At one level, Tehran was anxious to bury the legacy of the Israeli-Iranian alliance of the Pahlavi era, and thus was very keen to draw itself closer to the Palestinians. This it attempted to do, first by Islamicizing the Arab struggle against Israel, and second, in the absence of any viable Islamic Palestinian factions in first half of the 1980s, through developing contacts with the radical and rejectionist factions, particularly with those endorsed by Syria.

By the late 1980s, military and political developments in the region had forced a reassessment of the rejectionist/militant strategy of the republic. Even though a real pragmatist strand had been in evidence in Iran since 1984–1985, the turning point seems to have come with the U.S.-Iranian naval engagements of 1987, the UN's passing of Security Council Resolution (SCR) 598, and Iran's battlefield defeats of early 1988. The appointment of (Majlis) Speaker Rafsanjani as the commander-in-chief of the armed forces illustrated the ascendance of the pragmatists in power and Iran's unconditional acceptance of SCR 598 owes much to his appointment and his wish to end the war before a complete collapse of the Iranian war effort. For want of a better phrase, I have termed this third stage in Iran's foreign relations the *reorientation* phase, one of transition from radicalism to accommodation. This period started in earnest in June 1988 and lasted until August 1990, by which time we see the end of the transition to pragmatism and the establishment of the *pragmatist* line in Iran's foreign policy, the fourth phase. The ascendance of the pragmatist line can be detected in Iran's decision to end the eight-year war with Iraq, which also marked the point from which the "Thermidor" of the Iranian revolution could be said to have commenced.[22]

The most important development of the *reorientation* phase was Iran's unconditional acceptance of UN Security Council Resolution 598, almost a year after its unanimous passing by the Security Council. At the time, Iranian leaders insisted that peace was now in the best interest of the republic and that in accepting SCR 598 and suing for peace, Iran was countering the direct intervention of the "satanic" powers (i.e., the United States) in the Gulf region, which Iran could no longer either ignore or confront militarily. This is the first policy watershed of the republic that needs to be noted. It is important for three main reasons. First, it indicates the reversal of a major foreign-policy objective: defeat of Saddam Hussein of Iraq and his overthrow. Second, Iran's acceptance of SCR 598 opened the door to normalization of relations with its other Gulf Arab neighbors, so that by the end of 1988 Tehran had managed to reestablish cordial relations with all of the Gulf states, barring Iraq and Saudi Arabia. Third, in accepting SCR 598, Iran also indicated its interest in developing a viable security structure for the subregion in cooperation with all of its Arab neighbors.[23]

Apart from these strictly regional dimensions of the cease-fire, the cessation of hostilities between Iran and Iraq (one of the Soviet Union's Arab allies and its main military customer) removed the obstacles to closer contacts between Tehran and Moscow, a process that was helped in no small way by the Soviet withdrawal from Afghanistan. During 1989, a flurry of diplomatic contacts between the two neighbors culminated in Soviet foreign minister Shevardnadze's trip to Tehran and Speaker Rafsanjani's high-level visit to Moscow in June. The latter trip resulted in the signing of a multibillion-dollar trade and military cooperation agreement between Iran and the USSR. Relations developed then paved the way for close military, political, and economic ties between Russia and Iran since the collapse of the Soviet Union.

The cease-fire also enabled Iran to reaffirm its ties with its non-Arab neighbors, Pakistan and Turkey. Better relations with these countries, bilaterally and in the context of the Tehran-based Economic Cooperation Organization (ECO), of which all three were founding members, became a new imperative for Iran. ECO and Iran's relations with Pakistan and Turkey were particularly important to Tehran in the post–cease-fire Gulf environment, if for no other reason than the fact that by 1989 Iran had found itself surrounded by Arab alliances; Iraq had formed the four-member Arab Cooperation Council in 1989 and the Gulf Cooperation Council (GCC) had managed to consolidate itself as a key Gulf-based organization.[24]

Although close contacts between Tehran and its Arab friends were maintained after 1988, the rapprochement in Syrian-Egyptian relations in 1990, and the success of the Saudi-Syrian–sponsored Taif agreement for Lebanon, raised the prospects of a reemergence of the same tripartite alliance between Egypt, Saudi Arabia, and Syria that had existed in the mid-1970s. The danger from Tehran's perspective was that the presence of such an Arab alliance could only lead to the marginalization of Iran's regional role. While in the 1970s the shah's regime had been relatively successful in containing the influence of this alliance in the Persian Gulf subregion, in the absence of the same resources at its disposal, Iran's post-Khomeini leadership clearly could not do likewise. It had no diplomatic relations with Saudi Arabia or Egypt, and seemed to have few, if any, incentives to offer Syria to resist the lure of Saudi oil and petrodollars and Egyptian diplomatic clout. Furthermore, Tehran feared that the Saudi-hosted Taif process could reduce substantially Iran's influence in Lebanon, a country in which it had invested a great deal of energy and had viewed as the vehicle in which it could secure a politico-military foothold in the front line of Arab affairs. However, Rafsanjani, prioritizing relations with Syria, cooperated in the stabilization of Lebanon under Syrian hegemony in return for the pivotal role accorded its Hizbollah client in Lebanese politics and in the resistance to Israel in South Lebanon.

The fourth phase of Iran's regional policy, *pragmatism,* would emerge as a response to the Iraqi invasion of Kuwait and its aftermath.

The Kuwait Crisis: Iranian Pragmatism in Operation

For Iran, the Iraqi invasion of Kuwait in August 1990 was a mixed blessing, even though in Tehran's eyes the Baghdad regime's behavior seemed to have vindicated its policies toward Iraq in the 1980s, which many GCC countries came to acknowledge after the invasion. The immediate impact of the invasion on Iran was twofold: on the one hand it raised Iran's profile and highlighted its significance as a regional player (the crisis helped in opening all of the frozen channels of communications with Iran's Arab neighbors); but on the other, the crisis raised regional tensions and provided the catalyst for the return of Western powers to the Gulf subregion, thus weakening Tehran's ability to influence the policies of the GCC and to forge ties with the Gulf sheikhdoms aiming at collective security in the Persian Gulf.

Iran's position during this crisis was in sharp contrast to its interventionist and adventurist policies of the postrevolution period. Tehran's neutralist and nonaligned stance and support for the UN position throughout, coupled by its condemnation of the invasion, brought the republic substantial kudos. In 1990, Iran thus stood on the side of the West and restoration of Kuwait's sovereignty, and, by extension, the right of the Al-Sabah family to continue to rule the sheikhdom—indicating a complete change of heart toward the Kuwaiti regime.

While Iran did not actively encourage the war against Iraq, it did expect the war to weaken significantly its most stubborn regional competitor. President Rafsanjani was clear on Iran's position, despite grave reservations by the more radical forces: "The Iraqis must definitely pull out. . . . Here, we have no objection to [the 'foreign forces'] obstructing aggression; anybody may help in any way."[25] Neutrality in this conflict gave Tehran a large measure of flexibility in its foreign relations. It gave it scope to deal with Iraq as well as the antiwar Arab forces, while its insistence on the reversal of the aggression and an unconditional Iraqi pullout brought it closer to the anti-Iraq Gulf monarchies. Its restraint and neutrality also obtained for Iran renewed diplomatic relations with Jordan, Tunisia, and Saudi Arabia, and some constructive contacts with Egypt and Morocco.

Most importantly of all, as a consequence of the crisis, Iran was to win the victory over Iraq that had eluded it on the battlefield. Iraq capitulated to Iran fully and accepted the full implementation of SCR 598 and the 1975 Algiers Treaty concerning their border dispute. By December 1990 the UN had also recognized Iraq as the "aggressor" party in the Iran-Iraq war and had cleared the way for Iranian war reparations claims from Iraq of billions of dollars.

Despite Iran's efforts to limit Western military presence in the Gulf subregion, in the aftermath of the war a series of bilateral defense pacts between the main Western players and a number of GCC states paved the way for a permanent Western military presence in the Persian Gulf—something Iran had thought its acceptance of SCR 598 would have avoided. Moreover, the creation in March 1991 of the "6+2" Gulf security pact between the GCC and Egypt and Syria worried Tehran that its backyard was being developed as an exclusively Arab area.

The end of the Gulf war renewed pressures to address the Middle East's most serious problem, the Arab-Israeli conflict. For Iranian diplomacy, the Madrid process was a minefield not only because it threatened to subsume Syria in a Western-oriented peace agreement with Israel, but also because it was Iran that was being left out of the unfolding post-1990 regional order. Iran was especially concerned that the emergence of new agendas between Israel and the Arab states and the Palestinians left no room for Iranian involvement except in opposition to the whole process.[26] This role Iran readily adopted on the grounds that the Madrid process was U.S.-inspired (i.e., that Washington had a hidden agenda) and that it was designed to rob the Palestinians of their rights in favor of Israel's regional ambitions and aspirations. Also, Tehran's overtly Islamic profile did necessitate its formal opposition to the peace process on religious grounds.

Also problematic for Iran was the way in which the peace process was sucking in Iran's Gulf Arab neighbors, and thus adding to Tehran's sense of isolation and loss of influence in the Persian Gulf subregion. This sense of diminishing influence was heightened after 1993, with many GCC states opening direct channels of communication and trade talks with Israel and their willingness to bring the process (through multilateral and bilateral meetings) to the Gulf itself.[27] Nonetheless, Tehran's declared strategy toward the peace process was one of nonintervention; Iranian leaders stated more than once that there is no gain in Iran trying to be "more Palestinian than the Palestinians." It would not endorse the process, but nor would it stand in its way.

The fifth phase in the Islamic Republic of Iran's foreign policy emerged with the rise of the "Second Khordad" movement,[28] which marked the 1997 presidential election victory of Hojjatoleslam Khatami. Khatami's foreign policy reinforced the nonideological aspects of Rafsanjani's foreign policy, but it also went further, preaching compromise, rule of law, and moderation.[29] This fifth phase in Iran's foreign policy can suitably be termed the drive for *moderation*. It is symbolized by Khatami's overtly moderate and nonconfrontational approach to foreign policy, the president's declared aim of establishing a "dialogue of civilizations," and attempts at reaching an understanding with the West (including the United States). In foreign-policy terms, the Khatami administration has tried very hard to put to rest the ghosts of the revolution. Thanks to the president's efforts, Iran managed to make several new friends in a very short period of time after his election, and has rediscovered many old acquaintances as well. Khatami and his policies continue to capture international headlines and keep the West deeply interested in developments in the country. During his first term in office he made scores of overseas trips and visited no less than seven countries, more than any other Iranian leader since the revolution. In the first half of his presidency, his travels took him to such nontraditional Iranian destinations as Italy, France, and Saudi Arabia.[30] He also visited the Far East and Central Asia and received high officials from such pro-Western Arab states as Jordan, Morocco, Tunisia, and Egypt.

Iran in the Post–Cold War World Order

The end of the Cold War has brought to the fore the importance of the "three Gs" in Iran's foreign relations: geopolitics, geostrategic instabilities, and globalization. With over a decade of the post–Cold War order behind us at the time of this writing, Iran is still trying to make sense of the systemic changes that took place between 1989 and 1991, and in this endeavor is struggling to find its natural place in the increasingly interdependent and globalized international system. Since the late 1980s, Tehran has had to respond to systemic changes around it, and has been compelled to function as much as possible within the new international system, which not only witnessed the end of the Cold War and the demise of the Soviet superpower, but also the emergence of the United States as the undisputed extraregional power in the Middle East.[31] Concern with the country's territorial integrity has also been heightened with ethnic resurgence becoming the order of the day. Fear that secessionist movements in Iran and on its borders could be used by outside powers to destabilize the country and the regime have struck a chord with Iranian Islamists and nationalists alike.

At least two schools of thought about the new international system have prevailed in Iran.[32] One school welcomes the changes that have occurred in the international system since 1989. Proponents of the "positive" school hold that with the demise of the Soviet Union and prospects for more maneuverability due to the end of the Cold War and the strategic competition between Moscow and Washington in regions such as the Middle East, Iran can emerge as a more independent and powerful regional power. In the absence of superpower pressures, Tehran is better placed to create a new regional order in which Iran would be holding the balance of power. In the new situation, power derived from a combination of the Islamic revolution, a sound and pragmatic foreign policy, and the country's hydrocarbon wealth would enhance Tehran's ability to influence regional developments more fully and directly. Therefore, Tehran should grasp the nettle and adopt a proactive strategy in the Middle East and in the Asian territories of the former Soviet Union. To do this successfully, Tehran needs to create new ties and deepen its existing regional alliances. Proponents of this school also argue that continuing competition between the United States, the European Union, and Japan over the resources of the Persian Gulf, Central Asia, and Azerbaijan will inevitably generate new rivalries at the international level that, with careful planning, Tehran will be able to exploit at the regional level. In other words, they believe that while the old "negative balance" arguments may no longer apply, continuing rivalries at the international level will, in the medium term, allow Iran to apply the same model to the new situation and secure independence of action and enhance Tehran's room for maneuver.

The second school views the end of the Cold War and the demise of the USSR with deep anxiety. This "negative" school worries that Iran can no longer rely on the tried and tested strategy of the negative balance between Washington and Moscow, fearing that effectively Iran has been sidelined. With the superpower competition now effectively over, Iran has become less valuable strategically to the superpowers. It has no value to the West in terms of "containing" the Soviet threat to vital Western interests in the Middle East. Moreover, as there appear to be no external checks to U.S. power in the Middle East, the latter will inevitably increase its pressure on those regional states such as Iran that manage to function outside of its sphere of influence, and that have the potential to undermine its vital interests in the Persian Gulf subregion and the rest of the Middle East (particularly in the Arab-Israeli arena). Even in Central Asia and the Caucasus, the proponents of this school argue, Washington is bent on freezing Iran out of its emerging markets and the strategically important pipeline routes. Elements in this school also maintain that it is wrong to assume that in the "new world order," the hydrocarbon needs of the Western countries would stimulate rivalry among them that Iran could exploit; rather, they believe, the West would likely unite against any threat to its access to oil resources by any unfriendly local power.

So, if we can identify a general foreign-policy strategy followed by Tehran in the post–Cold War era, it is perhaps captured by the notion of "both North and South," which Ramazani popularized in 1992.[33] On the one hand, Iranian strategy needed to develop the techniques to exploit the growing voids between the United States and its European allies and Japan over regional and international economic issues as a way of blunting the U.S.-imposed sanctions on the country. Tehran's strategy also sought to attract non-U.S. Western capital into the country, in an attempt to draw closer to Washington's economic competitors who also happen to be its global strategic partners. On the other hand, as the post–Cold War order tended to encourage regionalization of the international system, Tehran opted to do two things: to found its own regional groupings and deepen the scope of existing ones (ECO, Caspian Sea Organization), in addition to trying to work with the GCC and the South Asian grouping of states; and, to improve its alliances with states such as Syria in the Middle East and deepen its ties with China, North Korea, Russia, and lately India, Greece, and Georgia outside of the Middle East. Iran, in short, has been developing links with both the North and the South poles of the international system.

The post-1990 changes in Iran's geopolitical environment and systemic changes since the end of the Cold War have reinforced the oil-weighted tendency in Iranian strategic thinking and the primacy of economics in Iranian foreign policymaking. This, however, does not mean that ideology and strategic ambitions have been completely displaced. Iran's leaders have asserted on more than one occasion that the republic's strategic ambitions cannot be realized without the country's economic renewal. Conversely, a weak economic base in the globalized economic system has increasingly been viewed by many Iranian leaders, including Presidents Rafsanjani and Khatami, as a recipe for further peripheralization.

At the same time, largely thanks to Iran's launching of its postwar Five-Year Plans and its continuing economic crisis, in broad terms the country's foreign policy has come to tally with its economic priorities. In this way economic necessities—need for foreign capital and expertise, trade links, importance of expatriate resources, the need to diversify the economy, and so on—have influenced foreign policy. Thus, in recent years a symbiotic relationship seems to have evolved between economic necessity and Iran's foreign policy. The main feature of this symbiotic relationship can be observed in the behavioral change in terms of Tehran's moderation and its realpolitik policy toward its neighbors and the European powers, and the abandonment, at the formal level at least, of the "export" of the Islamic revolution.

However, as the post-Khomeini regime's legitimacy is almost entirely based on the revolution and the system founded by Ayatollah Khomeini, it cannot negate Khomeini's principles without negating itself. So, while it is true to say that Tehran has been redefining its priorities in recent years and has been reconsidering Iran's place in the world, it would be unrealistic to expect it to abandon the system's modus operandi, nor indeed to forgo its Islamic profile only for the sake of economic gains. Furthermore, and as Amirahmadi notes, "As long as Iran and the Islamic movements [in the Muslim world] espouse the same ideals and radical ideology, this congruity of purpose will enhance the visibility of Iran and its strength in international politics."[34] One only has to consider Iran's successful involvement with the Islamic Conference Organization since autumn 1997 to realize that Tehran will continue to capitalize on Islam in its international profile.

Conclusion

Iran's foreign-policy course remains the subject of considerable controversy among analysts. It is still argued by some that while nominally the orientation of the republic remains similar to that advocated by the republic's founding fathers, in practice Rafsanjani and Khatami chose to subordinate ideological foreign-policy posturing to the resolution of domestic problems (the first prioritizing economic reconstruction and the latter the strengthening of civil society and the rule of law).[35] Still others argue that the steady triumph of the moderates in the power struggle in the 1990s should be viewed with caution because these forces could prove to be more dangerous to the West than their predecessors, especially if they strengthen Iran. With regard to the Rafsanjani administration, for example, Clawson has argued that "Iran's moderates do not differ profoundly from its radicals with respect to foreign policy."[36] He also expressed concern about the negative consequences of the "economization" of Iranian foreign policy: "The push for prosperity by the moderates is not necessarily a stabilizing influence. Indeed, Tehran's focus on economic growth rather than Islamic purity as the main activity of the government could become a new source of instability in the region, if Iranians conclude that the shortest and least painful route to prosperity lies in pressuring their neighbors."[37]

But since the mid-1990s, and certainly since 1997, the opposite trend has been in evidence; wherever possible, Tehran has tried hard to mend its diplomatic and political bridges and fences in order to enhance its economy and create the conditions for prosperity. Indeed, in many ways President Khatami's administration has made a virtue of Iran's economic ills to argue for more drastic political reforms and the opening up of all sectors of the economy to foreign investment.

Furthermore, it is increasingly clear that the changes in some key personnel, power structures, policymaking processes, and the material needs of the state count for a great deal when analyzing post-Khomeini Iran, even though there is much truth in Chubin's argument that due to the fractured nature of policymaking in Iran, foreign-policy initiatives are at best compromises between competing perspectives and interests.[38] This partly explains why Tehran is seemingly unable to project and pursue a clearly defined and consistent foreign policy, even though presidential leadership has tried very hard to institutionalize a break from the past since 1989. More time is needed before we can truly assess the extent of President Khatami's successes in this regard, but the available evidence suggests that he has significantly advanced moderation, dialogue, and détente as three of the principles guiding Iran's foreign policy in the new millennium.[39]

Notes

1. James Piscatori, "Foreword," in Anoushiravan Ehteshami and Manshour Varasteh, eds., *Iran and the International Community,* London: Routledge, 1991, p. ix.

2. Fred Halliday, "Introduction—Iran and the World: Reassertion and Its Costs," in Anoushiravan Ehteshami and Manshour Varasteh, eds., *Iran and the International Community,* London: Routledge, 1991, p. 3.

3. Richard Cottam, *Nationalism in Iran,* Pittsburgh: University of Pittsburgh Press, 1979.

4. Graham E. Fuller, *The "Center of the Universe": The Geopolitics of Iran,* Boulder, CO: Westview Press, 1991, p. 2.

5. The phrase and its tone are much less flattering when expressed in Persian: "Amrika Hich Ghalati Nemitavanad Bekounad."

6. For discussion of the "negative balance" concept, see Rouhollah K. Ramazani, *Iran's Foreign Policy: A Study of Foreign Policy in Modernizing Nations,* Charlottesville: University of Virginia Press, 1975.

7. For a full analysis, see Anoushiravan Ehteshami, *After Khomeini: The Iranian Second Republic,* London: Routledge, 1995; Jahangir Amuzegar, *Iran's Economy Under the Islamic Republic,* London: I. B. Tauris, 1993; Hooshang Amirahmadi, *Revolution and Economic Transition: The Iranian Experience,* New York: State University of New York Press, 1990.

8. G. Barthel, ed., *Iran: From Monarchy to Republic,* Berlin: Akademie-Verlag, 1983.

9. See Hossein Amirsadeghi, ed., *The Security of the Persian Gulf,* New York: St. Martin's Press, 1981.

10. Shahram Chubin and Sepehr Zabih, *The Foreign Relations of Iran,* Berkeley: University of California Press, 1974, p. 214.

11. Mohammad Reza Pahlavi, *The Shah's Story,* London: Michael Joseph, 1980.

12. Faramarz Rafipoor, *Touse-a va Tazad: Kousheshi dar Jahat-e Tahlil-e Enghelab-e Islami va Masaa'el-e Ejtemaiy-e Iran* (*Modernization and Conflict: An Attempt Toward the Analysis of the Islamic Revolution and Social Problems of Iran*), Tehran: Enteshar, 1998.

13. See Ehteshami, *After Khomeini*.

14. See Jahangir Amuzegar, *Iran's Economy Under the Islamic Republic*, London: I. B. Tauris, 1993.

15. See Massoud Karshenas and M. Hashem Pesaran, "Economic Reform and the Reconstruction of the Iranian Economy," *Middle East Journal* 49, no. 1, winter 1995, pp. 89–111; Anoushiravan Ehteshami, *The Politics of Economic Restructuring in Post-Khomeini Iran*, Durham, England: Centre for Middle Eastern and Islamic Studies, 1995.

16. Bahgat Korany, "From Revolution to Domestication: The Foreign Policy of Algeria," in Bahgat Korany and Ali E. Hilal Dessouki, eds., *The Foreign Policies of Arab States: The Challenge of Change*, Boulder, CO: Westview Press, 1991, pp. 103–155.

17. Hojjat Morteji, *Jenahay-e Siyasi Dar Iran-e Emrouz (Political Factions in Today's Iran)*, Tehran: Naqshou Negar, 1999.

18. Shaul Bakhash, "Iran: The Crisis of Legitimacy," in *Middle Eastern Lectures 1*. Tel Aviv: Moshe Dayan Center for Middle Eastern and African Studies, 1995, pp. 99–118.

19. See Ehteshami, *After Khomeini*.

20. Dilip Hiro, *Islamic Fundamentalism*, London: Paladin Grafton Books, 1988.

21. Hussein J. Agha and Ahmed S. Khalidi, *Syria and Iran: Rivalry and Cooperation*, London: Pinter, 1995.

22. Mehdi Mozaffari, "Changes in the Iranian Political System After Ayatollah Khomeini's Death," *Political Studies* XLI, no. 4, pp. 611–617.

23. Indeed, from November 1988 onward Iran made repeated references to the need for finding regional collective security structures for the Gulf area, and raised these ideas in many of its discussions with its GCC neighbors.

24. By the end of the century, however, there was some disagreement over Iran's relations with Pakistan and Turkey. Elements within the military were increasingly worried about Pakistan's support for the Taliban, its close ties with Wahhabi forces in Saudi Arabia, the escalating anti-Shi'a violence in Pakistan, and of course Pakistan's nuclear weapons. Others in the establishment, however, were less convinced that Pakistan posed a direct threat to Iran and its regional interests. They tended to subscribe to the view that Iran needed good relations with both India and Pakistan if it was to realize its ambition of becoming a major west Asian power. On Turkey also there seems to have been consensus since the early 1990s that tensions are not in Iran's interests, but Tehran worries about the Israeli-Turkish alliance and the access to Iran's borders that this alliance offers Israel. Iran's leaders have expressed their fears to Ankara, and have responded by drawing closer to Syria and also broadening their regional contacts by working more closely with Greece, Armenia, and Georgia.

25. BBC, *Summary of World Broadcasts*, 27 August 1990.

26. With regard to Israel, there is almost universal agreement that the Jewish state is an active regional rival bent on checking its political and military power and undoing Iran's achievements. Military leaders and their political masters seem to be convinced that Israel is planning a confrontation with Iran. Thus, as Israeli diplomacy and economic force reach the shores of the Persian Gulf and the Caspian Sea, so it is seen in Tehran as further concrete evidence of Israel's encirclement strategy.

27. Note Oman's hosting of the multilateral talks on water in April 1994, which included Israel, the visit of Prime Minister Rabin to Muscat in December 1994, and the establishment of direct trade links between the Jewish state and Oman in September 1995, and Qatar's increasingly overt contacts with Israeli business and political leaders.

28. The Second Khordad (Dovoum-e Khordad) movement refers to the day of Khatami's May 1997 election victory and the new reforms and reformist forces that it helped bring to the surface.

29. More darkly, there was a view during his first term in office that Khatami, despite his popularity, might fall victim to the Gorbachev syndrome— his reforms failing, he himself being eventually removed from office, and he being replaced by a hard-liner Islamist from the old guard.

30. With regard to the Persian Gulf, clearly Iran's pro-GCC strategy has borne some fruit, as seen by its successful courting of Saudi Arabia since 1996. The two countries' defense ministers have met more than once and Iranian naval vessels have visited the Saudi Red Sea port of Jeddah, arguably the country's most strategic maritime facility. But, Tehran still regards Saudi Arabia as an ideological rival, in Central Asia and elsewhere in western Asia, as well as a close ally of the United States. Riyadh also is conscious of the latent threat Iran poses to its interests in the Persian Gulf and beyond, but is keener at present to develop the friendship with the pragmatic Iranian leadership and carve for itself the role of a mediator in U.S.-Iranian exploratory discussions.

31. Akbar Mahdi, "Islam, the Middle East, and the New World Order," in Hamid Zangeneh, ed., *Islam, Iran and World Stability,* New York: St Martin's Press, 1994, pp. 75–96.

32. For a more detailed discussion of Iranian perspectives on the "new world order," see Anoushiravan Ehteshami and Raymond A. Hinnebusch, *Syria and Iran: Middle Powers in a Penetrated Regional System,* London: Routledge, 1997.

33. Rouhollah K. Ramazani, "Iran's Foreign Policy: Both North and South," *Middle East Journal* 46, no. 3, summer 1992, pp. 393–412.

34. Hooshang Amirahmadi, "Iran and the Persian Gulf: Strategic Issues and Outlook," in Hamid Zangeneh, ed., *Islam, Iran and World Stability,* New York: St Martin's Press, 1994, p. 118.

35. Shaul Bakhash, "Iran Since the Gulf War," in Robert O. Freedman, ed., *The Middle East and the Peace Process: The Impact of the Oslo Accords,* Gainesville: University Press of Florida, 1998, pp. 241–264.

36. Patrick Clawson, *Iran's Challenge to the West: How, When, Why?* Washington, DC: The Washington Institute for Near East Policy, 1993, p. 46.

37. Ibid., p. 37.

38. Shahram Chubin, *Iran's National Security Policy: Capabilities, Intentions and Impact,* Washington, DC: Carnegie Endowment for International Peace, 1994.

39. For an in-depth discussion of President Khatami's foreign-policy agenda during his first term in office, see Ali Ansari, "Iranian Foreign Policy Under Khatami: Reform and Reintegration," in Ali Mohammadi and Anoushiravan Ehteshami, eds., *Iran and Eurasia,* Reading, England: Ithaca Press, 2000, pp. 35–58.

14

The Foreign Policy of Turkey

Philip Robins

Prior to the end of the Cold War, foreign policy was an area of Turkish studies that tended to be relatively neglected. This was partly because of the geopolitical and normative marginality of Turkey: for realists and liberal institutionalists alike, Turkey was a bit player in altogether more important issues, from East-West rivalry to the Helsinki process; for area studies specialists, notably Europeanists and Arabists, Turkey was disdained as an insular country where people had unpronounceable names and spoke a strange language. For Turcophiles, the lack of interest may be explained differently: foreign affairs was an area of policy consensus, hence there was nothing very interesting to study or explain.

That does not mean to say that there was no interest in Turkey's external relations. But here the preoccupation tended to reflect the concerns and efforts of the Turkish elite.[1] By and large, Turkey's foreign relations were reduced to such hoary old subjects as Cyprus, relations with Greece, and the prospects for Turkey's admission to the European Community. The absence of any interest whatsoever in, for instance, Turkish–Middle Eastern relations was staggering.

Since the end of the Cold War the situation has changed, at least to some extent. Geostrategists have revalued Turkey as a strong state located amidst a collection of shaky or conflict-ridden subregions. Though hardly enthusiastic, Europeanists and Arabists alike have accepted that Turkey can no longer be ignored. A new generation of Turkish academics have emerged who are concerned to examine an important aspect of their state, especially mindful of the country's emerging pluralism. Though such expertise is often partisan and stubbornly compartmentalized, Turkish foreign policy is fast becoming a vigorous and contested field of study.

Against such a backdrop of external and internal change, it is indeed timely to reconsider Turkish foreign policy. This chapter seeks to explore the subject widely, ranging historically and eschewing regional compartmentalization. In doing so, it is intended to explore the dynamics of policymaking, as well as the principal decisionmakers. The chapter ends with three contemporary case studies that emphasize the continuity of foreign policy, even in a post–Cold War context.

Foreign-Policy Determinants

Turkey and the International System

Owing to its geostrategic location and, more recently, its growing power as a state, Turkey has been regularly subject to the attentions of great powers and the systemic forces that have been generated by their dynamic interaction. During certain periods, this has sharply constrained Turkey. But for most of the first seventy-five years of Turkey's existence as an independent state, Ankara has proved rather adept at fending off great-power pressures to act in a clientelist fashion. It is precisely this resilience that prompted Annette Baker Fox, in her seminal study of the power of small states, to describe Turkey as having acquired a position of "mounting influence." And this for a state, she noted, that had begun life as "the Cinderella of the eastern Mediterranean."[2]

The most momentous illustration of the power of independent action can be seen in the Turkish nationalists' refusal to accept the post–World War I settlement. The victorious powers sought to foist a victors' peace on Istanbul and its Anatolian hinterland. The 1920 Treaty of Sevres enshrined this vision, with the rump territories of the Ottoman Empire, including the emerging state's Anatolian heartland, threatened with dismemberment without input from the peoples themselves. Only through the robust actions of a relatively small group of Turkish nationalists, led by Mustafa Kemal (Ataturk), was this historical alternative suppressed. Turkey succeeded in rebuffing the newly emerging international system, and in fashioning its own destiny.

The first occasion when Turkish foreign policy was most constrained by systemic factors came in the wake of this struggle, when it had to compromise with the great powers of the day in order to consolidate the gains of the war of independence. In the early years of the existence of the modern state of Turkey, the international system was critical to the recognition and hence the consolidation of the republic. The

1923 Treaty of Lausanne settled all outstanding issues, save for the territorial dispute between Britain and Turkey over the fate of the *vilâyet* of Mosul. Though Mosul had been part of the lands included within the National Pact,[3] and hence was regarded by Turkish nationalists as legitimately part of Turkey, Ataturk, the pragmatist, recognized the choice that had to be made. Faced with the superior diplomatic and military standing of Britain, Ataturk yielded on the Mosul question in return for membership of the League of Nations. The future of the war-torn and impoverished territories of the nascent state and Ataturk's vigorous internal reform program required the respite of the certainty of status that only international recognition could bring. The settlement embodied in the Lausanne Treaty formally overturned Sevres and acknowledged Turkey's sovereignty.

Thereafter Turkey's policy manifested a high level of autonomy. In the runup to World War II, Turkey maneuvered adroitly to exploit systemic dynamics, which led to it being "actively wooed" by several great powers.[4] This helped Turkey to preserve its neutrality, while pocketing the gifts of more powerful yet increasingly supplicant states, the most obvious example being the acquisition of the Sanjak of Alexandretta from France in July 1939. Ankara then succeeded in remaining a non-combatant until February 1945, only finally declaring war on Germany when the threat of conflict across its borders had evaporated.

The second period when Turkish foreign policy was subject to powerful systemic pressures came amidst the birth of the new bipolar world order. As World War II was ending, Turkey was faced with a truculent and expansionist Soviet Union, which coveted both territory in northeastern Anatolia and control of the (Bosporus and Dardanelles) Straits. Turkey consequently sought security in the emerging Western alliance, which it eventually received once it had displayed its commitment to the U.S.-led fight against world communism through participation in the Korean War. Turkey became a full member of the North Atlantic Treaty Organization in the first NATO enlargement, which also included Greece, in 1952. A decade later, Turkish foreign policy was still subordinate to Cold War systemic factors. Thus, the United States could decide to remove its Jupiter missiles from Turkey as part of an overall arrangement with the USSR to end the 1962 Cuban missile crisis without even a reference to Ankara. Turkey would remain locked into a subordinate position in NATO within the broader context of superpower bipolarity until 1964.

In that year, however, a similar piece of high-handedness by the U.S. administration helped to curtail this extended period of systemic determinism. The turning point took place over Cyprus, with Ankara outraged at the political changes implemented by the Greek-dominated government on the island to the detriment of the Turkish population. With Ankara examining its options, President Lyndon Johnson subsequently sent the infamous Johnson letter of June 1964, which warned Turkey directly against intervention in Cyprus on pain of the United States refusing to honor its NATO commitments to protect Turkey against the USSR. Though shocked by the use of existential security guarantees as diplomatic leverage, the Johnson letter only crystallized latent thinking in Ankara that a more pragmatic regional policy was required, especially in order to win votes among the newly decolonized countries at the UN over Cyprus. With the new, post-Khrushchev triumvirate in the Kremlin making overtures toward a more flexible Ankara in an emerging atmosphere of détente, and trade and diplomatic relations following, never again would Turkey be so emasculated by the overall context of Cold War dynamics.

After 1964, Turkey's regional policy, too, was increasingly unfettered by its ties with the United States, the best example being its Cyprus intervention/invasion of 1974, when Washington failed to impose the restraint of a decade earlier. Turkish perceptions of the United States as a less than entirely reliable ally were, in turn, further strengthened by the congressionally inspired military sanctions after the Cyprus intervention/invasion of 1974. The rescinding of sanctions by the United States then grudgingly gave way to the 10:7 arms sale formula toward Turkey and Greece.[5] By the late 1970s and the onset of the "Second Cold War," Washington was in a more conciliatory mood toward Ankara, with the United States soft-pedaling its criticism of the September 1980 military coup d'état, and of Turkey's recognition of the so-called Turkish Republic of Northern Cyprus in 1983.

Turkey and Regional Systems

Not since the heyday of Byzantium has the city of Constantinople/ Istanbul been the center of the world; not since the early nineteenth century, and the accelerating decline of the Ottoman Empire, has a state ruled from Istanbul been a leading, proactive player in the international system. Since its emergence as an independent state, Turkey has lain at the geographical periphery of a number of regional systems: the Middle East, Europe, the Balkans. It further lay at the periphery of the East-West tensions of the Cold War, together with Norway being the epitome of a flank state.

Lying at the margins of subsystemic dynamics has proved to be both a blessing and a curse for Turkey. Examples of the positive benefits abound. For all of Stalin's initial bluster, Turkey was not subject to a concerted attempt to install a communist regime in the second half of the 1940s, as was the case with the states of Eastern Europe. Similarly, Turkey's peripheral position in the Middle East meant that in the 1950s and 1960s, when the post–World War I state system was under particular pressure from radical revisionism, such as the Nasserism that threatened other pro-Western regimes, Turkey's borders were never seriously threatened. A third example of the benefits of being at the geopolitical margins would be the strategic depth that Turkey enjoyed vis-à-vis potential security threats from the Middle East, such as the risk of ideological expansionism emanating from the newly installed Islamic regime in Iran in 1979. This strategic depth has, though, been much reduced since the late 1980s, owing to the proliferation of weapons of mass destruction and advanced delivery systems in the region, Turkey itself possessing neither missiles nor a nonconventional arsenal.

In escaping the worst excesses of subregional pressures, Turkey was aided by its own subjective ethnic and objective linguistic particularism. The Turks tend to regard themselves, culturally at least, as a people who originated from the Central Asian steppes. Small groups of Turks are to be found in Balkan states such as Bosnia, Serbia, and Albania, as well as, in slightly larger numbers, in Cyprus, but these tend to be communities left behind as the Ottoman Empire rapidly contracted in its final years. Turks, then, tend to regard themselves and in turn are perceived as being a distinct people, compared to majority communities in neighboring states. Similarly, the Turkish language is linguistically very different from those languages, such as Arabic, Persian, Greek, and the Slavic group of languages, in use in states that lie adjacent, in turn adding to this sense of discreteness.

Yet geographical marginalization has also had its drawbacks. Perhaps most tangible has been the relative ease with which the European Community parried Turkey's 1987 application to become a full member. It would have been much harder for the European Union (EU) to give Turkey the brush-off, as it also did at the Luxembourg summit in December 1997,[6] had Turkey been located closer to the heart of Europe.

A second downside of Turkey's marginal regionalism has been the dissipation of its considerable state power. With eight land borders and up to a further six neighbors if maritime boundaries are taken into consideration, Turkey's ability to sustain diplomatic engagement with any one region is limited, without, that is, incurring costs with respect to others.

The overall effect of Turkey's relations with subregional systems has tended to be that Turkey has pursued a regionalist strategy as a matter of agency rather than necessity. This helps to explain why Turkey's involvement with the EU has been sustained and intense, while its involvement with the Middle East has been spasmodic and uneven. Relations with yet other regions, notably Eastern Europe under communism and Transcaucasia and Central Asia during the Soviet period, have tended to be limited, and channeled through the hegemonic power center of Moscow. It has only been since the 1990s that the option of a regional policy toward either southeastern Europe or the former Soviet south has presented itself to the Turkish state.

Key examples of Turkey's subregional involvement may be seen during the interwar years, during the span of the Baghdad Pact in the mid- to late 1950s, and after 1964. Following its settlement with Britain and the League of Nations over Mosul, Turkey spent the next two and a half decades pursuing a strategy of "neutralism"[7] and seeking to stabilize relations with its neighbors in order to be able to pursue a domestic agenda of reform unhindered.[8] At the regional level, it stabilized relations with Greece through the Ataturk-Venizelos rapprochement of 1930, thereby opening the way for the conclusion of a Balkan Pact in 1934.[9] It set about managing relations with revolutionary Russia, with which it signed a treaty of neutrality and nonaggression in 1925; the two states were then to enjoy an uninterrupted period of stable relations until toward the end of World War II. Turkey's regional strategy was formally completed with the conclusion of the Saadabad Pact in 1937, with Afghanistan, Reza Shah's Iran, and Iraq, which aimed both to allay mutual security fears and to deter an Abyssinia-style colonial expansionism.[10]

One area where the option of a regional strategy continued beyond the onset of the Cold War was the Middle East. The ideologically inspired strategy, of which Turkish participation in the Korean War was an early example, ultimately led to Ankara's enthusiastic embrace of the Baghdad Pact. This proved to be a rare instance of Turkey implementing a systemic agenda, in this case of anticommunism, at a regional level. The aim of the Democratic Party government of Adnan Menderes was spatially to join up NATO and the Southeast Asia Treaty Organization, and hence contain the spread of Soviet-led communism. However, the nationalist current in the Arab world, with Nasser at its head, interpreted the Baghdad Pact as a Western-backed attempt to thwart its anticolonial independence drive, and sought to undermine it.

Faced with such a situation, Turkey showed its inexperience of operating a regional policy, especially with regard to the Middle East.

Ankara's injudicious pursuit of Jordanian membership in the pact almost precipitated regime collapse in Amman; its overbearing attitude toward Syria drove Damascus into a closer relationship with Moscow, hence enabling Soviet influence to vault over the northern tier alliance; then in July 1958 revolution in Iraq removed Baghdad from the Baghdad Pact. The whole affair remains arguably the most embarrassing debacle sustained by Turkey's foreign policy throughout the history of the republic.

With Turkey reeling from the blow of the collapse of the Baghdad Pact, Ankara flirted with the idea of an alliance of non-Arab states in the form of the Israeli-led "Periphery Pact." But before this could crystallize, the Menderes government had been overthrown in a military coup, and a more traditional caution had returned to Turkish foreign policy. In the 1960s it would be the pursuit of votes within the non-aligned movement in support of Turkey's Cyprus policy that would increasingly come to characterize Ankara's calculations, rather than an alliance of outcast states. Turkey would go on to play a balanced role during the 1967 Arab-Israeli war, though it would tilt toward the Palestinians in the 1970s, not least as a result of Arab oil power.

State Formation and Identity

Relative autonomy from regional determinants have meant that state-level factors have tended to dominate in Turkish foreign policymaking, especially since 1964, and the waning of systemic-level determinants. At the state level, two factors have been particularly outstanding drivers of policy: the quest for security and Kemalist ideology.

Though there is a 1,500-year-old history of states being based on the territory of today's Turkey, its security predicament is in many ways more a reflection of Third rather than First World preoccupations. For all the history of state existence, the Turkish republic was created less than eight decades ago and its story is intimately intertwined with European power politics. Though the Turkish state and its boundaries were born of indigenous agency, unlike so many other "imposed" states in the Middle East, the sense of existential insecurity, epitomized by the Sevres blueprint, resonates for Turkey's decisionmaking elites.

Against such a background, the state-building project in contemporary Turkey has often been synonymous with the overriding issue of security. The Turkish state was itself born of a bloody conflict with the armies of Greece, which misguidedly had sought to exploit the post–World War I vacuum in pursuit of territorial expansionism. Having defeated the Greeks, the army was then instrumental in state consolidation, especially in the military suppression of tribal uprisings in the predominantly Kurdish southeast of the country. After momentary flirtations with democratic practice, the first governmental structures and processes of the state were firmly based on single-party rule, in the interests of stability.

More recently, security considerations have often dictated foreign policy, especially as far as the Kurdish insurgency in Turkey is concerned. In the 1990s, Turkish foreign policy has often appeared to be "indexed" to the issue of Kurdish ethnonationalist radicalism, and especially the issue of the Kurdistan Workers Party (PKK). A simple equation has determined foreign relations: if you abhor the PKK you are our friend; if you (are perceived to) help or nurture the PKK you are our enemy. Thus, for example, the convening of the now defunct Kurdish "parliament-in-exile" in different European countries led directly to a deterioration in relations with states as diverse as the Netherlands and Russia. Anglo-Turkish relations, arguably the most stable and enduring between Turkey and a European state, were blighted between 1995 and 1998 by the broadcasts of the Kurdish-run MED-TV. Most vivid by way of example was the impact of the issue on Turkish-Syrian relations between 1987 and 1998, and especially its denouement. In October 1998 Ankara issued what amounted to an ultimatum to Damascus to expel the PKK leader Abdullah Ocalan from its territory or face military consequences.

In terms of regional integration, a premium has invariably been placed on security matters. Reference has already been made to Ankara's pursuit of full membership in NATO. More illustrative, perhaps, has been Turkey's dogged attempts to gain full membership in the Western European Union (WEU). A weak organization with a track record of inactivity and subject to thinly veiled contempt, not least by its very member states, Ankara's strenuous attempts to join the WEU have been wholly disproportionate to the importance and potential of the organization.

Of equal importance with, and often underpinning, security has been the role of ideology in foreign policy. The invention of an ideology was an essential part of the creation and consolidation of the Turkish republic. The twin foundations of the ideology of the new state were the notion of Turkish nationalism and the adoption of a variant of secularism. Ataturk's conception of nationalism was a subjective one. He decreed that being a Turk was a state of mind rather than of biology, hence the organizing principle of state nationalism: "Ne mutlu Turkum diyene" ("Happy is he who *calls himself* a Turk").

Ataturk's attempt to create a national identity for his new state has been remarkably successful, binding together an otherwise eclectic set of peoples. However, the existential necessities of the 1920s helped to forge an inflexible notion of nationalism, which both the successful nature of the project and the normative demands of the post–Cold War period have failed to soften. Turkish nationalism may indeed be inclusive for those who bow before it; for those who insist on asserting an alternative form of primary identity, Turkish nationalism is harsh, disapproving, and ultimately exclusive. Predictably, perhaps, the greatest tensions have emerged between Turkish nationalism and the ethnonationalists of the country's substantial Kurdish population, consisting of some 15 percent of the total.[11] With the exclusivism of Turkish nationalism and the radicalization of Kurdish nationalism, it is little wonder that security and ideological considerations interacted with one another throughout most of the 1990s.

In turn, Turkish foreign policy tends to reflect and reproduce this fierce and uncompromising notion of Turkish nationalism. It is perhaps most evident in the case of Cyprus, where Ankara, apparently supported by the bulk of the population, defiantly maintains its right and duty to protect the Turkish population of the island. Other illustrations of this proud nationalism would range from the haughty dismissal of the criticisms of Turkey's human-rights record by the European Parliament and nongovernmental organizations such as Amnesty International, through to Turkey's almost routine military incursions across the border into northern Iraq in search of PKK commandos.

Ataturk's secularism enshrined the division between the temporal and the spiritual. But it was very much a French conception of laicism, with its harsh anticlericalism and Jacobin overtones of atheism, overlain with the positivism of the day. For many of Ataturk's disciples, secularism is equated with modernity, civilization, and European values, while Islam is regarded as being synonymous with premodernity, superstition, and backwardness.

This secularism and its accompanying baggage, which in turn is the guarantor of the position of privilege of those who subscribe to it, helps explain why the Turkish elite has so obsessively pursued the grail of European integration, increasingly identified with membership in the European Union. In spite of the fact that member peoples and governments are, to say the least, ambivalent about Turkey's full membership aspiration, the relentless pursuit of the EU has continued. For the Turkish elite, to call a halt to the chase would be to accept defeat, encourage Islam back into the public space, and hence leave themselves vulnerable to challenge from a newer, Anatolian-based counterelite.

On those occasions when the rebuffs from Brussels have been too public or difficult to bear, the Turkish elite has fallen back on either the fantasy of an alternative notion of community focusing on, for example, Israel and the United States, or on a particularly defiant form of nationalism. The latter has usually taken the form of a tough and largely uncooperative policy stance toward Cyprus or a swath of bilateral disputes with Greece. It has also manifested itself in the form of bluster over the perceived increase in racism and xenophobia in Europe.

Foreign Policymaking

It has become a cliché of political commentary to say that in Turkey the state is strong and government is weak. It is certainly the case that coercive power is concentrated in the hands of the four main branches of the military. The bureaucracy, with its strong Ottoman tradition of organization and high status, is a relatively coherent and effective administrative apparatus.[12] The Ministry of Foreign Affairs, in keeping with its preeminent position during Ottoman times, is widely regarded as the cream of the Turkish bureaucracy, its cohesion and shared world view being underpinned by the homogeneity of the social and educational background of its diplomatic personnel.

By the same token, governments are indeed often weak, especially when they exist within a fragmented political-party system. For long periods of Turkey's recent history, notably 1973 to 1980 and 1993 to the present, multiparty coalitions of divergent ideological components have uneasily presided over the executive branch. Governments come and go, but the state establishment is relatively permanent.

This state establishment, in particular, has often sought to inculcate such a strong-weak view of Turkish politics. The military has been assiduous in promoting solidarity within its ranks, especially following the public displays of factionalism of 1960–1963. The rise to prominence of the National Security Council in 1961[13] has provided the military with a formal conduit through which to dispense its advice to government on security-related matters. Senior members of the state apparatus are fond of stating that, while government is responsible for policy, it is the institutions of the state that lay down the strategic parameters within which such microdecisions can be made.

As is often the case with such caricatures, the reality only approximates. Turkey has enjoyed periods of strong government: most obviously under the single-party system and the civilianized military leadership of

Ataturk himself; certainly under the majoritarian leadership of Menderes, who governed virtually unopposed between 1950 and 1958;[14] and arguably under the recivilianizing leadership of Turgut Ozal, especially from 1987 to 1991. During this time, Ozal demonstrated that firm government was possible, even vis-à-vis the security establishment. The resignation of the chief of the General Staff in October 1990 in protest at Ozal's handling of Turkish policy toward the Gulf crisis was a notable symbol of the primacy, though ultimately fleeting, of a civilian system of governance.

Insider Actors

Coherence in foreign policymaking in Turkey is helped by the fact that there is considerable consensus on the part of the Kemalist elite as to the priorities and orientation of policy. It is no coincidence that, for all the changes in the international system since the end of the Cold War, there is much continuity in Turkish policy. Turkey is in many ways a status quo power par excellence.

Constants in Turkish foreign policy include: NATO membership and support for the maintenance of the organization as a tight and effective body, with a leading role for the United States; a European vocation, reflected in the collection of membership cards to European clubs and most often articulated through the aspiration to assume full membership in the EU; solidarity with the Turks of northern Cyprus, and a commitment to their security based on the maintenance of ethnic separation; wariness of the Russian Federation to the north, mindful that the two states and their predecessors are estimated to have fought thirteen wars in the past; the subordination of relations with the Middle East (Israel increasingly excepted) and the Islamic world to that of European integration.

On a day-to-day basis, such constants are maintained and renewed by the foreign ministry, which has a clear sense of its own mission, and which provides continuity of implementation. More strategically, they are maintained by the military, with its assumed role of guardianship of the state. The general staff has shown itself to be quite willing to take a lead in foreign policymaking, as the three military agreements with Israel in 1996, and the personal diplomacy of the former chief of staff, General Ismail Hakki Karadayi, have illustrated. On the whole, however, both the ministry and the generals regard it as being the responsibility of government to make and preside over foreign policy.

Undoubtedly, Turkey's most effective prosecution of foreign policy takes place when its government, generals, and diplomats see eye to eye and enjoy one another's trust. The country enjoyed a golden moment between 1991 and 1993–1994, when Suleyman Demirel was prime minister, Hikmet Cetin was foreign minister, and Ozdem Sanberk was the undersecretary at the ministry. With the generals, no doubt relieved at the political eclipse of Ozal, in the background, Cetin and Sanberk in particular managed Turkish foreign policy in an effective, though unspectacular, way during arguably the most testing time during the post–Cold War period. Consequently, Turkey kept itself from being directly drawn into either the Karabakh or Bosnian conflicts, and stabilized and developed relations with the successor states of the Soviet Union.

By contrast, Turkish foreign policy has often degenerated into disarray, either as a result of instability in government, or where there is an ideological mismatch between government and the state establishment. A good example of the former occurred, ironically, almost immediately after the end of the golden moment. Between July 1994 and the general election in December 1995, Turkey had no less than six different foreign ministers. Even in a context of bureaucratic continuity, the conduct of foreign policy periodically descended into shambles, with foreign diplomats unsure of exactly what Turkish policy was on a range of different subjects, and tiring of having to repeat briefings to successive ministers.

The most traumatic episode involving the ideological mismatch between government and state undoubtedly came between June 1996 and June 1997. During that time, Turkey was governed by a two-party coalition, which was led by the Islamist Welfare Party. Uniquely, and incongruously, Turkey was led for twelve months by an Islamist prime minister, Professor Necmettin Erbakan, alongside a state machinery that was decidedly Kemalist in complexion. Ironically perhaps, foreign policy was only contentious during this time as an exception rather than as the norm,[15] and the government eventually fell more as a result of conflict in the realm of education than foreign policy.

The main reason why foreign policy was not the focus of ideological struggle was because the coalition tended consciously to eschew the controversial in foreign and defense policy. This was at least in part because the Islamists were constrained in power. The Welfare Party did not enjoy a majority in parliament, while their coalition partner, the True Path Party, which actually held the foreign-policy portfolio, was mainly secular and conservative in orientation. Moreover, cognizant of the coercive power of the military, Professor Erbakan was careful to steer clear of challenging any of the sacred cows of Kemalist foreign policy.

Even so, two related areas of foreign policy did emerge as controversial during this twelve-month period. These were both largely symbolic: first, Erbakan's two foreign tours, which took in seven developing countries with large or majority Muslim populations;[16] and second, the establishment of a so-called D-8 group of rising powers from within the developing world, incorporating some of those states he had previously visited.[17] Erbakan defended the initiatives on the grounds of a more rounded foreign policy, taking fully into account Turkey's geopolitics and, he might have added, the predominantly Islamic nature of its society. For the Kemalist establishment, the moves were regarded with great suspicion lest they threaten to undermine Turkey's strong sense of foreign-policy priorities. Since the demise of the coalition, the D-8 initiative has been allowed to wither on the vine.[18]

Outsider Actors

Beyond the government, the military, and the foreign ministry, all are "outsiders" as far as foreign policymaking in Turkey is concerned. This reflects the hierarchical nature of Turkish politics and society, and the "*memur* [state official] syndrome," namely a residual deference as far as the individual's view of the state is concerned.

In the 1990s there was a growing debate about whether such factors as public opinion, the media, and organized lobby groups were becoming more influential in foreign policymaking than before. It may be the case that this was true, but incrementally so and starting from a very low base. During the Bosnian conflict, for instance, public opinion, though routinely exposed to the horrors of war through the media, was not mobilized on the issue, in spite of populist attempts to exploit the tragedy. The leading example of this was the attempt to convene a mass rally on the Bosnian issue in February 1993, during the height of the conflict, under the potentially precipitous slogan "Turks to Bosnia." In spite of the efforts of the organizers, which included the by now much less influential President Ozal, only around twenty thousand people took part, the vast majority of those being Islamists and ultranationalists, a reflection of the marginal politics of its organizers. At no time during the prolonged conflict did the Turkish government or military come under real pressure to abandon the central strategy of Western-oriented multilateralism.

Arguably the only foreign-policy issue that has repeatedly excited the passions of the Turkish public has been Cyprus. It is no coincidence that Cyprus has been the focus of considerable consensus within the state institutions and government of Turkey, not least in 1974 when the original intervention/invasion took place. Cyprus has taken on an elevated importance, not just because of the presence of a substantial Turkish minority and its rough treatment at the hands of a dominant Greek population, but also because of the national prestige invested in the island over the last twenty-seven years.

In summer 1992, a relatively rare public disagreement over Cyprus policy took place in Turkey, with President Ozal supporting a more cooperative response to the latest UN-led mediation, and Rauf Denktas, the leader of the Turkish Cypriots, attempting to discourage such a response. After some vacillation, the Demirel government declined to clash with Denktas for fear of the public reaction, a relatively rare occurrence of the critical importance of popular sentiment.

The media too is more important than it was, but has not emerged as the watchdog on foreign policy that it has, for example, in the area of domestic corruption since 1996. A sizable number of daily columnists of the leading mass-circulation Turkish newspapers write regularly on foreign affairs. These are mostly career journalists who are well established in Turkey and have the respect of Turkish and foreign diplomats alike. Figures such as Sami Kohen, Mehmet Ali Birand, Cengiz Candar, and Semih Idiz lead the list of those specializing in foreign affairs; their number is supplemented by a number of weighty politicians who write regularly on such matters, such as Mumtaz Soysal and Coskun Kirca, and in turn by a new generation of academic commentators such as Mensur Akgun and Gun Kut. While the above list is dominated by independent spirits, in the case of lesser figures their writings appear heavily influenced by the nonattributable briefings of diplomats, ministers, and military figures.

One of the best examples of the prominent role of newspaper columnists in public debate about foreign policy was in relation to the Cyprus example cited above on the Butros-Ghali "set of ideas" in 1992. On that occasion, a small number of newspaper columnists led by Soysal and Candar trenchantly debated future Turkish policy toward Cyprus. However, while a laudable and largely transparent exercise, this was not quite what it seemed. Soysal was also acting as an adviser to Denktas at the time, and therefore was leading the defense of a policy position that he presumably had a significant role in elaborating; Candar, meanwhile, was a close confident of President Ozal, and was therefore also very much his master's voice. Since the heyday of expectations in the early 1990s, the press in Turkey has become somewhat less independently minded, with the onset of monopoly ownership and a growing dependence on cheap credits dispensed by the state.

Organized lobby groups are yet a third area to which commentators have looked with expectation in terms of the widening base of influence on Turkish foreign policy. Indeed, it is certainly true that there has been a growth in the establishment of particular ethnically oriented groups since the late 1980s. The reasons for this are probably twofold: first, the increasing self-awareness of a growing number of Turks as to their ancestors' places of origin, especially if those places were located outside the boundaries of the modern republic,[19] and second, the onset of a number of regional and often ethnically oriented conflicts adjacent to Turkey. Consequently, a number of associations have been established in Turkey, in particular to assist peoples enduring hardship in the Balkans and Transcaucasia.

Core activities of such groups have tended to concentrate on the organization of humanitarian assistance to trouble spots, and, where relevant, on the assistance of refugees who have found their way to Turkey. In the case of the Turks from Bulgaria, who arrived under the last months of the Zhivkov regime, the numbers involved have sometimes run as high as hundreds of thousands. Some organizations have attempted to broaden their activities in a bid to affect the policy debate in Turkey through, for example, organizing visitor programs for politicians from the conflict areas concerned, and attempting to gain access for their ideas to the Turkish media, parliament, and government.

While such organizational activities have achieved some success, attempts actually to influence policy have been much less so. Either ethnic lobbies have tended to cancel one another out, as was the case with the Abkhaz and Georgian groups in relation to the civil war in Georgia in 1992, or, where the lobbying has been exclusively one-sided, most notably with respect to the 1994 Chechen conflict in the Russian Federation, the Turkish state has simply refused to compromise on what it regards as core state interests. While Ankara allowed Chechen solidarity groups to take a lead in organizing humanitarian relief, and constantly repeated the plea that a peaceful outcome to the conflict should be sought, the Turkish authorities were also adamant in reiterating their commitment to the sovereign unity of the Russian state. With the Kurdish analogy in mind, Ankara could not risk a policy to which the Russians might respond in kind by sponsoring the PKK.

Foreign-Policy Behavior Since the Cold War

Selecting case studies of Turkish foreign policy is fraught with difficulty. How, for example, does one address state-to-state relations? Does one focus on relations of power (e.g., the United States), on historic threats (e.g., Russia), on new relationships (e.g., the former Soviet south), on relations characterized by tension (e.g., Greece)? In turn, how does one address thematic issues of great importance, from security cooperation to commercial relations to the interstate politics of water, electric power, and hydrocarbons infrastructure? And what of the newer dynamics in international relations? A study of Turkey that ignores "transnational" elements, from refugee flows to diaspora communities to cross-border violence to illicit drugs, would lose much of the informal complexity of Turkey's foreign relations.

A brief list of the dilemmas faced in selecting key case studies in Turkish foreign policy draws attention to the diversity and multiplicity of subject areas that have to be considered in studying Turkey today. Nevertheless, difficult decisions do have to be taken. Three cases have therefore been chosen. First, the Gulf crisis, because for Turkey too it was the first test after the seismic changes at the end of the Cold War. Second, relations with Russia, and attempts to manage the state that remains Turkey's most proximate and enduring external threat. Third, relations with the EU, because the European vocation remains a key core value of the Kemalist elite, and, in being so intimately bound up with its own sense of self, goes well beyond simply the domain of foreign policy.

The Gulf Crisis: Creating Precedents in a New Era

The 1990 Gulf crisis was of pivotal importance as far as Turkish foreign relations in the post–Cold War era were concerned. This was for two reasons. First, it marked the end of the conventional wisdom that Turkey need not be an actor in the Middle East subsystem, either as a function of the Kemalist disdain for the region or as part of the post–Baghdad Pact trauma. Second, it drew attention to and underscored the continuing geostrategic importance of Turkey, especially among policy insiders of the executive branch in Washington. It also raised questions about the extent to which Turkish foreign policy would change as a result of the new era.

Turkey did not welcome the crisis in relations with Iraq in August 1990. During the eight-year Iran-Iraq war, Turkey had built up a relationship of complex interdependency with Iraq. This was primarily economic in focus, being based on bilateral trade, transit trade, and the construction of two oil pipelines from the northern Iraqi oil fields to Turkey's Mediterranean coast. Moreover, common concern in Ankara and Baghdad at Kurdish political activism, harnessed to the use of violent resistance, made the two states obvious potential partners. However, by the time of Iraq's invasion of Kuwait, the relationship, which had rarely been entirely smooth, had become complicated by an emerging dispute over Euphrates and Tigris waters, and growing evidence of Iraq's intent on acquiring weapons of mass destruction.

Systemic pressures, in the form of the early UN resolutions on the Gulf crisis and the United States' emerging hostility to the invasion, meant that many of Turkey's early actions were as near as possible to being inevitable. To have refused to cease trading with Iraq or to have refused to close the oil pipelines would have been to defy UN Chapter 7 resolutions and the international legitimacy they embodied; it would have been to reject the new liberal institutions-based order on which the emerging post–Cold War era appeared likely to be predicated. Furthermore, and perhaps most importantly, such actions would have undermined Turkey's four-decades-old strategy of multilateral cooperation with the West, and, more particularly, jeopardized Turkey's bilateral relations with the United States. No actor of real importance, from President Ozal with his admiration of Reaganomics, through the general staff, would seriously have countenanced such a step, given the premium the Turkish military places on NATO solidarity. For Turkey, the Iraqi invasion was more an international than a regional crisis, and one deserving of a response accordingly.

While the general contours of strategy may have been clear from the outset, that does not mean that there were no tactical choices to be made. The rhetorical response of bureaucrats and ministers to the invasion fell back on the political culture of Kemalism, with its instinctive caution and wariness of being drawn into intra-Arab conflict. While Ankara was resigned to implementing the UN sanctions, it did not approach the task with relish, cognizant of the material damage that would accrue to Turkey. Ankara would have closed the pipelines, but seemed reluctant to do so while Iraq's pipeline across Saudi Arabia continued to pump oil. It was against this background of systemic, regional, and state institutional influences that the role of the individual leader came into play. President Ozal stepped in and, with a decidedly un-Turkish flourish, announced the immediate closing of the lines, to the evident embarrassment of both Turkish diplomats and the country's foreign minister. It was more a triumph of style rather than of substance, but it was the sort of breathtaking gesture that Washington's policy insiders still remember with awe and appreciation a decade later.

Ozal continued to dominate Turkish policy toward the Gulf crisis for the remainder of its duration. He luxuriated in the personal telephone diplomacy with President Bush. Turkey duly permitted the Incirlik base to be used for air attacks on Iraq when Operation Desert Storm began; Turkish land forces also tied down significant numbers of Iraqi troops through their deployment near the border. For those who found Ozal's style unbearable, there was no choice but resignation or, in the case of opposition politician Bulent Ecevit and his visits to Baghdad in the somewhat implausible professional capacity of a "journalist," the grand but empty gesture. The one area where Ozal's nerve failed him, however, was in the deployment of Turkish troops to join the international contingent in the Gulf. Though only of symbolic value, the profundity of the trauma of the fate of Turkish troops "in the sands of Arabia" during World War I deterred Ozal from taking liberties with public opinion.

Russia: Managing a Historic Threat

For most of NATO's European states, the security threat from the Soviet Union evaporated rapidly. The end of the Cold War removed the possibility of a nuclear conflagration; Gorbachev's de-ideologization of foreign policy neutralized Marxism-Leninism as a vehicle for transnational ideological threats; the collapse of the communist regimes of Eastern Europe removed the proximity of any residual conventional threat from the East.

For Turkey, the perspective of a strategic threat removed was not entirely shared with the old European frontline states. Turkish generals remained preoccupied with military threats from the Soviet Union, almost up to the demise of the USSR as a state in 1991. Moreover, Turkey, unlike the Western Europeans, never received the boon of the creation of a chain of substantial buffer states; even the establishment of a flimsy set of buffer states in the Transcaucasus was to prove fleeting, as Russian troops never actually left Armenia and quickly reestablished themselves in Georgia. While threat perceptions of Russia between Turkey and the rest of NATO continued to diverge, the view in Ankara was that current circumstances only provided a temporary respite from the unwanted attentions of Russian power.

As if to confirm this new reality, a whole raft of issues seemed to emerge that threatened to blight bilateral relations. These included the future orientation of the former Soviet south, which Turkey wanted to diversify away from a continuing dependence on Russia; conflict in the Transcaucasus, with the Russian Federation widely regarded as supporting Armenia against Azarbaijan over Nagorno-Karabakh and the Abkhaz rebels against the Georgian state; the old issue of access through the Straits, with Russia reserving the right to send a new generation of oil supertankers through the Bosporus and the Dardanelles; the former Yugoslavia, with Moscow backing the Serbs and Ankara supporting the Bosnian Muslims and Albanians, and with some even fearing a new Orthodox Christian–Islamic struggle in the Balkans; support for one another's secessionist movements, with Russia perceiving Turkish backing for its Chechen rebels, and, in turn, periodically flirting with the PKK.

During a period between roughly 1991 and 1994, any one of the above agendas could have emerged to create real bilateral tensions and proxy conflict between Russia and Turkey. Ankara certainly was conscious of the potential for a sudden deterioration in relations, as the earnestness of the Turkish diplomacy of the day attests. With leadership turmoil in the Kremlin and the international system yet to settle down in the post–Cold War period, there seemed like little respite from growing volatility. The maverick Russian-nationalist leader Vladimir Zhirinovsky appeared to personify the zeitgeist, combining as he did a fluency in the Turkish language and personal experience of the country with a visceral antipathy toward Turkish culture and history.

If, almost in spite of these dark atmospherics, Russo-Turkish relations have proved to be remarkably stable since then, it is because of state-level and, in particular, economic factors. Again, Turgut Ozal's leadership was also pivotal at a moment of change. In the 1980s he realized that Turkey, with its rapid economic and population growth, needed to secure new sources of energy imports; he also recognized early on the environmental benefits of natural gas. A great believer in complex interdependency as a means to secure bilateral stability, Ozal thus turned to the Soviet Union as a primary energy supplier. In 1987, Turkey began to import Soviet gas, exporting in turn domestic manufactured goods and contracting services in what was principally a countertrade relationship.

Once established, the costs of discontinuing the relationship began to grow for both sides. For Turkey, a retreat would have resulted in electricity blackouts, a return to burning sulphurous coal in Ankara and Istanbul, and the loss of good business for its large and influential holding companies; for Moscow, a collapse of the gas trade relationship would have curbed a flow of consumer imports, as well as bringing to an end a range of construction projects, from large supermarkets to sugar refineries, most of them built and run as joint ventures. With vested interests for the continuation of such a relationship building up rapidly on both sides, the volume of the gas trade continued to grow throughout the 1990s, and hence these potentially destructive areas of political difficulty have been ameliorated.

Europe: A Vocation in Jeopardy

For all the changes in the international system and in the regions around Turkey in the 1990s, it is the relationship with Europe that remains pivotal for the Turkish elite. The reason for this is that Turkish-European relations transcend the domain of foreign policy. The relationship is about the very identity, aspirations, and, in turn, the maintenance of the privileges of that elite. For the Kemalist elite, being recognized as European is about being acknowledged as civilized and sophisticated. Rejection is tantamount to being dismissed as no better than the Anatolian peasantry that they themselves despise. For the elite, membership in the EU is a panacea for ending their collective insecurity, and guaranteeing the continuation of privilege and secularism, much in the same way that earlier southward expansions of EU membership were regarded as shoring up processes of democratization.

In its pursuit of full membership, history has not been kind to Turkey. The European Commission eventually parried Ozal's 1987 formal application to join after two years of somewhat embarrassed reflection. At that stage, Turkey was one of the most plausible potential new members, after the European Free Trade Agreement countries. Ankara was a member of NATO; it had a functioning democracy, at least at the formal level; and it could point to an economy that had been made export-oriented and increasingly subject to liberal reform since the late 1970s.

Within a matter of months, however, it had become possible to contemplate an EU of thirty members without Turkey being among that number. Turkey had been overtaken, at a bewildering speed, by the Visegrad countries, the Baltic states, and even some of the states of the former Yugoslavia. By December 1997, and the EU's Luxembourg summit, a nadir had been reached: even states such as Bulgaria and Romania, which had languished in the immediate aftermath of the fall of communism, had been placed ahead of Turkey as candidate members.

The Luxembourg summit was followed by two difficult and rancorous years, during which Ankara made its displeasure known by suspending political dialogue with the EU. With incremental adjustments in the EU position, such as at the Cardiff summit, failing to retrieve the situation, the feeling began to grow in Europe that the awkwardness of Luxembourg had to be set aside. In turn, the ideological standoff over Europe inside Turkey was softened by Islamist pragmatism, which came to see in European standards of human rights and pluralism the guarantee of their own continuing participation in domestic parliamentary politics. The EU eventually adopted a new approach toward Turkey in December 1999 at the Helsinki summit, at which Turkey was formally made a candidate for membership.

The Kemalist elite greeted the Helsinki decision with an elation commensurate with its importance in Turkish identity politics. In so doing, the pragmatic rather than strategic nature of the decision was largely missed. The decision was much more about "managing Turkey," a large and important power, with a growing economy located in the midst of a series of present or potential dangers, than about clearing the way for its speedy accession to full membership. With Ankara required to put its house in order politically even before accession negotiations could begin, the scene seemed set for further periods of difficult relations between the two sides in the medium term.

Conclusion

A review of Turkish foreign policy, either in historical or contemporary perspective, indicates that, while relations with the Middle East have featured importantly at certain times and over certain issues, the relationship is by no means prominent, let alone dominant. Relations with Middle Eastern states have been eclipsed or relegated in three main ways. First, in the preferences of the Turkish elite, which have been focused on Turkey's relations with the EU and NATO. Second, in Turkey's main threat perceptions since World War II, where Moscow has cast the longest shadow. Third, in the center of gravity of the Turkish economy, which lies in Western Europe. In terms of foreign relations, as in other ways, it therefore makes little sense to speak of Turkey as an exclusively Middle Eastern state.

Having stated that, it is nevertheless right that Turkey should have a dedicated chapter in a book such as this. In spite of its Kemalist predilections, Turkey has never been able entirely to avoid interaction with the region. At crucial historical junctures, the Middle East has forced its way onto the agenda of Turkish diplomacy and in one key case, that of the Baghdad Pact, even became its obsession. For the states of the Middle East, that are in the main less populous and weaker in coercive terms, even a half-distracted Turkey simply cannot be ignored in regional calculations. It should not then be a surprise that in the post–Cold War era, baptized as it was by the Gulf crisis, and marked by the resurgence of the regional over the systemic, the interactions between Turkey and the Middle East have if anything increased. Issues as diverse as drug smuggling, the Kurdish question, water, and weapons of mass destruction will ensure that this trend continues. Though for Turkey the Middle East is likely to remain a region among many, it is one that it never again will be able to contemplate ignoring.

Notes

1. In his wide-ranging study of Turkish foreign policy, Ferenc Vali is explicit and hence symptomatic of this view when he writes: Turkey's "condition and aspirations must be appreciated in the manner in which they appear to her own leaders and not as they may appear to outsiders." See *Bridge Across the Bosporus,* Baltimore: Johns Hopkins University Press, 1971, p. xii.

2. Annette Baker Fox, *The Power of Small States,* Chicago: University of Chicago Press, 1959, p. vii.

3. The National Pact was adopted on 28 January 1920 by the nationalist-dominated parliament in Istanbul. It represented a mission statement for the state that was to emerge, in particular prescribing full independence; the integrity of the territory lying inside the armistice line inhabited by the Ottoman-Muslim majority; and opposition to restrictions of a political, juridical, or financial nature.

4. Fox, *The Power of Small States,* p. vii.

5. This was an informal formula operated by the U.S. Congress whereby for every $10 worth of assistance rendered to Turkey, Greece had to receive $7 worth.

6. At Luxembourg, the EU refused to bestow candidate status on Turkey, thereby effectively placing it in a category of one behind other states seeking full membership.

7. David Barchard, *Turkey and the West,* London: RIIA/RKP, 1985, p. 12.

8. See Vali, *Bridge Across the Bosporus,* p. 25.

9. Signed on 9 February 1934, the Balkan Pact also included Greece (with which Turkey had concluded a ten-year nonaggression pact in September 1933), Romania, and Yugoslavia.

10. William Hale, *Turkish Foreign Policy, 1774–2000,* London: Frank Cass, 2000, p. 62.

11. For a discussion of Kurdish demographics, and a serious attempt to come up with a working figure for Turkey's Kurdish population, see Servet Mutlu, "Ethnic Kurds in Turkey: A Demographic Study," *International Journal of Middle Eastern Studies* 28, 1996, pp. 517–541. Mutlu estimates the Kurdish population at 12.6 percent of the total in 1990, though this figure, based on successive censuses, may be underestimated. With Kurdish demographic growth greatly exceeding the average for Turkey, using Mutlu's approach the Kurds were probably around 15 percent of the population by 2000.

12. The four branches are the air force, army, gendarmerie, and navy. On the bureaucracy, see Martin Heper, *The State Tradition in Turkey,* Beverley, England: Eothen Press, 1985.

13. The National Security Council was in fact first established in Turkey in 1933. The body rose to prominence in 1961, when its existence was given a constitutional basis. Interview with NSC secretary-general Cumhur Asparuk, Ankara, 7 December 1999.

14. After three election victories, Menderes finally lost political power in May 1960 with the country's first military coup d'état.

15. For a discussion of foreign policy under the Welfare (Refah)–True Path coalition, see Philip Robins, "Turkish Foreign Policy Under Erbakan," *Survival*, summer 1997.

16. These were: Iran, Pakistan, Indonesia, Malaysia, Egypt, Libya, and Nigeria. Erbakan also visited Singapore as part of the itinerary of his "Asian" tour.

17. The D-8 states were: Turkey, Bangladesh, Egypt, Indonesia, Iran, Malaysia, Nigeria, and Pakistan.

18. For example, while Turkey established a D-8 secretariat in Istanbul it did so under a retired ambassador and with minimal resources.

19. One Turkey expert, David Barchard, estimates that "probably well over 50 percent" of urban and middle-class Turks have grandparents who came as refugees to Turkey from adjacent regions. See Barchard, *Turkey and the West*, p. 13.

15

Conclusion: Patterns of Policy

Anoushiravan Ehteshami and Raymond Hinnebusch

The foreign policy of any individual Middle Eastern state at a given time can only be adequately understood as the outcome of an interaction between the state, sub/transstate, and state-system levels. In the Middle East, the state system is—by contrast to neorealism's static and ahistorical model[1]—both contested and under construction, shaped by two forces: (1) a series of periodically erupting system-wide transstate forces—imperialism, nationalism, war, oil, Islam, and globalization; and (2) the behavior of the individual states that collectively "construct" the system. On the other hand, the state system and transstate forces constrain and shape the individual states, but not in any deterministic way. On the contrary, their distinctive geopolitical/economic positions and state-formation histories determine the specifics of the individual foreign policies by which states respond to these forces.

Imperialism and Nationalism

Ever since Napoleon's intervention in Egypt, outside forces have played a major part in the birth and development of the regional system. European powers took control of significant areas of the region, stimulated modernization, brought about the demise of the Ottoman Empire, and, in the process of carving new Middle East and North Africa (MENA) states from territories under their control, created the regional state system. In doing so, they built instability (conflict, revisionism) into the system and not so much from the anarchy inherent in a state system per se, as from the profound flaws in the particular architecture of the resulting system, notably the poor fit between state and identity, the

335

uneven fragmentation (by which large dissatisfied states were juxta-posed to small client states), and the ongoing penetration of the region by the core.

The impact of imperialism on the region inevitably generated a re-action, namely the rise of nationalism, variegated into at least four rival species: Arab, Iranian, Turkish, and Zionist. What Mustafa Kemal Ataturk and his modernizing and secularist "Young Turks" accom-plished in post-Ottoman Turkey in the 1920s was soon copied by others, first of all by Iran's first nationalist leader, Reza Khan, who actually modeled himself on Ataturk and whose reforms closely mirrored those of the new Turkish republic. Arguably, these two leaders' nationalist state building, which unashamedly copied Western practices, gave birth to the modern state in their respective countries.

Zionism, which was born in late-nineteenth-century Europe and en-joyed considerable following among Ashkenazi Jews, provided the ide-ology for the construction of a new Jewish state in the heart of the Arab and Muslim worlds, which became a reality in May 1948. Zionism pro-vided Israel's founding fathers, led by David Ben Gurion, with a state-building blueprint and an ideological underpinning of their foreign policy.

Elsewhere in the region, nationalist sentiments were inflamed by the Ottoman Empire's demise. In the interwar years, Syrian, Lebanese, and Egyptian intellectuals were adopting nationalism as an ideology, but it was not until 1952 in Egypt that Arab nationalism burst on the scene as a major political force. The Free Officers' overthrow of the Egyptian monarchy opened the way for the surge of Arab-nationalist sentiments across the region, fueled by the establishment of Israel, the example of Third World nationalism elsewhere, and the joint Israeli-Western attack on Egypt in the 1956 Suez war. Egypt's Nasser added Pan-Arabism to the regional agenda and used it to challenge traditional political elites in Syria, Iraq, Yemen, and later Libya and Sudan, where radical military republics rose to power.

Thus, the impacts of imperialism, above all the imperialist imposi-tion of the regional state system and the indigenous reaction to it, were the first major forces shaping and differentiating regional states and their foreign policies. The most crucial differentiating factor was the level of damage thus inflicted: the more the state system thwarted in-digenous interests and identity (whether creating "artificial" states in Syria and Iraq or leaving irredentist ambitions unsatisfied, as in Israel where parts of "Eretz Israel" remained outside its original borders), the more status quo social forces inside the states were weakened and the more radical, middle-class, or even plebeian forces were mobilized.

Where this issued in revolutions, revolutionary coups, or transforming elections that turned states over to these forces, they harnessed state power and foreign policy to their revisionist ambitions. Conversely, the more the new state system satisfied indigenous interests and identity, as in Turkey, Tunisia, Saudi Arabia, and possibly North Yemen, the more relatively status quo elites survived and newly independent states followed policies accommodating their states to the West. A secondary variable was the intensity of the external impact on a state. Thus, the longer and more intense the independence struggle, the more radical the nationalist reaction (Egypt, South Yemen), while the relative level of modernization also helped determine whether status quo monarchies collapsed (Egypt, Iraq, Libya) or survived (Saudi Arabia, the Gulf states).

Ideological Heterogeneity: The Arab Cold War

In the Arab world, states' differential experiences with Western imperialism issued in a basic ideological cleavage. The nationalist republics that sought to challenge the Western-sponsored regional disposition were ranged against the conservative monarchies that, created with Western assistance, relied on Western protection against nationalist forces.

Indeed, by the late 1950s, this domestically driven ideological heterogeneity had interlocked with the strategically driven competition of the world's two superpowers to project their influence into the Middle East. The aid and protection they gave to the opposing regional camps consolidated the polarization of the regional system in an Arab cold war that mirrored bipolarity at the global level.[2] The Cold War division was also briefly replicated in a distinctive local form in the conflict between conservative-tribal North Yemen and Marxist South Yemen.

Most importantly, the system's ideological heterogeneity, and specifically the "nationalist outbidding" it encouraged, prepared the way for the 1967 Arab-Israeli war, thus unleashing a new force on the region—hot wars.

War and State Formation

As constructivists insist, the struggle for power is not inherent in a state system, but "constructed" by the states that make it up through the insecurity they feel and the threats they pose to their neighbors. As realists would argue, however, once such a security dilemma is established, it takes on a life of its own. Indeed, in the Middle East, two of the most powerful and dissatisfied states, Israel and Iraq, contributed disproportionately to the unrestrained use of military power, hence the deepening of the struggle for power. Thus, Clive Jones's analysis shows how Israel's use of its superior power to address its insecurity actually spread insecurity and the tradition of power politics to its neighbors. This was not inevitable, but Ben Gurion's view of regional politics as a zero-sum game became a "self-fulfilling prophecy." Thus, it was Israeli attacks on Gaza that set Nasser on the road to Pan-Arab militancy while Asad's later transformation of Syria from a victim into a regional military power was a response to the Israeli occupation of Syrian territory. Charles Tripp's analysis of Iraq adds a domestic dimension to the "constructedness" of insecurity, showing how Iraq's foreign policy under Saddam, a main source of insecurity in the Gulf, was an external projection of the extreme ruthlessness of the *internal* power struggle; this, in turn, was a function of the extreme difficulty of ruling a fragmented and artificial state imposed from without.

Although there are numerous other conflicts in the region, the regional system has been disproportionately shaped by the wars on the Arab/non-Arab fault lines, the Arab-Israeli and the Gulf conflicts. The Arab-Israeli conflict grew from a localized substate struggle between Palestinian Arabs and Jewish settler groups in the 1930s to an interstate war in 1948. From its birth through the early 1980s, Israel fought five wars with one or more of its Arab neighbors (1949, 1956, 1967, 1973, and 1982). To say that this conflict shaped the politics of the region for over fifty years is no exaggeration, for not only did it drive the rapid militarization of both the Israeli and Arab states, but it also dictated intra-Arab relations and dominated the domestic agenda in the Arab countries of the Levant. Causing major casualties across the board, irredentism-stimulating changes to territorial borders, and great economic damage to the warring parties, the Arab-Israeli conflict also invited the superpowers into the region on opposing sides and their arms transfers escalated the level of militarization.

In the region's other major war of the Cold War era, the Iran-Iraq war, neither superpower wanted revolutionary Iran, which rejected both East and West, to triumph and spread its revolutionary influence. Both sides provided enough arms, however, to keep this war going for eight years, resulting in an estimated 1 million casualties and economic damage to the tune of $900 billion. By the time the parties accepted an UN-brokered cease-fire in July 1988, neither combatant could claim that it had achieved any of its declared war aims.

If the states, in launching wars, constructed a system fraught with insecurity, that system, in turn, reconstructed the states to survive in this dangerous environment. The imperatives of survival in the system tended to shape its parts, the individual states, spurring advances in defensive state formation and socializing elites into realpolitik prudence and a preoccupation with the accumulation of power needed to balance against threats. Thus, the priority that each member of the system—each regime—put on its own survival tended to turn them into equilibrating agents ensuring the survival of the system. Realism's most useful and penetrating insight is that state systems, once sufficiently formed, enjoy the main feature of any "system," namely, a tendency to self-preserving equilibrium.

Thus, the 1967 and then the 1973 and 1982 Arab-Israeli wars, and particularly the experience of defeat or high costs incurred in these wars, tended to recast the states, whether status quo monarchies or nationalist republics, in similar neopatrimonial molds and/or forced a significant convergence in their foreign policies toward more moderate, nonideological, "realist" policies. The radical states, most clearly in Egypt and Syria, abandoned risky revisionist policies (while the monarchies adopted some of their populist and nationalist policies to secure their fragile legitimacy at home). Similarly, revolutionary Iran, chastened by the Iran-Iraq war, was forced into more "realist" foreign policies. States that had a mixed experience—"high-cost victory" and/or special access to resources to buffer the costs—were less decisively pushed toward moderation. Thus, the costs of the 1973 and 1982 wars pushed Israel into more moderate policies, but the long-term territorial consequences of the 1967 victory kept it locked into irredentist revisionism (incorporating the West Bank and Gaza) and U.S. aid relieved it of much of the cost. Iraq's high-cost semi-victory in the Iran-Iraq war first moderated but then radicalized its foreign policy, leading to the second Gulf war. On the other hand, in states on the peripheries of the core conflicts, which were less threatened or evaded entanglement in wars, other factors dominated foreign-policy agendas: thus, in Tunisia economics remained more salient, while in the Yemens the need to secure the external resources to consolidate fragile states at home dominated policy.

The second Gulf war also left a profound mark on the regional system. By its end, Kuwait had been liberated, certainly, but Iraq had effectively been destroyed as a major regional power. This, the post–Cold War era's first major war, ushered in a new era of U.S. hegemony in the region. The Kuwait crisis also provided the basis for the redefining of the MENA regional system: it freed Arab regimes from Pan-Arab constraints and enabled them to pursue their own state interests, and it opened the way for dialogue between the main parties still engaged in the Arab-Israeli conflict. Thus, the Kuwait war was soon followed by the ground-breaking Madrid talks in autumn 1991 that initiated the Arab-Israeli "peace process."

Foreign-Policy Differences: Seeking Exit from War

Even if the system level induces a certain uniformity in the way individual states seek survival in a war-prone environment, the systemic level, per se, can never wholly explain the foreign policy of a particular state. Neither, however, can domestic politics: similarity of state formation does not necessarily induce uniformity in foreign-policy behavior. Indeed, even states with similar origins and geopolitical positions can pursue quite different foreign policies, as the differential courses of Egypt and Syria illustrate.

Both Egypt and Syria were ruled by authoritarian nationalist regimes; they also shared the watershed disaster of 1967 from which arose similar "pragmatic" leaders—Sadat and Asad. Their alliance launched the October 1973 war for recovery of their occupied territories and thereafter they began exploring a diplomatic settlement of the Arab-Israeli conflict. Yet, in the end, Egypt pursued a separate peace with Israel and a close U.S. alliance while Syria, left out, continued to champion the Palestinians (i.e., rejected a separate peace on the Golan) and was branded a rejectionist state by the West. This divergence can only be explained by a complex interaction between domestic factors and systemic situation.

Differences in state formation, including identity and power structure, shaped different conceptions of the state's interest. For Egypt, a homogeneous society with a long history of separate statehood and confident in its own particular identity, pursuit of Egyptian "national" interest was a viable alternative to Arab nationalism. The high costs of Arab involvement generated an Egypt-first attitude that made the sacrifice of Arab-nationalist principles less than fatal for regime legitimacy. Syria, lacking a history of statehood, embraced Arabism as its identity and service to the Arab cause was the main claim of the Ba'thist regime to legitimacy. A separate peace that abandoned the Palestinian cause would have been seen as a dishonorable offense against Arabism, fatal to regime legitimacy.[3]

There were also associated variations in the pillars of power of the two regimes. One prop of Sadat's state was the military elite, which in the early 1970s was resentful of the USSR owing to disputes over weapons deliveries, and attracted by promises of U.S. weapons. Another prop was the Egyptian bourgeoisie, which also wanted U.S. economic ties and a peace settlement. In Syria, state formation relied on power pillars that were resistant to a separate peace: the Ba'th Party, which institutionalized Arab-nationalist ideology, and the Alawi minority, which, in a Sunni-majority society, had to be seen as even more Arab-nationalist than the Sunnis. Asad could not afford to antagonize these pillars of his regime.

The geopolitical situation faced by the two countries also differed sharply. Israel's resistance to a comprehensive settlement put a separate one on the agenda for Egypt. As the most powerful Arab state, it had a strong bargaining hand since Israel had a strong interest in a separate peace that would take Egypt out of the Arab-Israeli military balance and effectively end the Arab military threat. Sadat saw his choice as either to accept a separate peace or insist on a comprehensive one and risk getting nothing. Syria held a much weaker bargaining hand, as Israel had little interest in a settlement with it, especially once Sadat showed his willingness to settle separately. Hence, Damascus remained adamant for a total comprehensive settlement.

Differing economic positions also counted. Egypt's economic crisis was particularly acute; war-associated economic losses were high (the loss of Suez Canal tolls, Sinai oil revenues, and tourism) and gains from their recovery and from U.S. economic aid potentially very high; once, by the late 1970s, Egypt had become dependent on U.S. aid, the costs of defying the United States over acceptance of a separate peace had become too high. Syria's economic crisis was less severe and the Golan had only limited economic value; on the other hand, Arab aid given to Syria in its role as frontline state against Israel bolstered its smaller economy much more and Asad had diversified his economic dependencies so that they could not be used to leverage his foreign policy.

Finally, the power needs of the leadership varied. Sadat, lacking Nasser's Pan-Arab stature, had little regional leadership to lose by abandoning the Arab cause. Asad, having lost the Golan for the sake of Palestine, had to recover it without abandoning Palestine; he built and legitimized his regime amidst this struggle and to settle for less would mean his whole career was a failure. Hence Sadat's willingness to make concessions to Israel and Asad's stubborn refusal to do so defined a completely different approach to negotiations with Israel.

This case shows how the way a state responds to similar systemic pressures varies according to: (1) its *position* (power position in the regional state system as stressed by realism and its economic position in the core-periphery system as stressed by structuralism); and (2) its distinctive pattern of *state formation* (state identity and structure). The two halves of Yemen also underline how different colonial experiences—core-periphery relations—can produce sharp differences in state-formation trajectories. And in the end, the "idiosyncratic factor," leadership, cannot be disregarded. Egypt's different courses under Nasser and Sadat or the quite differing styles of two leaders presiding over similar states, the cautious Asad and the reckless Saddam, suggest how far this is true.

In short, a state's actual foreign-policy choices, even if driven by similar logics of state interest (regime survival), may be very different depending on the specific interaction between the broader system and a state's unique features.

Oil and Political Islam

By the 1970s, war had precipitated the rising influence of two new forces that would also impact on the regional system and its constituent states. The 1967 war, in discrediting secular Arab nationalism, opened the door for the revival of a new revisionist ideology in the region, militant political Islam. The 1973 war precipitated the oil price explosion that flooded the region with new wealth. These two forces threatened to push the region in opposite directions—oil largely in a conservative direction while Islam was pushing toward reradicalization.

Much of the interest in the Middle East since the start of the twentieth century has been based on the presence of oil in abundant quantities. Oil has been a strategic commodity and access to it became an important stake in the Cold War. Oil generated a new interdependence between the fortunes of the "capital-surplus" oil-exporting countries and the economic performance of the main consumers—the developed countries who depended on "recycling" of the sheer amount of capital that oil exports generated. To put the magnitude of oil-generated wealth in some perspective, while OPEC members' total income in 1973 was an impressive $37 billion, it had gone up to $143 billion in 1977, reaching a staggering $285 billion in 1980.[4] In 1980, Saudi Arabia, with a population of around 14 million, amassed nearly $110 billion from its petroleum exports.

The new oil wealth had a profound, largely conservatizing effect on the region. It drew the Western powers further into the region to protect the Western-leaning oil producers and to defend the free flow of oil through the Strait of Hormuz. The subsidies of the oil producers helped moderate the foreign policies of the radical republics and ended the

Arab cold war. The spread of oil wealth marked the end of ideology among the formerly Arab-nationalist middle classes, while the rising wealth and prestige of Saudi Arabia encouraged the spread of Islamic movements used against the left in countries such as Sadat's Egypt. However, the corruption and inequality that oil money encouraged inside regional states contributed to the rise of a more radical version of political Islam.

The region has a long tradition of Islamist politics that, in the twentieth century, began in Egypt with the 1920s rise of the famous Muslim Brotherhood movement. However, the 1979 Iranian Islamic revolution was the high mark of a movement that had been growing across the region for the best part of the twentieth century. The Iranian revolution, whose ideology bucked the secular trend in twentieth-century revolutions, ended the reign of a pro-Western and secular regime in a large and strategically important Middle Eastern country. Like other revolutionary regimes, Tehran was determined to export the revolution and despite the fact that the revolution had occurred in a non-Arab and Shi'a-dominated country, its ripples were inevitably felt across the region. In 1980, Islamists assassinated Egyptian president Anwar Sadat; in 1982 Syrian forces put down an Islamist challenge; in 1988 and 1989 the Tunisian Islamist movement had been pushed underground for its antigovernment activities; in the late 1980s the Palestinian Hamas and Islamic Jihad organizations unleashed terror on the Israeli population and took on the secular Palestinian groups; and, throughout the 1980s, Lebanese Islamist groups attacked Western targets in that country, took Westerners hostage, and started a military campaign against the Israeli occupation forces.

MENA states responded to the challenge of political Islam through suppression, cross-border cooperation, introduction of reforms, and increasing the Islamic content of their rhetoric and public policies. By the end of the century, some Islamist forces had managed to enter mainstream politics in some regional states (Jordan, Kuwait, Morocco, Sudan, Turkey, Yemen). As Milton-Edwards suggests, a new generation of Islamists is learning from the past mistakes of their leaders and is seeking "to grapple and engage with the current global order."[5] But political Islam as a whole had not quite managed to shed its violent streak. Indeed, the more radical brand of revolutionary Islam was a product of Afghani resistance to the Soviet occupation of that country in late 1979. Ironically, Western security agencies not only trained and supplied the Afghan *mujahadin* but helped recruit Muslim volunteers from the MENA region for the battlefields of Afghanistan; they thus inadvertently generated a network of militants that, after the second Gulf war, turned their resistance against the new Western penetration of the region. The September 11 terrorist attacks in the United States were an unforeseen consequence of this policy.

At the suprastate level, however, Pan-Islamism, rather like Pan-Arabism before it, proved unable to create a sustainable international and intra-Islamic structure. Even where the Islamists managed to gain access to the levers of power (as in Turkey in 1997) or amassed influence in the legislature (as in Jordan, Kuwait, Morocco, and Yemen), they have been unable to effect a significant change in the external orientation of the state. Moreover, the region's overtly Islamic states (Afghanistan, Iran, Pakistan, Saudi Arabia, and Sudan) can hardly be said to be providing incentives for the further Islamization of the Middle East. The five Islamist states are very different from each other, profess different versions of Islamic ideology, and, far from forming a cohesive unit of Pan-Islamic states, often find themselves in open conflict with each other.

Early post–Cold War fears of an all-powerful Islamic threat emerging from the MENA region to replace the force of international communism in international affairs proved unfounded. In the region, Iranian revolutionary Islam was contained, not least by the alignment of the mildly Islamic Gulf states with secular Iraq in the Iran-Iraq war. Even where political Islam is in power, it is attached to and legitimizes state interests; as with oil, the incorporation of Islamic forces into the individual states seemed to strengthen them. But whether this supra-state force is, like Arab nationalism, being tamed and coopted by the state system, or whether it is taking on a new trans-state life outside the control of states, as the al-Qa'ida network suggests, remains to be seen.

The Varieties of Islamic Rentierism

That even such a potentially potent combination as oil wealth and religious zeal has proved unable to generate Islamic power in the international or regional arenas is explained by the cases of Saudi Arabia and Iran. Both claim to be Islamic states and both have partial rentier economies. Yet these features of their domestic political economies have not prevented them from following contrary foreign policies: while Saudi Arabia continues to bandwagon with the United States, the Islamic revolution's transformation in ruling elites turned Iran from the main regional surrogate of the United States into its main regional challenger. As with war, the impact of oil and political Islam differed greatly, depending on a state's particular systemic position and history of state formation.

As realists might expect, the differences in their geopolitical power positions tended to bias their policies in opposite directions. Saudi Arabia's low military capability could be said to explain its bandwagoning (its seeking of U.S. protection), while Iran is capable of and sees itself as naturally exercising regional leadership. Yet, power positions divorced from domestic politics cannot adequately explain such radical behavioral differences. On the one hand, it is partly the nature of the Saudi regime—its unwillingness to conscript an army that could threaten the royal family—that keeps it so militarily weak and dependent; a similar low-population oil state, Libya, with a different type of regime, has pursued foreign policies that are the antithesis of Saudi caution. On the other hand, Iran under a different regime, that of the shah, saw regional leadership as compatible with serving U.S. interests. A state's geopolitical rank defines its situation but not how it reacts to it.

Both regimes legitimate themselves by Islam, but Iran's Shi'a Islam is revolutionary while Saudi Arabia's Sunni Islam currently legitimizes the status quo. More than Shi'a-Sunni differences, though, this expresses different experiences of the West in the stage of state formation: while Saudi Arabia never experienced colonialism and actually achieved independence with British and U.S. support, Iran was victimized by the West, which was perceived to manipulate its rulers, notably the last shah. Iran's revolutionary Islam was a vehicle of power for utterly un-Westernized elites who mobilized a constituency among the disinherited, while in Saudi Arabia the militant elements, notably the Ikhwan (Wahhabis), were pushed out of the regime coalition in favor of tribal elites and conservative *ulama.*

Oil also had a contrary effect. In Saudi Arabia, it fostered a new petro-bourgeoisie with assets invested chiefly in the West while a favorable oil/population ratio allowed the regime to co-opt and dampen earlier radical sentiment among the working and middle classes. Iran's much lower oil revenues per capita meant oil development under the shah only fueled social mobilization, inequality, and frustration; the revolution displaced client elites with a stake in the Western economy and oil revenues were thereafter invested at home. In the one case, foreign policy was shaped by oil-created shared interests between the regime and the West; in the other case, oil helped bring to power an anti-Western regime. Thus, the two states ended up in quite different positions in the core-periphery structure.

To be sure, under Rafsanjani, Iran subsequently adopted more moderate policies, having learned the costs of radicalism in the Iran-Iraq war and being aware that economic development could not proceed isolated from the world economy. Systemic forces—war, "socializing" Iran's elites into the realist rules of geopolitics, U.S. manipulation of the levers of the world economy—pushed Iranian policies back toward the moderate center. But the contrasting relationships to the United States remain: while the Saudis still bandwagon, Iran now seeks to balance U.S. regional power. Since both oil and Islam seem compatible equally with revolution against and co-optation into the world capitalist system, neither explains much except in combination with the specifics of state formation. This was also the lesson of the differential response to defeat in war by Egypt and Syria.

Unipolarity and Globalization

Since the 1990s, the Middle East is being reconstructed yet again. Those states that had developed a dependence on Cold War relations for aid or protection, particularly from the USSR, had to accommodate themselves to U.S. hegemony. At the same time, the seeming globalization of democratic capitalism unleashed pressures in the region for economic and political liberalization. The instinct of the republics and monarchies alike was to shield themselves from these threats by controlling communications access and evading economic and political reform. However, the confluence of chronic economic crisis and new opportunities presented by such developments as the EU's Euro-Med initiative have led some MENA states to grab onto the globalization bandwagon.

Middle East states were not uniformly situated in the emerging new order and the main new differentiation among them was between those standing to profit from it and those standing to be victimized. Some states were locked into enduring costly conflicts at the regional core; those on the peripheries were more ready to detach themselves from these and look outward. Some were better situated in the core-periphery structure to profit (candidates to be newly industrializing countries [NICs]), while others were less prepared to liberalize or were targeted by the economic sanctions of the U.S. world hegemon and were more likely to be victims.

Among the seeming winners was Israel. It was immune from most economic constraints: not only was it able to command continued U.S. subsidies by virtue of its penetration of the U.S. policy process, but it had become a major player in globalized markets through its high-tech exports and inflow of foreign investment. Its one liability was its continued conflict-sustaining irredentism (i.e., dominance of the Palestinian territories), which retarded its smooth integration into the global core. Another winner was Saudi Arabia, which, by virtue of its role as oil "swing producer" and its heavy investments in the core, had achieved an asymmetrical interdependence between the ruling family and the West. Its main liability was the continued threat emanating from the Gulf conflict center.

Fairly well positioned were those North African Arab states that, accepting the principles of the Barcelona talks,[6] put European economic partnerships over attachment to Arab core issues. Thus, as Murphy shows, Tunisia, determined to be a winner rather than a victim of globalization, deployed its foreign policy to access economic resources and markets in the core. The internationalist coalition around Ben Ali, whose own extended family were among the ranks of capitalist entrepreneurs, restructured the regime to repress all resistance, often inspired by identity, to economic globalization and Western policy in the region that it believed jeopardized this project. Similarly, as Robins shows, Turkey's elite, always seeing itself as European, has prioritized economic growth through access to EU and U.S. markets. To reach NIC status, it is prepared to sacrifice economic and strategic interests with Middle Eastern states, especially Iraq, and to alienate the Islamic part of the population. At the same time, however, Iran and Turkey were instrumental in promoting the Economic Cooperation Organization, which tied them to the former USSR's Muslim republics and Afghanistan and Pakistan; such regionalization was a potential alternative to full globalization.

The losers are easily identified, namely the formerly radical nationalist or Islamic states. While oil or oil subsidies formerly gave militant states such as Libya, Iraq, Syria, and Iran the means to pursue nationalist ambitions, their dependence on sharply fluctuating oil revenues and on the import habit that oil fostered made them particularly vulnerable to U.S.-manipulated economic punishments. This increasingly tempered their revisionism, except in Iraq, which resisted only at great cost. Somewhat similarly, Yemen's sharp dependency on external resources forced it, with the end to alternative Soviet aid, to flip-flop from supporting Saddam's Iraq to giving facilities to U.S. forces being used against Iraq.

Egypt is perhaps the most ambivalent case, caught between geopolitical ambitions and economic constraints and opportunities. It still aspires, by virtue of its geopolitical centrality, to Arab leadership, but its geo-economic situation puts major constraints on this: its dependence on U.S. aid, insufficiently balanced by its importance to U.S. interests in the region, forced it to compromise its otherwise "natural" Arab role, beginning with its separate peace with Israel and continuing with its service to U.S. interests in the Gulf war and its capitulation to U.S. pressures to sign the Nuclear Non-Proliferation Treaty. At the same time, like North Africa, it aspires to achieve NIC status through integration into globalized markets. Syria and Iran are pulled, albeit less starkly, by somewhat similar contrary impulses.

The September 11 events in the United States may have reshuffled the deck among winners and losers in ways that cannot be fully anticipated at the time of this writing. While regimes such as Syria, Iran, Iraq, and Libya, which are on Washington's "terrorism list," feared they could be the next targets in the war on terrorism, the need for the United States to establish a broad coalition against Osama bin Laden meant that it might try to coopt them. Syria, in particular, had reason to hope its participation in the anti-terrorism campaign could be traded for U.S. pressure on Israel over the occupied territories. On the other hand, Israel's policies in the occupied territories suddenly became a liability for Washington as it sought to maximize its support in the Islamic world. Most unexpectedly, Saudi Arabia, long the closest Arab ally of the United States, incurred U.S. displeasure for its reluctance, in the face of Islamic militancy at home, to overtly support the war on Afghanistan or to attack the terrorist networks on its own soil from which many of the 11 September terrorist were apparently recruited.

Resisting the Zone of Peace:
Pluralist State Formation and Foreign Policy

Globalization is expected to bring democratization and spread zones of peace; however, the war-induced insecurity of the Middle East threatens to leave it out of the post–Cold War "pacific" world order. If zones of peace were to appear anywhere, they should, according to pluralists, start with the region's most democratic states. However, the foreign policies of Turkey and Israel suggest these expectations are premature. To be sure, pluralistic political institutions have incorporated significant levels of mass participation in each country. This, however, in strengthening identification with the state, has merely facilitated the national mobilization of the population for defense; its effect on policymaking has been neither as important or as "pacific" as the democratic-peace thesis expects.

Turkey's military and diplomatic establishment long made foreign policy relatively insulated from popular pressures and according to defensive geopolitical considerations that avoided foreign entanglements and, remarkably given its fraught location, enabled Turkey to stay out of costly wars. Elected politicians, by contrast, have been more likely to advocate adventurous regional policies such as Menderes's enlistment of Turkey against Arab nationalism and Ozal's involvement of Turkey, against the caution of the state establishment, in the Gulf war. When popular forces have impacted on foreign policy, it has usually been to inflame nationalism or Islamic sentiment, whether over Cyprus or the post–Cold War temptations of involvement in the Balkans and Central Asia.

In Israel, neither elections nor deepening party pluralism have altered the disproportionate recruitment of the policymaking elite from a security establishment that sees military force as a main instrument for dealing with Israel's neighbors. Given the powerful irredentist sentiment in a significant portion of the Israeli public (the Likud-settler bloc), electoral politics has, with few exceptions, rewarded politicians who profess hawkish rather than dovish sentiments.

The fact is that in both Turkey and Israel foreign policy is shaped first by elite conceptions of security and geopolitical interest; when nonelite influences impact on policy, they tend to express irredentism, not pacifism. The region's most pluralist states are also its most assertive. Israel, Turkey, and Morocco are the only ones to have colonized a neighbor's territory—Morocco's annexation of Western Sahara, Israel's of the occupied territories, and Turkey's of northern Cyprus. Turkey and Israel are leading the regional arms race and have formed an alliance meant to cement their overwhelming military superiority over their Middle Eastern neighbors. This suggests that as long as irredentism and insecurity remain basic features of the regional system, the foreign policy impact of the *form* of government will be relatively limited. The democratic peace may therefore be chiefly an artifact of regions dominated by status quo powers with secure identities.[7]

Summary

In conclusion, the following pattern emerges from the record:

- Reaction to the differentiated effects of imperialism set states on differing status quo or revisionist paths, but the wars this unleashed pushed their convergence toward moderation.
- Oil and Islam started to differentiate them again, but in the end had similar effects as oil money was circulated among states and Islam co-opted by them.

- The peculiarities of *position* (power in the regional system, economic status in the core-periphery structure), and of *state formation and identity,* differentiated state response to these system-wide forces. The differentiating force of identity was particularly underlined by Halliday's analysis of Yemen, where imperialism, Arab nationalism, the Cold War, oil, and political Islam each swept over and left their residues on the country, but where, by the 1990s, the irreducibly distinctive Yemeni political culture had reasserted itself and reunited the country's once-sundered two halves.
- Globalization is now also differentiating the states into winners and victims, but it has yet to deconstruct the insecurity-driven power struggle so pervasive in the region. The peculiarities of states' formation and power positions continue to distort and deflect the homogenizing effects of globalization on their foreign policies.

Notes

1. John Gerard Ruggie, "Transformation and Continuity in the World Polity: Toward a Neo-Realist Synthesis," *World Politics* 35, January 1983, pp. 261–285, makes the case for the historical evolution of the international system.

2. Malcolm Kerr, *The Arab Cold War: Gamal Abd al-Nasir and His Rivals, 1958–1970,* London: Oxford University Press, 1971

3. Murhaf Jourjati, "An Institutional Perspective on Why Asad Did Not Emulate Sadat," Ph.D. dissertation, University of Utah, 1998.

4. Data extracted from OPEC's *Annual Statistical Bulletin,* Vienna: OPEC, 1980.

5. Beverley Milton-Edwards, *Contemporary Politics in the Middle East,* Oxford: Polity Press, 2000, p. 137.

6. Barcelona is host to a new round of discussions between the European Union and the Mediterranean countries on the nature of politics, economics, society, and cultural relations in this area in the twenty-first century.

7. James M. Goldgeier and Michael McFaul, "A Tale of Two Worlds: Core and Periphery in the Post–Cold War Era," *International Organization* 46, no. 2, spring 1992.

Glossary

Anarchy: The absence of government, seen by realism as the main distinction between domestic and international politics.

Balance of power: A key realist concept referring to a balance between the power of states or alliances of states, and seen as the main way of preventing dominance and establishing order. Classical realists see it as the result of artful statesmanship, while structural realists view it as a natural or probable response to the insecurity of the system.

Bandwagon: In realist parlance, the opposite of balancing against a threat, that is, to appease a superior, potentially threatening power, either in order to help balance a more proximate threat or to share in the spoils of a winning coalition.

Bureaucratic politics: Concept developed by Graham Allison. Policy is seen as a product of struggle within governments by rival branches of the bureaucracy, each defending its own interests, possibly at the expense of coherent "rational" policymaking; the reverse of the rational-actor model.

Complex interdependence: Concept in pluralism developed by Keohane and Nye, the result of the multiple transnational and interstate ties, often economic, that tie states together and potentially mute conflict.

Constructivism: Proponents, for example, Alexander Wendt, argue that the state system is an intersubjective (cultural, not material) set of norms and expectations created by the interactions of states. The system, in

351

turn, shapes (constitutes) the identities of states and this, not simply power considerations, explains their behavior.

Democratic peace theory: The claim that the spread of democracy would lead to greater international peace and security, as democratic checks and balances make it harder to make war and democratic processes predispose states to a peaceful resolution of their conflicts. (A branch of neoliberal/pluralist thinking.)

Globalization: The speedup and intensification of worldwide social relations, driven by the internationalization of business and communications. It both partly bypasses states and ties them into a mutually interdependent world society that reduces their self-sufficiency and sovereignty.

Hegemon (hegemony): A hegemon is a dominant or leading state (e.g., the United States and the United Kingdom, at different times) that supposedly maintains order and economic stability in the world system, normally in the name of a certain normative ideology, such as liberalism.

Level of analysis: Refers to alternative foci of explanation for international behavior. The system level refers, in realism, to the anarchic structure of the states system and, in structuralism, to the hierarchic core-periphery global division of labor. It is seen by these approaches to shape the behavior of the unit level (the states). Substate phenomena, including individual leaders, government (executives, interest groups, bureaucracies), and civil society (political culture, public opinion), may be other identified levels; these are argued by pluralism to equally affect states' international behavior.

Neorealism (or structural realism): A version of realism that stresses the predominant influence of the state system (especially insecurity from anarchy) in shaping states and their behavior. Key text: Kenneth Waltz, *Theory of International Politics*, Reading, MA: Addison-Wesley, 1979. See also *realism*.

Pluralism: Acknowledges a plurality of forces shaping international relations besides states, notably suprastate (international organizations), transstate (transnational corporations), and nonstate (professional associations, social movements) actors. The resulting complex interdependence constrains states, especially deterring warlike behavior. Seeing states as less than unitary actors, pluralism also focuses on the role of substate domestic actors, such as competing bureaucracies, interest groups, and public opinion, as determinants of a state's behavior. It also stresses the role of leadership beliefs and images, including the irrationality caused by misperceptions. Subsumed within a broader school of "liberalism." Key text: Robert Keohane and Joseph Nye, *Power and Interdependence,* Boston: Little, Brown, 1977.

Rational actor: The notion that states, ideally, act as unitary actors, making decisions after collecting full information, surveying all feasible options, weighing costs and benefits, and matching ends and means. See also *bureaucratic politics* and *realism.*

Realism: Traditionally dominant school of international-relations theory. States are seen as unitary rational actors advancing their national interests amidst the insecurity of the anarchic international arena. International politics is a struggle for power, war is an ever-present possibility, and order depends on a balance of power. Decisionmaker rationality means careful "realistic" matching of goals and resources (the more commonsense use of the world *realism*). Key text: Hans Morgenthau, *Politics Among Nations,* New York: Knopf, 1978.

Regime: In the domestic context, refers to an existing governmental order. In international politics, refers to principles, norms, and procedures voluntarily agreed by states, which restrain their behavior.

Security dilemma: Coined by John Herz. In an anarchic system each state increases its power for defensive purposes but, in doing so, is seen as more threatening by its neighbors, who respond in kind, setting off arms races, with the result that all end up less secure.

Structuralism: As used here, the broad view, inspired by Marxism, that the hierarchical structure of the international capitalist system determines state options. Specifically, in the international economic division of labor, the core (developed) states subordinate and exploit the less developed countries (LDCs) or "periphery," whose function is to supply the latter with primary products. The system is maintained by transstate alliances between dominant classes in the core and periphery and by the economic dependency of LDCs. Dependency theory and world systems theory are seen here as varieties of structuralism. Key Text: Immanuel Wallerstein, *The Capitalist World Economy,* Cambridge: Cambridge

University Press, 1979. Not to be confused with "structural realism," another term for *neorealism*.

Transnational (or transstate): Refers to ties and nonstate groups that cross state boundaries.

Bibliography

Aarts, Paul (1999). "The Middle East: A Region Without Regionalism or the End of Exceptionalism?" *Third World Quarterly* 20, no. 5, October, pp. 911–925.

Adelson, Roger (1995). *London and the Invention of the Middle East: Money, Power, and War, 1902–1922*. London: Yale University Press.

Agha, Hussein J., and Ahmed S. Khalidi (1995). *Syria and Iran: Rivalry and Cooperation*. London: Pinter.

Ajami, Fuad (1977–1978). "Stress in the Arab Triangle." *Foreign Policy* 29, pp. 90–108.

——— (1981). *The Arab Predicament*. Cambridge: Cambridge University Press.

Al-Khalil, Samir (1989). *The Republic of Fear*. London: Hutchinson Radius.

Almadhagi, Ahmed, and Kassim Noman (1996). *Yemen and the United States: A Study of a Small Power and Super-State Relationship 1962–1994*. London: I. B. Tauris.

Alnasrawi, Abbas (1991). *Arab Nationalism, Oil and the Political Economy of Dependency*. New York and London: Greenwood Press.

Al-Suwaidi, Jamal, ed. (1995). *The Yemeni War of 1994: Causes and Consequences*. London: Saqi Books.

Al-Yassini, Ayman (1985). *Religion and State in the Kingdom of Saudi Arabia*. Boulder, CO: Westview Press.

Amin, Samir (1978). *The Arab Nation: Nationalism and Class Struggles*. London: Zed Press.

Amirahmadi, Hooshang (1990). *Revolution and Economic Transition: The Iranian Experience*. Albany: State University of New York Press.

———, ed. (1993). *The United States and the Middle East: A Search for New Perspectives*. Albany: State University of New York Press.

Amuzegar, Jahangir (1993). *Iran's Economy Under the Islamic Republic*. London: I. B. Tauris.

Anderson, Irvine H. (1981). *Aramco, the United States and Saudi Arabia*. Princeton, NJ: Princeton University Press.

Ayubi, Nazih (1995). *Overstating the Arab State: Politics and Society in the Middle East*. London: I. B. Tauris.

Bakhash, Shaul (1998). "Iran Since the Gulf War," in Robert O. Freedman, ed., *The Middle East and the Peace Process: The Impact of the Oslo Accords.* Gainesville: University Press of Florida, pp. 241–264.

Baram, Amatzia, and Barry Rubin (1994). *Iraq's Road to War.* Basingstoke, England: Macmillan.

Barchard, David (1985). *Turkey and the West.* London: RIIA/RKP.

Barkey, Henri (1998). *Turkey's Kurdish Question.* Lanham, MD: Rowman & Littlefield.

Barnett, Michael (1990). "High Politics Is Low Politics: The Domestic and Systemic Sources of Israeli Security Policy, 1967–1977." *World Politics* 17, no. 4, pp. 529–562.

——— (1992). *Confronting the Costs of War: Military Power, State and Society in Egypt and Israel.* Princeton, NJ: Princeton University Press.

——— (1993). "Institutions, Roles and Disorder: The Case of the Arab States System." *International Studies Quarterly* 37, no. 3, September.

——— (1995). "Sovereignty, Nationalism, and Regional Order in the Arab States System." *International Organization* 49, no. 3, summer.

———, ed. (1996). *Israel in Comparative Perspective: Challenging the Conventional Wisdom.* Albany: State University of New York Press.

——— (1996–1997). "Regional Security After the Gulf War." *Political Science Quarterly* 111, no. 4, pp. 597–617.

——— (1999). *Dialogues in Arab Politics: Negotiations in Regional Order.* New York: Columbia University Press.

Barnett, Michael, and F. Gregory Gause III (1998). "Caravans in Opposite Directions: Society, State and the Development of Community in the Gulf Cooperation Council," in Emmanuel Adler and Michael Barnett, eds., *Security Communities.* Cambridge: Cambridge University Press.

Bar-Siman-Tov, Yaacov (1998). "The United States and Israel Since 1948: A 'Special Relationship'?" *Diplomatic History* 22, no. 2, spring, pp. 231–262.

Barzilai, Gad (1996). *Wars, Internal Conflicts, and Political Order: A Jewish Democracy in the Middle East.* Albany: State University of New York Press.

Battah, Abdullah, and Yehuda Lukas, eds. (1988). *The Arab-Israeli Conflict: Two Decades of Change.* Boulder, CO: Westview Press.

Ben-Eliezer, Uri (1997). "Rethinking the Civil-Military Relations Paradigm: The Inverse Relation Between Militarism and Praetorianism Through the Example of Israel." *Comparative Political Studies* 30, no. 3, June, pp. 356–374.

Bengio, Ofra (1998). *Saddam's Word—Political Discourse in Iraq.* New York and Oxford: Oxford University Press.

Bennett, Andrew, Joseph Lepgold, and Danny Unger (1997). *Friends in Need: Burden Sharing in the Gulf War.* New York: St. Martin's Press.

Bennis, Philip, and Michel Moushabeck, eds. (1991). *Beyond the Storm: A Gulf Crisis Reader.* New York: Olive Branch Press.

Binder, Leonard (1958). "The Middle East as a Subordinate International System." *World Politics* 10, no. 3.

Blundy, David, and Andrew Lycett (1988). *Qaddafi and the Libyan Revolution.* London: Corgi.

Bowker, Robert (1996). *Beyond Peace: The Search for Security in the Middle East*. Boulder, CO: Lynne Rienner Publishers.

Brand, Laurie (1995). *Jordan's Inter-Arab Relations: The Political Economy of Alliance Making*. New York: Columbia University Press.

Brecher, Michael (1972). *The Foreign Policy System of Israel*. London: Oxford University Press.

Bresheeth, Haim, and Nira Yuval-Davis (1991). *The Gulf War and the New World Order*. London and New Jersey: Zed Books.

Bromley, Simon (1990). *American Hegemony and World Oil: The Industry, the State System and the World Economy*. Oxford: Polity Press.

——— (1994). *Rethinking Middle East Politics*. Oxford: Polity Press.

Brown, L. Carl (1984). *International Politics and the Middle East: Old Rules, Dangerous Game*. Princeton, NJ: Princeton University Press.

Buchta, Wilfried (2000). *Who Rules Iran? The Structure of Power in the Islamic Republic*. Washington, DC: The Washington Institute for Near East Policy.

Burrowes, Robert (1986). *The Yemen Arab Republic: The Politics of Development 1962–1986*. Boulder, CO: Westview Press.

——— (1999). "The Republic of Yemen: The Politics of Unification and Civil War, 1989–1995," in Michael Hudson, *Middle East Dilemmas: The Politics and Economics of Arab Integration*. London and New York: I. B. Tauris.

Calabrese, John (1994). *Revolutionary Horizons: Regional Foreign Policy in Post-Khomeini Iran*. New York and London: St. Martin's/Macmillan.

Chaudhry, Kiren Aziz (1991). "On the Way to the Market: Economic Liberalization and Iraq's Invasion." *Middle East Report* 170, May–June.

——— (1997). *The Price of Wealth*. Ithaca: Cornell University Press.

Chourou, Béchir (1998). "The Free-Trade Agreement Between Tunisia and the European Union." *The Journal of North African Studies* 3, no. 1.

Chubin, Shahram (1994). *Iran's National Security Policy, Capabilities, Intentions, Impact*. Washington, DC: Carnegie Endowment for International Peace.

Chubin, Shahram, and Sepehr Zabih (1974). *The Foreign Relations of Iran*. Berkeley: University of California Press.

Chubin, Shahram, and Charles Tripp (1988). *Iran and Iraq at War*. London: I. B. Tauris.

Clawson, Patrick (1989). *Unaffordable Ambitions: Syria's Military Buildup and Economic Crisis*. Washington, DC: Washington Institute for Near East Policy.

——— (1993). *Iran's Challenge to the West: How, When, Why?* Washington, DC: The Washington Institute for Near East Policy.

Cobban, Helena (1991). *The Superpowers and the Syrian-Israeli Conflict*. New York: Praeger, The Washington Papers, no. 149.

——— (1999). *The Israeli-Syrian Peace Talks: 1991–96 and Beyond*. Washington, DC: U.S. Institute of Peace Press.

Cordesman, Anthony (1987). *Western Strategic Interests in Saudi Arabia*. London: Croom Helm.

Cottam, Richard (1979). *Nationalism in Iran*. Pittsburgh: University of Pittsburgh Press.

——— (1988). *Iran and United States: A Cold War Case Study.* Pittsburgh: University of Pittsburgh Press.

Cremeans, Charles. (1963). *The Arabs and the World: Nasser's Arab Nationalist Policy.* New York: Praeger.

Davis, B. (1990). *Qaddafi, Terrorism and the U.S. Attack on Libya.* New York: Praeger.

Dawisha, Adeed (1976). *Egypt in the Arab World: The Elements of Foreign Policy.* New York: Wiley.

——— (1980). *Syria and the Lebanese Crisis.* London: Macmillan.

——— (1983). *Islam in Foreign Policy.* London: Royal Institute of International Affairs and Cambridge University Press.

——— (1990). "Arab Regimes: Legitimacy and Foreign Policy," in Giacomo Luciani, *The Arab State.* London: Routledge.

Dawisha, Adeed, and I. William Zartman (1988). *Beyond Coercion: The Durability of the Arab State.* London: Croom Helm.

Deeb, Mary-Jane (1991). *Libya's Policy in North Africa.* Boulder, CO: Westview Press.

Deeb, Mary-Jane, and Ellen Laipson (1991). "Tunisian Foreign Policy," in I. W. Zartman, *Tunisia: The Political Economy of Reform.* Boulder, CO: Lynne Rienner.

Dekmejian, H. R. (1971). *Egypt Under Nasir.* Albany: State University of New York Press.

Dessouki, Ali E. Hillal (1991). "The Primacy of Economics: The Foreign Policy of Egypt," in Bahgat Korany and Ali E. Hillal Dessouki, eds., *The Foreign Policies of Arab States: The Challenge of Change.* Boulder, CO: Westview Press.

Dodd, C. H. (1992). *Turkish Foreign Policy: New Prospects.* Huntingdon, England: Eothen.

Drysdale, Alasdair, and Raymond Hinnebusch (1991). *Syria and the Middle East Peace Process.* New York: Council on Foreign Relations Press.

Ehteshami, Anoushiravan (1995). *After Khomeini: The Iranian Second Republic.* London: Routledge.

——— (1995). *The Politics of Economic Restructuring in Post-Khomeini Iran.* Durham, England: Centre for Middle Eastern and Islamic Studies.

Ehteshami, Anoushiravan, and Raymond A. Hinnebusch (1997). *Syria and Iran: Middle Powers in a Penetrated Regional System.* London: Routledge.

Ehteshami, Anoushiravan, and Manshour Varasteh, eds. (1991). *Iran and the International Community.* London: Routledge.

El-Shazly, Nadia (1998). *The Gulf Tanker War.* Basingstoke, England: Macmillan.

El Warfally, Mahmoud (1988). *Imagery and Ideology in US Policy Toward Libya, 1969–82.* Pittsburgh: University of Pittsburgh Press.

Evron, Boas (1995). *Jewish State or Israeli Nation?* Bloomington: Indiana University Press.

Evron, Yair (1973). *Nations, Superpowers and Wars.* London: Elek Books.

——— (1987). *War and Intervention in Lebanon: The Syrian-Israeli Deterrence Dialogue.* Baltimore: Johns Hopkins University Press.

Evron, Yair, and Yaacov Bar-Simantov (1976). "Coalitions in the Arab World." *Jerusalem Journal of International Relations* 1, no. 2, pp. 71–72.

Fahmi, Ismail (1983). *Negotiating for Peace in the Middle East*. Baltimore: Johns Hopkins University Press.

Fandy, Mamoun (1999). *Saudi Arabia and the Politics of Dissent*. New York: St. Martin's Press.

Farouk-Sluglett, Marion, and Peter Sluglett (1990). *Iraq Since 1958*. London: I. B. Tauris.

Fraser, T. G. (1989). *The USA and the Middle East Since World War II*. London: Macmillan.

Freedman, Lawrence, and Efraim Karsh (1993). *The Gulf Conflict, 1990–1991*. London: Faber and Faber.

Fuller, Graham E. (1991). *The "Center of the Universe" : The Geopolitics of Iran*. Boulder, CO: Westview Press.

Fuller, Graham, and Ian O. Lesser (1993). *Turkey's New Geopolitics*. Boulder, CO: Westview Press.

Gause, F. Gregory III (1990). *Saudi-Yemeni Relations: Domestic Structures and Foreign Influence*. New York: Columbia University Press.

——— (1991). "Revolutionary Fevers and Regional Contagion: Domestic Structures and the Export of Revolution in the Middle East." *Journal of South Asian and Middle East Studies* 14, no. 3, spring.

——— (1994). *Oil Monarchies*. New York: Council on Foreign Relations Press.

——— (1997). "Sovereignty and Its Challengers: War in Middle Eastern Interstate Politics," in Paul Salem, *Conflict Resolution in the Arab World*. Beirut: AUB Press, pp. 197–215.

——— (1998). "The Arabian Peninsula," in Robert Freedman, ed., *The Middle East and the Peace Process: The Impact of the Oslo Accords*. Gainesville: University Press of Florida.

——— (1999). "Systemic Approaches to Middle East International Relations." *International Studies Review* 1, no. 1, spring, pp. 11–31.

Gerges, Fawaz (1994). *The Superpowers and the Middle East: Regional and International Politics, 1955–1967*. Boulder, CO: Westview Press.

Gershoni, Israel, and James Jankowski (1995). *Redefining the Egyptian Nation, 1930–1945*. Cambridge: Cambridge University Press.

Goldberg, Jacob (1986). *The Foreign Policy of Saudi Arabia: The Formative Years, 1902–1918*. Cambridge: Harvard University Press.

Graham-Brown, Sarah (1999). *Sanctioning Saddam: The Politics of Intervention in Iraq*. London: I. B. Tauris.

Guazzone, Laura (1997). *The Middle East in Global Change: The Politics and Economics of Interdependence Versus Fragmentation*. London: Macmillan.

Haikal, Muhammed Hassanein (1975). *The Road to Ramadan*. New York: Reader's Digest Press.

——— (1983). *The Autumn of Fury: The Assassination of Sadat*. London: Corgi Books.

Hale, William (2000). *Turkish Foreign Policy, 1774–2000*. London: Frank Cass.

Haley, Edward (1984). *Qaddafi and the United States Since 1969*. New York: Praeger.

Halliday, Fred (1974). *Arabia Without Sultans*. New York: Vintage Press.

——— (1990). *Revolution and Foreign Policy: The Case of South Yemen 1967–1987*. Cambridge: Cambridge University Press.

——— (1994). "The Gulf War 1990–1991 and the Study of International Relations." *Review of International Studies* 20, no. 2, April 1994.

Harik, Iliya (1987). "The Origins of the Arab State System," in Ghassan Salame, *The Foundations of the Arab State.* London: Croom Helm.

Harknett R., and J. VanDenBerg (1997). "Alignment Theory and Interrelated Threats: Jordan and the Persian Gulf Crisis." *Security Studies* 6, no. 3, spring, pp. 112–153.

Helms, Christine Moss (1981). *The Cohesion of Saudi Arabia.* Baltimore: Johns Hopkins University Press.

Hinnebusch, Raymond (1985). *Egyptian Politics Under Sadat.* Cambridge: Cambridge University Press, 1985.

——— (1991). "Revisionist Dreams, Realist Strategies: The Foreign Policy of Syria," in Bahgat Korany and Ali E. Hillal Dessouki, eds., *The Foreign Policies of Arab States: The Challenge of Change.* Boulder, CO: Westview Press.

Hiro, Dilip (1989). *The Longest War.* London: Grafton Books.

——— (1992). *Desert Shield to Desert Storm: The Second Gulf War.* New York: Routledge.

Hopwood, Derek (1992). *Habib Bourguiba of Tunisia: The Tragedy of Longevity.* Hampshire: Macmillan.

Hudson, Michael (1977). *Arab Politics: The Search for Legitimacy.* New Haven: Yale University Press.

——— (1995). "Bipolarity, Rational Calculation and War in Yemen." *Arab Studies Journal,* no. 3.

———, ed. (1999). *Middle East Dilemmas: The Politics and Economics of Arab Integration.* London and New York: I. B. Tauris.

Inbar, Efraim (1990). "Attitudes Toward War in the Israeli Political Elite." *Middle East Journal* 44, no. 3, summer, pp. 431–445.

——— (1997). "Israel's Predicament in a New Strategic Environment," in Efraim Inbar and Gabriel Sheffer, eds., *The National Security of Small States in a Changing World.* London: Frank Cass, pp. 155–174.

Ismael, Jacqueline (1993). *Kuwait: Dependency and Class in a Rentier State.* Gainesville: University Press of Florida.

Ismael, Tareq Y. (1986). *International Relations of the Contemporary Middle East: A Study in World Politics.* Syracuse, NY: Syracuse University Press.

Ismael, Tareq, and Jacqueline Ismael (1994). *The Gulf War and the New World Order.* Gainesville: University Press of Florida.

Jawad, Haifaa (1997). *The Middle East in the New World Order.* London: Macmillan.

Joffé, George, ed. (1999). *Perspectives on Development: The Euro-Mediterranean Partnership.* London: Frank Cass.

Joffé, G., M. J. Hachemi, and E. W. Watkins (1997). *Yemen Today: Crisis and Solutions,* London: Caravel.

Jones, Clive (1997). "Ideotheology: Dissonance and Discourse in the State of Israel." *Israel Affairs* 3, nos. 3 and 4, spring–summer, pp. 28–46.

Karpat, Kemal H. (1996). *Turkish Foreign Policy: Recent Developments.* Madison: Wisconsin University Press.

Karsh, Efraim, ed. (1987). *The Iran-Iraq War: Impact and Implications.* London: Macmillan.

Katz, Mark (1986). *Russia and Arabia: Soviet Foreign Policy Towards the Arabian Peninsula*. Baltimore: Johns Hopkins University Press.

Keller, Adam (1987). *Terrible Days: Social Divisions and Political Paradoxes in Israel*. Amstelveen, Netherlands: Cypress.

Kerr, Malcolm (1971). *The Arab Cold War: Gamal Abd al-Nasir and His Rivals, 1958–1970*. London: Oxford University Press, 1971.

Kerr, Malcolm, and El Sayed Yassin, eds. (1982). *Rich and Poor States in the Middle East*. Boulder, CO: Westview Press.

Keyder, Caglar (1987). *State and Class in Turkey: A Study in Capitalist Development*. London: Verso.

Khalidi, Rashid, et al. (1991). *The Origins of Arab Nationalism*. New York: Columbia University Press.

Kienle, Eberhard (1990). *Ba'th Versus Ba'th: The Conflict Between Syria and Iraq*. London: I. B. Tauris.

Korany, Bahgat (1986). *How Foreign Policy Is Made in the Third World*. Boulder, CO: Westview Press.

——— (1987). "Alien and Besieged Yet Here to Stay: The Contradictions of the Arab Territorial State," in Ghassan Salame, *The Foundations of the Arab State*. London: Croom Helm.

Korany, Bahgat, and Ali E. Hillal Dessouki, eds. (1991). *The Foreign Policies of Arab States: The Challenge of Change*. Boulder, CO: Westview Press.

Korany, Bahgat, Paul Noble, and Rex Brynen, eds. (1993). *The Many Faces of National Security in the Middle East*. London: Macmillan.

Kostiner, Joseph (1987). "Shi'i Unrest in the Gulf," in Martin Kramer, ed., *Shi'ism, Resistance and Revolution*. Boulder, CO: Westview Press.

——— (1993). *The Making of Saudi Arabia*. New York: Oxford University Press.

——— (1996). *Yemen: The Tortuous Quest for Unity, 1990–1994*. London: Pinter.

Lackner, Helen (1986). *PDR Yemen: Outpost of Socialist Development in Arabia*. London: Ithaca Press.

Lenczowski, George (1990). *American Presidents and the Middle East*. London: Duke University Press.

Lesch, David (1996). *The Middle East and the United States: A Historical and Political Reassessment*. Boulder, CO: Westview Press.

Long, David (1985). *The United States and Saudi Arabia: Ambivalent Allies*. Boulder, CO: Westview Press.

Love, Kenneth (1969). *Suez: The Twice-Fought War*. New York: McGraw-Hill.

Luciani, Giacomo, and Ghassan Salame, eds. (1988). *The Politics of Arab Integration*. London: Croom Helm.

Lustick, Ian (1997). "The Absence of Middle Eastern Great Powers: Political Backwardness in Historical Perspective." *International Organization* 51, no. 4, pp. 653–683.

Maddy-Weitzman, Bruce (1993). *The Crystallization of the Arab State System, 1945–1954*. Syracuse, NY: Syracuse University Press.

Marr, Phebe (1985). *The Modern History of Iraq*. Boulder, CO: Westview Press.

McDowall, David (1996). *A Modern History of the Kurds*. London: I. B. Tauris.

Mohammadi, Ali, and Anoushiravan Ehteshami, eds. (2000). *Iran and Eurasia*. Reading, England: Ithaca Press.

Ma'oz, Moshe (1988). *Asad, the Sphinx of Damascus.* New York: Grove Weidenfeld.
Ma'oz, Moshe, and Avner Yaniv (1986). *Syria Under Assad.* London: Croom Helm.
Ma'oz, Zeev (1997). *Regional Security in the Middle East.* London and Portland: Frank Cass.
Mufti, Malik (1995). *Sovereign Creations: Pan-Arabism and Political Order in Syria and Iraq.* Ithaca, NY, and London: Cornell University Press, 1995.
——— (1998). "Daring and Caution in Turkish Foreign Policy." *Middle East Journal* 52, no. 1, winter.
Murden, Simon (1995). *Emergent Powers and International Relations, 1988–1991.* Reading, England: Ithaca Press.
Nahas, Maridi (1985). "State Systems and Revolutionary Challenge: Nasser, Khomeini and the Middle East." *International Journal of Middle East Studies* 17.
Newman, David, ed. (1995). *The Impact of Gush Emunim: Politics and Settlement on the West Bank.* London: Croom Helm.
Niblock, Tim (2001). *"Pariah States" and Sanctions in the Middle East: Iraq, Libya, Sudan.* Boulder, CO: Lynne Rienner.
Noble, Paul (1991). "The Arab System," in Bahgat Korany and Ali E. Hillal Dessouki, eds., *The Foreign Policies of Arab States: The Challenge of Change.* Boulder CO: Westview Press, pp. 65–70.
Nonneman, Gerd (1997). "The Yemen Republic: From Unification and Liberalization to Civil War and Beyond," in Haifaa A. Jawad, ed., *The Middle East in the New World Order,* 2d edition. London: Macmillan.
Owen, Roger (1981). *The Middle East in the World Economy, 1800–1945.* London: Methuen.
——— (1992). "Arab Nationalism, Arab Unity and the Practice of Intra-Arab State Relations," in *State, Power and Politics in the Making of the Modern Middle East.* London: Routledge, pp. 81–107.
Page, Stephen (1985). *The Soviet Union and the Yemens: Influence in Asymmetrical Relationships.* New York: Praeger.
Parker, Richard B. (1984). *North Africa: Regional Tensions and Strategic Concerns.* New York: Praeger.
Peleg, Ilan (1998). "The Peace Process and Israel's Political Kulturkampf," in Ilan Peleg, ed., *The Middle East Peace Process.* Albany: State University of New York Press.
Penrose, Edith, and E. F. Penrose (1978). *Iraq: International Relations and National Development.* London: Ernest Benn.
Peri, Yoram (1983). *Between Battles and Ballots: Israel's Military in Politics.* Cambridge: Cambridge University Press.
Petran, Tabitha (1972). *Syria.* London: Benn.
Pipes, Daniel (1990). *Greater Syria: The History on an Ambition.* New York and London: Oxford University Press.
——— (1996). *Syria Beyond the Peace Process.* Washington, DC: Washington Institute for Near East Policy.
Piscatori, James (1983). "Islamic Values and National Interest: The Foreign Policy of Saudi Arabia," in Adeed Dawisha, ed., *Islam in Foreign Policy.* Cambridge: Cambridge University Press.

———— (1986). *Islam in a World of Nation-States*. Cambridge: Cambridge University Press.

Porath, Yehoshua (1986). *In Search of Arab Unity, 1930–1945*. London: Frank Cass.

Quandt, William B. (1993). *Peace Process: American Diplomacy and the Arab-Israeli Conflict Since 1967*. Washington, DC, and Berkeley and Los Angeles: The Brookings Institution and University of California Press.

Ramazani, Rouhollah K. (1975). *Iran's Foreign Policy: A Study of Foreign Policy in Modernizing Nations*. Charlottesville: University of Virginia Press.

———— (1992). "Iran's Foreign Policy: Both North and South." *Middle East Journal* 46, no. 3, summer, pp. 393–412.

Rathmell, Andrew (1995). *Secret War in the Middle East: The Covert Struggle for Syria, 1949–1961*. London: I. B. Tauris.

Riad, Mahmoud (1982). *The Struggle for Peace in the Middle East*. London and New York: Quartet Books.

Roberson, B. A., ed. (1998). *The Middle East and Europe: The Power Deficit*. London: Routledge.

Robins, Philip (1991). *Turkey and the Middle East*. London: Royal Institute of International Affairs.

———— (1997). "Turkish Foreign Policy Under Erbakan." *Survival,* summer.

Rossi, Pierre (1967). *Bourguiba's Tunisia*. Tunis: Editions Kahia.

Rugh, William (1996). "The Foreign Policy of the United Arab Emirates." *Middle East Journal* 50, no. 1, winter.

Safran, Nadav (1985). *Saudi Arabia: Ceaseless Quest for Security*. Cambridge: Harvard University Press.

Salame, Ghassan (1987). *The Foundations of the Arab State*. London: Croom Helm.

Salloukh, Bassel. (1996). "State Strength, Permeability, and Foreign Policy Behavior: Jordan in Theoretical Perspective." *Arab Studies Quarterly* 18, no. 2, spring.

Sayigh, Yazid, and Avi Shlaim, eds. (1997). *The Cold War and the Middle East*. London: Oxford University Press.

Schiff, Zeev, and Ehud Ya'ari (1985). *Israel's Lebanon War*. London: Allen & Unwin.

Schofield, Richard (1991). *Kuwait and Iraq: Historical Claims and Territorial Disputes*. London: RIIA.

Seale, Patrick (1965). *The Struggle for Syria*. London: Oxford University Press.

———— (1988). *Asad: The Struggle for the Middle East*. Berkeley: University of California Press.

Segev, Tom (1994). *The Seventh Million: The Israelis and the Holocaust*. New York: Hill and Wang.

Sela, Avraham (1998). *The End of the Arab-Israeli Conflict: Middle East Politics and the Quest for Regional Order*. Albany: State University of New York Press.

Sheehan, Edward (1976). "How Kissinger Did It: Step by Step in the Middle East." *Foreign Policy,* no. 22, spring.

Sifry, Micah, and Christopher Cerf (1991). *The Gulf War Reader*. New York: Times Books, 1991.

Simons, Geoffrey (1996). *The Scourging of Iraq: Sanctions, Law and Natural Justice*. London: Macmillan.

Skeet, Ian (1988). *OPEC: Twenty-Five Years of Prices and Politics*. Cambridge: Cambridge University Press.

Smith, Charles (1992). *Palestine and the Arab-Israeli Conflict*. New York: St. Martin's Press.

Smolansky, O. M., and B. M. Smolansky (1991). *The USSR and Iran—The Soviet Quest for Influence*. Durham, NC: Duke University Press.

Sprinzak, Ehud (1991). *The Ascendance of Israel's Radical Right*. London: Oxford University Press.

St. John, Ronald (1987). *Qaddafi's World Design*. London: Saqi Books.

Taylor, Alan (1982). *The Arab Balance of Power*. Syracuse, NY: University of Syracuse Press.

——— (1991). *The Superpowers and the Middle East*. Syracuse, NY: Syracuse University Press.

Telhami, Shibley (1990). *Power and Leadership in International Bargaining: The Path to the Camp David Accords*. New York: Columbia University Press.

——— (1990). "Israeli Foreign Policy: A Static Strategy in a Changing World." *Middle East Journal* 44, no. 3, summer, pp. 399–416.

Tibi, Bassam (1990). *Arab Nationalism, A Critical Enquiry*. Ed. and translated by Marion Farouk-Sluglett and Peter Sluglett. London: Macmillan.

——— (1998). *Conflict and War in the Middle East: From Interstate War to New Security*. London: Macmillan.

Tripp, Charles (2000). *A History of Iraq*. Cambridge: Cambridge University Press.

Troeller, Gary (1976). *The Birth of Saudi Arabia*. London: Frank Cass.

Vali, Ferenc (1971). *Bridge Across the Bosporus*. Baltimore: Johns Hopkins University Press.

Van Crevald, Martin (1998). *The Sword and the Olive: A Critical History of the Israeli Defense Forces*. New York: Public Affairs.

Vandewalle, Dirk (1995). *Qadhafi's Libya, 1969–1994*. Basingstoke, England: Macmillan.

——— (1998). *Libya Since Independence: Oil and State-Building*. London: I. B. Tauris.

Vitalis, Robert (1997). "The Closing of the Arabian Oil Frontier and the Future of Saudi-American Relations." *Middle East Report,* no. 204, July–September, pp. 15–21.

Walt, Steven (1987). *The Origin of Alliances*. Ithaca, NY: Cornell University Press.

Yaniv, Avner (1987). "Alliance Politics in the Middle East: A Security Dilemma Perspective," in Auriel Braun, ed., *The Middle East in Global Strategy*. Boulder, CO: Westview Press.

Yavuz, M. Hakan, and Mujeeb Khan (1992). "Turkish Foreign Policy Toward the Arab Israeli Conflict." *Arab Studies Quarterly* 14, no. 4, fall.

Zangeneh, Hamid, ed. (1994). *Islam, Iran and World Stability*. New York: St. Martin's Press.

The Contributors

Anoushiravan Ehteshami is director of the Institute for Middle Eastern and Islamic Studies and professor of international relations at the University of Durham. He is also vice-president of the British Society for Middle Eastern Studies (BRISMES). His most recent publications include *Iran's Security Policy in the Post-Revolutionary Era* (coauthor, 2001), *Iran and Eurasia* (coeditor, 2000), *The Changing Balance of Power in Asia* (1998), *Syria and Iran: Middle Powers in a Penetrated Regional System* (with Raymond Hinnebusch, 1997), *Islamic Fundamentalism* (coeditor, 1996), *After Khomeini: The Iranian Second Republic* (1995), and *From the Gulf to Central Asia: Players in the New Great Game* (editor, 1994).

F. Gregory Gause III is associate professor of political science at the University of Vermont and director of the university's Middle East studies program. He is author of *Oil Monarchies* (1994) and *Saudi-Yemeni Relations: Domestic Structures and Foreign Influence* (1990), as well as a number of articles on the international politics of the Middle East and the Gulf region in journals and edited volumes.

Fred Halliday is professor of international relations at the London School of Economics, where he teaches courses on international relations theory and on the international relations of the Middle East. His books on the Middle East include *Arabia Without Sultans* (1974), *Iran: Dictatorship and Development* (1978), *Revolution and Foreign Policy: The Case of South Yemen, 1967–1987* (1990), *Islam and the Myth of Confrontation* (1994), and *Nation and Religion in the Middle East* (2000). He is currently working on a book for Cambridge University Press on the international relations of Middle Eastern states.

Raymond Hinnebusch is professor of international relations and Middle East politics at the University of St. Andrews, Scotland. He is the author of *Egyptian Politics Under Sadat* (1985); *Authoritarian Power and State Formation in Ba'thist Syria: Army, Party and Peasant* (1990); *Syria and the Middle East Peace Process* (with Alasdair Drysdale, 1991); *The Syrian-Iranian Alliance: Middle Powers in a Penetrated Regional System* (with Anoushiravan Ehteshami, 1997); *Syria: Revolution from Above* (2001).

Clive Jones is senior lecturer in international politics and Middle East studies, University of Leeds. His publications include *Soviet Jewish Aliyah 1989–92* (1996), *International Security in a Global Age* (co-editor, 2000), *Israel: The Challenge of Identity, Democracy and the State* (with Emma Murphy, 2001).

Emma C. Murphy is lecturer in Middle East politics at the University of Durham. Her main research interests have been Palestinian and Israeli politics, North African politics, and the political economy of the Middle East. Her publications include *Economic and Political Change in Tunisia: From Bourguiba to Ben Ali* (1999) and *Israel: Democracy, Identity and the State* (with Clive Jones, 2001).

Tim Niblock is professor of Arab Gulf Studies and director of the Institute of Arab and Islamic Studies at the University of Exeter. He works on the political economy and international relations of the Arab world, with particular emphasis on Sudan, Iraq, Libya, and the Arabian peninsula. Among his publications are *"Pariah States" and Sanctions in the Middle East: Iraq, Libya, Sudan* (2001), *Economic and Political Liberalisation in the Middle East* (coedited with Emma Murphy, 1993), and *Class and Power in Sudan* (1987).

B. A. Roberson, University of Warwick, is editor of and contributor to the following: *The Middle East and Europe: The Power Deficit* (1998), *International Society and the Development of International Relations Theory* (1998), *The Challenges to Lebanon in the Future Middle East,* a special issue of *Mediterranean Politics* (vol. 3, no. 1, summer 1998), and *Postwar Lebanon: The First Decade* (forthcoming).

Philip Robins is university lecturer in politics, with special reference to the Middle East, and a fellow of St. Antony's College, Oxford, positions that he has held since 1995. He spent the previous eight years at the

Royal Institute of International Affairs, Chatham House, where he was head of the Middle East Programme. He is the author of *Turkey and the Middle East* (1991) and is currently completing a book on Turkish foreign policy.

Nadia El-Shazly is analyst on Middle Eastern affairs, especially security issues. She is author *of The Gulf Tanker War: Iran and Iraq's Maritime Swordplay* (1998).

Charles Tripp is reader in the politics of the Middle East at the School of Oriental and African Studies, University of London. He is coeditor of *The Iraqi Aggression Against Kuwait* (with W. Danspeckgruber, 1995), coauthor of *Iran and Iraq at War* (with S. Chubin, 1988) and *Iran-Saudi Arabia Relations and Regional Order* (with S. Chubin, 1996), and author of *A History of Iraq* (2000).

Index

About the Book

This important new textbook offers a theoretically grounded, systematic examination of the foreign policies of twelve Middle East states.

The authors first establish a common analytical framework for studying the individual cases; they also delineate the broader regional and global arenas within which Middle Eastern governments operate. Subsequent chapters assess the foreign policies of the region's key players (Egypt, Iran, Israel, Saudi Arabia, Syria, and Turkey), two "pariah states" (Iraq and Libya), and two smaller states (Tunisia and Yemen).

Designed for use in both politics and IR courses, the book combines an exceptional range of empirical case-study material with thematic, comparative analysis.

Raymond Hinnebusch is professor of international relations and Middle East politics at the University of St. Andrews, Scotland. **Anoushiravan Ehteshami** is professor of international relations at the Institute for Middle Eastern and Islamic Studies, University of Durham, England. The two are coauthors of *Syria and Iran: Middle Powers in a Penetrated Regional System.*